Making Fathers Pay

David L. Chambers

Making Fathers Pay

The Enforcement of Child Support

With a Methodological Appendix by
Terry K. Adams

The University of
Chicago Press
Chicago and London

DAVID L. CHAMBERS is professor of law
at the University of Michigan Law School

The University of Chicago Press, Chicago 60637
The University of Chicago Press, Ltd., London

© 1979 by David L. Chambers
All rights reserved. Published 1979
Printed in the United States of America
83 82 81 80 79   5 4 3 2 1

Library of Congress Cataloging in Publication Data

Chambers, David L
  Making fathers pay.

  Bibliography: p.
  Includes index.
    1. Desertion and non-support—Michigan.
  2. Support (Domestic relations)—Michigan.
  3. Parent and child (Law)—Michigan.   I. Title.
  KFM4304.8.C48   346'.773'017   79-11953
  ISBN 0-226-10077-4

To Mary

Contents

Preface

One afternoon during the fall of 1971, I crossed the grounds of the Detroit House of Corrections with one of the guards. DeHoCo, as it is known locally, is a jail at the edge of Detroit for men convicted of offenses carrying sentences of up to one year. Law students for whom I served as a faculty adviser provided legal assistance on civil matters to some of DeHoCo's inmates. "Over there," my companion casually observed, nodding toward a long low barracks, "is where we keep the runaway pappies."

"The what?" I asked naively. He explained that on that day—and almost any other day—there were fifty or sixty Detroit men serving time for failing to make court-ordered payments for child support. A few questions asked of others revealed that he was correct and that Detroit's practice was common in other parts of Michigan. I could, however, learn little of the practice in other parts of the country. Indeed, I found that there was little written about any aspect of child support.

Curiosity led me to a public agency in each Michigan county known as the Friend of the Court. All parents under support orders are expected to make their payments through it. What I found at these agencies was a cornucopia of information—about parents' payments, about individual enforcement efforts, and about the characteristics of families. It quickly became apparent that these files could permit learning not only about jailing and its effects but also about payments of child support in general and, together with information from other sources, about the broad range of financial problems of broken families.

It is now seven years, several grants, and hundreds of thousands of coded pieces of information later. Along the way, I have sought to learn enough about the tools of social science research to make an acceptable, if rudimentary, use of them. I am a lawyer by training, an amateur in a sophisticated field. I have come to stand in awe of those who illuminate for the rest of us the forces affecting human behavior.

For whatever I have learned over these several years, there are many persons to whom I am deeply indebted. The first two are Terry K. Adams and Ray M. Shortridge, who served as the principal research associates on the project. Each arrived with experience in the techniques of social science research and with knowledge of computer programming. Terry, who served as my research associate from 1972 to 1974, designed much of the study of families in Genesee County, Michigan, the county we examined most closely. He then oversaw its execution. In the years since, he has continued to serve as my principal adviser and critic, cautious and caustic, intimidatingly well informed about the income problems of American families. He is the author of the methodological appendix at the end of this volume. Ray Shortridge served as research associate from 1974 to 1976 and designed most of that part of the study in which we examined collections in twenty-eight Michigan counties. He then ably directed the twenty-eight-county study in the field and guided the initial stages of the analysis. During the last four years of the project, Ray, Terry, and I were aided by Priscilla Cheever, who performed with skill the computer work for the project and provided an inexhaustible reservoir of indignation over the transgressions of fathers.

I owe no less a debt, although one of a very different order, to the heads of the Friends of the Court in the twenty-eight counties we examined. I am particularly indebted to Robert Standal, the Friend of the Court in Genesee County, and to Robert Benedict, Betty Church, Emil Joseph, and Victor Morgan of his staff, as well as to Richard Benedek, the Friend of the Court in Washtenaw County. These indulgent administrators tolerated a platoon of researchers in their offices over long periods of time. In all the counties, it was continually refreshing to find public officials who were proud of their work and receptive to the inquiries of outsiders. How many other researchers can boast that they approached twenty-eight public agencies, proposing an investigation of their effectiveness, and found that all twenty-eight agreed without an arm-twist?

Of yet a third order is the debt I owe to those who have provided funds for the project. The Center for Studies in Criminal Justice of the University of Chicago Law School and its directors, Norval Morris and Franklin Zimring, made a leap of faith and provided funds for the first two summers of the project. Frank continued to provide valuable comments stage by stage over the years. During an early part of the project, Princeton University's Woodrow Wilson School also lent an especially gracious form of support by providing me with an office and secretarial support for a sabbatical term that allowed me not only to write but also to sit in on social science classes and read widely. I especially relish the help I received from Jameson Doig of Princeton's Department of Politics and Robert Scott of the Department of Sociology.

When it became clear that the appropriate scale of the project would be a larger and more ambitious one than was at first anticipated, the Law and Social Sciences Division of the National Science Foundation provided three substantial grants. Walter Probert, Robert Berry, David Baldus, and H. Laurence Ross each served for a time as director of the division over the term of the project and offered advice and encouragement.

During all the years of the project, substantial further support was provided from the William W. Cook research funds of the University of Michigan Law School. My colleague, Richard Lempert, who chaired the Law School's research committee during the formative stages of the project, goaded me to expand its scope and provided supportive advice (and telling criticism) in the years that followed. His careful review of the penultimate draft provided the most meticulous scrubbing the manuscript ever received. At earlier stages, I also received fortification and advice from William Birdsall, economist and professor of social work at the University of Michigan, and Kenneth Eckhardt, sociologist at the University of Delaware and author of an earlier study of child support.

Over a score of persons worked with Terry Adams, Ray Shortridge, and me on various stages of the gathering and coding of the data. Lists of names are tedious to everyone except those listed, but I am so grateful for the aid of many people that I wish to make at least this brief recognition. Those who aided in the gathering of data in the field during the summers of 1972 through 1975 and in coding the data during the falls' and winters included: Janet Findlater, Clark Andrews, Mary Margaret Bolda, Raymond Boryczka, Carolyn Daitch, Paul Fisher, John Kinney, Paul Kowtna, Paul Lee, Duane Moore, Thomas Plumb, Ann Poulin, Frances Prevas, John Quinn, Kathleen Ricke, Gregory Robbins, Marcia Robbins, Richard Sanders, Robert Schwartz, Chuck Schmidt, Steven Silverman, and David Weisberg. There were also those who aided in the early computer work on the project. This group included Shawn Benbow, Shirley Stevens, and Michael Thomas. For secretarial help I am indebted to many people but particularly to Theresa Kappes and Peggy Morgan.

Finally, the tale of one family whom I call the Neals weaves through the entire book. I am deeply grateful to them for the time they gave talking with me. Their lives have not been easy. They have lived at the edge of poverty for twenty years. May their next several decades be brighter, much brighter, than their last two.

Part One

Introduction

"I'm Going To Teach You a Lesson"

The Court:	All right, Mr. Connors, bring up Mr. Neal. (Whereupon Mr. Connors [the enforcement officer] and Mr. Neal approached the Bench.)
The Court:	Mr. Neal, do you know why you're here?
The Defendant:	Yes.
The Court:	I can't hear you.
The Defendant:	Yes.
The Court:	Why are you here?
The Defendant:	Back alimony.
The Court:	It's not alimony; I never ordered alimony.
The Defendant:	No.
The Court:	You were never ordered by Judge Johnston to pay alimony.
The Defendant:	No, support.
The Court:	That's right. You were ordered to pay support for your children, not alimony for your wife. And that was back in '63, and he only made you pay ten dollars per week per child. You have five, is that right?

The Defendant: Yes.

The Court: Do you know how much you're in arrears?

The Defendant: Yes.

The Court: How much?

The Defendant: It's over ten thousand.

Jerry Neal is about to be held in contempt of court for failing to obey his court order to pay child support.* He had been divorced six years before, paid steadily for a while, and then stopped paying altogether four years before the hearing we are reading. Jerry is one of four to six million Americans, nearly all males, who are under child support orders after a divorce or an adjudication of paternity. At the time of his hearing in 1970, Jerry's position among the millions of parents then under orders was unusual, but not because he was failing to pay. Most parents under orders of support in this country, then and now, are irregular payers. What was unusual was that he happened to live in a place that took the collection of child support seriously. He lived in Flint, Michigan.

In most cities in 1969, Jerry Neal, regardless of his payments, would not have ended up before a judge. He might well not even have received any reminders that he was behind in payments. In Flint's county—Genesee—and in every other Michigan county, a public agency known as the Friend of the Court collects money from parents and pursues those who fail to pay. The agency has always taken its work seriously. Despite the impression conveyed by Jerry's payment performance, Genesee and many other Michigan counties are remarkably successful at their job. Michigan as a whole collects more money per case from its fathers than any other state in the country. Over the last few years, collecting child support has become a major enterprise of state governments all across the nation, largely because recent federal legislation conditions the full statutory reimbursement to the states of their welfare expenditures on their making much more substantial efforts than in the past to collect support. During this period, Michigan has frequently been put forth as a model for other states to emulate. This book was written partly to report why Michigan collects so much—and why within Michigan, though all of its counties

*Here and elsewhere in the book, I have changed the names of men under orders of support and members of their families as well as the names of judges and staff members of Friends of the Court. I have also altered several details in the lives of the Neal family members to help insure that their actual identities will not be recognized.

have Friends of the Court, some counties collect vastly more than others.

Not surprisingly, at the time of Jerry Neal's hearing, the judge was more interested in the reasons for Jerry's failure than in the reasons for Michigan's success.

The Court: Well, why are you that far behind? Why haven't you paid something on it?

The Defendant: Well, I had other bills and trying to make a living myself; I just couldn't seem to pay nothing.

The Court: Well, what do you mean "other bills"? You knew you had these children.

The Defendant: Yes.

The Court: These children didn't ask to be brought into the world, Mr. Neal. How did you expect those children to get food in their little stomachs and clothes on their back, shoes on their feet, boots in the wintertime? Where were you working all this time?

The Defendant: I had different jobs.

The Court: Well, why haven't you held a steady job? What's your trouble? I'd like to know.

The Defendant: Nothing.

The Court: Well, then, why haven't you held onto a steady job if nothing's wrong with you?

The Defendant: Just trying to find something that pays more money.

The Court: But you can't do it—

The Defendant: No.

The Court: —going from one insignificant job to another. Were you born here in Flint?

The Defendant: Yes.

The Court: You know that you could make a hundred and fifty, hundred and sixty dollars in the factory here. Why didn't you apply to the factory?

The Defendant: I did. They won't take me back because I got a hernia and I couldn't pass the test again.

The Court: You got married [a second time] in '65. Did you marry a Flint woman?

The Defendant:	Yes.
The Court:	Is she working?
The Defendant:	No. She can't work; she's a diabetic now.
The Court:	Now, isn't that too bad. That's just too bad. And so you've been paying her bills; is that what you've been doing?
The Defendant:	Yes.
The Court:	You knew you had these five children before you married her. These are the ones that come first. I don't care about your second wife. If and when you have enough money to have a second wife, then you get a second wife. But these children are too small and I'm not going to let them go around in garbage cans looking for food or something, or to put shoes on their feet. If you're strong enough to marry a second time and go to bed, you're strong enough to get a job that will pay and feed these children. You have no business assuming that responsibility when you had five little tots to take care of. They didn't ask to be brought into this world, Mr. Neal. You've defied this court. You think that laws were made for everybody but you. Well, I'm going to teach you a lesson.

Jerry Neal's case seemed simple enough to the judge. She saw a man who had worked but had not paid, a man who had remarried but put his own needs and the needs of his new wife ahead of those of his children. He didn't say so at the hearing—"You couldn't say nothing to her," he later told me—but he regarded himself very differently. He saw himself as a man barely making do at one unskilled job after another and as a man no less entitled than any other to stay coupled, even if serially, over the course of his life.

Jerry knew that his children were not scavenging out of garbage cans but were living on a public assistance grant that, though modest, was higher than the fifty dollars a week he was supposed to have paid in support. He also knew that any amount he paid would be sent to the welfare department, not to his children. The judge and Jerry's former wife each also knew this but certainly did not believe that it justified nonpayment. To the judge, the children's receipt of welfare made Jerry's failure to pay seem more irresponsible. As she complained when jailing another man at about the same time, "I'm getting sick and tired as a taxpayer of supporting your children and other fellows' because they are just too doggone lazy to support their own."

Much of our study has been devoted to trying to understand why, even in places that collect from most men, many, like Jerry, still fail to pay. Jerry talked about having trouble making ends meet and no doubt he did; but he nearly always held a job, and many other Genesee men, no better off financially than Jerry, paid their support regularly. We have tried to learn the relationship to men's payments of their background characteristics and of various aspects of their marriages, as well as the impact of events that occur after divorce, events such as their remarriage or the children's receipt of welfare benefits.

Whatever Jerry's reasons for failing to pay, the judge had just grounds for concern about Jerry's children. How would they get food in their little stomachs and boots in the wintertime? If Jerry had trouble making ends meet, the plight of his former wife, Dolores, with five small children, was far bleaker. Like the vast majority of divorced women with children, Dolores found that her separation from her husband produced a sudden and calamitous decline in the income available to her. Child support can be important for easing the crisis. On the other hand, sad to say, if she had tried to live on Jerry's fifty dollars a week, which represented about 40 percent of his take-home pay at the time of divorce, she would have been unable to keep food in her children's stomachs or afford boots for the wintertime, even if Jerry had paid in full. Twenty-six hundred dollars for a woman and five children would barely pay the rent.

One aspect of our study has been to try to grasp the economic position of women with children after divorce and the place in their lives of other sources of income—not only child support but also income from their own employment and welfare benefits as well as income provided indirectly through remarriage. Nearly all women do in fact turn to one or more of these other sources. Dolores Neal, who turned to the welfare system and to remarriage and found each wanting, remained bitter over the years at Jerry's apparent lack of concern. She would have enjoyed sitting in the courtroom.

The Court:	Do you have anything to say why I shouldn't cite you for contempt of Court?
The Defendant:	(No audible response.)
The Court:	Do you have anything to say, I asked you?
The Defendant:	No.

The Court:	You have nothing to say in mitigation of what you've done to these children?
The Defendant:	I know I did wrong.
The Court:	Yes. If you would have sent at least ten dollars a week for the five of them, at least we would have seen that you were making an effort. You didn't even send a nickel.
The Defendant:	I did send money off and on, but right to them; I didn't send it to the court.
The Court:	Oh, really, and you expect the court to believe that?
The Defendant:	No.
The Court:	You're darn-tooting I don't believe it. This court finds nothing wrong with you. Hernia or no hernia, you had no business leaving the Fisher Body when you were building up seniority, fringe benefits, everything. You take a leave of absence and go to Florida with a new wife. You may have gotten that hernia at Fisher's for all you know.
	Anyhow, the court finds you in contempt of court for violating this support—violating the judgment of divorce, wherein support was made for five small children at ten dollars per week [per child]. And that isn't even enough. The court finds nothing wrong with you, hernia or no hernia. There are many men who work with hernias; they are physically and mentally able. If you are capable of remarrying, you are capable then of supporting your children. You are to be confined to the county jail for one year unless you come up with half, at least five thousand dollars, and a wage assignment of at least the current fifty dollars, plus twenty-five dollars on the back.

One year in jail or five thousand dollars, a common sentence in Genesee County for a man with a large arrearage. Five thousand dollars is about what Jerry had earned the year before. Jailing for failure to pay support is an everyday occurrence in Michigan. In Genesee, during the period we studied, one of every seven divorced men with children was sentenced to jail at least once for failing to pay support during the life of his support order. In several Michigan counties, on any given day, more men are sitting in the county jail for failing to pay support than are there under sentence for all other jailable offenses combined.

The jailing of men who fail to pay looms large in the study that follows. It does so in part because, in one important sense, jailing seems to work. At the end of our study the evidence is strong that, in the context of child support, the use of jailing, when coupled with a well-organized system of enforcement, produces substantial amounts of money both from men who are jailed and from men who are not. At the same time, the process that leads to jail has many worrisome aspects. In reading the transcript, one notices that Jerry had no attorney and was not informed of a right to call witnesses in his behalf. He was not told what would constitute a defense. He was not told the range of dispositions the judge had the power to order. The hearing is in fact simply the last of several stages in which peremptory actions are taken against nonpayers.

The Court: You are to be confined to the county jail for one year unless you come up with half, at least five thousand dollars, and a wage assignment of at least the current fifty dollars, plus twenty-five dollars on the back.
                    Let him make two or three telephone calls and see if he can get somebody to take him out.

Mr. Connors: Thank you, your Honor.

Jerry didn't bother to make any calls. He knew no one would come. He served ten months with two months off for good behavior. He served two more sentences later. After his third sentence, he started to pay, for a while.

Two

Seeking Answers

The Friends of the Court and Their All-Knowing Files

Jerry Neal's marriage lasted eight years. At separation, Jerry began a relationship with the Friend of the Court that lasted twice as long. The rich files of this agency furnished the information on which our study is based.

Among American jurisdictions, the Friend of the Court is somewhat unusual. In nearly all states, an arm of the state welfare department enforces orders of support in welfare cases and, by many different names, operates in these cases like Michigan's Friend of the Court. Even within the welfare setting, however, such agencies have existed in most states for only a few years in anything but the most primitive form. More significantly, in most states, there is no agency comparable to the Friend of the Court for cases in which the custodial parent is not receiving welfare. Federal law now requires that states also provide assistance in collecting support for custodial parents not receiving welfare benefits, but in most states such services are available haphazardly at best. While many states now have an office connected with the court that receives payments and disburses them to the custodial parent, only a small number of states have an agency made freely available to the parent not on welfare that will help her enforce her support order. In general a woman must turn to her own attorney.

Michigan's Friend of the Court was founded in 1917, because the private system of support enforcement had proven ineffectual. A description given by a Michigan judge in an interview over forty years ago looked back on Michigan's system before 1917. It will sound like a description of 1979 to divorced women in much of the country today:

> If the husband failed to pay alimony [or child support], the wife must employ an attorney and get an order to show cause, get it served, be present at the hearing; if an attachment was ordered, the wife must supervise the issuing of the same, accompany the officers, point out the defendant, and then, if he was brought in on an attachment, be present at the hearing and persuade the judge to send the husband to jail if he did not pay the alimony, averaging probably five dollars a week. If the woman's and the lawyer's patience were not completely exhausted by one experience such as this, they were the type whom the court began to look upon as persecutors and their zeal was thus thwarted by their own efforts. If the attorney took all the money collected, he was not paid for one-tenth of the time he necessarily devoted to the case. The result was the collection of practically no alimony, and what was collected never reached the children.[1]

In 1917, the judges in Detroit responded to the inadequacy of private enforcement by appointing Michigan's first Friend of the Court. The judges charged the lawyer they appointed with the sole duty of collecting support for minor children. In 1919, Michigan's legislature authorized other counties to appoint a comparable person and, two years later, changed the authorization into a mandate to the counties to create such a position.

Today, the "Friend of the Court" is the title for both the person heading the agency in each county and for the agency itself. The Friends of the Court themselves are now appointed by the governor at the recommendation of the local circuit judges. These Friends of the Court oversee all official matters relating to divorce and paternity. Their staffs provide advice to the court on child custody and visitation provisions and on the appropriate size of orders of support. They receive all payments from the support-paying parent and remit them to the custodial parent, guardian, or welfare department. And they serve as investigators, warning-senders, and prosecutors for the entire enforcement process. Their duties extend equally to welfare and nonwelfare cases.

The Michigan agencies have grown and flourished. What began in Wayne County as a single lawyer in 1917 is now, in Wayne alone, a sprawling agency with a staff of over three hundred persons, including more than forty lawyers. In Michigan today, there are sixty-three Friends of the Court, some in the northern part of the state serving several counties through a single office. In 1974, the last year we surveyed, these Friends of the Court collected slightly over $200 million in child support from about 240,000 parents under orders of support in divorce, paternity, and other cases. By the end of 1977, the total annual collections had risen to $288 million from 296,000 parents under support orders.

The offices of the Friends of the Court are as varied as the counties they serve. A few still operate out of the basement of a county courthouse and are staffed only by a bookkeeper and a part-time Friend of the Court, who is sometimes a local lawyer in private practice. On the other hand, seventeen of the agencies have fifteen or more full-time employees; five have more than fifty. Though they operate under a single statutory framework, the Friends of the Court vary widely in their conceptions of their roles. Nearly all view as their primary function the collection of child support payments, but some place much more emphasis than others on professional social work, with staff members who deal with problems of child custody and visitation. Similarly, some Friends of the Court are lawyers whose staffs are dominated by lawyers, while others, including some in large counties, are not lawyers and have no lawyers on their staffs.

Much of the latter portions of this book deal with the effects of a well-organized system of enforcement on payments of child support. At this point, the significance of this system is that it generates information, and this information was the basis for our study. The files of Michigan's Friends of the Court made it possible to learn a great deal about the characteristics of divorced families with children. The near uniqueness of Michigan makes it difficult to reproduce the study today in many other parts of the country. Ours has been an entirely file-based study. Though interviewing has been conducted, such as the interviews with Jerry Neal and his family, the only information systematically gathered has been culled from agency files.

No couple with children can be divorced in Michigan without becoming a file in the office of the Friend of the Court. For this reason, the agency records provide a repository from which representative samples of divorced families with children can be drawn. Of central importance to the inquiry here was the fact that judges in each county entered support orders in nearly every case in which a mother received custody of the children and that, except in unusual circumstances, the payments under all orders were to be made through the agency. Thus, the agency's records reveal week by week whether payments have been made. These payment records formed the cornerstone of our entire study. We have used them in two ways. First, we have used them to compare the rates of collections for a large number of Michigan counties—twenty-eight in all. We drew a sample of payments in each of these counties and used other information that we gathered about their enforcement systems and their socioeconomic composition to try to account for the differences among them in rates of collections. It is this part of the study that has provided the basis for our conclusions about the effects of jailing on the general payment levels of the counties.

Second, we have used the payment records to learn why some men within a single county pay much more than others. In two counties—Genesee and Washtenaw—we drew large random samples of individuals under orders of support. In Genesee and one other county—Macomb—we also drew substantial samples of men who had been jailed.

The files of the Friends of the Court are a treasure trove of information beyond their records of payments. Because the agency staff makes recommendations regarding custody of children and gathers information used in fixing the appropriate amount of support, the staff members record information about the ages of the parties, the number of children, the parents' occupations and earnings, the parents' reasons for wanting the divorce, and much more. After the entry of a support order, the staff also keeps track of all enforcement efforts used on the fathers and of some other events in the parents' lives such as the mother's receipt of public assistance. In one county, the files even contained copies of the transcripts of nearly all appearances by delinquent fathers before the judges, permitting us to learn about the employment status of the father and his asserted reasons for nonpayment at the time of the imposition of the sanction.

Figure 2.1 illustrates for a single hypothetical case how the kinds of information we culled from agency files interact to synergistic advantage. We can, for example, learn from an enforcement log the date of a given enforcement effort and then turn to the payment records to learn what payments followed the effort. In the figure, the warning letter of November 6 is immediately followed by payments but the letter of April 18 is not. (We followed such responses across thousands of efforts in hundreds of cases.) We can in turn enrich the payment and enforcement information with personal information about the man and the members of his family—occupation, age, sex, race, and a dozen other factors; and, after examining large numbers of cases, we can

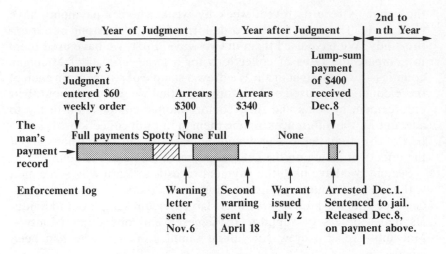

Fig. 2.1 Hypothetical case indicating records available in Genesee County.

learn whether there are different patterns of payments by different
groups after warning letters or jailing or other measures. Do white-
collar workers respond after warning letters any differently than blue-
collar workers? Do men with a history of alcohol problems pay better
after jailing than men without such a history? Or we can simply
examine payment records over the lives of entire orders and learn what
sorts of men pay overall at higher rates than others.

   The interaction of the payment records and the enforcement efforts
thus permits us to gauge the effects of sanctions on individuals with
greater precision than has typically been possible in studies of other
behavior that leads to incarceration. Comparable records could exist
for burglaries and armed robberies only if the burglar called in each
Monday to report what stores he had broken into during the preceding
week.

   Our random samples of entire caseloads were generally drawn in
the most straightforward way imaginable: cases were arranged alphabetically in the agency files, and we simply picked an interval—every
fifteenth case, for example—and started at the beginning at a random
point among the early A's and worked our way to the end of the
alphabet. (Appendix table 2A provides a list of our principal samples
and some summary information about the uses we made of them.)
In the text, we discuss our samples and methods of analysis as we

reach specific topics relevant to them. Thus, for example, our discussion of the several ways we measured payments that followed enforcement efforts will be found in Chapter 7, on the effects of specific efforts. Additional detailed information on methods will be found in the Methodological Appendix.

We have said earlier that our samples of families with orders of support permit us to give a general description of the characteristics of divorced familes with children. It is not, however, quite the case that all divorcing families with children end up with a support order directed against the noncustodial parent. Some small groups of families are underrepresented in our study to the extent that we seek to portray divorced families generally. One significant missing group are the families in which the father received custody and the mother was the parent under the support order.[2] These cases are omitted because, during the period we studied, support orders were rarely entered against mothers. Courts did not enter orders against women in part because many of the mothers in the cases in which the father was awarded custody were disabled or otherwise considered unable to provide support (or satisfactory custody) and in part because courts simply treated men and women differently. In the two counties we examined most closely, our random sampling in each county of over four hundred families identified not one mother under an order of support. For this reason, throughout the book, we will typically refer to the custodial parent as the "mother" and as "she" and to the noncustodial parent as the "father" and as "he," even at the price of reinforcing old notions of proper responsibilities. This and other limits on the range of families we include does not affect the representativeness of our samples of families actually under support orders. It affects only our efforts to describe the position of all families with children in divorce.

The Michigan Counties Studied

All our samples have one aspect in common: they were drawn from certain Michigan counties. A little more about these counties may be useful before we embark on a discussion of our findings about the families who lived in them. The map of Michigan's lower peninsula has frequently been likened to a hand, with the "thumb" on the right. The map on page 16 displays the lower peninsula and the twenty-eight counties we studied. The twenty-eight are all below the knuckles. The three counties that we examined most closely—Genesee, Washtenaw, and Macomb—are outlined more heavily, freckles on the thumb.

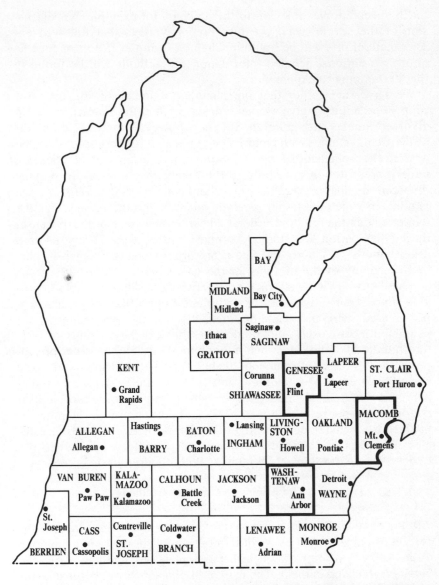

Map of lower peninsula of Michigan, with the twenty-eight counties included in the study. Cities indicated are county seats.

Most of Michigan's population lives in its southern counties. The counties we studied were twenty-eight of the thirty in the state with a Friend of the Court caseload in 1973 of more than one thousand cases. Although the state has eighty-three counties, these twenty-eight contain nearly 85 percent of the state's population. On the other hand, our twenty-eight were by no means uniformly urban. Although the three counties near the southeast corner that form the core of the Detroit metropolitan area—Wayne, Oakland, and Macomb—had a total population in 1970 of 4.2 million (close to half the population in the state), half of the counties in our twenty-eight had populations under 100,000.

How do the residents of the counties we studied compare to residents of other parts of the country? As a group, the residents of our twenty-eight counties suffered unemployment problems that were somewhat more severe than those for the nation as a whole, but they were nonetheless somewhat more prosperous as a group when measured by median family income or the proportion of the population having low incomes. The three counties we examined most closely— Genesee, Washtenaw, and Macomb—were in turn more prosperous by either of these measures than the average of the twenty-eight counties as a whole. Appendix table 2B provides a detailed comparison of several characteristics culled from census information.

Throughout the study, Genesee is our focal point. Whenever we describe the operations of a system, or the characteristics of a caseload, or seek to understand the behavior of particular groups of persons, Genesee serves as our base. The other two counties, Washtenaw and Macomb, were chosen for the contrasts they offer to Genesee.

Genesee County has an urban core surrounded by suburban towns and a rural fringe. It had a population of 480,000 in 1970. Its principal city, Flint, is an automobile town. During times of economic prosperity, nearly a third of the county's male labor force works in one of the manufacturing plants of the Chevrolet, Buick, or Fisher Body divisions of General Motors. The county's fortunes rise and fall with the auto industry. When the United Auto Workers struck General Motors in 1970, the receipts of the Friend of the Court took a sudden plunge. Like so many urban centers in America, Genesee also reveals the paradox of high unemployment amid general prosperity. In the last five years, Genesee's unemployment level rarely dropped below 8 percent. We picked Genesee for close examination because its Friend of the Court had an aggressive enforcement system and maintained especially thorough records.

The county from which we developed the next greatest amount of detailed information, Washtenaw, also has several automobile plants and a mix of urban, suburban, and rural areas, but it is different in some significant ways. The county contains both the University of Michigan and Eastern Michigan University and thus has a large student and faculty population. Ann Arbor is Washtenaw's principal town. As appendix table 2B reveals, a much greater portion of the county's labor force works in white-collar occupations than is the case in Genesee or in the rest of the nation.

We chose Washtenaw because its Friend of the Court employed a much less aggressive system of enforcement than Genesee during the period we examined. While Genesee had a large full-time staff of support enforcement officers, Washtenaw during much of this period had no one working solely on enforcement of support. During a year when Genesee's judges sentenced 224 persons to jail for nonpayment, Washtenaw's sentenced no more than five. Washtenaw thus offered an opportunity to view closely overall payment behavior and responsiveness to mild enforcement efforts in a place with a strikingly different pattern of enforcement.

Macomb, the last of the three counties, has a larger population than either of the other two, but shares a common bond with Genesee—a very high portion of its labor force works for the automobile companies. Macomb has no large central city. Rather it contains prosperous blue- and white-collar suburbs of Detroit. Macomb was chosen for a narrow purpose. Like Genesee, it has an intensive system of support enforcement and judges who rely heavily on sentences to jail. Macomb's judges, however, typically impose much shorter sentences than the judges in Genesee, and the sentenced men in Macomb spend much shorter periods of time in jail. We drew a sample of jailed men in Macomb solely to compare the effects of a different sentencing strategy.

With this background, we are ready to meet the couples whose marriages ended in divorce.

Part Two

Families in Divorce

Three

The Divorced Families in Genesee County

Jerry Neal, the man shipped to jail in the opening pages of this book, looked back on his marriage to Dolores Schiller. They first met, he told me, in 1952, when a friend introduced them at a roller rink in Flint. Jerry was twenty-two and a high-school graduate. Dolores was sixteen, a high-school junior. They had each grown up in Flint. Jerry, his father, his three brothers, and Dolores's father all worked on the assembly line at plants of General Motors. Jerry asked Dolores for a date and they dated steadily for eight months. From the outset, Dolores's mother had misgivings about Jerry: he was too old, he was a Catholic, he was Polish. Jerry's summary of the courtship, like his view of nearly everything, is free of clutter: "I just met her through some friends we knew and just started going together and I just married her."

Of all the men in our samples, Jerry is the only one I interviewed at length. To avoid losing sight of people for numbers, I interviewed Jerry four times, his current wife twice, his mother and his first wife each once, and his enforcement officer at the Friend of the Court and his supervisor at the jail during the last of his three sentences once each. Jerry and his family share many characteristics with other jailed and unjailed men in our samples—families that we will generally view through bits of data from the agency's files.

Dolores and Jerry were married in the summer of 1953. Dolores did not return to high school that fall and soon became pregnant. For the first several years of their marriage, Dolores gave birth to a child nearly every year. By the time she had reached twenty-three, their five children had been born. Dolores views the children as having created a stress on the marriage. "Perhaps we had too many too quick," she reflected dryly. A change in the economy darkened the family situation. From boom employment in their first years, Flint slid into the recession of the late fifties, and Jerry found himself frequently laid off from his job at the Buick plant. He started drinking more and more in the evenings with unmarried male friends and coming home erratically. He and Dolores never talked much—"Jerry's not much of a talker"— and now talked even less.

When he couldn't find work in Flint, he commuted to a job at a Chevrolet plant sixty miles away, returning on weekends to the small, saltbox house that they had bought on the edge of Flint. By Dolores's own admission Jerry always worked when he could and always brought home his paychecks. As we find with a large number of men in our sample who are identified by their wives as having an alcohol problem, alcohol never prevented Jerry from holding a job. Apart from the paycheck and the children there became less and less of a relationship in any other way: "She started going her way and I went my way." At some point in about the eighth year of their marriage, Dolores decided that she'd had enough, but, in Jerry's view, she believed she could not divorce him because she had no grounds. He gave her grounds in the form of an unwelcome Christmas present in 1962:

> Well, it was just before Christmas, just a couple of days before, I guess.... It'd been going on a long time. She'd been threatening, "Well, lay a hand on me and that's all I need to get the divorce," because she didn't have no grounds. She kept pushing it into me and finally there was a Christmas party and I come home. I'd just built up enough in me. I just hit her then.

Drunk, he hit her on the head with a hammer. He drove her to a hospital, was arrested, and then held on a bond of ten thousand dollars. Dolores, who had a large knot on her head and a slight concussion, decided, after a month had passed, to drop charges and to file for divorce. Jerry was then released from jail.

Looking back, more than a decade after their divorce, Dolores remembered the painful goose egg but also remembered Jerry with greater fondness than either of her later husbands. "Nice," "usually even-tempered" were terms she chose. Jerry claims not to understand why Dolores wanted to divorce him. That they talked little, that he spent most of his free time with male companions, did not distinguish him from many men he knew whose marriages had survived. "I'd have kept it going," he told me.

And indeed, the files of the Friend of the Court reveal that at Jerry's predivorce interview, he expressed a strong desire to reconcile. Dolores had no such inclination, and in early 1963, ten years after their marriage, their divorce became final. The court's final decree provided a decent burial:

> It is ordered and adjudged, and this court by virtue of the authority therein vested, and in pursuance of the statutes in such cases made and provided, doth order and adjudge, that the marriage between the plaintiff, Dolores Neal, and the defendant, Jerry Neal, shall be and is hereby dissolved.

Backgrounds

Nearly all the information we have about the backgrounds of the remaining couples in our Genesee samples comes from the interviews conducted by the staff of the Friend of the Court before divorce as a part of the process of developing information and recommendations for the court regarding custody, visitation and the amount of child support. The profile we obtained in Genesee County from this information is hardly as rich as might be wished—the Friend of the Court needed to know some things we did not and did not care about other matters we wanted to know more about. We can, nonetheless, draw a rough sketch of the divorced families in general and what they passed through.

There were 411 couples in our random sample in Genesee County. All the couples had four characteristics in common: they had been married, they had had children, they had been divorced, and the fathers were under court orders entered in or before 1970 to pay support.

The information about them thus serves both to paint a picture of urban families with children who pass through divorce and to provide background for our inquiry into payments and enforcement. Below, we report the high levels of payments in most Michigan counties. When we do so, the reader may picture an "average" American couple with minor children that may well not correspond to the "average" couple within our sample.* For these high levels of payments are obtained from men who were typically young at marriage, young at divorce, and

*The means within our sample on a broad range of characteristics are set forth in the last column of appendix table 3I.

earning less than the mature mid-career worker in our society. Divorce, though occurring among all groups, does not strike at random.

Of the education or ethnic backgrounds of our Genesee families, we can say nothing directly. Our principal background information is limited to the occupation of family members, their race, and their religious affiliation. The families in our sample, like those of the county in which they reside, are predominantly headed by white, Protestant, blue-collar workers. There are nonetheless some significant differences between our divorced families and the families in the county population as a whole. As figure 3.1 reveals, 62 percent of the fathers in our sample were unskilled blue-collar workers, whereas only 46 percent of the male workers in the county population as a whole were unskilled workers. Conversely, a much smaller proportion of the men in our sample than in the county as a whole worked in white-collar jobs. The over-

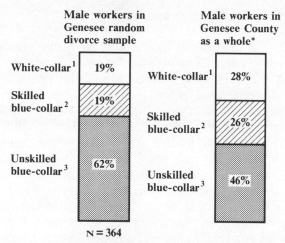

Fig. 3.1 Occupational status of working men in Genesee County.

*From U.S., Bureau of the Census, *1970 Census of Population,* vol. 1, pt. 24, table 122.
[1]Professionals (including teachers), managers, clerical, sales. In both our sample and in Genesee as a whole, 39% of the white-collar group were clerical or sales and 61% were professionals or managers.
[2]Skilled blue-collar included craftsmen and foremen.
[3]Most of the unskilled blue-collar workers in the county and in our sample worked in the automobile industry. Of those remaining, a small portion in both our sample and the county population represents a group that is hard to categorize otherwise: public-service workers, including police, fire, and postal workers.

representation of blue-collar workers among the divorced population is not peculiar to Flint. In the nation as a whole, the divorce rate is higher among blue-collar families.

Genesee's unskilled labor force has a distinctive and cohesive character. Nearly two-thirds of the unskilled workers in Genesee County in 1970 worked in the auto industry. So also did 60 percent of the unskilled workers in our sample. They all worked in plants of General Motors or, in a small portion of cases, in the plants of one of the suppliers of parts to GM. As General Motors workers, these men are among the most highly compensated assembly-line workers in the country, with strong traditions in Flint of long service within the company. As we have seen, Jerry Neal, his three brothers, his father, and Dolores's father all worked for General Motors. All but Jerry have spent nearly their entire careers at one of the body or assembly plants.

A great many of the women in our sample also worked during marriage, but we had trouble determining how many. Our only information about the women's employment comes from their interview with the Friend of the Court just before the divorce became final. Although 58 percent of the women in our sample were employed at the time of the interview, 1970 census figures report for Genesee that only 35 percent of the married women with minor children were employed. It thus seems probable that many of the women in our sample had entered or returned to the labor market only after separation. Since this chapter seeks to reveal some of the characteristics and situations of our families during their marriage, we have saved a discussion of women's earnings until the next chapter, which deals with the economic consequences of divorce.

The earnings of the men in our sample varied widely at the point of divorce, in part because of an artifact of the study: having drawn a sample of all support cases alive in 1970, we included families divorced as far back as the early 1950s and as late as the early 1970s. Only at the point of the divorce did the agency have earnings information on nearly all the men. After standardizing the men's wages in relation to 1977 dollars, we found little that was unexpected (see appendix table 3A).

White-collar workers earned more than blue-collar. Skilled blue-collar workers earned more than unskilled. On the other hand, the white-collar classification yokes together two very different groups— white-collar clericals on the one hand and managers and professionals on the other. Clerical workers not merely earned far less than professionals and managers, they also earned less than skilled blue-collar workers and about the same as unskilled auto workers.

We cannot be certain whether the earnings of the men in our sample were lower, on average, than the average for all men in similar occupations in Flint. It seems likely that they were because most of the men were under thirty at divorce, a point earlier than their peak earning years.

Just as the substantial majority of our population worked in blue-collar jobs, so likewise the substantial majority were white. Ten percent of Flint's population was black in 1960 and 14 percent was black in 1970. Thirteen percent of our sample for which we had adequate information was black. (We had no information about race for forty-four of our cases.) The black fathers in our sample, as everywhere in America, were far more likely than whites to be employed in unskilled blue-collar work than in skilled blue-collar or in white-collar employment. It is somewhat surprising, however, that among the unskilled blue-collar workers in our sample black men were more likely than whites to be working in the automobile plants. Among unskilled workers, 71 percent of blacks and 57 percent of whites worked in the auto industry. Unskilled black workers as a group earned about the same as unskilled white workers.

When we put race and occupation together, we find, not surprisingly, that we have an overwhelmingly white and blue-collar group among our divorced families. The men in two-thirds of our sample were, like Jerry Neal, white men working in blue-collar jobs.

The one other background characteristic about which we have some information is religion. At the interview by the Friend of the Court, each party was asked, "What church do you attend?" A slight majority of men and a third of the women said they didn't attend any church. For the men and women who did attend church, about three-quarters attended Protestant churches and nearly all the rest attended a Roman Catholic church. Of the Protestants, most were members of the less "conservative" denominations. They were almost twice as likely to attend Methodist, Lutheran, Presbyterian, or Episcopalian churches as they were to attend Baptist or other fundamentalist churches (see appendix table 3B).

The high number of "none" answers to the question about religion is almost certainly due to the form in which it was asked—"What church do you attend?" In Washtenaw County, where the question asked was "What is your religion?" many fewer persons of either sex answered "none." Because of the way the question was asked in Genesee, we learned little when comparing mothers' and fathers' religion of the incidence of divorce for couples in which each spouse is of a different religion. In the 128 cases in our sample in which both parents named an attended church, the vast majority were married to persons within the same classification. Eighty-seven percent of "liberal" Protestant men were married to "liberal" Protestant women; 78 percent of "conservative" Protestant men were married to "conservative" Protestant women; and 83 percent of Roman Catholic men were married to Roman Catholic women. Interestingly, when there had been marriages across faiths, liberal and conservative Protestants were as likely to have been married to Roman Catholics as they were to Protestants of the opposing degree of "liberality." (Our one practicing Jewish male was not married to our one practicing Jewish female. Each had been married to a Protestant.)

The Marriages and the Children

For most of the couples, the dissolved marriage that we are dissecting was the first for each spouse. For a quarter of the couples, however, one or both of the partners had been married before. When there had been a previous marriage, it was somewhat more often the father who had been married.

Other studies indicate that second marriages tend on the whole to be successful[1] and nearly as likely to endure as first marriages among the population as a whole.[2] We have no evidence to dispute those findings, since ours is solely a sample of marriages that broke apart. It is nonetheless the case that, within our sample, when a marriage was the second for either or both parties, divorce occurred significantly sooner (after an average of 5.9 years), than when the marriage was the first for both parties (an average of 8.3 years).[3]

Those in our sample for whom the marriage was their first had typically married when quite young—at a substantially earlier age than that at which most persons first marry in Michigan (see appendix table 3C). In Michigan in 1970, of all men and women in the state who had ever married, only 8 percent of the men and 29 percent of the women had first married when they were eighteen or younger. In our sample, however, 27 percent of the men and 61 percent of the women had married when that young. Dolores Neal was thus not an exceptional case among divorced women in having married at seventeen. She was indeed close to the median within our sample. Demographers would find nothing surprising in our figures. It is a commonplace observation that persons marrying in their teens are far more likely to divorce than persons marrying later.[4]

The overrepresentation of persons married when eighteen or younger accompanies an overrepresentation of marriages in which the woman either was pregnant at marriage or had already given birth to the couple's first child.[5] A third of the women in our sample had conceived their first child before marriage, the youngest brides being the ones most likely to have been pregnant (see appendix table 3D). From estimates by the Department of Health, Education, and Welfare, of the portion of women married between 1955 and 1959 who conceived their first child before marriage, it appears that the proportion of couples in our sample with premarital conceptions was nearly twice the national average among married couples.[6]

These gossipy surface facts about early marriages and shotgun marriages tell us little about the actual quality of the marriages. People do not divorce "because" they married when young or even because they "had to get married." As we have warned, a rounded view of the life of the couple when married was not available from the file. What we have is information about the number, timing, and ages of children, the reasons given to the Friend of the Court by each spouse at the end of the marriage for wanting a divorce, and the couple's attitude toward reconciliation.

Most of the couples in our sample began having children right away. We have seen that a third of the women were pregnant before marriage. By the end of the first calendar year after the year of the marriage, nearly three-quarters of the couples had had their first child.[7] Over the years that followed before divorce, two-thirds of the families had at least one more child after the first. By the time of divorce, the average number of children for all our couples was 2.26 (see appendix table 3E). About a third of the families had three or more children. The Neals were a part of a small minority—one in fourteen—who had as many as five children.

Even though there were children in all the marriages in our sample, many of the marriages did not last long (see appendix table 3F). Half the couples separated after no more than six years together; a quarter stayed together no more than three years. Only one in seven marriages lasted more than fifteen years.

Among our families, the number of children and the length of marriage are closely related.[8] When someone asks of an older couple whose marriage remained intact, "How many children did you have?" the answer tends to be regarded as reflecting the total number of children desired by the couple over a lifetime. For the couples in our sample, however, the number of children seems often to have been a function simply of the marriage's length. At divorce, most of the mothers were still of childbearing age—over 80 percent were under thirty-five—and many had more children later by different men. Dolores and Jerry Neal each had one more child in later marriages. (Appendix table 3G shows the close relation between marriage length and several other factors, including the number of children of the marriage.)

Reasons for Wanting Out: The Divorce

Our couples separated after varying periods together. The legal system which intruded mildly with blood tests and a few days' waiting period when they were married intruded now in a much more cumbersome way. All of our couples ended their marriages in court—the manner prescribed by law. We do not have within our sample those who parted company without one party seeking to formalize the division. In our cases, the wife was the moving party for the divorce in seven out of every eight cases, a national pattern that, as others have pointed out, may well reflect little about which partner first wanted out of the marriage.[9] To some people, the male who files for divorce lacks gallantry and even manliness. When we looked within our sample to see what characteristics distinguished the one-eighth of the men—fifty-four in all—who had either been plaintiffs or cross-plaintiffs, we were more surprised by what we did not find than by what we did.

White-collar fathers were no more frequently the plaintiffs than blue-collar fathers. Nor were fathers who were divorced in more recent years more likely to have been plaintiffs than fathers in earlier years. As might be anticipated, men with signs of alcohol problems rarely took the initiative in filing for divorce. Men whom women complained about in their interview as having alcohol problems or who have other indications in their files of an alcohol problem were only a third as likely as other men to have filed first.[10]

After filing for divorce in Michigan, the plaintiff with minor children must wait six months before a court will enter a final decree, a procedural device designed principally to encourage reconciliation.[11] During the pendency of the divorce proceedings, the Friend of the Court was responsible for framing recommendations to the judges regarding custody and for providing information or recommendations regarding the appropriate amount of support. In only about 8 percent of our cases was there ever any formal dispute over custody. Whether there was a dispute or not, however, the Friend of the Court in Genesee sought to interview each party and paid a visit to the home of the proposed custodial parent.

In custody matters, the court had the choice not merely of awarding custody to one parent or the other. It could, and occasionally did, award "custody" to the Friend of the Court with "placement" in the mother, a quaint disposition used when the parent considered preferable for custody was nonetheless believed not fully adequate. This device supposedly gave the Friend of the Court power to remove the child from the home of the parent without a hearing in advance and without claiming neglect or abuse. As a matter of stated policy, for example, the judges in Genesee and several other counties refused to grant a final award of custody to any parent who was living with an unrelated person of the opposite sex in the period prior to the divorce. One of the predivorce interviewers in Genesee said he typically telephoned the mother before going to visit in order to avoid any embarrassing encounters. For this reason, perhaps, the number of cases in which final custody was withheld from either parent was very small. In the vast majority of cases, the parents agreed between them by discussion or default that the children would live with the mother, and the agency and judge ratified the arrangement without conditions.

Nearly all the mothers in our sample attended the predivorce interview with the Friend of the Court, but about sixty-seven men, a sixth of our sample, failed to attend. All were men who had been served or were eventually served with the divorce complaint (if they had not been served, they would not have been in our sample because no support order could have been entered), but some had apparently been served and then left the county before the interview. The interview was typically held shortly before the final hearing on divorce, usually several months after the plaintiff had filed the complaint.

The group that failed to show is of considerable interest because most of the men in it were far less reliable payers of support than the remaining men and were the target of a disproportionate share of the enforcement efforts. They have been nearly as elusive a group to us as they were to the Friend of the Court. The interview they missed, which might have served as an opportunity for the agency to underscore the obligation to pay, would have served for our study as the occasion when the men's earnings, religion, and attitude toward reconciliation would have been recorded. For those who missed this meeting, we generally have no information on these matters. Fortunately for us, their wives were interviewed and were asked some questions about their husbands.

What is most remarkable is how few distinguishing characteristics the no-shows have: they are not significantly younger or older than those who attend the interview, not significantly more likely to be blue-collar than white-collar workers or to have been partners in short marriages. They are not even more likely to be complained of as having alcohol problems. Their wives are, however, more likely to be receiving welfare at divorce, more likely to complain of inadequate support during the marriage, and less likely to be interested in reconciliation than are the wives of men who showed.

A couple of questions asked of all those who did attend the interview poked slightly beneath the skin, giving us more than the surface statistics of age, earnings and other numbers. Each party was asked their attitude toward reconciliation and their reasons for wanting a divorce. Regarding reconciliation, far more men than women were willing to reconcile or to consider reconciling—a third of the men but only 11 percent of the women (see appendix table 3H). White-collar men were no more willing to reconcile or to consider reconciling than blue-collar men. On the other hand, men who were older at divorce were more willing than younger men to consider reconciling (without regard to the length of the marriage).[12] Among the men least likely to be willing to reconcile were those accused by their wives of infidelity.[13] Many of these men apparently had other plans.

The fathers and mothers who came to the interview were asked their reasons for wanting a divorce. The agency staff primarily recorded assertions of misconduct, often failing to note mere assertions of inability to get along. This practice may have derived in part from the staff's primary focus on information relevant to a decision about custody. As table 3.1 reveals, wives were far more likely to complain than husbands. Many wives made more than one complaint. When they did complain, they were most likely to claim physical abuse, infidelity, alcohol problems, or failure to support. Most husbands did not complain of any specific misconduct, but those who did were most likely to complain of infidelity. They never complained of inadequate support.

We have had to use the parents' assertions of misconduct with considerable caution for they may have been seeking to impress the agency that they had good reasons for wanting a divorce and that they were worthy of sympathy. Thus, complaints by mothers about alcohol, infidelity, and inadequate support were all significantly more common in the divorces in our sample that became final in the 1950s and early 1960s, when judges more typically required a showing of some cruelty, than they were in the divorces of later years when the courts had largely abandoned any pretense of a requirement of fault. In later years, interviewed women were apparently more likely to offer generalized explanations framed in terms of marital discord.

Table 3.1   Misconduct Asserted by Husbands and Wives as Reasons for
                             Wanting Divorce, Genesee Random Sample

Type of Misconduct	Number of Wives Asserting	% of Total Wives Asserting	Number of Husbands Asserting	% of Total Husbands Asserting
Physical abuse	90	23%	3	1%
Infidelity	85	21	46	14
Alcohol problem	81	20	9	3
Failure to support	75	19	0	0
Verbal abuse	40	10	15	4
Misconduct toward children	31	8	18	5
Sexual demands	14	4	0	0
Desertion	11	3	16	5

NOTE: Some spouses made more than one complaint. The
percentage is computed on the basis of the 400 wives and 340
husbands who were interviewed by the Friend of the Court.

We cannot know, of course, whether in the earlier years the partners
frequently lied about the misconduct they asserted. It seems likely that
most of the wives and husbands believed they were telling the truth.
The incidence of adultery and physical abuse seems little higher than is
commonly reported among American couples generally.[14] What is
wholly unascertainable, however, is the degree to which the reported
misconduct, assuming it did occur, was in fact an important motive for
seeking the divorce. As we saw in table 3.1, the kinds of misconduct
wives most frequently alleged were physical abuse, infidelity, alcohol
problems, and nonsupport. Although any one of these could cause a
marriage to collapse, they were also the kinds of behavior that women
and their attorneys might have picked out, among all the sources of
unhappiness in marriage, as those that would be most readily accepted
by the court as a satisfactory basis for awarding them a divorce and
custody of the children.

Let us look a bit more closely at these asserted reasons for divorce.

Physical abuse was, by a slight margin, the most frequently alleged
form of misconduct, mentioned by 23 percent of all mothers. Even in
the post-1969 period, when the incidence of reporting misbehavior declines significantly, the incidence of reporting physical abuse remains
at 17 percent, a decline that is substantially less than that for each of

the other most commonly asserted complaints. Some of the notes taken by staff members of the Friend of the Court are vivid—and numbing: reports of repeated beatings, of beatings during pregnancy, of threats to kill, of assaults continuing even after the man had moved out of the home. Assault is mentioned by the wives of 20 percent or more of the men in all blue- and white-collar occupations, except by wives of professionals or managers, who may have had special reasons for not mentioning abuse that in fact occurred. There also appears no relation between abuse and length of marriage. Twenty-three percent of the 119 mothers whose marriages lasted more than ten years complained of physical abuse. Recent research by others suggests that assaultive behavior is far more common within families than has typically been recognized.[15] What we have seen tends to confirm these reports.

Although physical abuse is the most commonly asserted reason for wanting a divorce, there is reason to believe that it is not regarded as the most unforgivable of the sins of marriage. Physically abused women were as likely to be willing to reconcile as women who did not complain of physical abuse. On the other hand, among the women who complained of inadequate support, far fewer were willing to reconcile than the sample average, suggesting that the husband's repeated failure to support signaled the most irretrievable breakdown of a marriage. To be sure, we would be unwise to see a complaint of nonsupport as reflecting a marriage that had failed for want of money alone. Many of the men who had failed to provide for their families were probably estranged from them in other ways. Men portrayed by their wives as nonsupporters were, for example, significantly less likely than other men to attend the predivorce interview with the Friend of the Court.

Complaints by women of their husbands' alcohol problems, of physical abuse, and of nonsupport were closely intertwined. Many women who complained of one, complained of one or both of the other two. Alcohol forges the strongest links with the other two: two of every three mothers who complained of alcohol problems also complained of either physical abuse or nonsupport or both (see figure 3.2).

A Summary Synthesis

Recall Jerry and Dolores Neal: their anger and disengagement; their many children and little contact; Jerry's hard drinking and hard work; Dolores's loneliness and frustration. In some regards these few interviews make our statistical information from the Friend of the Court seem nearly as unsatisfying as the statistics of a football game when

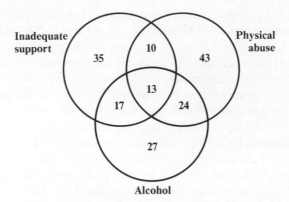

Fig. 3.2 Interrelation of mother's complaints of alcohol, physical abuse, and inadequate support (Genesee Random Sample). Number of women who complained (numbers are actual number of complaining mothers).
42% complained of nonsupport or alcohol or physical abuse
67% of those complaining of alcohol complained of at least one of the other two
52% of those complaining of physical abuse complained of one of the other two
53% of those complaining of inadequate support complained of at least one of the other two

offered as a substitute for watching the game itself. We can, however, infuse more life into our statistical information by regrouping it in terms of the age of the men at the time of their divorce. (We could as easily have grouped the cases by the age of the women since, as one might guess, husband and wife were typically within a few years of each other.) When we do group our cases in this way, we can picture younger and older couples who make it easier to imagine—or recall, if the reader has been married—where people stand at various stages of their lives. (Full details are found in appendix table 3I.)

Consider first the quarter of men in our sample who were twenty-five or under at divorce. These ninety-one men, most in their early twenties and nearly all of them blue-collar workers, had married, produced children, and were divorcing before many of their contemporaries had married for the first time. These were men compelled to face family responsibilities when they were young—they were under twenty, on the average, when their first child was born—and for them and their even younger wives this alone may have caused strain. Over half the marriages lasted less than two years before separation, and at separation few of either sex indicated a willingness to reconcile or to consider reconciling. On the other hand, however young they were, it was not possible without flouting law and custom to wipe the slate clean and start afresh. It is not merely that partners to short marriages form emotional attachments stronger than either recognizes before separation. There was something more than emotional attachment that continued to bind them: one or two very young children and a court order for support that would last nearly as many years into the future as the parents had been alive in the past.

Compare with this youngest group the position of the oldest quarter of our cases—those involving men who were over thirty-five at divorce. These 112 men, averaging about forty-one years of age, had been married an average of fourteen years before separation, most of them having married in their mid-twenties—after the age at which the younger men had been divorced. Over half had three or more children. The youngest was typically in grade school, the oldest in junior high school, at the time of separation. At the point of divorce, this group was in general fully established in their careers. Though the unemployment rate among them was as high as among the youngest men, far more were working in skilled blue-collar or white-collar jobs. They were, on the average, earning over 50 percent more each week than the younger men. With school-age children, far more of their wives were working at the time of divorce. Far fewer were receiving welfare benefits. Nearly 40 percent of the men in this group—about twice the percentage found among the youngest men—expressed a willingness to reconcile or to consider reconciliation at divorce. On the other hand, like the wives of the youngest men, very few of the wives of the older men (only 9 percent) were interested in considering reconciliation.

The group in between—the men who were twenty-six to thirty-five at divorce—were in between as well in most other characteristics: two children, marriage lasting five to ten years, the older child in grade school by the time of divorce. This group earned more than the younger men and less than the older. Jerry Neal was one of these men. Like Jerry, many of them had bought their first home not many years before. Now the disposition of that home became just another painful clause in the divorce decree.

These three groups, roughly arrayed by age, convey some flavor of the differing situations and experiences of the men at the point of divorce. Even if we know little of the quality of the day-to-day life of the couple, the men and their positions at divorce provide some basis for hypotheses about expectable patterns of payments of support after divorce, hypotheses we will soon be testing. They also provide a setting for understanding the general economic position of the families at divorce. We might guess that the older women, more of them working, with husbands able to pay higher orders of support, would be better off financially. To some extent this is true. As we are about to see, however, whether the women are younger or older, working or not working, nearly all mothers with children face a severe financial crisis at divorce that simply varies in degree. In this sense, our three groups are again one group, and this one group feels pinched.

Four

The Economics of Divorce

In some societies that are considered "primitive" couples divorce with only the slightest ceremony. The father (or the mother, depending on the custom) takes the children, returns to his village, and rejoins a unit that typically includes his own parents. The other parent is reabsorbed for as long as she chooses into the household of her parents. There is no dispute over custody and, though there will be a division of belongings upon separation, and a bride price perhaps returned, neither parent makes payments of support through any tribal Friend of the Court. Partners may be bitter on departure, but the process is swift and final.[1]

In our "civilized" society, we are more deliberative. On divorce, either parent may receive custody, and the increasing recognition that parents of either sex may be amply suited to raise children makes competing claims for custody difficult to resolve. Returning to a home "village" to live with grandparents is acceptable only as a transition to living again in a separate unit. Thus Dolores and Jerry Neal parted angrily in the socially prescribed way. Dolores and the five children stayed as a unit in the small house at the edge of Flint. Dolores's parents, who lived in a small house, could not absorb their daughter and five grandchildren. Dolores felt lonely and isolated but would not have chosen to live with her parents even if invited. Jerry, after his sojourn in jail for assaulting Dolores with a hammer, moved into a basement apartment of his own.

The tradition in our society of parents and children living alone without other relatives serves functions some people would consider useful: workers can more easily move to available jobs and consumption is maximized by small, inefficient units. Divorce, however, is an inconvenience, rarely useful to the economy, frequently costly to taxpayers. The mother and children maintain a separate unit but generally lack the capacity to maintain their former standard of living. Jobs are available to some but, as we shall see, mothers, when they are employed, often cannot earn enough to sustain their families at a level even close to that they maintained before. Most women remarry, but some prefer not to; and those who do marry again often wait for some time before doing so. Because of the obvious plight of the "single" mother, American governments have developed two systems of income support. The first takes the form of court-ordered child support paid in weekly installments. The second is welfare. Under each system enormous numbers of dollars change hands, but most of the people affected by each system are unhappy: fathers and taxpayers feel they pay out too much; mothers receive too little to survive in decency. These are the marks of civilization.

Our focus is child support. Let us look first at the way that courts fix the orders of child support and then examine the comparative well-being of the mothers relying on various forms of income support—their own employment, welfare payments, remarriage, and child support.

Fixing the Order of Support

Dolores Neal filed for divorce and applied for a temporary order of support. When the divorce became final, the court entered an order of ten dollars per week per child—a total of fifty dollars per week. At that point, Jerry earned about $120 a week after taxes. Thus his order was slightly more than 40 percent of his take-home pay.

How did the court fix the size of the order?

For income taxes—the other large compulsory transfer of income affecting Jerry—elaborate published schedules fixed to the dollar the amount Jerry owed. Michigan law, however, sets forth no specific formula for fixing orders of child support. Like statutes in many states, the Michigan statute authorizing courts to enter orders for child support gives the court no guidance whatever. The only section dealing with orders for support simply provides that, at the time of granting the divorce, the "court may make such further decree as it shall deem just and proper concerning the . . . maintenance of the minor children of the parties.''[2]

"Just and proper." Nothing more is said to steer the judge's decision. Is the "just" order one that requires the noncustodial parent to pay the full costs of support for the children and for their custodian at the standard at which they previously lived? Or is the "just" order one that requires the noncustodial parent to pay the difference between what a custodial parent can be expected to earn and the amount needed for the family to live at its prior standard? Or, if the custodial parent is expected to meet her own needs, is the noncustodial parent to be required to meet only half the remaining needs of the children, however defined? Is a "just" order reduced or terminated when the woman remarries? Is it reduced if the father has new children who need care? The legislation in Michigan and most other American states is silent. Appellate court decisions provide the trial judges little guidance. The divorcing parents may accordingly find the amorphous Michigan statute much like the legislation that accords a criminal court judge discretion to impose on a burglar a sentence of any term of years up to life. And, indeed, the imprecision of the divorce and criminal laws may have a comparable origin. In each setting, the legislators may have believed that fixed rules would not meet the requirements of individual cases, though much the same claim can be made about rates of taxation. They may also have believed, when they enacted the "just and proper" language in the nineteenth century, that divorcing persons, like criminals, have no compelling claims to predictability or even-handedness.

Despite the statutory language, Michigan's local judges have devised a system that has produced some measure of regularity and rough equity, even though it fails to reflect a coherent set of principles. In nearly all Michigan counties, the judges and Friends of the Court rely on a locally devised schedule that fixes the orders of support in relation to two factors only: the number of children in the family and the net earnings (after taxes and Social Security) of the noncustodial parent. Although each county has its own schedule, the percentage rates fixed for earnings in relation to the number of children differ little across counties, in part because many counties borrowed from their neighbors. In Genesee, for example, a circuit judge wrote all the other Friends of the Court and developed a schedule based on the responses. Table 4.1 shows the common range of orders within our samples, as prescribed by the support schedules, as well as orders fixed under a

Table 4.1   Orders of Support as Proportion of Father's Net Earnings

No. of Children	% Range Within 28 Counties According to Schedules	Actual % Among Full-Time Workers, Genesee Random Sample (mean)	% in "Model" Schedule, King County, Washington
1	18–23%	23.3%	24%
2	30–35	36.7	35
3	38–42	39.5	42
4	45–48	43.8	48

"model schedule" about which we shall say more below. No Friend of the Court or judge regarded the schedule as binding, but in about two-thirds of the counties in our twenty-eight-county sample the Friend of the Court believed that the actual order differed from the support schedule in fewer than 20 percent of cases.

The actual orders in our cases at the point of divorce averaged about twenty-seven dollars a week for men who were employed full-time at the point of divorce and represented an average of 33 percent of their after-tax earnings. The dollar figure may sound meager, but the reader needs to remember that our sample was drawn from cases alive in 1970 and included men divorced as early as 1951, when average earnings were less than a third of what they are today. The average weekly order entered in Genesee County in 1978 would be closer to seventy dollars a week or about thirty-five hundred dollars a year.

How do Michigan's orders compare with those in other states? There are no other recent studies we could find that report for a random sample of divorce cases the relation of order size to parents' earnings. I have reported our findings at conferences across the country and find that child support enforcers believe that Michigan's orders are as high as, or higher than, orders elsewhere. In many places, no child-support schedule is used, the statutory language is as cloudy as Michigan's, and lawyers bargain over child support in each case as part of a common package that includes alimony and the division of real and personal property.

The most notable aspect of the rates in the Michigan support schedule is their origin in custom. None of the schedules, so far as we can learn, were developed after a study of the actual costs of raising children or after determining the earnings of working mothers. An effort to approach the setting of orders more "scientifically," however, has produced strikingly similar results that may cast some light on the judgments implicit in the Michigan schedules. The judges of Seattle, Washington, recently sought to develop a support schedule reflecting actual needs of families of varying sizes and invited Florence T. Hall, a professor of home economics, to work with them.[3]

Professor Hall developed for the Seattle committee a new schedule based on three premises: (1) the support amount should be directly related to the predivorce family income rather than some abstract notion of a child's basic needs; (2) orders should be set on the assumption that the custodial parent has an income to meet his or her own needs and that each parent should contribute an equal portion of earnings to the cost of supporting the child; and (3) children should share in the decreased standard of living necessarily resulting from the costs of maintaining one parent in a separate unit. In the end, using cost-of-living information from the Bureau of Labor Statistics, the committee produced a schedule identical in form and similar in detail to those we found in Michigan—identical in form because orders were to be fixed taking into account only the noncustodial parent's earnings and the number of children, and similar in detail in that the percentages of earnings set for families of various sizes were only a few points higher in Seattle than in Genesee (see table 4.1, above).

That Michigan's system, originating in custom, should come so close to the carefully developed system of Seattle may seem surprising but should not be. Those who undertook the revision of the support schedule for Seattle knew they could not depart too dramatically from old ways and retain wide support, and Seattle's old ways were close to Michigan's. They also wished, quite openly, to develop a formula that was easy to apply.

Knowledge of the way the Seattle schedule was formulated illuminates several aspects of the Michigan system. The most important of these is that while the orders of support typically seem high to fathers—a third of their net income seems a lot of money—the amount the schedules prescribe is not enough to permit the wife and children to live at their former standard. Far from it. Under the Seattle and Michigan schemes, only if the woman earns enough to sustain herself at her former standard and enough more to provide a large share of the costs of maintaining the children at the standard will the support payments of the father permit a continuation of the prior standard of living for her and the children.

A few other aspects of the Michigan and Seattle systems bear observation. Although the Seattle system assumed that the custodial parent would be supported by other income, in neither Michigan nor Seattle does a custodial parent's earnings enter into the formula for determining the amount of support. The exclusion of the custodial parent's income provides her with the maximum incentive to enter the labor market and earn as much as she can, since the support amount will not decline as her earnings increase. Michigan courts also do not reduce support orders upon the remarriage of either the husband or the wife or upon any later order of support entered against the father. Explained on the ground that the noncustodial parent's obligation is not justly affected by any of these events, the policy has the effect of creating the maximum incentive for the custodial parent to remarry and the maximum incentive for the noncustodial parent to remain single, even celibate.

Finally, in neither Michigan nor Seattle does a support-paying parent have a guaranteed "cushion" to meet his or her own needs. A noncustodial parent earning so little that he cannot afford to live alone at the poverty line will nonetheless be ordered to pay the schedule-fixed percentage of his earnings. This is true, even though the unit of the other parent and children, if similarly poor, will be eligible for federal welfare benefits, while the low-earning other parent alone probably will not be eligible. Today there is no federal system of income support for the nondisabled person of very low earnings who lives alone.

Financial Positions after Divorce

Child Support and the Family's Standard of Living

How well do parents and children get along financially after divorce? One judge in Flint commented to me, "I tell these people when they come to my courtroom that even though they cannot stand living together, they're not going to be able to afford living apart."

The judge was partly right. Divorce works a financial catastrophe for most people who pass through it. But, as hinted above, at least initially, the financial crisis is usually far more acute for the newly separated woman taking care of children than it is for the man on his own. The man faces crises readjusting to life on his own—anger, remorse, loneliness, depression. The woman faces these and the financial crisis as well. In a well-regarded study of peoples' attitudes toward their own lives, women who had divorced and not remarried reported less satisfaction with their lives than Americans in any other marital status, including widows and women who had never married.[4] Divorced women were especially likely to fear being unable to meet their bills. Seventy percent of divorced women but only 42 percent of divorced men said they often worry about making ends meet. The women's fears have foundation. Accustomed to life at one standard, newly divorced women suddenly find themselves several "notches" worse off.

To understand the financial situations of the parties we need to look at the financial position of the family when it was intact and then compare the positions of the separated units. The comparison is a gloomy one. There are problems posed, however, in making comparisons. Since an eight thousand dollar income for the man living alone will permit him to live considerably more comfortably than the same eight thousand dollars will permit the woman and three children to live, we need some acceptable standard of living figures that account for units of varying sizes. The United States Department of Labor has developed several such standards and has inherited another—the Poverty Line—from the Social Security Administration. These somewhat artificial standards are useful bases for making comparisons and yield some startling results when applied to our families.

The Poverty Line was devised by Mollie Orshansky of the Social Security Administration in 1963.[5] Its construction was very simple. Surveys in 1955 had indicated that most families spent about one-fourth of their income on food, very large families as much as one-third. The Department of Agriculture had devised and priced several model diet plans, the lowest-cost of which was the "Economy Food Plan." The original measure was obtained by multiplying the cost of the Economy Food Plan by three. Since that original computation (based on the 1961 Economy Food Plan), the measure has been revised annually to reflect changes in the "cost of living."

Orshansky never intended her measure as anything more than a first approximation. However, White House pressure to devise a standard against which to measure progress in the "war against poverty" led to almost immediate and uncritical adoption of the Orshansky standard. It remains today the principal measure of economic "well-offness" of the poor, despite its well-recognized inadequacy;[6] we use it solely because it is so prevalent.

The three "standard budgets" of the Bureau of Labor Statistics were devised in 1967, although the "intermediate" standard is simply a continuation of something called the "moderate" standard used since 1946. These standards are also in part based upon Department of Agriculture standardized food plans, the "low-cost," "moderate-cost," and "liberal" plans. But the remainder of each budget was originally set by specifying and pricing a quantity and quality of goods and services for each living level, and has been updated since by adjustments for "cost-of-living" changes in each component.[7]

The Lower Standard Budget was devised in part in response to appeals from state welfare agencies and legislators formulating public-housing income criteria for a budget more consistent than the Moderate Budget with public-assistance program objectives and funding constraints. The Intermediate Budget has always been thought of as a "modest but adequate" level, attained by the average American urban working family. The Higher Budget level is not so well specified, having apparently been devised mainly to provide symmetry with the lower budget, but it certainly defines a standard of living well below what most Americans would consider luxurious. In 1969 roughly 11 percent of all American families were below the Poverty Line, 18 percent above the Poverty Line but below the Lower Standard, 25 percent above the Lower Standard but below the Intermediate Standard, 24 percent above the Intermediate Standard but below the Higher Standard, and the remainder—23 percent—above the Higher Standard. For simplicity of exposition in the materials that follow, we have merged the groups below the Poverty Line and the Lower Standard Budget into one group below the Lower Standard. The Lower Standard Budget seems to us to convey better the line below which most people would feel they are living in poverty.

Let us try to convey these standards of living a bit more graphically. The food component of the Lower Budget is heavily weighted with potatoes, dry beans and peas, and flour and cereals. It is light on meat, poultry, fish, fruits, and other vegetables. Meat, when purchased, is the cheapest cuts, the vegetables can be purchased only "in season," no "convenience foods" can be purchased, and food away from home can be purchased only rarely and then only at fast-food stands. It takes extraordinary shopping and cooking skill to produce a nutritionally adequate diet on the money available from the Low-Cost plan. It is not surprising that studies by the United States Department of Agriculture have found that only about a quarter of families with earnings at this level attain minimal nutritional adequacy.

The food component of the Intermediate Standard Budget allows for more and better cuts of meat, for more fruits and vegetables (even out of season), for milk and eggs, and for some convenience foods. It also permits dining out at moderate-cost restaurants several times a year. The Higher Budget's food component is different from the Intermediate Budget's primarily in allowing for more expensive grades of food and more frequent visits to more expensive restaurants. Similar gradations of differences in the styles of life at varying living standards can easily be pictured for housing, clothing, transportation, and other costs: from a cramped, rented apartment to a purchased home with a yard; from patched and repatched hand-me-downs to several new sets of clothing a year; from no car or an old used car to two cars.

Where in relation to these standards did our families in Genesee County live before and after separation? The short answer is that most lived moderately well before separation but that the women and children fared miserably afterwards.

After adjusting earnings at divorce, whenever that occurred, into constant dollars, we find, as figure 4.1 reports, that the combined earnings of the men and women in our families permitted over two-thirds of the families, when intact, to live at or above the Intermediate Standard Budget line.* These figures somewhat exaggerate how well-off our families were when intact because the earnings of some of the women we have included almost certainly came from jobs they did not acquire until after separation. If we assume that some but not all of these women were employed before separation, it is probable that around 35 to 40 percent of the families lived above the intermediate line when the parents were together. The number living below the Lower Standard Budget when the family was intact would probably have been around 30 to 35 percent.

For two reasons, the picture changes dramatically at the point of divorce. The first reason is that no matter what the parents' joint income was when the family was intact, the same income cannot be divided at divorce in such a way that the now separated family can live as well as before. As soon as one parent is living in one place and the other parent and children in another, the total cost of housing will almost always be higher—and will always be higher if the custodial parent remains in the residence in which the family had been living before separation. Similarly, if there had been only one automobile in the family before separation, there will now be a need for two. To maintain the same standard of living, total income of the two parents will have to rise between 10 and 25 percent.

The second reason for the dramatic change is that income will not in fact be distributed between the two units in a way that permits approximately the same standard for each unit, even though the standard

*The process we used to adjust earnings in order to render all cases comparable is explained in the Methodological Appendix, pp. 291–92.

will be slightly lower for each than before. In almost all cases a smaller portion of the income needed to maintain their former standard will be available to the mother and children than will be available to the father. To have lived at the intermediate standard before the separation, the family of four in 1978 would have needed a total income of $18,600. To maintain the same standard after divorce, the mother and two children would have needed a total income of $14,100, or about $270 each

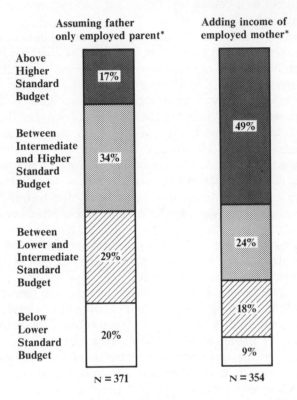

Assuming father only employed parent*

Above Higher Standard Budget — 17%

Between Intermediate and Higher Standard Budget — 34%

Between Lower and Intermediate Standard Budget — 29%

Below Lower Standard Budget — 20%

N = 371

Adding income of employed mother*

49%

24%

18%

9%

N = 354

Fig. 4.1 Standard of living maintained by families prior to sep-aration (Genesee Random Sample).
*Over half the mothers in the Genesee sample were employed at the time of their predivorce interview with the Friend of the Court. Unfortunately, the Friend of the Court records did not reveal how many of these women had been employed prior to separation. The columns of the figure here assume that the father was employed before separation but make alternative assumptions regarding the mother's employment.

week. Can she in fact obtain $270 every week through earnings and support payments—or even 10 or 20 percent less? Probably not. The same will be true for mothers who had lived at other income levels before divorce.

In most of our families, it was probably the case that immediately prior to separation the father was employed full-time but the mother was not employed. (Two-thirds of our mothers had a child three or under.) Consider the position of each parent, if we assume for the moment that there is no such thing as court-ordered child support and the father made no voluntary payments for his children's support. Figure 4.2 illustrates the financial situation after separation of the father in the Genesee cases if we assume that he was the only employed person in the family and retained all his earnings for his own use.

There is no need here for a column illustrating the position of the mother and children. By hypothesis, if she is not employed or receiving welfare benefits and the father is making no payments, she and her children will have no income. In the figure, they would be an all-white

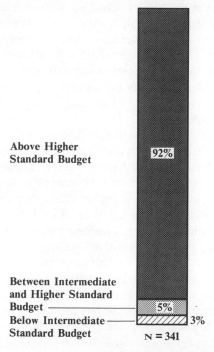

Above Higher
Standard Budget   92%

Between Intermediate
and Higher Standard
Budget ────────────── 5%
Below Intermediate ───── ///////// 3%
Standard Budget   N = 341

Fig. 4.2 Position of working fathers after divorce if they lived alone and failed to pay support (Genesee Random Sample).

column living below the Lower Standard Budget. A pillar of salt. The father's column is noteworthy, however. By separating himself from his family and hoarding all income to himself, the father improves his standard of living dramatically. When with their families, over a third of working men lived at or below the level of the Intermediate Standard Budget. Living apart, only 3 percent, most of them part-time employed, are left below that budget level. Over nine in ten suddenly attain the Higher Standard Budget for a single person.

Fortunately for the financial well-being of women and children, courts upon separation do order absent fathers to pay support. Unfortunately, as we will later see, many fathers fail to pay. After divorce, Jerry Neal paid for about a year and then stopped. Dolores's anger at his nonpayment now becomes even more understandable. She was not employed when she separated from Jerry. She was at home taking care of five children, all of them under nine. The youngest was only two. Jerry was earning high wages for 1962—a gross of $122 a week from General Motors. When living together as a unit of seven, the family had been able to live at the Lower Standard Budget level. On leaving, Jerry was suddenly earning enough to live at the Higher Standard Budget level for a person living alone: enough for a newly purchased home, a car, a steak diet. Dolores, when child support stopped, had five young children and no income, unless she turned to welfare.

What if the father *does* pay the support ordered by the court? What then is the standard of living of the mother and her young children if she is not employed?

As we know from the discussion above, so long as there is no increase in family income, both units cannot retain their former standard when living apart. Figure 4.3 makes clear, however, that under the levels of child support that are in fact ordered in Michigan—orders that are, we believe, as high as, or higher than, those in most parts of the country—it is only the women and children whose standards of living decline even when the father is making payments. With child support payments alone, only 3 percent of mothers can maintain a standard above the Lower Standard Budget. Put another way, a mother with two children needs between 75 and 80 percent of the family's former total income to continue to live at the prior standard. The father will have been ordered by the court to pay around 33 percent of his income. There remains a painful gap. On the other hand, the father who pays child support and retains two-thirds of his income still remains better-off financially than he was before divorce. Four in five fathers can live at or above the Intermediate Standard Budget.

The gap between the father's position and that of the mother and children in many cases widened over time. Orders were fixed in dollars based on the man's earnings at the point of divorce. Courts were willing to increase the dollar amount upon proof that the father's earnings had increased, but in only a small portion of our cases were there ever any increases in the dollar amount of the order. Thus for most women the order size remained the same over the years, while the costs of living rose.

In the first year after divorce, Jerry Neal paid the court-ordered support of fifty dollars a week, about 40 percent of his take-home pay. With the remaining 60 percent of his pay check, Jerry, like most other

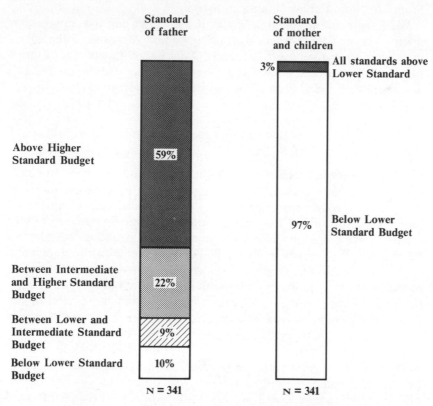

Fig. 4.3 Standards of living after divorce if father paid support and mother tried to live on support only (Genesee Random Sample).
NOTE: Compare these standards with those in figure 4.1.

fathers, lived above the Higher Standard Budget. From the fifty dollar payments each week, however, Dolores and the five children had income equal to only three-fourths of the Poverty Line, not enough to make do in even the most rudimentary way. Remember how little even the Lower Standard Budget provides—mostly beans and starch, an eight-year-old used car, around $140 for rent in today's market. Fifty dollars every week in 1962 seemed an enormous amount of money to Jerry Neal but too little to Dolores. Both were right in some important psychological sense. The gap in psychological perception between many divorced persons about the value of the payments surely operates to widen other gaps in the postdivorce relations between parents—gaps in perceptions about "fault" in the marriage, the appropriate care of children, and so forth.

We have made it sound so far as if the father can live in splendor upon divorce. Later we will see that when he lives alone, although he may be comparatively well-off, he is likely to feel lonely and bitter; if he remarries and has a new family, he may in fact eventually live at a lower standard than before, if he pays child support to his first family.

Additional Sources of Income for the Mother and Children

We have seen that unemployed mothers can rarely survive on child-support payments alone. Within our sample, it is apparent that few tried to do so. In the initial months after separation, a substantial number returned to live for some period with their own parents or other relatives. We did not code this information for our random sample, but for the sample of men who were jailed in Genesee, who mirror in many regards the blue-collar families in our random sample, about 40 percent of the mothers were living either with their parents or with other relatives at the time of the predivorce interview with the Friend of the Court. We have no way of knowing from the Friend of the Court files whether many mothers continued to live with other relatives for a substantial period after divorce. Other literature about divorce leads us to guess that for most Genesee mothers, as for most other American families in divorce, the return to living with other relatives was probably regarded as transitional—a way station on a road that led toward the reestablishment of a new and separate unit.[8]

The majority of mothers lived in a unit with their children and no one else. For them especially—but also for most of those living with relatives—a strong need existed to develop a source or sources of income to supplement the father's support payments.Three sources, not mutually exclusive, were available: earned income from employment, income from public-assistance benefits, and income from a man with whom they established a new living relationship. At least nine of every ten mothers in our sample turned to one or more of these three at some point after divorce. Half the women turned to two sources or all three, a high portion taking or retaining employment, then remarrying, but never applying for public assistance. The portions in our sample who were employed by the time of their divorce or who received welfare benefits or remarried over the lives of the orders in Genesee are revealed in table 4.2. Since we had employment information for mothers only at the point of their divorce, the table understates the portion of the mothers who were later employed. The true figure for those ever employed after divorce is probably closer to 80 percent than it is to the 59 percent whom we record as employed at the moment of divorce.[9]

Table 4.2	Other Income Sources of Women, Genesee Random Sample		
Sources		N	%
None: not employed at divorce, no welfare, no remarriage		35	10%
Employed: no welfare or remarriage later		71	20
Welfare: not employed, no remarriage		39	11
Remarriage: no welfare, not employed		39	11
Employed and welfare: no remarriage		15	4
Employed and remarriage: no welfare		102	28
Remarriage and welfare: not employed		36	10
All three: employed, welfare, remarriage		23	6
Total		360	100%
		N	%
Portion of women who were:			
Employed, part- or full-time at divorce		211	59%
Ever received welfare benefits during life of records		113	31
Remarried during life of records		200	55

NOTE: "Employed" means employed part- or full-time at the point of divorce. "Welfare" and "remarriage" refer to receipt of welfare benefits or to remarriage at any time up to our coding in the summer of 1973.

Only thirty-five women, 10 percent of those who remained in Genesee County and for whom we had full file information, were not employed at divorce and did not either remarry or turn to public assistance during the lives of our records. They are a special group. In comparison to the women who were then employed, or who remarried, or who received welfare (or any combination of these), this group, on average, received from child-support payments a higher portion of their needs than any other group. Their orders were larger, though they had no more than the average number of children, and their former husbands paid at a particularly high rate. Even given this payment rate, however, very few even of these women were able to maintain their former standard of living or even the next lower standard budget level. Yet more of this group could survive in some fashion on support alone. We cannot know how many of these women not employed at divorce later joined the labor force. It may well be that most were employed at some later point but had enough resources to tide them over during the period immediately after separation at the time that the only information we had about their employment was recorded.

The reason that few of this group ever received welfare benefits may possibly be the high level of their support payments. It may also be due to reasons of class status—more of these women had been married to white-collar men, and other parts of our study suggest that such women, even when needy, less frequently received public assistance. The reason that fewer of this group remarried may be a function of age. Together with the women who were employed but never remarried or received AFDC, this group was older (32.3) at the point of divorce than any of the other groups (the rest averaged 27.0).[10] We have found that the woman's age is importantly related to remarriage.[11]

This group of women who were not employed at divorce and who never remarried and never received welfare benefits nonetheless may well have sensed their economic vulnerability at the point of divorce: 29 percent of this group, but only 8 percent of other mothers, indicated in their predivorce interview a willingness to reconcile or to consider reconciling.[12]

Let us look now at the remaining 90 percent of our mothers who did turn to other sources of support.

Income from Employment

At the point of divorce almost exactly half the mothers in our sample were employed full-time. Another 8 percent were employed part-time. We can rarely tell from the file information available to us how many of these women had been employed when the family was intact and how many began to work only after separation. Census figures for Genesee County strongly suggest that many of the mothers in our study returned to the labor force after separation or in anticipation of separation. In 1970, in Genesee County as a whole, only about a third of married women in intact families with children under eighteen were in the labor force.[13]

Through their earnings, a few of the women in our study were able to sustain a comfortable standard of living for themselves and their children. For most, however, even with full-time employment, the family's standard of living was much lower than it had been. Part of the problem lay in the lower earnings women received. The women in our study who were employed earned, on the average, about 57 percent of what their husbands earned—$67 a week as opposed to $117 a week.

Why did women earn so much less than men? For some of the women, the answer surely lies in part in the recentness of their return to the labor market; they received entry-level wages while their husbands had been building seniority over several years in the labor force. But the problem runs deeper. In this country, women's jobs simply pay less well than men's regardless of seniority. The women in our study earned in relation to their husbands almost precisely the portion of men's earnings that women earn across the country.[14] A justification often offered for the lower pay in jobs available to women—that women are second earners in their families—rings particularly hollow when applied to the mothers in our study who must provide the principal support for their children.

Accordingly, few of the divorced women in our study, could, without depending on the father's contributions or some other source of income, maintain a decent standard of living for themselves and their children solely on the basis of their own earnings. As figure 4.4 indicates, two-thirds of the working women in our sample would, on their own earnings alone, have lived with their children below the Intermediate Standard Budget. Only 16 percent—fewer than one in six— would have been able to live above the Higher Standard Budget.

That standard was far lower than it had been for most of these women and children during the marriage. If we assume that both parents had been employed during the marriage and look at the combined earnings of the husband and wife, we find, of course, in almost every case that, despite the fact that the former unit in which the children lived was one person larger, these women and children were far better-off financially when the family was intact: with the father in the

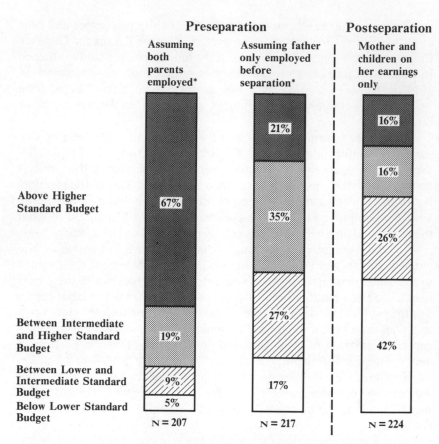

Fig. 4.4 Standard of living of the mothers employed at divorce (Genesee Random Sample).

*These columns differ from those in figure 4.1 in that all families were included in figure 4.1 whether or not the mother was employed at the time of the predivorce interview. Here only those employed at the time of that interview are included. We include a column here that assumes that only the husband was employed before separation, because many of the women employed at the time of the interview probably were not working at the time of the separation several months earlier.

home and both parents employed, 67 percent of the families could live above the Higher Standard Budget; on the mother's earnings alone, fewer than a quarter as many of the mothers and children could live as well. There were only thirty-eight divorced mothers who on their own earnings alone could maintain their families at the Higher Standard level. These women nearly all held comparatively high-paying jobs (averaging over 50 percent higher earnings than other working women in the sample). More striking, nearly all of them—thirty-five of thirty-eight—had only one child. Only three of the 278 women with more than one child earned enough to keep their family at the Higher Standard Budget level.

The figures at the other end of the earnings scale are fully as noteworthy. On the combined earnings of husband and wife only 5 percent of the families had lived below the Lower Standard Budget, but on the employed mother's income alone 42 percent of the mothers and children lived below this level. If we regard the Lower Standard Budget as the minimally decent level for subsistence in this country, it is distressing to recognize that on their own earnings nearly half the employed mothers would have been unable to feed or house their children with minimal adequacy.

We have not yet, however, considered child support. What if the father did pay the court-ordered support *and* the mother was employed? Was the combined income from these sources sufficient to permit the mother and children to sustain their former standard of living? For some courts, that has been the goal in fixing child support orders.

Figure 4.5 reveals a marked improvement for the mothers. On the combination of their earnings and the father's payments, if made in full, only about 15 percent of employed mothers were forced to live below the Lower Standard Budget level, as compared with the 42 percent we have just examined when the mother had to subsist on her earnings alone. Indeed, as a comparison of figure 4.5 with the second column of figure 4.4 reveals, the woman and children, on her earnings plus full child support, were approximately as well-off financially as they had been before separation, if the father alone had been employed before separation.

Can we conclude from these figures that a woman unhappy in marriage can improve her happiness and maintain her financial position simply by separating, obtaining a child support order, and working in the labor force? Far from it. In the first place, to live as well, the mother must actually collect the court-ordered support, and, as we shall see, many men simply do not pay. Moreover, even if the father does pay regularly, the comparative advantage here applies only for women who had not been employed before divorce. For those who were employed before separation (and not simply employed for the first time after separation but before divorce), the combined earnings of both parents in an intact family nearly always produce a higher standard than the mother's earnings plus child support (compare figure 4.5 with the first column of figure 4.4). Finally, even if a woman who has not been employed is confident that she can get a decently remunera-

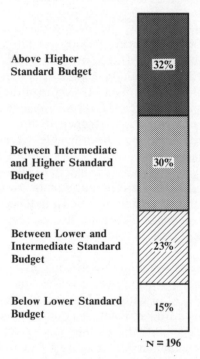

Above Higher
Standard Budget   32%

Between Intermediate
and Higher Standard   30%
Budget

Between Lower and
Intermediate Standard   23%
Budget

Below Lower Standard
Budget   15%

N = 196

Fig. 4.5 Standard of living of employed mothers and of children, if husband paid support in full (Genesee Random Sample).
NOTE: For a rough comparison of the positions of the fathers in these cases, see col. 1 of figure 4.3. That figure includes all families, whereas this one includes only the families with mothers working at divorce. If we look only at the fathers in cases in which the mother was employed, we find that, if they lived alone, 66% of the fathers could pay support and still live above the Higher Standard Budget level, as opposed to the 59% shown in figure 4.3.

tive job after separation and is confident that her husband will pay support, there is reason to believe that as a single parent on her own she will still feel economically less secure despite the fact that she is objectively as well-off as she was before separation.[15] She has no other adult to lean on as financial insurance. Moreover, she is a woman, and in this country women are less likely than men to have been raised to believe that they can handle financial matters.

There were within our sample seventy-one women who were employed at the point of divorce and who apparently neither remarried nor turned to the welfare system during the period we recorded. They raised their children on their earnings plus whatever child support their former husbands paid. This group was closely similar in its characteristics to the thirty-eight women described above who were not employed at divorce but who also never turned to the ADC system or remarried. Like them, they were older on the average at divorce, after longer marriages, than were the women who remarried or applied for public assistance. Indeed the only factor that clearly distinguishes this group of employed women from those who turned to none of the three alternative systems is the fact of their employment.

While employment in the labor force is an obvious way to ameliorate the financial problems after divorce, it is not a solution equally available to all women.

Within the data available to us, the age of the youngest child at the point of separation was the strongest factor associated with whether the mother was employed full-time at the point of divorce. The younger the youngest child the less likely the mother was to be employed (see appendix table 4A). Those employed full-time included two-thirds of the mothers whose youngest child was of grade school age but only a third of those whose youngest was twelve months or younger.

Most people would expect that mothers of young children would be less likely to be employed than mothers of older children. But much disagreement would arise over the implications for public policy of the finding that a third of single mothers with children twelve months or younger were in the labor force. Many would applaud their employment because it keeps them off welfare or, from a less selfish perspective, because it gives them financial independence as well as relief from full-time housekeeping. These persons would advocate expanded day-care facilities to permit even more women to become employed.[16] Others would conclude that welfare benefits should be raised substantially to permit the third of mothers of one-year-olds who were employed to stay at home nurturing their babies. They would feel much

the same way about the 47 percent of mothers of children of one to
three years who were also employed.[17]

The 231 mothers with children under three years constituted a
majority of the women in our sample—nearly 60 percent in fact. These
young women faced a grim choice. If they elected to remain at home
with their child (or children), child support alone would not bring their
family even to the Poverty Line and, as we will soon see, welfare
benefits would provide only a little more. On the other hand, if they
chose to take a job, they faced both the problems of finding suitable,
affordable day-care and doubts about whether they were serving their
children's best interests. Moreover, even within the range of jobs
commonly available to women, employers are often reluctant to hire
persons who have not been employed for several years and who are the
sole caretakers of small children and are needed at home whenever a
child is ill. Consider Dolores Neal. She did not in fact try to find
employment after separation, but imagine her appeal at that point to an
employer: she had never been employed in her life; she had never
finished high school; she was depended upon by five children under
nine. There appear to have been dozens of other women like her within
our sample.

Public Assistance

The program known as Aid to Families with Dependent Children addresses directly the income problems of custodial parents after divorce. This program, which is federally supported and in which all
states participate, provides aid to families with one parent absent from
the home, so long as the caretaker parent has income lower than the
grant level the state has set for a family of that size. Each state legislature decides for itself the level of grants that it will pay to eligible
residents who apply.

Parents who turn to public assistance assign their rights to child
support to the state. They do not, that is, receive welfare benefits in
addition to their child support payments; they receive the benefits in
place of the child support. In exchange, they receive a grant varying
with the size of their family and with the amount of their own earnings,
but not varying with the ups and downs of actual payments of support
by the other parent. The state bears the risk of his nonpayment.

In Genesee County in 1969, a parent with two children would have
been eligible for public assistance totalling about three thousand dollars
over the year, approximately the Poverty Line and not quite two-thirds
of the Lower Standard Budget. In 1976, the same family would have

been entitled to about forty-four hundred dollars, but, because of inflation, the grant would represent slightly less in purchasing power than did the 1969 grant of three thousand dollars. Imagine trying to raise two children today on forty-four hundred dollars a year. Michigan's grants are higher than the grants in most other states (see appendix table 4B for grant levels in Michigan in 1969 and 1976 in relation to the various budget levels).

Dolores Neal was one of many women in Genesee County with far less income than the amount granted for a family the size of hers. Even though Jerry paid his child support regularly during the first year or so after they separated, his fifty dollar weekly payment was less than the grant amount for a family of an adult and five children. At the point of divorce, about 40 percent of the women in our sample were similarly eligible for assistance, even if their former husbands regularly paid support. If none had paid support and earned income had been the only income available, over 60 percent of the mothers and children would have been eligible for assistance.

Dolores Neal did apply for public assistance. At the time of her divorce, all five of her children were under nine and the youngest was not yet two. Except during most of the few-year periods of her second and third marriages, she has remained on the AFDC rolls throughout the years since her divorce from Jerry. In 1962, at the time of her divorce, her grant was about $2,800 a year. In 1976 the yearly grant for a parent and five children had risen to about $6,756. In addition, under the Medicaid program adopted in the years since her divorce from Jerry, Dolores would today be entitled to free medical insurance coverage comparable to that which could be purchased at an annual premium of $1,625. Since AFDC and Medicaid benefits are not subject to taxation, their combined value is equal to gross earnings of about $9,500 a year.

Ninety-five hundred dollars will still sound to many Americans like a good deal of money. It was, in fact, approximately the median income of all American families in 1970. But a mother and five children constitute a large family, and costs of living have risen dramatically during the 1970s. A mother and five children with an income of $9,500 would live at slightly above the Poverty Line today but still well below the Lower Standard Budget, the level at which Dolores and Jerry had been living at the time they separated. In most other states, since grants are lower than they are in Michigan, Dolores and the children would live well below the Poverty Line.

However modest the standard of living that welfare benefits permit, they can nonetheless assure to a parent a dependable flow of income. Nonetheless, most mothers and children eligible for assistance in our sample never received it. About half the families in our survey were eligible for assistance at the point of divorce, given actual payments of child support. (If the woman's earnings coupled with child support payments she actually received exceeded the grant level set by the state for recipients, she was not eligible for a grant.) Because of periods of unemployment or nonpayment, a substantial additional number of mothers were eligible at some later time. Yet only 18 percent of the mothers in our sample had received public assistance by the end of the calendar year after the year of their divorce and only slightly more than 30 percent ever received assistance during the period of our coding. What marks the difference between the mothers who do and mothers who do not turn to the AFDC system for support after a divorce?

Within our data, we had many factors that might have differentiated women who received public assistance from women who did not: the number of children, the age of the youngest child at divorce, the employment status or occupation type of the father or mother, information about whether the mother ever remarried, and so forth. To sort out which of these, if any, were significantly related to welfare receipt, we relied on multiple regression analysis and a related technique called multiple classification analysis.[18]

After a series of analyses, we found several factors that helped to explain which mothers received welfare benefits. By far the strongest factor was the mother's employment status and occupation at the time of divorce (see figure 4.6). That employed women turn less frequently to welfare for support may hardly seem puzzling. It is striking nonetheless that women employed at the point of divorce are so much less likely to receive public assistance not merely at the point of divorce but at any time thereafter.

As the figure also reveals, women employed in different occupation groups turned to welfare at greatly different rates. Women working at divorce in blue-collar jobs outside the auto industry were, for example, more than twice as likely to receive public assistance at some point as women in white-collar clerical, secretarial, or sales jobs, despite the fact that within our sample the earnings of this white-collar group were not significantly higher than the earnings of blue-collar workers. Since women's earnings in dollars at divorce did not prove to be significantly related to receipt of welfare, the differences we found by types of employment suggest either that the white-collar workers had more dependable jobs, or more loyalty to them, or that other factors—social factors—inhibited them from applying at the same rate.

In our multiple classification analysis, three other sorts of women who proved particularly likely to receive assistance were those who were divorced in the last years of our sampling (1969–73), those whose former husbands paid nothing or nearly nothing in support over the lives of their decrees, and those with children under the age of one at the point of the divorce. (See appendix table 4C.) Of the three findings, one makes sense, a second is confusing, and the third is slightly surprising.

The finding that mothers with very young children are more likely to

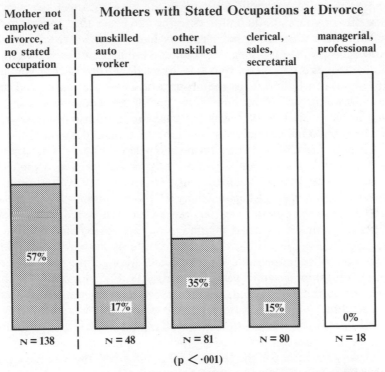

Portion Ever Receiving AFDC Benefits

Mother not employed at divorce, no stated occupation | **Mothers with Stated Occupations at Divorce**

unskilled auto worker   other unskilled   clerical, sales, secretarial   managerial, professional

57%   17%   35%   15%   0%

N = 138   N = 48   N = 81   N = 80   N = 18

(p < ·001)

Fig. 4.6 Relation of mother's occupation and employment status at time of divorce to her receipt of AFDC benefits then or later during period of support order (Genesee Random Sample).

receive welfare benefits seems to have an obvious explanation: mothers with babies wish more often to remain at home than to join the labor force. The second finding, that mothers who do not receive their child support payments are more likely to receive public assistance, would similarly appear to have an obvious explanation: women are more likely to need assistance when they are not getting support. In fact, the relation of welfare receipt and child support payment rates is more elusive, because in some cases the causal effect may well have been just the opposite: some men fail to pay because their wives are already receiving assistance and thus have an alternative source of support. We have had grave difficulty sorting out the direction of the causal link.[19]

The third finding is not so confusing but is somewhat unexpected: despite the fact that they had been in the files for fewer years by the time of our sampling, the mothers in the 126 cases that opened in 1969 or later were more than half again as likely to have received public assistance by 1973, when we collected information, as were the mothers in the 238 cases that had opened before 1969. Even more strikingly, nearly five times the proportion of mothers divorced in the post-1969 era received benefits by the end of the second year after their final order of divorce than was the case among those divorced in the pre-1969 era. One possible explanation, documented by others, is that throughout the United States during the period from the late sixties to 1971 a much larger portion of persons eligible for assistance applied for it than had previously been the case.[20] Apparently by the time that high-enrollment period began, many of those within our sample who had been divorced in the pre-1969 period had remarried or adjusted to living on their own earned income. For this earlier divorced group, welfare seems indeed to have been a source of support to which they turned only if other possible sources failed. Many of the pre-1969 group within our sample who ever turned to AFDC did so only after yet another marriage had failed. On the other hand, for more of the group divorced in 1969 or thereafter, a group which may have sensed fewer social barriers to welfare receipt, welfare was a first line of defense against the economic stress of the postseparation period.

As was the case for the women who turned to the welfare system only after a second divorce, so for others in our sample the receipt of welfare was not an always or never proposition. Of the 120 women in our sample who received welfare benefits, only twenty-seven (or 23 percent) received welfare in every year from the divorce to the end of our records.[21] Indeed, more women (thirty-two) received welfare benefits for one year only than received it in every year. Thus for many women, welfare served as a needed, temporary crutch during a period of readjustment. The stereotype of the welfare recipient as the person who enrolls and stays on until the youngest child is eighteen fails to describe most of the women in our study just as it fails to describe most parents who receive public assistance in this country as a whole.

Remarriage

After Dolores Neal divorced Jerry, she found financial support over time alternately through the welfare system and through remarriage. She remarried a few years after divorcing Jerry, had a sixth child, then divorced her second husband, lived on public assistance, remarried a few years later, and finally divorced her third husband and returned to public assistance. Most of the women in our sample remarried, although for most the second marriage seems to have lasted at least until the point at which we ceased collecting data. By that time in 1973, 57 percent of the women in our Genesee sample who had been divorced in 1970 or earlier had remarried. Of those divorced in 1965 or earlier—divorced at least eight years by the end of our records—67 percent had remarried.

We have no information whatever on the earnings of the men whom the women in our sample remarried, but the remarried women no doubt form a large majority of those women within our sample who were able to resume the standard of living they maintained during their earlier marriage. Let us play with a few assumptions. Because there was surely underreporting of remarriage by both men and women, assume for the moment that each mother in our sample remarried and that the man she remarried earned the same amount that her prior husband had earned before separation. Assume further that the new husband, her children's stepfather, made his income available to her and her children. She would then by hypothesis have been in a position to maintain her preseparation standard of living, even if the children's real father failed to pay his court-ordered child support. If the father did continue to pay support, she would, of course, have begun to live at a higher standard than she had before. Figure 4.7 displays in the left column the enriched standards of living our mothers and children would then have had.[22]

By contrast, the father who remarried may well end up living at a lower standard of living than his remarried first wife. As the second column of figure 4.7 reveals, if the father remarried and began to support a new child (either his own by his new wife or his new wife's by her own prior marriage), he would, if he paid his child support to his first family, have been less than half as likely as his first wife to have been able to maintain a standard of living at or above the Intermediate Standard Budget level. The economic positions of parents may well thus reverse after they have each remarried. Unfortunately, the records in Genesee contain such spotty information about the men's remarriage that we are unable to analyze whether the more financially pressed men within our study were any less likely to remarry.

For the woman, how ironic it is that a return to the state that had previously failed to satisfy should prove the only way for her to provide

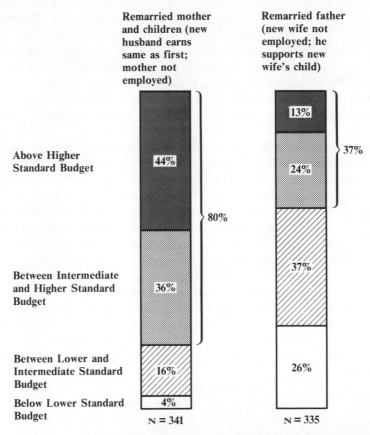

Fig. 4.7 Effects of remarriage on father's and mother's standard of living, if father continued to pay support to first family (Genesee Random Sample).

reliably for the security for her children! But the irony is less bitter than might be thought. Remarriage serves many values beyond income security. Most notably, there is companionship for the woman and a person with whom to share the responsibilities of guiding and caring for the children. There is also a return to the status our society regards as "normal" for adults. Men are even more likely to remarry after divorce than women,[23] although for them it may in some sense produce a reduction of the standard of living they can afford. Moreover, as we have mentioned earlier, studies of second marriages suggest that on the whole they work out well for both men and women.

Like employment, however, remarriage is not the answer for everyone. In some cases, the women does not wish to remarry; in others, she does but fails to find someone with whom she wants to spend her life. What factors tend to distinguish those women within our sample who did not remarry from those women who did? After repeated filtering we found, through regression analysis, two groups of women significantly less likely to remarry than others: women who were older at divorce and women who were black (see appendix table 4D).

By far the stronger of these two factors was the mother's age at divorce. As table 4.3 shows, there is a consistent negative relationship between age and remarriage. Four of every five women who were divorced before they were twenty-two, but only one in three of those over thirty-three, had remarried by the end of our records. Once the mother's age is taken into account, other factors that might have been expected to affect remarriage—particularly, the number of children the

Table 4.3   Mother's Age at Divorce in Relation to Remarriage,
                   Genesee Random Sample

Age at Divorce	N	% Who Remarried
17–21	62	83%
22–24	60	65
25–28	91	62
29–32	54	61
33–36	45	40
37–40	30	37
41–51	24	17
Total	366	58%

woman was taking care of and the age of her youngest child at the point of divorce—cease altogether to have any bearing on the incidence of remarriage. Mothers of three or four children are as likely to remarry as mothers of one.[24] Remember Dolores Neal. Although she had five young children at divorce, she was only in her mid-twenties and, perhaps for that reason, soon found someone to remarry.

Why black women were less likely to remarry than white women is unclear, but the difference is distinct. Black women are only half as likely to remarry as white women (33 percent vs. 60 percent). The difference holds after controlling for the other significant factors (mother's age and years covered by our records).

Some factors that bore no relation to the incidence of remarriage may also be of interest. Roman Catholic women, a group who might have been thought to have religious reasons for not remarrying, were no less likely to remarry than other women. Nor were the more financially secure women less likely to remarry than others. Through regression analysis, we found no relationship between remarriage and the fact of the mother's employment, or her earnings in dollars, or her total income from earnings and child support actually paid in the period after divorce. As suggested before, there are many reasons for remarriage other than financial security.

Summary

Our Genesee County sample included cases that had opened in each year between 1952 and 1970. Within this group, the average order of support for a woman with two children was thirty-three dollars per week. Today, with inflation, new orders in Genesee in divorces involving families with two children probably average about seventy dollars per week or over $3,500 per year.

Few divorced women are so well-off that they can regard $3,500 as pocket change. On the other hand, $3,500 is not enough today for a mother and two children to live on at the Poverty Line. (This amount is, in fact, less than 70 percent of the 1978 Poverty Line.)

As we turn to examine the rates at which men actually pay support and the elaborate system that exists in Michigan to ensure that they pay, we may tend to forget that the transfers of income that are the goal of this system and that seem so large to so many men are small in relation to the standards of living most Americans hope to maintain. We should also remember that even employed women who receive all child support payments due them often can not maintain their previous standard of living. For most women, child support at its best can mean the difference between living below the Poverty Line and living at a very modest standard of living somewhat above it, a critical difference but less of a difference than one might have hoped $3,500 to make.

How can a higher standard of living be assured for women raising children on their own? Producing full payments from fathers under the current system would help but cannot be enough. Much higher orders of support are conceivable, but only the vengeful would regard it as a success in public policy if we removed the mothers and children from poverty by putting the fathers there instead. Answers in full must lie outside the child support system—most probably through expanded employment opportunities for women. While default in payments of support may justly be seen as a problem, full payment of child support can only be part of the solution.

Dolores Neal is one of those for whom child support has offered no solutions. Her problem is not merely that Jerry has not paid, except sporadically. Even if he had paid, the quality of her life would have been little different. Her problems run deeper.

Like Jerry, she has been married three times. One step beyond Jerry, she has also been divorced three times. She has found neither the state of marriage nor the state of being single wholly satisfactory. Reflecting on the dozen years since her divorce from Jerry, she commented, "I feel smothered when married. People want to take care of me, but I can take care of myself." And yet, having had a paying job only once in her life (for three weeks), she finds herself "afraid" to try to find employment. Her youngest child from her marriage to Jerry will soon reach eighteen. Neither child support nor public assistance will then be available. After three husbands, she still lives in the little house she and Jerry bought twenty years ago. In another year or so, that is about all she will have left. She will be in her early forties, without an employment history and without any other sort of income. "I may need to get married again, you know," she forecast without pleasure.

She remains bitter toward all three of her husbands but particularly toward Jerry and her second husband, Carl, by each of whom she bore children and from each of whom she received little money after divorce. Referring to her five children by Jerry, she complained, "I didn't bring them into the world by myself, but I've had to raise them by myself. Other men have to pay. Why shouldn't he?"

Over the years, her bitterness has spurred her to call the Friend of the Court repeatedly, telling them where to find Jerry, even though she knew that, because she received public assistance, anything Jerry paid to avoid jail or to secure release from jail would be forwarded to the state, not to her. Partly because of information she provided, Jerry has been sentenced to jail three times for failing to pay. Carl has also served one term for nonsupport. Chatting with me on her front porch, Dolores chuckled as she remembered that for a few months Carl and Jerry served time in jail together.

Part Three

What Makes Fathers Pay?

Five

Payment of Support

Why Fathers Might Not Pay

If one knew nothing at all about actual levels of payment by American parents under orders of support, what would one guess they were? Would one guess that most parents would pay or that most parents would not? If I can reconstruct my own suppositions before I knew too much, I think that I naively assumed that most parents would pay without prodding. I would have guessed that, except for those who were unemployed or who earned so little they could barely survive, most would be propelled by affection or concern for their children into regular payments. How wrong I would have been.

When we began this study, only one earlier study not limited solely to welfare cases was available that examined payments by parents under orders of support. Completed in the mid-1960s by Kenneth Eckhardt, now of the University of Delaware, it reported on the enforcement of support in Dane County, Wisconsin, a prosperous county that includes the state capital and the principal campus of the state university.[1] Eckhardt studied all cases of families with minor children divorcing in that county in 1955 in which support orders were entered against a parent (always the father). For these 163 cases, he followed payments from the entry of an order through the tenth year after the divorce.

His findings have been widely and angrily reported in the women's literature of the last decade. Eckhardt found that in the first year under the support order 40 percent of fathers made no payments whatever. By the seventh year, over 70 percent were making no payments. Over the seven-year period, the mean level of payments by all fathers seems to have been no higher than about 30 percent of everything they owed. I have always found his findings startling, even shocking.

When we recall the calamitous financial circumstances of mothers with children at the point of separation, Eckhardt's findings suggest that most divorced fathers in Madison, Wisconsin, must have had a wanton disregard for the well-being of their children: "Let 'em starve." Perhaps we should let this judgment stand. As a group, the Dane fathers were, after all, reasonably well-off, largely white-collar, with orders no higher in relation to earnings than is the case elsewhere in the country.

"Wanton disregard" is a strong term, however, a term for the action of the landlord who evicts mothers and children during a snowstorm. A more understanding view of the fathers seems called for. As a growing literature makes clear, separation and divorce are a time of anger, confusion, and depression for men and women alike.

When a small portion of this study was published as an article and reported in some newspapers, I received letters from several men (and the second wives of two divorced men) who conveyed a very different view of the moral position of men who do not pay. One response took the form of a press release that had been issued by an organization called United States Divorce Reform, Inc.:

> Professor Chambers states "the sad finding of our study has been that, in the absence of sanctions, so many fathers fail to pay . . ."
> The "sad" part is the cruel treatment given to fathers in the divorce courts where they have no constitutional rights, and are exploited, persecuted, prosecuted and treated as non-persons, their only rights being that of paying child-support and alimony, being deprived of their children and homes and being shoved out into the street without any recourse, and, in most cases, without any justifiable reason.

Another letter came from R. F. Doyle, president of a group called the Men's Rights Association, enclosing a copy of his book *The Rape of the Male,* an attack on the mistreatment of men by women and judges. On the cover of the book is Christ nailed to the cross. And inside:

> No picnic, divorce is a suit that takes men to the cleaners. . . .

Divorce orphans are pitiful, but adult males are primary, more direct casualties. Financially and emotionally drawn and quartered, these unfortunates are to be found in all walks of life. Jails and skid row are overcrowded with the bitter, defeated flotsam and jetsam.

Angry at their former wives, angry at judges who mistreated them in court (in assuming, for example, that children naturally belong with their mothers), men may feel that they have few ways to communicate their feelings effectively except through nonpayment. The man may conclude that, if he pays, he is tacitly admitting his fault in the collapse of the marriage or ratifying the actions of a court he considers to have denied him justice.

Anger is not the only emotional state that can underlie nonpayment. Remorse and depression can serve as well. If recollection of the separation is painful, the writing of a check is a weekly stab from the past. One avoids pain by not thinking about payments.

Money itself may have special symbolic content between the man and his wife. Money talks. How much of his earnings the man turned over to his wife, how reliably he did so, his tone and attitude in doing so may well have communicated to the woman during the marriage his attitude toward her. The man who used his wife's access to money during marriage as a way of keeping her servile and dependent may maintain this pattern after divorce for the same purpose. Unpredictability in payments induces anxiety in the woman and is thus a source of power for the male, assuring him at once of her dependence on him and her comparative lesser worth.

On the other hand, money may have played another, very different, symbolic role. It may have represented to the man all his inadequacies in the marriage. Many men, particularly blue-collar men, feel that they fail to provide for their families adequately.[2] Arguments over money may have been a festering sore within the marriage, contributing to its dissolution. After separation, how will men who had such feelings tend to pay? If they are in fact often out of work, that alone may force nonpayment. Even if they are regularly employed, however, some such men may be subject to an especially strong need to repress a recollection of their financial obligations to their children.

Men with weak attachments to their children may also be expected to pay support irregularly. In America today, many fathers live in the same home with their children but participate very little in their upbringing. Even fathers who regularly spend time with their children may be affected by a sense of a special bond between the children and their mother if the mother has been the principal caretaker. Think of the many fathers who can comfortably describe themselves as having spent an afternoon at home "babysitting," even though they would never use the same term for the care given by the mother. Unconsciously, many men, especially those least involved with their children, may regard marriage as a contractual arrangement in which the wife agrees to take care of the husband and the husband in return agrees to support her and the children. Upon separating, she stops caring for him. He may feel at some level that he is no longer obliged to support her or "her" children.

Indeed, on separation, the man suddenly finds himself out of the house that his salary paid for, living in an undecorated, unfamiliar apartment. *The Rape of the Male* paints a picture that will seem only a slight caricature to many men: "a room furnished in early Salvation Army, an unmade bed, a bare bulb, an empty soup pan on the burner, a john down the hall, and a lonely man choking down meals of crackers and cheese." The man doesn't recall that his wife and children are struggling on a tiny fraction of the past income previously available to them. Even if the man recognizes that he has in fact more income available to him in relation to his needs than he did when living with his wife and children, he does not *feel* comfortable or happy. No one is making that unmade bed, washing that soup pan or putting the cheese on his crackers. Other excuses come easily: she's not taking good care of the children; she's sleeping with "him," let "him" support her; the kids don't have to obey me any more, so what do I really owe them? If the mother, for good or bad reasons, makes visiting with the children difficult or refuses to permit visits at all, the father may well respond by reducing payments to a trickle or cutting them off altogether. The reneging behavior of one parent will reinforce the reneging behavior of the other.

We referred earlier to the studies of others who report that divorced women are more unhappy than other women with the overall quality of their lives. Much the same can be said of divorced men. Though they are not as unhappy as divorced women, they report significantly lower levels of life-satisfaction than are reported by all groups of married men, with or without children.[3]

The unhappy man who forms a pattern of nonpayment in the early period after separation may resist beginning to make payments even after his initial intense feelings following separation have softened or passed. He may by then have become accustomed to having his full income available to him. As time passes he will probably begin to live with another woman or remarry. If he reattaches himself, and his new partner already has children, he will probably begin to support them. Or he and his partner may conceive additional children of their own. In either event, he will have substantial competing expenses on behalf of children whose daily needs he sees and hears about.

From all these perspectives, the dribs and drabs of payments found by Eckhardt in Wisconsin may still seem unjustified but they will at least be more comprehensible. The Wisconsin findings also provide a foil for the markedly different payment performances we are about to report from our study of Michigan. An explanation of the comparatively high payments we found in Genesee and other Michigan counties will form the core of much that follows.

Payment Performance in Genesee County

In Genesee County, as soon as a court entered an order of support, the new case was placed in the computer files. Thereafter the computer was programmed to charge against the account each week an amount equal to the weekly order in the case. In turn, the bookkeeping staff of the agency entered into the computer all payments as received and, with special symbols, all adjustments to the account other than from cash payments. Periodically the computer would spit out for each case the record of payments due, payments made, and adjustments. These payment histories were stored and always available whenever there was a dispute over payments.

We drew our sample in Genesee from the alphabetical list of the cases that were in the computer in November 1970 and used the printed payment records to follow the cases back to the dates they opened (for a few, as early as 1952) and forward until the summer of 1973, if they remained open until that point. By this process, we included no cases that were not open for at least eighteen months. Most of our cases had been open at least seven years.

The records of the agency permitted us to gauge men's payment performance in several ways. Our principal measure is what we call the "payments index," a straightforward measure of payments. For each year of payments, we computed what proportion each man had paid of all he had been ordered to pay—that is, his total payments in dollars divided by the product of the number of weeks the order had been in effect during the year (nearly always fifty-two except in the first year) multiplied by the weekly order amount. This produced a figure functionally comparable to a batting average.[4]

This payments index is directly comparable to the measure Eckhardt used in Wisconsin. When the index is computed for our men in Genesee, however, we find a markedly different pattern of perfor- mance. Figure 5.1 displays the comparison. In the first year, more Genesee men than Dane men pay all or nearly all and far fewer pay nothing or nearly nothing. Over time, despite all the reasons we suggested why payments might decline, the portion of full-paying men in Genesee actually grows. In Dane their number steadily declines. In the sixth year after divorce, Genesee County collected an average of about 72 percent of all moneys due, but Dane County collected only a third as much—about 24 percent of all that was due.

When we look back from the end of our records across the payment careers of the men in our sample, we find in Genesee only a small portion of men—one in seven—who had paid at an average annual rate of 20 percent or less of everything due over the life of their order. (We computed each man's lifetime payment index simply by averaging his annual indexes, weighting for partial years.) Nearly half the fathers had paid 90 percent or more of all that was due. (The median portion paid was 87 percent—see table 5.1.)

How applause-worthy is a payment rate of 87 percent? Many people will justly conclude that a payment rate of .87 by a man who is working full-time is unsatisfactory. Consider an eighty-dollar-a-week order—a common order today for a father with two children and take-home pay of $250 a week. After seven years, a man under such an order who had paid 87 percent of all he had owed would have made payments totalling over $25,300, but he would still have underpaid by nearly $3,800, or about forty-eight weeks' worth of payments. Even today, $3,800 will buy a lot of winter coats and hamburger.

When we speak, as we will, of the high levels of payments in Genesee, we intend a comparative statement only. Remember Dane. Half the Dane County men paid no more than 10 percent of all they owed. The portion of Dane fathers paying 87 percent or more cannot have been more than about one father in every five.

Asking why fathers in Genesee paid so much more than fathers in Dane is a way of asking one of the two central questions about pay- ments that this study has sought to answer. In the next chapter, we describe our inquiry into the payments in twenty-eight Michigan coun- ties, many of them very different from Genesee, in an effort to under- stand what accounts for the difference in payments among various places. It will come as little surprise that we conclude that much of the difference is attributable to Genesee's aggressive enforcement system

Genesee County*

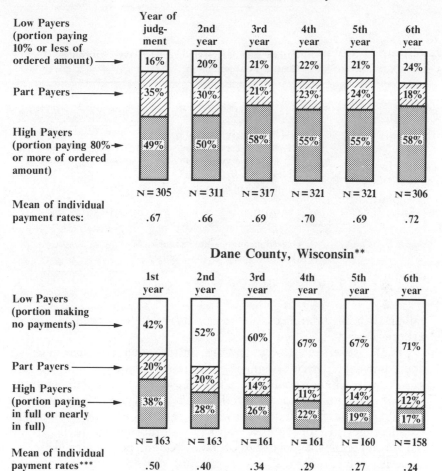

	Year of judg-ment	2nd year	3rd year	4th year	5th year	6th year
Low Payers (portion paying 10% or less of ordered amount) →	16%	20%	21%	22%	21%	24%
Part Payers →	35%	30%	21%	23%	24%	18%
High Payers (portion paying 80% or more of ordered amount) →	49%	50%	58%	55%	55%	58%
	N = 305	N = 311	N = 317	N = 321	N = 321	N = 306
Mean of individual payment rates:	.67	.66	.69	.70	.69	.72

Dane County, Wisconsin**

	1st year	2nd year	3rd year	4th year	5th year	6th year
Low Payers (portion making no payments) →	42%	52%	60%	67%	67%	71%
Part Payers →	20%	20%	14%	11%	14%	12%
High Payers (portion paying in full or nearly in full) →	38%	28%	26%	22%	19%	17%
	N = 163	N = 163	N = 161	N = 161	N = 160	N = 158
Mean of individual payment rates***	.50	.40	.34	.29	.27	.24

Fig. 5.1 Comparison of payments by divorced fathers in Genesee County, Michigan, and Dane County, Wisconsin, through sixth year of order (for cases open for at least that long).

*In this figure we have made an adjustment for a small group of low-paying cases opened prior to 1966, when the Friend of the Court in Genesee put its payment records on computer (see explanation in Methodological Appendix, pp. 299–301). For the six years tabulated here, the actual number of files prior to the adjustment is fifteen fewer than reported above in the first and last years and sixteen fewer than reported above in the years in between.

**Data from Kenneth Eckhardt, "Social Change, Legal Controls, and Child Support: A Study in the Sociology of Law" (Ph.D. diss., University of Wisconsin, 1965), p. 226.

***Computed by ascribing 100% as payment rate of full payers, 0% as rate of nonpayers, and 60% as rate of partial payers.

Table 5.1   **Portion Paid of Everything Owed, Averaged Annually,
                             Genesee Random Sample**

Men Paying over Life of Decree at Average Rate of:	N	% of Total Sample
.00–.20 of everything due	59*	14%
.21–.50 of everything due	43	10
.51–.80 of everything due	76	18
.81–.90 of everything due	47	11
.91 or more of everything due	199	47
Total	424*	100%

Overall mean for total sample—.74
Overall median for total sample—.87

*See the first footnote to figure 5.1.

rather than to differences in the quality of fathers bred in one or another county.

Chapter seven relates our findings on the other principal question about payments: What explains the differences among men in the rates of payments *within* a county such as Genesee? Who are the men (one-quarter of the total) who pay less than half of everything they owe, and how do they differ from the men who pay nearly everything? What are the characteristics of the men who pay well throughout the life of the decree and of the men who start off badly but end performing well? For these answers, we will be examining our random samples in Genesee—the same men whose marriages and economic circumstances at divorce we have already discussed. We will also be making use of our sample of men in Washtenaw County to look for the patterns of payments under a much less rigorous system of enforcement.

Six

Why Some Counties Collect More than Others

We are watching a television news special in 1976 on "Children of Divorce." Barbara Walters is staring at the camera—chilly, controlled, disapproving. She is deploring the circumstances of large numbers of American women who must raise children on their own, and she asserts that three million mothers are forced to live below the Poverty Line because of fathers who refuse to pay court-ordered support.

She continues to speak as the scene shifts to a busy office. Metal walls, pea-soup green, convey that we are at a public agency. The camera pauses briefly at a sign marked "Friend of the Court." We're in Genesee County.

"This office in Flint, Michigan," she informs us, "is the most successful in the country when it comes to collecting child support." The camera picks up a line of men in work clothes queuing up at a teller's window. "Here they get 80 percent of the husbands to pay in full. In the rest of the country the average is much lower. This office takes in about $25 million dollars a year. The money is taken in here and sent to the wife." A teller records a payment. A computer terminal winks and purrs. "She doesn't have to confront her husband when he doesn't pay. This office, the Friend of the Court, does that for her. And they're not very friendly about it."

Ominously, the scene shifts. We are peering through the bars of a jail cell at six inmates sitting around a table. They resemble the men in line in the preceding scene. The walls are the same green. This group, however, is playing euchre. One, with a glazed look like the rest, vacantly lights a cigarette.

"The man in Flint who doesn't pay child support has two choices: get out of town or go to jail. He can be jailed for nonsupport for up to a year. He goes before a judge and is sentenced for contempt of court. No trial, no defense, no appeal. These men are in for one year each. One man served thirteen one-year sentences!"

The greatly different levels of collections between Genesee County and Dane County, Wisconsin, that we have already noted beg for an explanation, and Walters, in the cavalier style of television journalism, supplies an easy one: Genesee collects more because it has an agency that does the "confronting" for mothers not receiving payments and because (cut to scene of jailhouse) those who are confronted and do not respond end up in jail. Walters is wrong about her claim that the financial plight of mothers and children is largely attributable to fathers who fail to pay. As we've seen, even with regular payments by the father, most women and children suffer grave financial difficulties. And she's wrong in her claims that Genesee collects more than any other child support "office" and that every nonpayer who doesn't leave town goes to jail. On the other hand, with a few important qualifications, our study suggests that she is essentially correct about the reasons for Genesee's high collections. This chapter tracks the way we sought to learn what accounted for the differences in collections between places.

Methods

How can one learn with accuracy why some places collect much more than others? With great difficulty. The reader must bear with us as we make an effort to reach an understanding of what makes such a system tick.

No matter how closely we examined our data from Genesee County, we could never be certain whether the high payment rates we observed were produced by the presence of the Friend of the Courts, by the fear of jailing, by the morals of its citizens, or by something else we could not imagine.

To explain the differences, we decided to look at payments in twenty-eight Michigan counties that differed from each other in many regards, in an effort to see what factors would explain differences in collections among them. A map of the twenty-eight counties we used appears in Chapter 2, but a map cannot convey the flavor of the differences we felt among them as we crisscrossed the state eating in places like Rose's Tiffany Restaurant or Hittler's Cafe. These counties are the stars of this chapter and we need to understand a bit about their widely varying characters and personalities.

Like New York, Michigan has an intensely populated corner, large stretches of agricultural land, and some secondary large cities on its western side. In the southeast corner is Detroit in Wayne County. Wayne is the nation's third most populous county, urban from border to border, a place where high incomes and high unemployment have long lived side by side. Next door to Wayne to the north and northeast are two massive suburban counties, Oakland and Macomb. Half of Michigan's residents, over four million, live in these three counties. For several decades, the fortunes of all three have risen and fallen with the fortunes of the automobile industry. On the other hand, there are important differences among them. For example, a quarter of Wayne's residents are black, but black persons comprise only 1 percent and 3 percent, respectively, of the population in Oakland and Macomb. Similarly, though the population of each is nearly all white, far more of Macomb's residents than Oakland's work at blue-collar jobs.

As one moves farther north and northwest of Detroit, one encounters other cities dependent on the auto industry—most notably, Flint, Saginaw, Bay City, and Lansing—but they are surrounded by rural areas. Thus although 80 percent of Genesee County's residents are classified as living in an urban setting, the county's edges are rural and some of the residents classified by the census as urban actually live on small farms. In two of Genesee's neighbors within our group of twenty-eight—Lapeer and Livingston Counties—only 11 and 12 percent of the residents, respectively, live in urban settings. Indeed in half of our twenty-eight counties, more persons live in rural than urban settings.

Moving westward across the state from Detroit, past Ann Arbor and Jackson, there are tiers of rolling and flat farmland, gentle to the eye. As we reach the western counties, we encounter several substantial cities—Kalamazoo, Grand Rapids, Battle Creek, and, at the shore of Lake Michigan, Muskegon (not included in our sample) and St. Joseph-Benton Harbor. The auto industry has far fewer employees here. Here there are large fruit and vegetable farms and manufacturing industries—cereals, furniture, appliances. Some of the western part of the state is conservative country, the home territory of Gerald Ford. Two of the counties—Kent, home of Grand Rapids, and Kalamazoo—are the most populous counties in the country for first- or second-generation Americans of Dutch descent.

It is these diverse counties that we examined. We found, as an initial matter, that they collected child support at vastly different rates. To learn the rates, we drew samples averaging 430 cases in each of the twenty-eight counties, including a fresh sample in Genesee. For each person in each sample we computed how much he had paid of all that he had been ordered to pay during a given period—that is, the "payments index" that we just described as our basis for examining payments in Genesee. The only difference between the payment information gathered in the earlier inquiry in Genesee County and in our inquiry in this part of the study was that in our look at twenty-eight counties we examined the parents' payments during one payment year only. For as many of the twenty-eight counties as we could, we coded payment information about the calendar year 1974; for some, because of the way the county's records were kept, we coded a different several-month or one-year period generally overlapping part of 1974.

After computing individual performance rates for each person in our sample in each county, we then computed three payment figures for each county as a whole: the mean of the individual payment rates within the county, a figure that is close, though not identical to the portion collected by the county of everything it was supposed to collect;[1] the portion of men in the county paying nearly nothing during the period (that is, 10 percent or less of the ordered amount); and the portion of men paying everything due or close to everything due (that is, 80 percent or more of everything due).

Table 6.1 reveals the widely varying patterns of payment that we found. (Appendix table 6A lists the rates of collection for each of the

Table 6.1   Mean Portions Collected of Everything Due from Divorced Persons under Orders of Support during Survey Period, 1974–75, 28 Michigan Counties

% Collected by County of Amount Due	No. of Counties Collecting This Amount	% of Counties Collecting in This Range	% of Fathers Paying 10% or Less of Amount Due	% of Fathers Paying 80% or More of Amount Due
41–50%	2	7%	47%	32%
51–60	5	18	38	42
61–70	13	47	24	50
71–80	6	21	16	60
81–90	2	7	8	72
Total	28	100%	25% (mean)	51% (mean)

twenty-eight counties.) In many respects, the payment rates within counties resemble those of Genesee or Dane. As was true in those counties, during any given year most men paid nearly everything or nearly nothing. That is true for 70 percent or more of the persons in every one of our counties. The minority of parents who during the period paid more than 10 percent of what was due but less than 80 percent were typically those who paid steadily for some part of the year and not at all in other parts. Few sent in a payment here, a payment there, in fits and spurts throughout the year. The striking differences among the twenty-eight counties were in the portions of payers at the bottom and the top: from two counties in which only a third of men paid nearly everything due to two where over two-thirds paid nearly everything; from a few counties in which nearly half the men paid nearly nothing to a few others in which only one man in ten paid so little. Accordingly, across the counties, the average portion paid by men of their amounts due varied widely—from a low in two counties of only 45 and 46 percent of the ordered amounts to a high in two other counties of 85 and 86 percent of everything due. Nearly half the counties straddle the midpoint, collecting 61 to 70 percent of the amounts due. (Genesee County, though collecting so much more than Dane County, was in fact one of the counties in the middle range: the men in our separate sample of Genesee in the twenty-eight-county-study paid during 1974 an average of about 68 percent of all amounts due.)[2]

We have used the counties' mean for reporting almost all of our findings, because we found that the portions paying at the bottom and the top correlated so overwhelmingly with the mean that separate reporting was superfluous.[3]

Factors That Might Explain Differences in Collections

After finding these widely varying payment rates among the counties, our goal was obvious but elusive: to explain why some counties collected so much more than others. From the outset of the study, we had been especially interested in measuring the effect on collections of the threat and use of jail. Thus, at the same time that we gathered information about collections, we determined for each county the number of persons sentenced to jail for contempt for nonpayment during a recent period, typically calendar year 1974, using records kept by the agency or the local courts. Judges in some counties jailed practically no men at all. Judges in several others jailed a significant portion of their nonpaying men every year. The heavy-jailing counties jailed ten times as large a portion of their caseload as the lowest-jailing counties. After gathering information about jailing, we found a close parallel between payments and jailing: the counties that jailed more did in fact collect more. (The correlation between the mean payment rate and the rate of jailing in relation to county population was +.492.[4] Appendix table 6B displays the relationship in somewhat different form.)

But the apparent relation between jailing and payments might well have been a mirage. Counties that jail more men might also take other enforcement steps more frequently, and the frequency of one of the other steps—for example, sending more reminders about nonpayment or holding more hearings—might more adequately or wholly explain what jailing appeared to explain. Or, apart from the enforcement process, perhaps what appeared to be the effects of enforcement were properly attributable to differences across counties in the characteristics of the persons under orders of support, differences that affect either their willingness or their capacity to pay support.

For this reason, the large remaining task in this part of our study was to catalogue all the plausible reasons apart from jailing that might explain differences in collection and to gather comparable information for each county that might capture those reasons in quantifiable form. The task was quite intimidating. Consider all the reasons that might explain why a large urban county such as Wayne County, with two and a half million residents, might collect at a vastly different rate from rural Barry or Branch Counties, each with under forty thousand residents. And then think of how few of those differences could be fully captured in hard numbers.

Except for order size and payment, we did not have individual information about the twelve thousand men in our samples from the twenty-eight counties. To look for differences that factors such as earnings or enforcement efforts might have exerted on collections, we had to rely on general information about each county, not about each man.

We sought first to develop, for each county, measures of county prosperity that might result in uneven capacities to pay among county residents under orders of support. To do so, we drew primarily on census information and on information about unemployment obtained from the Michigan Employment Security Commission. We found considerable variation in family incomes and in unemployment rates, variation that might well have produced differences in performance. (See the differences in six of these measures in appendix table 6C. See also the unemployment rates in 1970 in the twenty-eight counties in appendix table 6A.) Differences in unemployment rates were particularly noticeable. 1974 was a year of high unemployment generally, a period of recession that especially hurt the automobile industry and affected unevenly the counties in our study. The least affected five counties had unemployment rates averaging about 5 percent during the months we examined. At the other end, five counties had an average rate in excess of 15 percent. There was also considerable diversity in median family incomes with several counties having medians around $9,000 and several others having medians nearly half again as high.[5]

We also coded for each county one aspect of the divorce process that would unevenly affect the capacity of men to pay: the size of their court order in relation to their earnings. Lacking individual case information about earnings, we coded information from the support schedules the counties employ as the basis for setting orders. It turned out that the schedules were quite similar across our twenty-eight counties. For a couple with one child and a support-paying parent earning $160 per week in take-home pay, the order in twenty-two of our twenty-eight counties would have been $30, $31, or $32 per week. It thus appeared unlikely that variations in collections within the twenty-eight counties were linked to differences in portions of men's earnings consumed by support orders.

In addition to gathering information about factors that might have affected ability to pay, we sought to develop measures of possible differences among the counties in men's attitudes toward their children, toward payment of support, or toward the system of enforcement. We knew of no surveys of any sort, let alone any county-by-county studies, that asked divorced men what they thought of their children. We nonetheless coded certain information that we thought might provide indirect measures, not of attitude toward children, but of attitudes toward obedience to law. We also coded some other indications of social cohesion within counties that could operate either to create an atmosphere in which persons sense more informal pressure to live up to obligations or to provide a network for the spread of information about the enforcement process. We included such information as the counties' population, the portions of their population that lived in urban areas, the population growth over the preceding decade, the crime rate, and voter participation rates. (Nine of the factors we used and our findings as to each are included in appendix table 6D.)

Many of the indicators we used seem quite remote from considerations bearing on support payments. It takes a bit of imagination, for example, to perceive a link between the portion of eligible persons voting in the 1972 presidential elections and the average levels of payment of child support. Our dubious theory was that people who vote might be more likely to live up to other social obligations.

The third large body of information we coded concerned the enforcement systems of the counties. No such oblique relationship exists between the information we gathered about enforcement and the possible effects on collections. There our difficulty was capturing in quantifiable form the considerable diversity of enforcement approaches. While these numbers may satisfy for purposes of regression analysis and are at the heart of the findings we reached about the factors bearing on payments, they do not convey much of the rich variety among our counties in the ways they went about collecting money. We will later be examining minutely the system in Genesee County. A few thumbnail sketches of a couple of other counties may capture some of the flavor of their differences and permit the reader to judge how closely their processes are reflected in the numbers we actually used.

What all the Michigan counties have in common is the agency known as the Friend of the Court, which is charged with disbursing child support payments that do come in and pursuing payments that don't.

Barry County, with thirty-eight thousand residents in 1970, had the smallest population of any of our twenty-eight counties. Rural, but without particularly fertile soil, it has recently suffered Michigan's common problem of high levels of unemployment. At the time we coded the county's payment records in 1974, Barry's Friend of the Court had six full-time employees: Gerald Mahler, the head of the agency; two full-time bookkeepers; two persons with training as social workers who performed home visits; and a deputized enforcement officer, Mr. Sunior, who previously had been in police work. Mr. Mahler knew personally most of the families who had been in his caseload for several years. Younger staff members knew the remaining families Mr. Mahler did not. When he and I crossed the courthouse square into a coffee shop, he exchanged "good mornings" with other customers and then leaned over and said, "I won't tell you who, but there are three people in my caseload in here now." Later, when he and I reviewed some payment records I had found somewhat confusing, he remembered most of the specific events in men's lives that had produced the puzzling entries.

Barry's system of contacts with divorced families was thoroughgoing. The staff conducted two home visits with the custodial parent before divorce and annual visits thereafter, taking a particularly disdainful view of custodial mothers who lived with men to whom they were not married. They monitored the father's payments even more closely than the mother's sex life. The man who missed more than a couple of payments was sent a warning, whether the mother had complained or not. If he failed to respond to the warning, he received an order to show cause, directing him to appear at a hearing. If he again failed to respond, a warrant was issued for his arrest. (In many counties the Friends of the Court use the civil equivalent of a warrant known as a writ of attachment. Mahler used warrants because "most people think an attachment is some sort of order to pick up a chair or a car.")

Those brought to court when significantly in arrears stood a high probability of being sentenced to jail for contempt. During 1974, twenty-five men, or one in eight of those who ended the year paying less than 80 percent of everything due, were sentenced to jail. The two judges in Barry typically imposed sentences of thirty days on those they held in contempt, and most men purchased their early release by making a substantial lump-sum payment. Barry also extradited men who fled to other states, an expensive proposition, since two officers had to travel to the other state. Barry nonetheless brought back nine men during 1975 at an average cost of about seven hundred dollars. With a smile, Mahler explained that, during the winter, he rarely has difficulty finding officers willing to travel to somewhat warmer places to pick up miscreants.

Wayne County is seventy times as populous as Barry and, though the two counties are similar in the seriousness with which they take the enforcement of support orders, there are many differences in their approaches. In 1974, Wayne's Friend of the Court had three hundred employees spread across several floors of two downtown buildings in Detroit.[6] If paternity cases are included, the agency had a caseload of well over 120,000, by far the largest in the state. Unlike Barry, Wayne kept all payment records on computer. Also unlike Barry, but like nearly half the counties in our sample, Wayne removed from its active files cases that hadn't been paying for some substantial period, and stored them in a separate location. (We went to those separate locations—in Wayne, to tier after tier in the dusty basement of the old county courthouse—to include such cases proportionately in our sample.) Wayne had its own staff of arresting officers and mailed nearly twenty-five thousand orders to show cause during 1974. Its twenty-eight judges sentenced around nine hundred men to jail for contempt. Nine hundred is a large number, but if the Wayne judges had followed Barry's pattern in sentencing to jail one of every eight men who had paid less than 80 percent of everything owed during the year, they would have sentenced over eight thousand men, not nine hundred, during the year. Wayne's scale is too vast for intimacy. The head of the agency, a lawyer earning over forty thousand dollars a year, not only did not know very many of the divorced persons in his caseload, he barely knew, and could hardly have been expected to have known, all his employees.

The other twenty-six counties also exhibited diverse approaches to collection and enforcement. As of 1974, several large counties did not have computerized records, but several much smaller counties did. Half the counties sent warnings to nonpaying fathers whose former wives were not on welfare only on the request of the mother. The other half, which we called "self-starting," had a system similar to Barry's in which they acted to warn nonpaying fathers after a fixed number of weeks of nonpayment had gone by. Many counties had no arresting officers of their own and relied solely on the local sheriff; and so forth. One need not be a sophisticated social theorist to hypothesize that these differences of approach might well produce differences in rates of collection (see details in appendix table 6E).

The counties also differed greatly among themselves in the extent of their reliance on court hearings and jail for persons who failed to respond to warning letters. The tool that agencies use to force men to come to a hearing is an "order to show cause," an order directing the man to "show cause" to the judge why he should not be held in contempt. In each county, we counted these orders or obtained a count from the agency. Some agencies, we found, sent few orders, but their counties' judges jailed a large portion of the persons brought for hearings. Other agencies mailed large numbers of orders, up to eight times as many in relation to the size of their caseload, but their judges sent few men to jail. Still others did little of either or a great deal of both. When they did sentence men to jail, judges in almost all counties fixed a dollar figure short of the full arrearage that they would accept for early release, but the dollar amounts they demanded varied greatly, as did the jail terms they imposed as the alternative to the payment on the arrearage. In many counties, judges almost never imposed sentences of six months or more. In a few, however, judges routinely imposed sentences of a year, the maximum permitted by law. (See variations in appendix table 6F. A county-by-county list of the rate of jailing in relation to population is included in table 6A.)

There was one further aspect of the child support system that varied across counties and, though on the face of it this aspect had nothing directly to do with enforcement, it might well have exerted an effect on collections. As we mentioned earlier, men paying child support on behalf of children receiving welfare benefits have a disincentive to pay not shared by other men. The disincentive flows from the fact that the payments are never received by the child but are forwarded by the Friend of the Court directly to the welfare department. The father's payments make no difference in the standard of living of his child. While this policy exists in all Michigan counties—indeed, in every county in every state—there was great variation among the counties in the portion of the caseload that involved welfare cases. The one piece of information in addition to payments that we coded for every case in our own samples was whether the children in the case were currently receiving welfare benefits. In several counties we found that fewer than 20 percent of mothers were receiving assistance; in several others, more than 40 percent received assistance (see appendix table 6G). The rate of welfare receipt was high not only in Wayne County but also in several rural counties where unemployment was high and earnings comparatively low.

It was in our efforts to log for each county information about incomes, enforcement approaches, and other factors conceivably affecting payments that we have skated on thinnest ice. We ourselves computed parents' payment rates and developed confidence in our accuracy. We similarly counted with care the exact number of men sentenced to jail during a common time-period. But for factors that might have affected payment rates other than the incidence of jailing, we encountered all the problems that have bedeviled research on deterrence.[7]

We have already mentioned that for many factors that might plausibly have affected payments—especially those bearing on people's attitudes toward their obligations—we often had to resort to the most oblique sorts of indications. Even factors that seemed likely to have a more direct relationship to payments, such as unemployment rates, pose problems, for they reflect the conditions in each county as a whole and may not accurately reflect the conditions of the particular men under orders of support. Fortunately, our mode of analysis does not require that our sample rates faithfully mimic county rates. It is sufficient that the differences be more or less consistent across counties, for example, that counties with higher rates of unemployment also have proportionately more unemployed men under orders. While this proportionate relationship is a plausible one to expect, it is by no means necessarily the case, and we are unable to check for it given the available data.

We also had to worry whether apparently comparable information across counties was actually comparable in fact. Even the seemingly simple task of counting the size of county "enforcement staffs" forced us to grapple with different meanings given to the term "enforcement" by the agency heads we interviewed and with multiple functions of individual staff members. Even when information appeared comparable, it was often somewhat stale or unreliable.

Finally, some reliable and available information displayed so little variation among the counties that we were unable to assess the significance of certain elements of the enforcement process or of the demography of the population of supporting fathers. For example, we have noted that the counties made use of closely similar schedules for setting support orders in relation to the noncustodial parent's earnings and the number of children. Because of the similarity across counties, we were unable to test for differences in collections that might have accrued from larger or smaller orders in relation to incomes.

Why Rates of Collection Differ

After gathering as much information as we could about each of the twenty-eight counties on more than one hundred factors that we thought might serve to sort the high- and low-collecting counties, we strove to learn which factors actually bore some relation to levels of payments. When we completed a long series of regression analyses of our own data, three factors stood out as powerfully related to the levels of collections of support. The scores of other factors we had analyzed, some of which standing alone exhibited a substantial correlation with collections, explained very little after these three were taken into account.

The first of the three was an aspect of the enforcement process: counties that initiated enforcement efforts in nonwelfare cases without waiting for complaints from the mothers collected more than those that relied on complaints. These fourteen aggressive Friends of the Court, with what we have called "self-starting" systems, monitored men's payments and, after a few weeks of missed payments or the accumulation of an arrearage of a certain amount (say a hundred dollars), sent a warning notice to the nonpaying parent.

The second significant factor was linked to the first. It was the county's rate of jailing (in relation to its population). We reported above a strong positive correlation between collections and the rate of jailing. After controlling for other factors, we found that counties that jailed more men collected at higher rates—if, but only if, they also had self-starting enforcement systems. A county had to have both a

self-starting enforcement system and a substantial rate of jailing in order
to add appreciably to collections. Counties with a high jail rate but no
self-starting system of warnings collected little, if any, more than
counties that jailed almost no one.*

The third factor was population—the larger the county, the lower the
collections.[8] For example, none of the seven highest collecting counties had populations larger than 70,000. Conversely, nine of the ten
lowest collecting counties had populations greater than 110,000.

These three factors account for over 60 percent of the variation in
payment rates among the counties. Put another way, within our sample, if one knew a county's population, whether its Friend of the Court
was "self-starting," and the frequency of jailing, one could typically
predict within a few percentage points the average proportion of the
amounts men owed that the county actually collected.[9]

One other factor aids slightly in explaining differences in collections.
When unemployment rates are higher, collections are lower. It is not,
of course, surprising that payments should be lower in places where
unemployment is high. What was surprising to us was that unemployment rates did not account for more of the differences among the
counties. When we included unemployment rates with our other factors,
we could account for differences among the counties only to a slightly
greater degree than we could using the three dominant factors alone.
What was also surprising to us was that among several unemployment
figures we had for each county the figure that served to account for
some differences was the 1970 unemployment rate rather than the rate
for the exact months in 1974 or 1975 for which we had coded payments.
The figures for 1974–75 were not merely contemporaneous with our
payment data but were also much more varied than the rates for 1970
(see appendix table 6C).

Figure 6.1 presents our findings graphically with regard to the three
principal factors, although at the cost of simplifying for display the true
variations in population and rates of jailing actually used in our

---

*There were twenty counties that were not both self-starting and high-jailing. (See
appendix table 6G for a definition of high-jailing.) Within this group of counties—some
of which were self-starting but low-jailing, some of which were high-jailing but not self-
starting, and some of which were neither—the jailing rate and the self-starting factor add
nothing to the adjusted explained variance in collections, once population and the rate of
unemployment are taken into account. Thus, though there was considerable variation in
the collection rates among these counties, there was no reason to believe that the jail
rate helped to explain the variation. By contrast, when all twenty-eight counties were
considered, the jailing rate and the fact of a self-starting system were the two strongest
factors and together, even with population and unemployment, explained nearly 50
percent of the variance in collections.

analysis. Appendix table 6H presents the same and related data in more technical form.

The rate of jailing makes a difference in collections, but how much of a difference? As we have said, our analysis indicates that, for purposes of measuring differences, the jail rate and the factor of a self-starting enforcement process cannot be separated. When taken jointly, and

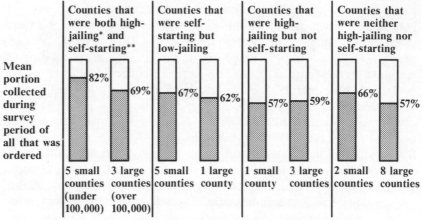

How much the county jails, whether Friend of the Court initiates enforcement without awaiting complaints, and county population

Fig. 6.1 Interrelation of three most important factors relating to collections in twenty-eight Michigan counties.

Mean collections:

13 small counties (under 100,000)—72%
15 large counties (over 100,000)—60%

12 high-jailing counties*—71%
16 low-jailing counties—61%

14 self-starting counties**—71%
14 non-self-starting counties—60%

5 small, high-jailing, self-starting counties—82%
8 large, low-jailing, non-self-starting counties—57%

*A high-jailing county, for our purposes, was one that jailed 4 or more men for nonsupport during 1974 for each 10,000 persons in the county population in 1970. The mean jailing rate for the high-jailing counties was 6.0 per 10,000. The mean rate for the low-jailing counties was 1.7 per 10,000. See further explanation in appendix table 6H.
**A self-starting county was a county that had had for some years a policy of initiating enforcement efforts in delinquent nonwelfare cases without waiting for complaints.

when population and unemployment are also taken into account, counties with both a high jailing rate and a self-starting policy collected an average of 25 percent more per case than was collected by the counties that did not have both.[10] For a county such as Genesee that collected $17.3 million in 1974 from all fathers, this finding suggests that had Genesee not been a high-jailing, self-starting county it would probably have collected about $3.5 million less than it did. That is a lot of money.

A Self-Starting Enforcement Process, the Rate of Jailing, and Population

We have dismembered a complex process—the payments across counties of divorced parents toward the support of their children. Payments go down with higher population, up with a self-triggering warning system, down with more unemployment, and up with more jailing. Though our findings have surface plausibility, those who cherish the complexity of humanity will be pleased that when we peered more deeply into our pool of data we found the waters muddier than they initially appeared.

In the first place, it is important to remember that while these variables explain much about the differences in the rates of collections, they do not explain everything. Consider just a couple of comparisons among our counties. One non-self-starting county collected more than 20 percent more than another non-self-starting county, despite the fact that the higher-collecting county was considerably larger and jailed far fewer men. (Compare counties 22 and 27 in appendix table 6A.) Similarly, as between two other counties of closely similar population, both with high rates of jailing, the non-self-starting county collected more, not less, than the self-starting county. (Compare counties 10 and 13 in appendix table 6A.) Clearly, other factors are also at work that we cannot fully identify. Had we information about the portion of fathers in our counties' caseloads who had moved out of the county or about actual rates of unemployment for the men in our samples, we might have been able to account for more of the differences.

Moreover, with each of our three most important factors relating to collections, there are problems in interpreting the factor's significance.

Our finding that counties whose Friends of the Court initiated enforcement without awaiting complaints collected more money than other counties is, at first glance, hardly surprising. One anomaly nonetheless persists about this self-starting factor. We defined a "self-starting'' county as one in which the Friend of the Court initiated enforcement efforts in nonwelfare cases without awaiting complaints from the custodial parent. We excluded welfare cases from the definition of a self-starting county because all Friends of the Court had self-triggering systems for initiating enforcement in welfare cases. Given our definition, one would have expected that when we analyzed the welfare cases from our samples in the twenty-eight counties, the self-starting factor would not have helped sort the high- and low-collecting counties. In fact, however, the self-starting factor is nearly as significant an explainer of the variations among counties in their collections in the welfare cases as it is for the caseload as a whole. This finding suggests that the counties that are self-starting simply collect support in both welfare and nonwelfare cases more effectively for reasons related to, but distinct from, the self-starting attribute alone. Several other aspects of the enforcement process—thoroughness of bookkeeping, size of the enforcement staff and dollar expenditures in relation to caseload, and so forth—correlate mildly with performance and with the self-starting factor. It appears that "self-starting" may simply capture best the sum of the attributes of an efficient and persistent organization.

That the presence of an effective collection organization and the rate of jailing work hand in hand is also not surprising. Under a self-starting enforcement system, a larger portion of men who falter are told to "pay up." The high rate of jailing seems to add, "and we really mean it." Neither message has potency without the other. We had expected, however, that the rate of jailing would not have been the only way to convey "we really mean it," but at least within our study no other aggressive aspect of the enforcement system served anywhere nearly as well to explain the differences in overall collections.

We looked, for example, at the use of orders to show cause—the orders to appear at hearings issued when men fail to respond to warning letters. As noted above, we had a reasonably accurate count of such orders during the same period for which we counted jailings and found that counties varied widely in their rate of use of such orders and in the ratio of orders to subsequent sentences to jail. We had hypothesized that, because they were sent to many more people than were actually jailed, the orders themselves, with their stern and official directive to appear in court, might well have served to communicate more effectively than the sentencing rate itself the seriousness of the enforcement agency. We found, however, that neither the rate of orders to show cause nor any combination of the show-cause rate and jail rate (to measure the conviction rate among those ordered to appear at hearings) helped sort the higher- from the lower-collecting counties nearly as well as the jail rate.

On the other hand, we found that long sentences to jail also appear to make no difference. An index that weighted the rate of jailing in each county by the average length of sentences imposed was far less valuable in explaining variations in county collections than the jailing rate alone and added nothing to the explained variation in the collection rate when used with the rate of jailing controlled. We will have more to say in Chapter 9 about sentence length when we look to see whether it has an effect on the men actually jailed. For now, we can state that, within the range of measures available to us, it is the sentence to jail rather than the length of the sentence that appears to communicate the necessity of paying.

It remains possible, nonetheless, that some unmeasured aspect of the enforcement process less stringent than jailing explains what the jailing rate appears to explain. We were, for example, unable to count the number of warning letters mailed in the twenty-eight counties during either a year we studied or any other year. We thus could not calculate the rate at which the agency sent warnings in relation to the number of cases in the caseload or in relation to the number of cases with arrears at some point during the year. Nor were we able to determine for each county the average time between the development of an arrearage and the mailing of a warning. While we believe it probable that our self-starting factor would correlate strongly and positively with each of these desirable measures, had we been able to develop them, the self-starting factor is unsubtle in its form—every county either was or was not self-starting in our definition. There were no gradations. It is thus possible that one or more of these other dimensions of the enforcement process would account for all or some part of the differences in collections that we have attributed to the rate of jailing.

A problem for analysis would persist even if we had found that the rate of jailing in our twenty-eight counties failed to explain variations in collections but that measures of milder enforcement efforts were powerful explainers of variation. Since the form warning-letters in nearly all counties carried threats of judicial action that many recipients probably read as a threat of jail, a finding that the heavy use of nonpenal enforcement efforts, but not the jail rate, helped sort the higher- from the lower-collecting counties could have either of two very different meanings. It could mean that the threat of jail was truly irrelevant and that men can be propelled toward payment by reminders alone, or it could mean that letters threatening judicial action are sufficient in themselves to create the fear of jail, regardless of the actual rate of jailing. If the latter were the case, then, even though the actual jail rate would not have affected collections, collections would still decline if jail were removed as a legally permissible sanction and men under orders learned of the change in the law.

The final significant factor apparently affecting collections was the county's population. Our findings suggest that even if two counties have a self-starting system of enforcement, jail at the same rate, and have the same rate of unemployment, the less populous county will still collect more money. Why should this be so? The lower collections in populous counties is unlikely to be attributable to lower incomes among the persons in our large-county samples. Among our counties, the portions of the population living in poverty were larger and median incomes were appreciably lower in the smaller counties than in the large ones.[11] It is, of course, possible that our samples mirror unevenly the income levels and unemployment rates of their counties as a whole and that a disproportionate number of poor people are among the divorcing population in the large but not the small counties. Although that interpretation is possible, it receives no support from other data within our own samples.[12]

Another possible explanation for lower payments in more populous counties was also untestable. Within Genesee County, we found that men who left the county after divorce paid dramatically less well than men who stayed.[13] It is possible that the portion of parents under orders who left town after divorce was much greater in the more populous counties than in the less populous ones. Unfortunately we have no reliable figures on out-migration either for the fathers in our samples or for the counties generally. The only migration figures available from census data are those for net migration—a projection of the probable net number of people moving into and people moving out of a county between decennial censuses.[14] For what it is worth, we found that only a small portion of the divorced men in Genesee moved away after divorce. For only about one-sixth of the men do we have any indication that they established residence outside Genesee County at any point during the life of their order, and some of these returned while the order was still in force. Jerry Neal, for example, lived in a neighboring county for a few years and then returned to Genesee.

Among all the explanations for the relevance of population, it is our best guess that the correct explanation lies in a greater insulation of city dwellers from the enforcement process. In several of the small counties such as Barry, but in none of the large, the director of the Friend of the Court knew personally a significant portion of the men in his county's caseload, a fact that probably affected some of the men under orders. The difference for the parent in the smaller county is probably not merely that someone whose esteem he values knows whether he is paying. It is also likely that he believes—correctly—that he is easily located. Staffs of the Friend of the Court in populous counties often reported grave difficulties in finding nonpayers, even when they had remained within the county.

Remember Barry County, our least populous county, where the Friend of the Court nodded to his clients in the coffee shop. Barry was our highest-collecting county—87 percent was collected of everything owed, almost eighteen dollars of every twenty dollars ordered was actually paid. Someone on the staff of the agency knew where almost every father lived, worked, or drank. And then recall Wayne County, seventy times more residents, over one hundred thousand cases, three hundred employees. Wayne was our lowest-collecting county—45 percent was collected, only nine dollars of every twenty dollars ordered was actually paid. And yet both counties took enforcement seriously. Barry did jail more persons in relation to its population and did have a self-starting enforcement system of much longer-standing, but the massive differences in collections between them is almost certainly attributable in large part to Barry's cozy manageability and Wayne's impersonal vastness.

Lessons from the Twenty-Eight County Study

In Chapter 5, we offered a startling comparison of payments in Genesee County, Michigan, and Dane County, Wisconsin. Genesee's payments started fairly high—in the first year fathers paid on the average about two-thirds of all they owed—and then, wonder of wonders, improved slightly over time. Payments in Dane started somewhat less well—in the first year fathers paid about half of all that was due—and then got steadily worse. The differences now seem more comprehensible. Since Dane's population was half that of Genesee, with unemployment no higher, the results of our study of twenty-eight Michigan counties support our original hypothesis that the collection system is critical.

In Dane County there was an agency, an office of the court that received payments from fathers, but it had no enforcement duties. Dane mothers not receiving welfare benefits, like mothers in most of

the country today, had to turn to private enforcement mechanisms—
typically a lawyer—that were no more satisfactory in Wisconsin in
1965 than they had been in Michigan fifty years before. The only ves-
tige of an enforcement system was the prosecutor's office. Focusing on
the small portion of fathers whose families received welfare and on
fathers charged with other criminal offenses more difficult to prove, the
prosecutor secured the jailing of as many men in Dane in relation to the
caseload as had the Friend of the Court in Genesee. The remaining
fathers—those without other pending criminal charges and whose
wives did not receive welfare—were essentially immune from serious
enforcement.

The contrast between Dane and Michigan thus suggests two
significant conclusions that complement and clarify our findings. The
first is that simply having a full-time enforcement agency available, at
least at the mother's request, will exert an immense effect on payments. Dane County collected far less per case than Wayne County,
ten times its size. Had Dane been a Michigan county with a Friend of
the Court and with the same population and the same rate of unemployment it had in 1970, our study suggests that, even if it had been
a low-jailing, non-self-starting county, it would probably have collected
over 60 percent of all that was ordered (not the 30 percent it in fact
received in an average year). Within Michigan, we found that the degree of the agency's organization and tenacity makes a difference. The
comparison suggests that just having some sort of integrated collection
and enforcement system charged with enforcement is itself critical. It
suggests, in short, that places that collect little today might collect a
great deal more simply by creating such a full-time agency with responsibilities for all areas of enforcement.[15]

The second message from Dane concerns the effects of jail as an
instrument of enforcement. We found within Michigan that in the absence of a self-starting enforcement system, a heavy jailing rate makes
little difference in collections. The Wisconsin county, collecting so
little but jailing as many men as Genesee, corroborates our own tenta-
tive conclusion about the futility of jail as an instrument of collection
except when potential offenders come to believe that they are likely to
end up there. That belief apparently does not arise for most men from
the mere fact that many other men are jailed but rather from the coupling
of jailing with an effective warning system pointing toward one's own
confinement.

Washtenaw County, Michigan, also offers us some further, more
subtle lessons. Washtenaw, in which we drew, as in Genesee, a de-

tailed random sample, was also one of the counties in our twenty-eight-county sample. The enforcement systems in Genesee and Washtenaw differed greatly. Two differences are familiar to the reader. For several years up to and including the years we studied, Washtenaw had not been a "self-starting" county: a woman not receiving public assistance had to make a complaint by letter or telephone before a form notice of arrearage was sent to the father, and she had to complain again, this time in writing, before a nonresponding father was sent an order to show cause. Moreover, although many Washtenaw men in the caseload had been arrested for nonsupport—often through the serving of a warrant when arrested for an altogether different offense like a traffic violation—Washtenaw's judges jailed far fewer persons for non-support. In the year that Genesee's judges sentenced 224 men, Washtenaw's sentenced no more than five.

In Washtenaw, as in Genesee and Dane, as time passed after the entry of a support order, some men ceased to pay, some began to pay, and some kept paying at the same rate. A comparison of overall patterns of payment performance of parents in Genesee and Washtenaw over the lives of their decrees sheds more light about the effects of a zealous enforcement process, for Washtenaw comes much closer to Genesee but still exhibits important differences.

In the first year in each county most men are paying either nearly everything or nearly nothing, and over the years more and more men end at the extremes, drawn into or falling out of the payment system. The difference between the two counties, subtle but distinct, lies in the changing proportion of fathers paying at high and low rates.[16] In Genesee in the first year, as viewed earlier in figure 5.1, half the men are high payers and 16 percent are low payers. By the sixth year, even more men—close to 60 percent—are high payers and 24 percent are low. The mean level of payments rises slightly over the years, from .67 up to .72. In Washtenaw, the pattern is better than Genesee's in the beginning but worse in the end. In the first year, 56 percent are high payers and only 12 percent are low payers. By the sixth year, however, the portion of high payers has slipped to 46 percent and the portion of low payers has risen dramatically to 36 percent. The mean level of payments falls somewhat every year, beginning at .70 but ending at .53. Were we able to control for population and unemployment, the earlier results suggest that Washtenaw, both smaller and with less unemployment, would appear even worse.

The patterns of payments in the two counties over time suggest that, in each county, a substantial number of men consciously or unconsciously tested the enforcement system in the early years. In Genesee many were burned and moved toward full payments. In Washtenaw, many who paid erratically apparently found that their haphazard payments were ignored or followed by hollow threats or that, even if they were arrested, they were released and then forgotten.

Table 6.2 illustrates the same point in somewhat different form. It reveals the pattern of payments in individual cases in the same two counties, showing the number of men in each county who started in the first years of the order paying at either high or low rates and whether they were still paying at high or low rates by the sixth and seventh years. The difference between the two counties does not lie in the men who started at high rates. In each county, 49 percent of the men started in the first year paying 80 percent or more of the amount due. Of these men who started at high rates, only slightly more of Washtenaw's than Genesee's slid into lower payments. The noteworthy difference lies rather in the men who started at a low rate of payment. In each county 51 percent of the men start low, but in Genesee County more than half of this low-starting group ends up as high payers whereas in Washtenaw only about one-fourth of the low payers move up.

What this pattern suggests, when taken together with Eckhardt's

Table 6.2	Payment Trends, Genesee and Washtenaw Random Samples		
	Percent of Men in Caseload Whose Payment Rate:	Genesee County	Washtenaw County
	Starts high, ends high	39%	35%
	Starts high, ends low	10	14
	Starts low, ends high	28	13
	Starts low, ends low	23	38
		100%	100%
		(N=229)	(N=167)

High = Payment rate was 80% or more of amount due.
Low = Payment rate was less than 80% of the amount due.
Start = Average for each person of payment rate in year of final order and first year thereafter. In cases with missing data for either year, the payment rate of the other year was used.
End = Average for each person of the payment rate in sixth and seventh year after the year of the final order. In cases with missing data for either year, the payment rate of the other year was used.

findings in Dane County, Wisconsin, is that when there is no enforcement system at all (Dane) most men who pay well át the outset will fall
by the wayside. On the other hand, if there is some enforcement system, even of the passive sort found in Washtenaw County, most high
payers will stay high payers. The presence of an especially rigorous
system such as that in Genesee, makes little difference to those who
start at a high level so long as there is at least some system. For those
men who start badly, however, only an ardent enforcement system
serves to bring many up to high payment levels. These findings are
consistent with a hypothesis that, while it takes some effort to maintain
payers in a pattern of steady payment behavior voluntarily begun, it
takes far more effort to undo an established pattern of poor payment.
Washtenaw's system is sufficiently effective to sustain the high starters
but insufficient to turn around many of the low.

Dollar Costs and Returns of Jailings

Within Michigan, counties that jail large numbers of men collect more
than those that do not. It remains possible, however, that the counties
that use jail will show a net loss for their policy because the dollar costs
of jailing exceed the returns. In fact, the gains in dollars are almost
certainly far greater than the dollar costs.

The financial costs of a self-starting jailing policy—of extra enforcement officers, extra court time, jail operations, and so forth—are considerable, but the additional amount of support collected is simply
greater. As we have discussed, counties with both a self-starting enforcement policy and a substantial reliance on jailing collected an average of 25 percent more than similar counties that did not have both.
Thus, in Genesee County, the marginal dollar costs of the arresting,
jailing, and self-starting policy in 1974 might have been as high as
$400,000,[17] but the amount of collections attributable to these en-
forcement efforts might have been nearly $3.5 million of the $17.3
million collected by the agency that year.[18]

We have so far been comparing costs and benefits among counties
with full-time agencies, some more ardent than others. If we compare
instead the probable costs and returns of two jurisdictions, one having
a full-time aggressive agency and the other having no agency at all and
leaving each parent to private devices, by hypothesis, the savings in
enforcement expenses would be even greater for the latter. Yet, as the
Dane County, Wisconsin, study suggests, we would almost certainly
find that the foregone collections would be vastly greater yet.

These calculations do not include conceivably determinable losses of wages by the men jailed (or the consequent losses in tax revenues from them), but these losses, while not trivial, need not necessarily be great. As we have reported, the deterrent effect of the sentencing rate turns not at all on the length of sentences imposed or on the number of days served (some of the highest-collecting counties imposed the shortest sentences). It thus appears that most men sentenced could be held only a few days, with little loss, if any, of the general deterrent effect.

We must remember when we are comparing dollar costs and benefits that we are often referring to costs to the taxpayers of producing benefits to individual families. Only in welfare cases does the government both bear the costs and reap the gains and, even in the welfare setting, federal, state, and local governments bear uneven shares of the costs in relation to their shares of the returns. At any given time, most divorced parents with children are not receiving welfare benefits. Across our twenty-eight counties, an average of 30 percent of the families were receiving welfare at the time we sampled. For the 70 percent of families not receiving benefits, the relevant cost-benefit question differs from that appropriately asked when the government is collecting for itself: in a society that normally relies on private enforcement of personal financial obligations the question is whether the value public enforcement offers over private enforcement is sufficient to justify the expenditure of public funds. Because public enforcement is so much more effective and because so many dollars are at stake for the benefit of children, most Americans would probably answer "yes," but reaching such an answer does require more than simply counting dollars.

Jail and Deterrence

Our findings that, under certain circumstances, jail works may lead some directly to the conclusion that jail ought to be widely used, especially since working men who willfully refuse to support their children are widely considered to be immoral and to "deserve" a term in jail. Regarding "oughts," I urge the reader to suspend judgment for a while. In the later chapters of the book, we will look carefully at those who are actually jailed, and their immorality can then be more justly measured. We will also be examining alternative systems of collections that may be as effective as—or more effective than—the threat-based system that exists in the high-jailing counties today.

It is also tempting to apply findings we have reached about collection of support to other forms of behavior regulated as criminal. If jail deters nonpayment of support, can we conclude that it will similarly deter rape or armed robbery? Not at all.

We can expect that a policy of jailing will have a greater effect when those tempted know that all their actions are observed. Most armed robbers and rapists hope that their identities will remain unknown. Most embezzlers and heroin dealers hope that even the offense itself will never be detected by anyone interested in securing an arrest. In the case of child support in Michigan, both the fact of the offense and the identity of the perpetrator are always known. The agency knows on Monday if Jerry Neal's payment came in on Friday. Thus the very factor that made our study possible—the all-knowing files of the Friend of the Court—makes our findings ungeneralizable to most other forms of conduct.[19]

In addition, each form of behavior has its own psychological setting. Persons considering aggressive sexual or physical assaults, even if they know that their identities will be learned, may well be typically less responsive to the threat of incarceration. "Nonsupport" is not an irreversible act committed in the heat of passion. However angry a man may be at his former wife, a "sudden" decision on Friday not to pay can be fully undone and punishment avoided the following Monday or even a week from Monday, after reflection on the consequences of nonpayment. A gun that has been shot in anger cannot be similarly unshot.[20]

Finally, most men do not, of course, deliberate each week about payment or nonpayment. Penal sanctions may operate in a much more subtle way to reinforce a person's sense of how much importance the community attaches to a certain form of behavior. In the context of child support, we have been unable to determine the contribution of jailing to this socialization process, and our inability to measure and make comparisons with other forms of behavior further reduces the utility of our study for understanding them. The probability seems substantial, however, that the divorced men who fall behind in payments, but who are otherwise, most of them, in the mainstream of "law-abiding" citizenry, are more susceptible to pressures toward lawful behavior than are the men in our society who are drawn toward "street" crime.

Despite all these cautions, the study may have one application to other sorts of behavior: recall that even with as visible an offense as nonpayment of support the rate of jailing had little effect on behavior except when a jailing policy was the capstone of an otherwise well-organized and well-announced enforcement system. If this is so, it would appear likely that the mere rate of jailing would have even less value as a source of terror for offenses such as drug use or burglary in which the offender perceives little likelihood of being identified.

At the same time, the study also appears to confirm one commonplace prediction: swift and certain punishment can reduce the incidence of some forms of undesired behavior, so long as the potential offender perceives himself likely to be caught.[21] If a policeman is watching and customers know it, fewer candy bars are shoplifted. The sad finding of our study has been that, in the absence of sanctions, so many fathers fail to pay. The remarkable finding has been the effectiveness of enforcement agencies in many Michigan counties in creating an impression of a policeman at the elbow.

Seven

Why Some Fathers Pay More than Others

Our discussions thus far help us understand why an agency in one county—Genesee County, for example—might collect so much more from divorced fathers than its counterpart agency in another county. On the other hand, our findings about rates of collections among counties cannot tell us why some men within a Genesee County—a Jerry Neal—pay so little while others pay so much. All men in Genesee County had to cope with this aggressive enforcement system. Jerry Neal was not merely a rare "deadbeat" in a county of saints. During the year we surveyed for the twenty-eight-county study, it is true that over half of the men in Genesee County paid nearly everything, but it is also true that a quarter paid nothing or nearly nothing.

When seeking to explain the vast differences among men's rates of payments within a single county, the twenty-eight-county study hints that we should search for aspects of men's background or situations likely to indicate imperviousness to a system of reminders or sanctions. Beyond that, the study tells us very little. We have thus used our detailed samples from Genesee and Washtenaw counties to examine the relation of payments to both the characteristics of the men and the events in their lives. Any attempt to dissect the factors affecting individual behavior is a risky enterprise. It may aid in understanding what follows if we set forth a general thesis about payments by individuals and how to think about the factors bearing on them. We will then turn to our findings from Genesee and Washtenaw.

A Commonsense Theory of Payments

Chambers: After the divorce, you paid fairly steadily for the
                   first year and then stopped. Later you were ar-
                   rested and jailed, and after release you still didn't
                   pay. Why so?

Neal: Well, you see I basically have this sociopathic
                   personality—very little commitment to anyone
                   or anything except my own short-run desires.
                   Then, too, I'm an unskilled blue-collar worker
                   with only a high school education. Besides that,
                   I'm Catholic.

That's all made up. Jerry Neal never said any such thing. Only the
most peculiarly detached or overeducated persons explain their own
behavior in terms of their background characteristics or personality
type. Like almost anyone else confronted with behavior that he knew
was socially unacceptable, Jerry's explanations for nonpayment were
excuses and his excuses were situational. He stopped paying after the
first year, he said, because Dolores had remarried and her new husband
was taking all the money. Later, after Dolores divorced her second
husband, Jerry had trouble with an old hernia and Dolores was on
AFDC anyway and wouldn't have received any money he might have
paid. At other times, he was working but having trouble making ends
meet. He too had remarried and his new wife was a diabetic who could
not work.

The mock and actual conversations with Jerry convey some of the
complexity of the problems facing anyone trying to understand what
makes fathers pay. In most of our cases, the period from divorce until
the couple's youngest child became eighteen was at least fourteen
years, over seven hundred weeks. From one view, the man who is not
paying needs not one excuse but seven hundred, and we need to understand not one nonpayment (or one murder or one robbery) but seven
hundred.

Here is a way of looking at the father's behavior over the fourteen-
year period. A court enters an order of support. Most men begin to pay
at the outset. Later, events occur or circumstances arise that invite, or
even necessitate, a lapse in payment. Sometimes these events or circumstances will have arisen before the order is ever entered, and there
will be no payments even at the beginning. What sorts of circumstances? Bitterness over the separation or the incidents that pre-

cipitated it. Layoffs or loss of a job that leave the man utterly without income or so pinched that he feels forced to forego payment in order to survive. Disputes over visits with the child. The mother's serious involvement with a new boyfriend or her happy remarriage. The man's dating of a woman who makes him feel good about himself. The mother's moving to a new town with their children. Rising living costs. After payments lapse, or never begin, there will similarly be later "events" that invite a return to (or commencement of) payment—twinges of conscience, a resumption of work, the mother's jibes or complaints, letters from the enforcement agency, threats of jail.

Whether the man will cease paying in response to the events inviting nonpayment and whether, if he does cease, he will begin to pay again turn on a combination of factors that determine at each point the place he accords the court-ordered responsibilities to his children in the hierarchy of the other demands on his earnings. The father will pay if he is able to pay and if the combined weight of the factors favoring payment (love, fear, guilt, whatever) exceed for him the weight of the factors favoring nonpayment.

A man's attitudes about duties that parents have toward their children or about duties to abide by societal rules may be among the factors that affect his response to the events inviting nonpayment as well as his response to efforts to persuade him to pay after a lapse. For some men, the fact of a court order may be enough to produce payments: one does what one is told to do. For others, the order alone may not be enough to produce payment, but official reminders may trigger guilt or a sense of responsibility, wholly apart from the consequences of nonresponse. Finally, of course, for some men, perhaps soon after the entry of an order and surely later if the threat is palpable, the desire to avoid jail or its alternative, flight, will become critical. Over the years from divorce at, say, age twenty-six to the end of the order at age forty-two the same events will have different meanings, the man's stake in the community or in a new family will alter, new attitudes will form. Life evolves; it is not static.

The 410 men in our Genesee sample, nearly all under weekly orders, enjoyed collectively about 140,000 opportunities to pay or not to pay over the years we logged. We cannot hope to explain in full the behavior of even one man—Jerry Neal or anyone else—for even one week, let alone that of 410 men for 140,000 weeks. What we can do, much more modestly, is use the random sample that we drew in Genesee to look for ways in which payment histories relate to background characteristics of the men and their marriages, characteristics that may indirectly affect men's willingness or capacity to pay. We can also look for the effects of visible events that might have affected some men's decisions either not to pay or to begin paying again. We can then turn to our closely comparable sample of over 400 cases in Washtenaw County to learn whether these same background characteristics and events interact with payments any differently in a county with little jailing and a less organized system of enforcement.

Payments and Background Characteristics

In an earlier chapter, we described the characteristics of the men, women, families, and marriages in our Genesee families. We discussed the many women who married when very young or pregnant and others who married much later; men's and women's occupations, earnings, and religious backgrounds; race; large families and small ones. We also described the attitudes about reconciliation expressed by each party at the predivorce interview and the reasons each gave for wanting a divorce.

What relationship do any of these have to payments? The short answer is that a few have some relationship but most have none.

Payments in Genesee County

The average person in Genesee County had paid about 74 percent of everything owed up to the point that we stopped recording payment information, a median of about six years from the entry of the final divorce decree. Nearly half the fathers had paid 90 percent or more of everything due. On the other hand, about 22 percent of them had paid less than half of everything due. We came to the task of explaining differences among men's rates of payments with few firm hypotheses about the way the various background and marital characteristics would relate to payments. The father's race, religion, and occupation at divorce seemed unlikely to signify much in themselves about divorced men's attitudes toward their children, although race and occupation seemed likely to have an indirect relation to men's capacity to pay. Similarly, the father's age at divorce indicated little in itself, although younger men might generally earn less and feel less able to pay.

We did have slightly greater expectations for the significance of certain aspects of the marriage; it seemed to us that, on the average, the longer men had been married and the longer they had lived with their children the more attachment and feeling of responsibility they might have to their children. Even these factors, however, seemed at best quite oblique indicators of attitude. Indeed, it seemed plausible that some men would feel more protective toward younger children, even though they had not lived with them for long.

When we learned the payment levels by various groups of men in relation to the social and economic data we had about them—for example, their occupations or the lengths of their marriages—by far the most striking finding was not the differences that emerged but rather how close in performance the various groups were: we found no sub-groups of thirty or more men with a common characteristic paying less than an average of 62 percent of the amounts due nor any of thirty or more paying over 86 percent of everything due. All are thus within twelve percentage points of the mean. On the other hand, our sample is fairly large and the difference between a rate of payment of 62 percent and a rate of 86 percent is substantial (especially when one remembers that the ceiling is 100 percent). Many of the differences are of statistical significance: the differences are large enough, that is, that we can be confident there are also differences within the total group of men under orders in Genesee from which we drew our sample.

When we examine payments in relation to various social and economic characteristics, we find, before controlling for the effects of one characteristic upon another, that men in white-collar occupations and skilled blue-collar jobs pay somewhat more fully over the lives of their decrees than unskilled blue-collar workers, especially blue-collar workers outside the auto industry. Similarly, men who earned $150 or more each week at divorce paid better over the life of the decree than those who earned less and particularly better than men who earned $60 or less or who were unemployed at divorce. And men who were in their thirties at divorce paid better than others and particularly better than men who were twenty-five or under. On the other hand, although there are slight differences among religious groups, the differences are small and not statistically significant. White persons paid on average at a slightly higher rate than black persons, but again the difference is not statistically significant. (See details on all factors in appendix table 7A.)

Even for the differences that are statistically significant, several warnings are necessary. First, we are talking only about groups. The differences here are so slight that they give almost no guidance about what payments to expect from a particular individual. At divorce, Jerry Neal was thirty-one years old, an auto worker, and a Roman Catholic. He was thus a member of several average- or higher-than-average-paying groups—yet his lifetime index was well below 50 percent.

Second, several of the categories here are closely interrelated. Un-skilled blue-collar workers are, of course, greatly overrepresented in the group earning sixty dollars or less per week. They are similarly somewhat overrepresented among the men divorced when twenty-five years old or under. While being under twenty-five or an unskilled worker or earning under sixty dollars are all associated with lower payments, the figures reported so far do not inform us which of these characteristics—only one or two or all three—are important after con-trolling for the others.

A final problem is caused by missing data. In relation to several characteristics (especially the father's religion and earnings), the group of men for whom we had no information paid far less well than even the lowest-paying identified group.[1] In relation to race, on the other hand, the missing group paid far better than men identified as either black or white.[2] Explanations for the aberrant payment rates of the missing-data cases are easily supplied, but the explanations do not solve the prob-lem. When there were missing data for the man's job or his earnings, it was almost always because he failed to attend the predivorce inter-view with the Friend of the Court, and we found that those who missed the interview in Genesee (and in Washtenaw) paid as a whole far less well than others.

Information about race was not recorded at the predivorce inter-view. Rather, it was noted by the enforcement officer on the sheets that he kept to aid him in tracking down nonpayers. Race was less fre-quently recorded for men who paid regularly, hence the higher pay-ments for those for whom race is missing. The problem posed for us is that we cannot be certain that men for whom we do not have informa-tion about race (or earnings or religion) would be proportionately dis-tributed across racial (or earnings or religious) groups. It might be the case, for example, that if we knew about race for all men, the apparent slight difference between whites and blacks would disappear altogether—or be somewhat magnified.

We cannot, in the end, fully evade the problem of the missing data, but we have used several different techniques to reduce the problem[3] and we will flag the reader's attention each time missing information may affect the reliability of what we report.

The problem caused by reporting on the relation to payments of social, racial, and occupational characteristics before controlling for simultaneous effects can of course be corrected through statistical techniques to impose the controls. Before we do so, let us thicken our broth with information about the relationship between payments and various characteristics of the men's marriages.

As with men's occupations and ages, we find differences in payments, modest but statistically significant, when we examine payments
in relation to various attributes of their marriages (appendix table 7B
provides greater detail). We find, for example, that men married to
women who were pregnant at marriage pay less well than others; we
also find lower payments by men whose marriages lasted less than a
year. The relation of payments to marriage length is, however, mixed:
lower among men of quite short marriages, higher among men with
marriages that lasted more than ten years, but, as the appendix table
makes clear, no coherent pattern for marriages that lasted more than
one year but less than ten.

We also found that the younger a woman was at the birth of her first
child the less well her husband paid after divorce. A third of the men in
our sample married women who were eighteen or under at the birth of
their first child and this group paid substantially less well than the
remaining men, whose wives were older, and especially less well than
the ninety men whose wives were twenty-three or over at the first
birth. The mother's age at this point proved much more strongly tied to
the father's performance than the father's age at marriage or the
father's age at the birth of the first child. Why this is so we cannot be
certain. Perhaps the mother's age at the birth of the first child reflects
some combination of other factors, not directly measurable, that bear
on the father's sense of attachment to his child.

When we move on to look at payments in relation to facts about the
children of the marriage, we find that the sex of the children tells us
nothing. On the other hand, we find that the older the youngest child
was at the point of separation, the better the father pays, though there
is no difference after the child is three (that is, over thirty-six
months—see appendix table 7C). Especially low-paying were the
twenty-nine men whose youngest child was not yet born at the time of
separation. The number of children produces an odd pattern, with
persons with one or two children paying around the mean, those with
three paying somewhat higher, those with four or more paying somewhat less well.

We used multiple classification analysis,[4] the variant of regression
analysis, to sort out which among the factors we have examined so far
about the men, their marriages, and their children were most
significantly related to performance. We found that five of these factors
can account for a substantial portion of the variation in payments, not
nearly as large a portion of the variance as we were able to explain in
the twenty-eight-county study but a set of results that should be reported, nonetheless.[5] In order, the five pieces of information most

strongly related to collections were the length of the marriage to separation, the father's occupation, his age at divorce, the number of
children, and the mother's age at birth of their first child. Information
about the father's race, age of the youngest child at divorce, the
father's earnings and religion, and whether the woman was pregnant
explain very little more of the variation once we have taken the first
five characteristics into account. (The full results are shown in appendix table 7D.)

After the effects of other factors are controlled, two interesting and
conflicting patterns emerge. Men with the longest marriages paid especially well, but even though marriage length correlated strongly and
positively with number of children (+0.49), men with four or more
children paid especially poorly.[6] Similarly, men whose wives were
over thirty at the birth of the first child child paid especially well, but
men who were themselves over forty at divorce paid especially poorly.
Hypotheses about ill-formed attachments to their children may possibly explain the low payments by men from short marriages or men
whose wives were very young at the birth of the first child, but the low
payments by men over forty at divorce remain a puzzle.

Controls help illuminate the relation of payments to the father's occupation. After controls, skilled blue-collar workers pay as well as
either group of white-collar fathers, and only the fathers who were
unemployed at divorce or worked at unskilled jobs outside the automobile industry pay markedly less well than others. Earnings at divorce cease to be a relevant factor. Eckhardt in his Wisconsin study
found that blue-collar workers paid less well than white-collar workers
of similar earnings at divorce. He invited a conclusion about difference
in class attitudes.[7] Our finding regarding the high payments of skilled
blue-collar workers and the closely comparable high payments of the
unskilled automobile workers suggests that what may in fact be important is not social class but simply steadiness of employment. In an
analysis in which we made use of our fragmentary information about
the stability of the man's employment over the years after divorce, we
found that for those few men for whom we had such information,
stability of employment was far more significantly related to performance than was their occupation.[8]

We had available to us a few pieces of information directly related to
the divorcing process whose bearing on payments we have not yet
discussed. The agency sought to interview each parent before divorce.
Nearly all mothers attended, but a sixth of the fathers did not. From
those who did attend the interview the agency staff learned about at-

titudes toward reconciliation and about reasons for wanting the divorce. We found that men who failed to attend the interview paid far less well than men who did—more than a third less of everything owed. On the other hand, almost none of the attitudinal information gathered at the interviews helps explain variations in payments (see more complete information in appendix table 7E). Men whose wives complain of alcohol problems, physical abuse, or infidelity paid as well as other men. Even men whose wives complain that they were inadequate supporters during marriage pay nearly as well as men about whom no such complaint is made. In multiple classification analysis that uses the background characteristics previously discussed, none of these factors, except attendance at the interview, offers any explanation of differences in rates of payments.

What does failure to attend the interview signify? The only direct relation between attendance and payments that seemed plausible to us was that those who failed to attend missed an occasion on which to become aware of the existence of the Friend of the Court and obtain a visual image of the seriousness of the payment process. At least as plausible is that the failure to attend simply indicates the father's lack of strong attachment to his children or his particularly strong feelings of anger or bitterness toward his wife.

Even though failure to attend is strongly tied to payments, when we included this factor in our multiple classification analysis, it did not remove any of the anomalies from our earlier analysis of the relation of payments to the characteristics of the men or their marriages. That is, for example, we had found, after controls for other characteristics, that men over forty at divorce paid less well than other men. Adding in the attendance at the interview did not explain this odd finding; it did not appear, that is, that a disproportionate number of older men missed their interview and that those who attended paid as well as others. The factors that had explained differences in payments before still explained differences after attendance was included.

The fact that the mother's complaints of alcohol problems or inadequate support did not identify fathers with especially poor payment records surprised us. It may well be that the vast bulk of men viewed by others as having a drinking problem still work full-time. Jerry Neal was one of millions of heavy-drinking men whose wives were injured by their conduct but whose capacity to hold some sort of job and hold it steadily was relatively unimpaired. For both the drinkers and the men labeled as inadequate supporters, we need to remember where we are: Genesee county, a place where support was strictly enforced. We have

found that, among the fathers in Genesee who paid more than 80 percent of their amounts due, enforcement efforts were used substantially
more frequently on those fathers said to have alcohol problems or said
to have been inadequate supporters than they were on men about
whom no such complaints were made. We will see shortly that the men
in Washtenaw County whose wives complained of alcohol abuse or
nonsupport paid far less well than other men.

We are nearing the end of our discussion of background characteristics. Before we turn to a brief comparison with Washtenaw County,
there are two other factors ascertainable at the time of the divorce that
merit examination. One is that, at the moment of divorce, an order was
set that differed widely among the men in terms of the portion that it
represented of their earned income. When we compare payment rates
with men's support-order sizes in relation to their income we do not
find what we had expected.

The men with orders representing less than 20 percent of their earnings pay no better than those with orders twice as high in relation to
their earnings (see appendix table 7F). Only men with the very highest
orders in relation to earnings pay significantly less well: the twenty-
seven men working full-time whose orders represented more than 50
percent of their take-home pay did pay less well (an average rate of
.68), but not as poorly as might have been guessed. Since orders are set
in relation to earnings and number of children, we had expected that
the link we had found between number of children and payments would
disappear once we took the order/earnings ratio into account. It does
not. After the order/earnings ratio is taken into account, the fathers
with four or more children still pay less well than others. Why this is so
we still cannot say.

A final factor that was determinable at divorce may well be
significant largely as an artifact of the way our study was conducted.
Fathers in our sample who were divorced in earlier years pay better
than the fathers who were divorced later. Those divorced in 1952 to
1961 paid at an average rate of over 20 percent higher (.81 as opposed
to .66) than those divorced in or after 1969 (see appendix table 7G). We
have little reason to suspect that fathers divorcing in recent years were
poorer or angrier than fathers divorcing earlier or loved their children
less. The significance of the year of the divorce seems rather to lie first
in the fact that in the years prior to 1966, when the agency put its
records on computer, the agency made a practice of putting into separate bins a few cases in which there were neither payments nor complaints, and we missed those cases in our analysis. We have explained

this problem in our Methodological Appendix and the adjustments we made for it. If we add to the pre-1967 cases in our sample a number of zero-payers to represent those who were lost by being prematurely closed—we believe that there should have been about ten or twelve zero-paying cases, no more—the difference between the pre-1966 and post-1966 cases is somewhat reduced.

There is a second reason for lower payments in cases opened in the later years. We have already seen that in Genesee men pay on the average slightly better over time regardless of the year that the case was opened. The men divorced in 1967 thus had more years of payments due by the time we recorded in 1973 than did the men divorced in 1970. In any event, whether we can explain away the problem of the year of the final order, we need to control for the year of the order in our regression analysis.

When we undertook a series of multiple classification analyses with all the factors ascertainable at divorce, sifting out those that retained a capacity to separate the higher- from lower-paying groups, we found that we could now account for around 32 percent of the variation in payments. Our full findings are captured in table 7.1. The strongest factor was the attendance of the man at the predivorce interview. The length of the marriage to separation, the father's occupation, the year of the final order, the mother's age at the first child's birth, the number of children and the age of the father at divorce then followed with the patterns revealed earlier still intact. Once controls were entered, the slight differences we had found between the rates of payment of most other groups almost wholly disappeared.

A Comparison of Payments in Genesee and Washtenaw Counties

Many groups that we had expected to pay poorly within Genesee County paid at almost the average rate. Recall, for example, the high rate of payments by men claimed by their wives to have alcohol problems. From the Genesee data alone, however, we could not determine whether these men paid nearly as well as the rest of the population because their alcohol problem (at least as reported by wives) did not have a significant bearing on their willingness or capacity to pay or because, though it did affect their willingness to pay, Genesee's enforcement system was sufficient to overcome their resistance. Similarly, for almost any high-paying group in Genesee—men with long marriages, men who were white-collar or skilled blue-collar workers— we could not sort out from the payment information alone whether they

Table 7.1   **Seven Factors Determinable at Divorce Most Closely Associated with Payments, Multiple Classification Analysis, Genesee Random Sample**

	N	Mean Payment Rate	Mean Rate after Adjustment for Other Factors
Total	409	.74	.74
Father's attendance at predivorce interview			
Failed to attend	68	.51	.56
Attended	341	.79	.78
			(Beta .26)
Length of marriage to separation			
12 months or less	42	.66	.66
13–36 mos.	55	.74	.74
37–60 mos.	79	.68	.69
61–120 mos.	112	.76	.73
121 or more mos.	118	.82	.84
(Missing data)	(3)	(.10)	(.18)
			(Beta .25)
Father's occupation			
Unskilled autoworker	135	.77	.77
Unskilled, nonautoworker	87	.66	.67
Skilled blue-collar	69	.80	.79
Clerical, sales	25	.86	.81
Managerial, professional	42	.85	.81
Public service (police, fire)	14	.75	.80
Unemployed, never reported	37	.54	.58
			(Beta .22)
Year of final order			
1952–61	64	.81	.84
1962–66	139	.78	.78
1967–68	75	.76	.75
1969–72	130	.66	.65
(No final order)	(1)	(.96)	(.93)
			(Beta .21)
Mother's age at birth of first child			
18 or under	140	.66	.67
19–22	163	.78	.79
23–30	68	.81	.77
31 or over	22	.85	.85
(Missing data)	(16)	(.69)	(.67)
			(Beta .18)

Table 7.1 (Continued)

	N	Mean Payment Rate	Mean Rate after Adjustment for Other Factors
Number of children			
1	138	.76	.80
2	134	.73	.74
3	67	.80	.75
4 or more	67	.66	.63
(Missing data)	(3)	(.86)	(.71)
			(Beta .17)
Father's age at divorce			
25 or under	91	.66	.71
26–30	126	.75	.77
31–35	69	.81	.78
36–40	60	.80	.79
41 or more	50	.77	.66
(Missing data)	(13)	(.58)	(.68)
			(Beta .16)

Portion of variance explained by seven factors: 32.2% (unadjusted), 27.0% (adjusted)

paid so well by reason of a greater predisposition to pay or because they were responsive to the enforcement process. Our information from Washtenaw County provides useful insights into the reasons that underlie the payments of particular groups.

Washtenaw, with the cities of Ann Arbor and Ypsilanti, was the other county in which we drew a detailed individual sample. We reported in chapter 6 that Washtenaw, one of our low-jailing counties without a self-starting enforcement system, collected considerably less per case than Genesee. Over the lives of the decrees to the point at which we sampled them, Genesee's men, as we know, had paid an average of 74 percent of everything due. Only 11 percent had paid 20 percent or less of all amounts due. Washtenaw's fathers, by contrast, paid an average of only 56 percent of all amounts due, with far more fathers (30 percent) paying less than 10 percent of all amounts due.[9]

When we turned to compare the performance of subgroups in the two counties—men of comparable earnings or occupations or common lengths of marriages—we had in hand our results from the twenty-eight county study. Since we had found there that rigorous enforcement capped by jailing apparently produces payments from men who do not respond to lighter measures, we thought that we could learn from a comparison of Genesee and Washtenaw whether men who are especially responsive or unresponsive to rigorous enforcement had any distinguishing characteristics we could identify. Here was our approach. Because of Washtenaw's far less aggressive system of enforcement, we expected, first, that when we found a comparable group in each country paying at similar high rates, we could conclude that these men were either entirely self-propelled toward payment and needed little pushing or, at the least, that for this group Washtenaw's milder efforts were fully sufficient. In either case, we could conclude that, for these men, Genesee's system provided no useful incremental pressure toward payment.

Second, and by the same token, we expected that when we found comparable groups in each county paying at essentially the same low rates, we would be able to conclude (as we had within Genesee alone) that these were groups with a high proportion of members either unable to pay or doggedly resistant even to Genesee's harsher efforts. Third, when we found groups that paid considerably better in Genesee than in Washtenaw, we expected to conclude that these were groups that were able to pay but resistant, groups goaded into higher payment by Genesee's harsher system but left unpersuaded by Washtenaw's milder system. Finally, if we found a group that paid at higher rates in Washtenaw than Genesee, we would perhaps have located a group receptive to Washtenaw's blander treatment but hostile to Genesee's. We had expected to find several sets of each of the first three of these comparative groupings.

In fact, we found that no identifiable groups of any substantial size paid at as high a rate in Washtenaw as their counterparts did in Genesee. Not one.

Rather, virtually all pairings were of the third sort. Just as the Genesee sample as a whole paid about 20 percentage points more than the Washtenaw sample of all that was ordered, so both the poorer- and better-paying subgroups within Genesee typically paid around 16 to 24 percentage points more than their counterparts in Washtenaw. Figure 7.1 provides several examples of this pattern. These results, repeated for characteristic after characteristic, suggest that whatever encourages high performance in Genesee's system operates nearly uniformly across most subgroups. If, as the twenty-eight-county study suggests, it is largely the aggressiveness of Genesee's system that makes the difference, the uniformity of our findings across most subgroups is striking and somewhat surprising. It suggests both that there are few identifiable groups so self-motivated toward payment that they pay as well as they are able without threat and, conversely, that there are few

groups so unable to pay that the threat of jail does not produce substantial additional payments.

There are a few exceptions to these findings. Consider, for example,
a group we have already discussed in Genesee: men whose wives complained of them as inadequate supporters during the life of the marriage. In both counties, the men considered poor supporters during
marriage pay less well than the men not so considered, but the difference between allegedly poor supporters and other men is much
greater in one county than in the other. They pay almost 40 percent less

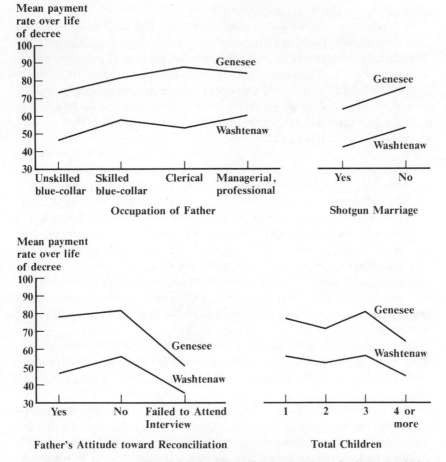

Fig. 7.1 Comparison of mean payments of subgroups within
Genesee and Washtenaw Counties (Genesee and Washtenaw
Random Samples).

well than the rest of the men in Washtenaw but only 10 percent less well than the rest of the men in Genesee (see appendix table 7H). This pattern suggests to us that in each county these men are as a group resistant toward paying (either because they are financially strapped or because they are otherwise ill-disposed toward paying support), but that the resistance is primarily psychological (since the men respond to Genesee's pressures). We find some internal corroboration for this finding in our Genesee sample where the gap between the asserted poor supporters during marriage and the others is considerably greater during the first years of the order than it is in the later years, suggesting a group that eventually hears a message.[10]

Two other groups who also paid especially less well in Washtenaw than their counterparts in Genesee were those whose wives asserted at divorce that their husbands had an alcohol problem (.42 payment rate in Washtenaw, .73 in Genesee) and those who were unemployed at divorce (.36 in Washtenaw, .62 Genesee). These groups probably include in both counties some altogether unemployable men, but it appears to be the case that Genesee's system cajoled many of them into at least significant partial payment.

Finally, the converse. There is one group that paid nearly as well in Washtenaw as its counterpart in Genesee. These were the men who were plaintiffs in their divorce suits. These men paid at an average rate of .70 in Washtenaw and .79 in Genesee. Conversely, in each county, the men who not only did not play the role of plaintiff but also failed even to attend the predivorce interview paid at similar especially low rates (see appendix table 7I). It appears that men who serve as plaintiffs are either an especially self-motivated group or that they respond especially well to Washtenaw's milder system. Later in this chapter, we turn to the effects of particular enforcement efforts on various groups and attempt to sort out which of these explanations seems most plausible.

Our ruminations for the last few paragraphs have been about exceptions to a general finding strong enough to bear repeating. The comparison of subgroups in Genesee and Washtenaw suggests that nearly all groups respond to the particular pressures and threats of the Genesee system in much the same degree. A corollary of this finding is thus that within Washtenaw, as in Genesee, the differences in rates of payment between the higher- and lower-performing subgroups are typically within a rather narrow range. We had expected to find in Washtenaw, with more lax enforcement, that there would be wider variations among groups, helping us identify those who were most psychologically resistant or receptive. As in Genesee, however, in most regards, the similarities—between persons of varying incomes or ages or lengths of marriage—are more striking than the differences.

That men of different occupational or racial groups pay at similar rates should be a source of relief, not disappointment. Had we been able to isolate some physical or class characteristic that identified men the great majority of whom were likely to pay very little, we would invite selective intensive enforcement against them—hostility even before nonpayment occurred, undue skepticism in response to explanations about a missed payment. Hasty enforcement based on class characteristics is one of America's most intractable problems in law enforcement. It is the problem of police assuming that a group of black, low-income teenagers on a street corner are planning illicit activities, while making no such assumption about a group of white, middle-income teens. Within our own sample, the only group in each county that is easily identified and strongly invites especially intense enforcement (in advance of actually failing to pay and failing to respond) is the men who fail to attend their initial interview with the Friend of the Court. At least with the men in this group it is their own conduct that has invited the skeptical treatment.

Effects of Postseparation Events

We have been examining the relation of payments to the circumstances and characteristics of the parties to a divorce that were ascertainable at the point of divorce. These unalterable facets of the parties' lives are not the only factors that might have affected later payments about which we had information. As we have earlier indicated, over the life of a support order dozens of events occur that prevent a father from paying or provide a wavering father excuses or justifications for stopping: layoffs at work, squabbles over visitation, remarriages, and so on. Unfortunately, not all these events were available to us to code. What we have is not the father's diary but the agency's. We are thus somewhat hobbled in our goal of learning the ways fathers responded to various sorts of occurrences. Nonetheless, we had fairly complete information in Genesee about the woman's remarriage and the woman's receipt of welfare benefits, each of which may operate as a disincentive to pay. We also have some information—too often incomplete—about the father's employment problems, the father's remarriage, and the father's or the mother's departure from the county. We have little similar information from Washtenaw, but we can make some useful comparisons with Eckhardt's study in Wisconsin.

Let us look first at the four circumstances that involve the father—

his employment problems, his visitation patterns with his children, his movement away from Genesee County, and his remarriage. We will then examine his reactions to three events that involve the mother— her remarriage, her receipt of welfare, and her participation in the labor force.

Events in the Father's Life

Employment Problems of the Father

A man with no income or resources cannot pay. Even for employed men, a sudden drop in income—say, from a shift to part-time work— may well produce a drop in payments. In Genesee County, men who, upon being laid off or losing their job, reported their problem to the agency were generally treated with some compassion. The enforcement staff tolerated a reduction in payments during the layoff and urged the men to pay an extra five dollars or ten dollars per week later to make up the loss. A simple and graphic illustration within our own study of a drop in payments for work-related problems can be seen through the annual pay indexes from 1969 to 1972 of the Genesee County men who were working in the auto industry at the time of their divorce (see Table 7.2). The four years from 1969 to 1972 were generally prosperous years except that from September to December of 1970 the factory workers at General Motors were on strike as a part of the general renegotiation of the contracts of the United Auto Workers with the "Big Three" American automobile manufacturers.

As is apparent, payments dropped markedly in 1970. Even though men received some strike benefits from their union, their total earnings

Table 7.2   **Annual Payment Rates of Unskilled Blue-Collar Workers in Auto Industry, Genesee Random Sample**

Year	N	Annual Payment Index
1969	118	.77
1970	123	.68 (strike year)
1971	122	.86
1972	111	.82

declined markedly during the strike period. In 1971 payments went above 1969 levels in part because some men were making up for their nonpayment during the strike. It is noteworthy, however, although not apparent from the table, that only a minority of the men who paid less well in 1970 made up for it during 1971. There were twenty-eight auto workers who paid well (over 80 percent of everything due) in 1969 and less well (under 80 percent) during 1970, the strike year. In 1971, most of this group whose payments had fallen off began to pay well again, but only twelve of the twenty-eight paid off some or all of their deficit from 1970 by paying more than 100 percent of what was due in 1971. Many of those who paid close to 100 percent, but no more, of all that was due in 1971 may well have believed that the agency could not justly require them to eradicate the 1970 deficit, since their income had declined for reasons they would consider beyond their control. If the marriage had still been intact, they might have reasoned, the whole family would have suffered together.

This payment pattern of many of the General Motors workers helps us understand one of the puzzling aspects of the payment records in Genesee. We have emphasized again and again the generally high payment rates in Genesee, but it is also the case that over half the men in the Genesee sample developed at some point an arrearage of at least twenty-six weeks' worth of payments, and most of those who built such an arrearage kept it for more than one year. (A person with a twenty-six-week gap in payments would still have a payment index of .95 after ten years if he met all other payments.) We suspect that one reason such arrearages accumulated was that a man was laid off or lost his job, then returned to work and to regular weekly payments but never made up the arrearage. Though enforcement officers tried to induce men who fell behind for employment reasons to pay a few dollars extra each week upon return to work, rarely, if ever, were men who were currently paying in full jailed for failing to make up for an old period of nonpayment related to a decline in earnings.

Unfortunately, we can follow the employment histories of none of our men week by week over the lives of their orders. Men were under no obligation to file monthly or even annual reports on their income. We typically read of work problems only as excuses made by fathers and recorded by enforcement officers after periods of nonpayment and the mailing of a warning letter. Thus to the extent that we have information about work problems year by year it is often of dubious value (after-the-fact explanations for nonpayment) and skewed toward the

lower-paying men. The labor-market problems of men who were suc-
ceeding in making regular payments might well not appear in the files at
all. We nonetheless had for seventy-seven men indications (apart from
payments) that they remained with the same employer throughout the
life of the decree.[11] This group paid at an average annual rate of .92, the
highest-paying subgroup among all those we classified. We also had
forty-six men repeatedly recorded as unemployed who paid at an average rate of .56 (see appendix table 7J). Unfortunately, since we have
inadequate information about the employment histories of over half the
sample, no safe conclusion can be drawn. We strongly suspect, however, that we could say much more about sources of periods of nonpayment if monthly employment or earnings information had been
available to us over the lives of men's orders.

Men Leaving Genesee County

Among the 410 men in our random sample of Genesee cases, at least
seventy men moved away from the county at some point. Some moved
to other counties within Michigan. Others left the state. One or two left
the country. As a group, they paid at a miserable rate: an overall index
of .33. No other identifiable group paid so poorly (see table 7.3).

The powerful relation between payments and leaving the county is
even more apparent when we examine the portions of low-, middle-
and high-payers who left. Twenty-five of thirty of the lowest-paying
men (those paying 10 percent or less of all owed) but only 7 of the 237
highest payers (those paying 80 percent or more of all owed) appear to
have left town (see appendix table 7K).

Table 7.3	Relation of Payments to Father's Leaving the County after Separation, Genesee Random Sample		
		N	Overall Payment Rate
Fathers who apparently left the county		70	.33
Fathers whose files contain no indication that they left the county		339	.83
Total		409	.74
			p < .001

Insulation from the enforcement system occurred when men left the state, because the only way to enforce a Michigan order in any other state was for the Friend of the Court in Genesee to find the man and then, through Genesee's prosecutor, enlist the aid of the prosecutor in the man's new state to initiate an action in that state's courts under the Uniform Reciprocal Enforcement of Support Act, an act under which states enforce other states' decrees. At best, the enforcement in the other state was no better for collecting from the Genesee man than it was in collecting from those divorced in the other state, and most states' systems were far more rudimentary than Michigan's. Even if the man moved within Michigan, it was often difficult to enforce the order; the man was subject to arrest anywhere in the state, but the sheriffs in the rest of the state often showed little interest in tracking down nonpaying fathers from other counties.

In two aspects, our figures about very low payments for men who left Genesee do somewhat overstate the dimensions of the low performance of these men. In the first place, some high-paying men probably moved away but no notation was made of their new addresses because no one became concerned about payments. From the large number of regularly paying men whom we are certain remained in Flint, we are nonetheless confident that the leaving rate was dramatically higher for the low-paying men.

In the second place, our sample excludes altogether a small group of men who moved out of state and who, on the whole, paid somewhat better than the men within our sample who stayed in town. These were men who were divorced in Genesee County but whose cases had been transferred for enforcement purposes prior to 1970 to courts of the state to which they moved. Such transfers could be arranged pursuant to the Uniform Reciprocal Enforcement of Support Act (URESA). We excluded such cases because we were looking for the effects of the Genesee system on the people for whom the agency was responsible for enforcement. As is explained in the Methodological Appendix (Dataset G), had we included such URESA cases proportionately in our random sample (and we could have justified doing so because they were persons divorced in Genesee at the relevant time) they would have increased the number of cases in our sample by about 5 percent—22 to 25 cases on top of our 410. Most of these cases were enforced for some period in Genesee before the man moved. From a sample we drew of payments in URESA cases, we found that, although the overall payment rate for these cases was significantly lower than payments in the sample of cases enforced continuously in Genesee, it was higher than the payments for the group of men who left town but remained in the Genesee caseload. If we add to our seventy men who left town an additional twenty-five URESA men within our sample and impute to the twenty-five a payment rate of .65, the mean for the URESA sample we drew, the ninety-five men who left town would have had an average payment of .41, still the lowest-paying large group within our sample.

Having located a group of substantial size that moved out of the county, we tried to ascertain whether there were any distinguishing characteristics identifying those who left. With the social or economic characteristics we have for the seventy men for whom we coded information, we could identify no groups of men over half of whose members left the county. Nonetheless, there were some significant differences in rates of leaving. Through multiple classification analysis, we found that men who were unemployed or only employed part-time at divorce were over twice as likely to leave as were men who were employed full-time. Conversely, we found that men who were from thirty-one to forty at divorce or who were white-collar workers were considerably less likely to leave than men who were much younger or men who were blue-collar workers.[12] These findings may simply reflect men with stronger attachment to jobs in Genesee County. We did, however, find it somewhat puzzling that, among blue-collar workers, those working in the automobile plants at divorce were as likely to leave the county as other unskilled blue-collar workers, even though as a whole auto workers made payments at significantly higher rates than other unskilled workers.

What was the causal relation between lower payments and leaving the county? The most logical explanation is that the men who left knew the consequences of nonpayment and wanted to avoid them. Nearly all these men had been the subject of enforcement efforts before leaving. Indeed, a few had already been jailed for nonpayment before they left. This discussion of men who leave the county may thus seem inappropriate in a chapter on causes of nonpayment, since leaving town appears not to be a "cause" of nonpayment but the result. In fact, the causal relation between payment and departure may well be more complex, and in some men's cases departure may appropriately be considered a contributor to nonpayment. Some men surely left Genesee County for reasons that had nothing to do with avoidance of an obligation to pay. Having moved, they were insulated from Genesee's enforcement process. Facing little formal pressure to pay, especially if they left the state, they might easily have fallen into patterns of nonpayment that might have been corrected had they remained in town. It is in this sense that their moving may be said to have caused or contributed to their nonpayment.

Even if a man had moved expressly to avoid the consequences of nonpayment, his later payments might well have been affected by the move. As we will see, many men who stayed in Genesee but had periods of nonpayment were cajoled or frightened into resuming regular payments through the efforts of the Friend of the Court staff. While men who were unemployed at divorce were overrepresented among those who left town, it is nonetheless the case that at least forty-seven of the seventy who left were employed full-time; thirty-eight of this group were working for General Motors or at skilled blue-collar or white-collar jobs. Thus, if the men who moved had stayed in town (or if, having moved, they had found themselves subject to a national enforcement system as effective as Genesee's was locally), many would probably have been brought back into the legion of regular payers.

Do our findings that many men leave town suggest that Genesee's aggressive system backfires—that for each extra dollar gained from tough enforcement more is lost from those who flee? No. For more to have been lost than gained, one must first assume that, had these men stayed, gentler methods would have brought a significant number of them into line. Moreover, even if gentler methods could have persuaded some to pay, the study of twenty-eight counties strongly suggests that the net gain in dollars of an aggressive system that depends in part on jail exceeds whatever losses there are from the men who leave but might have been nudged into regular payment. As in Chapter 6, we are discussing here the dollar costs, not the social costs, of a jailing policy. The social costs, too high in the author's view, are discussed in Chapters 8 and 10.

Fathers' Visitations with Children

When men move they become isolated from more than the enforcement process. They also become isolated from their children, as well as from friends or relatives who might remind them about the children and arouse feelings of guilt. Of course, the move itself signifies that the men did not place weekly visits with their children as their highest priority, but once the move is made further diminution of contact is likely. There were twenty-nine fathers in Genesee whose files indicated that they never had any contact with their children after divorce. Some of these men moved away from Genesee but many did not. This group of twenty-nine paid at a mean rate of .34 over the life of the decree.

Except for the men who moved away, we found no other group with a common identifiable behavior or characteristic that paid so poorly. (The significance of "no contact" persists even after controlling for whether the men left town.) Conversely, the sixty-five men for whom we have indications of regular contact paid at the especially high average rate of .85 (see appendix table 7L). In reporting our information about father-child contacts, we must warn that for almost two-thirds of our fathers we have no relevant information about visitation and that, if we had obtained such information in all cases, we might find that the group of men who had no contact with their children paid as well as the group who visited regularly.

We must also warn that even if we assume a link between visitation and payments the nature of the link is not fully clear. For most men, both payments and visitation probably flow from a common source— affection for the child. In some cases, perhaps many, visitation may help induce continued payments by keeping the child's needs vivid in the father's mind. If the latter is the case, policies that encourage visitation may help produce higher collections.

The relation of payments and visitation is more subtle than our few numbers convey. Many families with fathers who do visit with their children encounter occasional crises in payments precipitated by disagreements over visitation. When we surveyed enforcement officers in Genesee County about factors they thought might lead to lower payments, nearly all believed that squabbles over visitation resulted in lower payments. That such a relationship should exist is almost inevitable. For many divorced couples, visitation is the one event within the mother's control that she knows the father cares about, and child support payments are one event within the father's control that he knows the mother cares about. If one parent is perceived by the other as reneging on obligations to pay or permit visits, the other begins to withhold on the corresponding item. Visitation and support payments may thus become weapons for continuing the battles that occurred during the marriage. As one mother told a Friend of the Court worker in another county, "It's the same old story. He used to say, 'No sex, no grocery money.' Now he says, 'No visits, no child support.'"

Thus, officers hear frequently of visitation problems when they send warnings to fathers about nonpayment. Sometimes, on close inquiry, the father seems to have precipitated the squabble over visitation in order to have an excuse not to pay: he arrives for the children half drunk, leaves them in his car while he sits for an hour in a bar, or repeatedly arrives at the wrong time; the mother understandably responds by insisting on different behavior; he claims she is interfering in his relationship with the children and begins to withhold payments. Sometimes it is the mother who starts the process. One Friend of the Court told me of a particularly vindictive mother who asked her former husband to switch his visiting day from Sunday to Saturday, then told their son that because his father had insisted on the change he could not participate in a Saturday afternoon baseball league. It took the father several weeks to figure out why the boy was so sullen every Saturday afternoon.

Whatever the problems with visitation in cases in which the father wishes to visit, their relation to payments appears in most cases to be short-term and remediable. We do not have week-by-week records of the parents' disputes over visits. We did code whether there was any record in the files of complaints by either parent about visitation. On the whole, the men in cases in which there were such complaints paid over the life of the decree as well as or better than the men in cases in which there were no such complaints. Indeed, the eighteen men in our sample who complained frequently paid far better than the average—perhaps feeling that their high payments gave them a special right to complain. These findings about payments and visitation are not at all inconsistent with the enforcement officers' beliefs that a squabble over visitation produces a withholding of payments. Rather, they suggest simply that over the life of the decree men who fight over visitation are those who are, on the whole, involved with their children and that involvement is a good sign for high lifetime payments.

Remarriage of Mother or Father

The relinking of either partner with a new partner can affect the father's desire to continue paying, even though it has no effect on his legal obligations to his children. His own reattachment to a new woman may lessen his attentiveness to the needs of his original family. Moreover, if his new partner is not employed, his living costs will increase. Each of these aspects of his realignment—diverted attention and diverted income—grows more powerful as a disincentive to payment if his new wife or companion already has children of her own who live with them or if the two beget new children. We have already seen in Chapter 4 that men who continue paying their child support after remarrying and having a new child often end up living at a lower standard of living than their former wives.

The man whose former wife remarries or has a new companion does

not, by her act, become any less able to pay, but her relinkage may
operate in several ways to make him less willing to pay. He may first be
simply jealous or angry that she has found someone else: she should
prefer to be lonely than happy with somebody new. If the new man
earns high wages, the father may persuade himself that the children do
not need his money. He may even persuade himself that his own responsibility has ended: the new man has the companionship benefits of
the father; let him pay the costs. If the new man does not earn a high
salary, the father may see his continuing payments as being siphoned
off to support a wastrel. Regardless of the sort of person the new
husband is, the wife's remarriage provides excuses. We may recall, for
example, that Jerry Neal, who paid steadily for the first year after
divorce, said he stopped because of Dolores's remarriage. Jerry's excuse was the last in my list: "I quit paying because he'd just sit on his
butt and . . . take the money and not give it to the kids. Nobody was
getting it but him. She said [later] she was glad I quit paying because
that made him get off his butt and go out and . . . have to get a job." I
found the excuse a bit unlikely: "Could he really support them [on your
support payments]? Live in that house and feed all of them on fifty
dollars a week?" Jerry persisted: "Well, he was taking the money,
though, and leaving them with nothing. That's the heck of it."

The further "heck of it" is that some mothers hope that the new
stepfather will replace the father as the "father figure" in their children's eyes. Some women may thus be willing to tolerate nonpayment
or even to encourage it in return for the former husband's reduction in
frequency of visits.[13]

Given all these considerations, Eckhardt's finding in his study of
collections in Wisconsin, that the remarriage of either parent was followed by an immediate and precipitous decline in payments in a
significant number of cases does not run counter to our expectations.[14]
Remarriage's invitations not to pay were widely accepted.

We find no such pattern in Genesee County. Our evidence of relinkage for each parent was, like Eckhardt's, the formal step of remarriage,
not the less formal arrangements that could well have the same effects.
(We are thus in somewhat the same position as criminologists who
must study the effects of sanctions through evidence of repeat arrests
or convictions, so-called "recidivist" rates, rather than through direct
evidence of the actual incidence of the prohibited conduct.)

Our evidence of fathers' remarriages was spotty, because men had
no obligation to report remarriages to the Friend of the Court. The files
of a quarter of the men included some evidence of remarriage, but

national statistics strongly suggest that the actual incidence within our sample should have been over 60 percent. We will thus say little of this group, except that for those men within our sample who are noted as remarrying, there is no evidence of a decline in payments after the apparent time of their remarriage. Moreover, the men whom we know to have remarried paid as well over the lives of their orders as the rest of the population (a rate of .75 as compared to a rate of .73 for the remaining men—see appendix table 7M). As a more indirect indication of the relation of payments to men's sexual activities, we similarly found no lower payments by men accused at divorce of infidelity (a large portion of whom remarried almost immediately after divorce).

Our data on the women's remarriage are more nearly complete, though it is probable that the actual incidence was slightly higher than we report it. As we reported in Chapter 4, we have information that about 58 percent of the women in our sample had remarried by the end of our records. Two in every five who remarried did so very quickly: by the end of the year following the year of their divorce, they had reported a name change to the Friend of the Court. (Since Michigan law at that time did not permit a woman with custody of children to return to her maiden name upon divorce, the name change was a reliable indication of remarriage. The principal reason that women reported the change was to insure that their support checks would be issued in their new name.)

Within our records, we find that men whose wives remarried, and even men whose wives remarried early, paid as well over the lives of their decrees as men whose wives apparently remained single. The lifetime payments index was .73 for men whose wives remarried and .76 for the men whose wives did not, a difference of no statistical significance (see appendix table 7N). We also find, for those whose wives did remarry, no pattern of declining payments at the point of remarriage. Figure 7.2 shows the pattern of payments. The group who remarry displays the same slight rise in payments over time of the caseload as a whole. We found this surprising.

We also found interesting another aspect of the high payments of these men whose wives remarried. Even after learning that they paid as well over the lives of their orders, we had still thought it likely that, among men who paid well, enforcement efforts might have been used more frequently on the men whose wives remarried than on men whose wives did not. Even this did not prove true. The frequency of efforts over the lives of their decrees was virtually identical for the two groups.

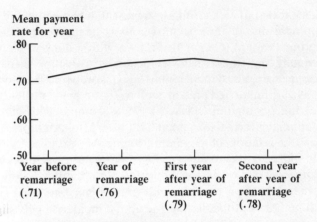

Fig. 7.2 **Father's payments before and after mother's remarriage (Genesee Random Sample, N=162).**
NOTE: Included are 162 cases in which there is a full year's payment information in the year immediately before the mother's marriage and through the first year after the marriage. In the figure shown here, 131 cases remain for the second year. Excluded altogether are many cases in which the mother remarried soon after divorce and there was no payment information for a full year before remarriage.

For the vast bulk of men in the Genesee caseload, the general atmosphere of the enforcement process and the normal incidence of specific efforts were apparently enough to keep them paying. The Wisconsin study indicates that many men, in the absence of enforcement, will cease to pay if their wives remarry. Many Genesee men must have had the same urge but few apparently acted on it.[15]

Events in the Mother's Life

The Mother's Receipt of Welfare Benefits

From an interview with Jerry Neal while he was serving time in jail:

Chambers: One reason she says she is [angry] is that she's had to raise these kids by herself without any real help from you and that it's not been easy.

Neal: I don't think it has. But she's telling me, well, don't worry about it because she's drawing ADC.

Chambers: Did she tell you not to worry about paying?

Neal: Well, she's getting, she's getting money from ADC.

Chambers: Yes. And if you paid what would have happened?

Neal: Well, she wouldn't have got it anyway.

Among the forms of income available to mothers and children, one derives from a system highly likely to destroy a father's motivation to pay. Women who receive welfare benefits under the program of Aid to Families with Dependent Children must assign their support rights to the state. They then receive the same amount each month whether or not the father pays. The government assumes the risk of noncollection. While the government's bearing of the burden operates to the woman's financial advantage, the man who knows that his children are receiving welfare benefits is also likely to know that his children are no better off if he pays than if he doesn't. If the man has remarried and has new children, every dollar he pays in support reduces resources for his new family without any corresponding benefit to his old family. Under these circumstances, a man who loved his children by each marriage equally would not pay support to the Friend of the Court for the earlier ones unless forced to or overcome by a sense of civic duty. As an alternative to nonpayment, the loving father might slip money to his former wife under the table, though he would do so at his peril, and she, if she accepts it and fails to report it, risks being prosecuted for fraud.

Just as the father loses his incentive to pay, the mother receiving welfare payments loses her incentive to keep the agency informed of the nonpaying father's location. A few women are so angry that they will continue to inform the agency where to find their former husbands—Dolores Neal did so more than once while receiving welfare benefits—but most others will no longer care as much whether the father pays or not.

Despite these gloomy prospects for lower payments, measuring the actual effects of the woman's receipt of welfare on the payments of the father has proven nettlesome. Within our Genesee sample, it is clear as a starting point that men whose wives receive welfare benefits do pay significantly less well over the lives of their decrees than other men. As table 7.4 reveals, the fathers whose children ever received welfare benefits paid at an average annual rate of .63, while the remaining fathers paid at a rate of .81, nearly 30 percent more.

On the face of that statistic alone, however, any of three plausible explanations could be offered for the lower payments of the "welfare" men. The first grows out of the disincentive: men pay less *because* their wives receive welfare benefits. The second is the converse: women apply for welfare *because* their husbands have not been paying support. And the third is that some other characteristics of the "welfare"

Table 7.4   **Payments by Fathers in Relation to Mother's Receipt of Welfare Benefits, Genesee Random Sample**

	N	Mean Payment Rate
Fathers whose former wives ever received welfare benefits	143	.63
Fathers whose former wives never received welfare benefits	263	.81
Total	406	.74
		p < .001

men—lower incomes, shorter marriages—account for what welfare receipt appears to explain, and that welfare receipt has nothing directly to do with payments at all. (A fourth explanation would be some combination of the other three.)

After analysis, it appears that the lower payments by men whose wives receive welfare can be explained primarily through the third of the possible explanations: that is, the cases of welfare recipients differ from the nonwelfare cases in ways other than welfare receipt, and it is these other characteristics that largely explain the differences in payment. We earlier identified certain characteristics that corresponded with higher and lower payments within Genesee: length of marriage, father's occupation, number of children, father's age at divorce, the mother's age at the birth of the first child, and the year of the final order (see table 7.1 above). When we ran multiple classification analysis of payment performance, using these six variables and a variable indicating whether the mother ever received welfare, we found striking results. Before we ran the MCA, welfare receipt had the second strongest relation to payments of the seven factors. After controlling for the other six factors, welfare receipt lost most of its explanatory value and became the weakest of the seven.[16]

Thus, lower payments in welfare cases seem to be largely due to the fact that a disproportionate number of men whose wives receive welfare have other characteristics such as short marriages or many children or unskilled blue-collar occupations that are also strongly associated with lower payments. When we have controlled for these other factors, the payment rate in the welfare cases rises from .63 to an adjusted rate of .69, and the payment rate in the nonwelfare cases declines from .81 to an adjusted rate of .78. Instead of a difference of 18 percentage points between the welfare and nonwelfare cases, there is a difference of only 9. To be sure, the after-controls difference between .69 and .78 does remain sufficiently large to be statistically significant (p <.01), but the difference is slight enough now for one to marvel at the closeness of the groups rather than to bemoan the distance between them.

Neither of our other two hypotheses—that welfare receipt causes lower payments or vice versa—seems to explain the remaining differences between welfare and nonwelfare cases. A look at the payment rates of the "welfare" men before and after the year in which their wives began to receive assistance suggests that if either causal force is at work, it works to a modest extent only.

As a group, the men whose wives never receive public assistance pay better from beginning to end than the men whose wives do receive assistance, and the disparity between them grows somewhat as time passes. Though we know that many women have severe income problems even when men pay at the rate of the higher group, it seems highly probable that some additional women are brought into the welfare system by reason of the lower payment rates.

On the other hand, when we look closely at the men whose wives do receive welfare benefits, we find no significant decline in payments after they first begin to receive assistance. We have only fifty-one men for whom we have a full year's payment information before their former wives began receiving AFDC, coupled with two full years thereafter. As figure 7.3 reveals, the payments of the men in this group remain nearly stable. The slight decline we find is insufficient to sustain any theory about the disincentive effects of welfare receipt. (Indeed for a slightly larger group of sixty-eight men who include the fifty-one and seventeen additional men for whom we have payment information only for the first year after the mother's first receipt of welfare, we find no decline in payments at all from the year before first receipt through the year of first receipt and the first year thereafter. See appendix table 7O.) It thus appears that, as with remarriage, Genesee's enforcement system is successful in keeping most men whose wives receive welfare from giving expression to their reduced incentive to pay.

We have generally postponed discussion of the policy implications of our findings until the last chapter of the book. Since this is not a book with a principal focus on collections in welfare cases, however, our

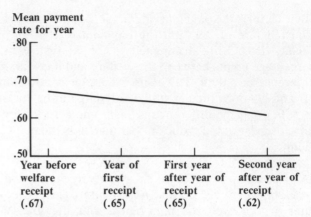

Fig. 7.3 Father's payments before and after mother's welfare receipt (Genesee Random Sample, N=51).
NOTE: Included are the 51 cases in which there is a full year's payment information in the year immediately before the mother's first welfare receipt and through two years of payments afterwards. See also appendix table 7O.

discussion here seems the most suitable place for a brief reflection on the special problems of payments in welfare cases from the perspective of those seeking to collect.

In all but four of the twenty-eight counties we surveyed, the men whose former wives were currently receiving welfare paid, as a group, less well than the men whose wives were not. Across our counties the average portion collected in welfare cases was about 25 percent less than it was for the nonwelfare cases. There were, to be sure, four counties in which the collections were about the same in both welfare and nonwelfare cases, but these counties cannot provide models for collecting in welfare cases, for they were all distinguished not by the special success of their efforts in AFDC cases but by the comparative ineffectiveness of their systems in both welfare and nonwelfare cases. (They were four of the seven lowest collecting counties overall.) In short, all signs within our own study suggest that public agencies will have to expect that they will collect less money in AFDC cases than they can collect with the same efforts in other cases, even if they make as strenuous efforts as Michigan's counties generally did.

The point is not, of course, that vigorous efforts are pointless. Efforts at collections pay off for the welfare cases just as they do for the nonwelfare cases. Indeed, enforcement efforts appear to be able to overcome much of the psychological disincentive to pay that would appear likely to flow from the father's knowledge of the mother's welfare receipt. The point is simply that equal efforts will predictably produce less in welfare cases for reasons largely beyond the capacity of public officials to control.

The Mother's Labor Market Employment

The three common alternative sources of income for a woman are her own earnings, welfare, and the earnings of a man with whom she lives. We have seen that an intensive enforcement process appears effective at overcoming whatever resistance men whose wives remarry have toward continued payment. The process can be nearly as effective for combating disincentives that flow from the woman's receipt of welfare. What effect does the father's knowledge that his former wife is employed have on his willingness to pay? Very little, apparently, at least within Genesee County. Within Genesee County, we find that men whose former wives were employed at the point of divorce (the only point at which we have systematic information about her employment or her earnings) pay as well as or better than men whose wives were not employed (see table 7.5).

We also find that in cases in which both father and mother were working and income figures were available for both, the more the

Table 7.5   Relation of Man's Payments to Mother's Employment
and Earnings, Genesee Random Sample

Mother's Status	N	Overall Payment Index
Employment		
Working part or full-time at divorce	224	.77
Not working at divorce	151	.71
Missing data	(34)	(.71)
Earnings in comparison to father's		
Not working, father working	136	.75
Earnings equal up to 40 percent of father's	42	.77
Earnings equal 41–60 percent of father's	56	.81
Earnings equal 61–80 percent of father's	45	.87
Earnings equal 81 percent or more of father's	56	.73
(Earnings of one parent or the other missing or father unemployed)	(74)	(.60)
Total	409	.74

woman earned in relation to her husband the better he paid—up to a point. The one discordant note is that, if the women earned more than 80 percent as much as the father, the father paid slightly less well. The comparatively lower payments by this group hold after we control for the actual earnings of the father. This pattern of payments suggests that at most levels of earnings by the women, men are not deterred from payment. On the other hand, at least for a few men, when the woman's earnings became nearly as large as the man's or greater than his, the psychological setting seems to change, perhaps because the man felt upstaged by the woman or perhaps because he found a more ready excuse when weighing other expenses he faces.

Our findings about the minimal effects of the mother's employment are corroborated by our information from Washtenaw County. We found that men in Washtenaw whose wives were employed paid at essentially the same rate as men whose wives were not. Given the less stringent enforcement system in Washtenaw, this finding suggests that in general employment by women is not a disincentive that strong enforcement is required to overcome but rather that it is simply not a disincentive at all.

There are, of course, several reasons why a woman's earned income might have a different psychological content than her "income" from welfare or remarriage. Many women were employed before separation. In these cases, the man could not view her earnings as new dollars replacing his. For some men also, the woman's employment may have served a positive inducement to payment: she's doing her part, so I should do mine. Finally, of course, the man making payments to an employed woman not living with a new man knows that his money is neither being shipped to the welfare department nor slipped into the pocket of some lover who is in his view unworthy.

Effects of Enforcement Efforts

Thus far in this chapter we have been examining various events or circumstances that might cause men not to pay. Here we shift to examining the effects of efforts to induce men who have stopped to begin again.

Within our sample most men have lapses in payments. (Only twenty-two men—6 percent of the sample—paid with such metronomic regularity that they ended every payment year with no arrearage at all or an arrearage of no more than three weeks' worth of payments.) At the same time, most men who stop paying at some point do not stop forever. Something occurs to revive the payment habit. Sometimes, the lapse has occurred with the other parent's consent—the father has kept the children with him for several weeks while the mother is out of town—and he begins to pay as planned when the mother returns. Similarly, lapses due to layoffs or job losses may well end when the father returns to work. In these cases, no external stimulus is necessary.

A prod to recommence payments may, however, come from some external source: the child's mother, the child herself, other relatives to whom the mother has complained, or the Friend of the Court. Of all these, we have systematic information about only one, the enforcement efforts undertaken by the Friend of the Court. The balance of this chapter relates our findings about the responses of men in Genesee and Washtenaw to various warnings and to wage assignments. The responses of men to being jailed are saved for Chapter 9.

Responses to Warnings and Wage Assignments, Genesee County

We have already described the apparent effects of a well-organized enforcement process on the overall levels of collections across twenty-eight Michigan counties. It was certainly implicit there, and will be made explicit here, that the enforcement system operated as more than a brooding omnipresence inspiring men to pay. It was not a tornado that never touched down. Real men received real threats. And these men began to make payments in the wake of enforcement efforts directed specifically at them. Indeed, the payment stream of many men over the life of their decrees is composed of periods of steady payments ending for reasons we usually cannot identify and reviving shortly after some sort of warning from the Friend of the Court. Table 7.6 indicates the number and frequency of efforts directed to the men in Genesee County. Only about one in ten of the men received no reminders of nonpayment or other effort at persuasion over the life of their orders. Most of this untouched group were nearly perfect payers, though a few were persons who disappeared in the early weeks of the case and never paid a nickel. (We did not count a warning as an "effort" if it was returned "addressee unknown," since we were seeking to measure men's responses to efforts they knew about.)

What sorts of efforts were used and what responses did they induce? From whom? And for how long? In this section we will be answering these questions with respect to that vast majority of efforts, nineteen of

Table 7.6   **Number and Frequency of Enforcement Efforts over**
                             Life of Order, Genesee Random Sample

No. of Efforts	N	% of Sample	Average Time between Efforts	N	% of Sample
None	43	11%	6 months or less	57	16%
1	49	12	7–12 months	103	28
2 or 3	81	20	13–24 months	85	23
4 or 5	71	17	25–48 months	74	20
6 or 7	51	12⎫	49 months or more	45	12
8–10	55	13 ⎬39	Cases with no efforts	(43)	—
11 or more	60	14⎭	(Missing data)	(3)	—
Total	410	99%	Total	410	99%

every twenty in Genesee, that are carried out by the Friend of the Court staff without any active involvement of the judges.

In Genesee County, the Friend of the Court employed full-time staff members whose sole responsibility was to make certain that fathers paid. These "enforcement officers" were assigned to specific judges, each officer handling part of the caseload of one or two judges. Since 1966, when the agency's payment records were placed on computer, each officer has received every two weeks a computer-printed list of all the cases for which he was responsible. The list indicated the date and amount of each man's most recent payment, the total amount of his arrearage in dollars, and the number of weeks' worth of payments his arrearage represented. On the basis of this list, the officer decided which nonpaying men he wished to pursue. Though each officer carried about a thousand men in his caseload, at any given time each needed to watch only a small number of men: those men whose payments had become erratic and who were not believed to have totally disappeared.

On the 410 men in our sample, we found that by the time of our coding the agency staff had used over 2,100 efforts not involving hearings before a judge. Of these efforts, almost exactly three-quarters, over 1,600, were "pay-or-appear" letters, a one-page form letter reminding nonpayers of an arrearage and threatening court action. Of the remaining quarter of the efforts, half were "wage assignments," orders by a judge entered at the request of the staff that direct the fathers' employers to make payments directly to the Friend of the Court. The remaining efforts were divided among several sorts of other written or oral warnings. Table 7.7 reveals the distribution.

Table 7.7   Incidence of Efforts Not Involving Appearance before
                             a Judge, Genesee Random Sample

	No. of Efforts in 411 Cases	% of All Non-judicial Efforts	% of All Cases with This Type of Effort	% of All Cases with This Type of Effort in Cases with Any Efforts
Form letter threatening court action (pay-or-appear letter)	1,618	75%	87%	98%
Other forms of warnings				
a) Nonthreatening form "contact" letter	89	4	16	18
b) Nonthreatening personal letter	23	1	4	5
c) Threatening personal letter	24	1	5	6
d) Phone calls (unclear whether threatening or not)	77	4	10	11
e) Warning that warrant issued	21	1	4	4
f) Arrest with judicial appearance	38	2	8	9
Total: other warnings	272	13	32	35
Wage assignment	263	12	43	48
Total	2,153	100%	90% (% of cases with any efforts)	—

Effects of "Pay-or-Appear" Letters and Other Warnings

Imagine yourself to be a person in Genesee County under a recently entered order of support. You make payments for several months and then, after an argument with your former wife or during a period when changing from one job to another, you cease making payments. Within a few weeks, you receive from the Friend of the Court your first communication about an arrearage. It is the so-called "pay-or-appear" letter (see figure 7.4).

THE SEVENTH JUDICIAL CIRCUIT OF MICHIGAN

R. W. Standal, Friend of the Court
1101 Beach Street
Flint 2, Michigan

Dear Sir:

You are hereby notified to appear before me on ——————, the —————— day of —————————————— between 8:00 A.M. and 12:00 Noon or between 1:00 P.M. and 5:00 P.M. relative to the arrearage on your support order.

If you fail to appear as ordered, immediate court action will be taken.

This is your final and only notice.

Very truly yours,

Social Service Caseworker
Enforcement Division
Friend of the Court

Fig. 7.4 Example of "pay-or-appear" letter, Genesee County.

"Immediate court action will be taken."
"This is your final and only notice."
The Genesee enforcement staff flung this bucket of cold water at the first appearance of a significant arrearage. It remained by far the most common reminder they sent at the onset of any later period of arrearage, representing over 90 percent of all mailed warnings. They did not routinely use at the outset or later a letter that provided a modest nudge conveying an assumption that the man might well be doing the best he could.

As one might anticipate, about 70 percent of the pay-or-appear letters were followed by the father's making contact with the agency, typically by either a visit or a call. The high rate of contact is perhaps the clearest indication of the seriousness with which the recipients took the letters. Most bill collectors would feel proud to produce the same response-rate to their form notices, especially from a group of debtors like these who had never applied for credit in the first place.

In most instances, the officer's records were silent about whether the father stated a reason for missing his payments, but in the 424 instances in which an excuse was recorded, by far the most common excuse was a recent loss of income—through loss of job, a layoff, a strike, or sickness. The next most common claim was that the man had made payments directly to the woman. (See a full list in appendix table 7P.)

We cannot know, of course, whether men were telling the truth in the excuses they gave. A dragon was breathing down their necks and the excuses they used were especially suited to help them avoid being burned: I can't pay (income loss) or I have already paid (direct payments).[17]

Though our information about the reasons for lapsed payments is spotty, we do know a great deal about the sorts of revived payments that followed the warnings. What were they?

Perhaps an initial illustration from an actual case can convey both the variety of responses and the problems we have faced in conducting and reporting this part of our research. Jerry Neal cannot usefully serve as our example, because his responses to pay-or-appear letters were nearly always the same. He would receive the warning letter, call the agency, state some problem he claimed to be having, and then make no payments. We will use Herman Abbot, another disguised but actual case, instead.

Herman was divorced in 1968, after three years of marriage and one child. The court ordered him to pay eighteen dollars a week. Between 1968 and 1973, Herman was the subject of five enforcement efforts, all of them pay-or-appear letters. Like Jerry Neal and many other men, Herman always made contact with the agency in response to the warning. Unlike Jerry's payment responses, his were quite varied. Herman received his first letter before the divorce became final. According to the payment records, he had fallen behind by about six weeks' worth of payments on his temporary order. He called his enforcement officer and claimed that there must have been some bookkeeping error, but no credit was ever made to his account. Without further protest, he then resumed steady payments and continued making steady payments for about six months, after which, for a few months, his payments became spotty.

The second letter came after about two months of the erratic payments, three months after the divorce became final. His arrearage was then about $150. He made no recorded excuse for his failure to pay, although the file records do reveal that his former wife had remarried during the brief period since the divorce. In any event, on the day he made contact with the agency, he made a lump-sum payment of $120. This payment was not, however, followed by regular weekly payments. A few months later Herman made some payments, for reasons not apparent from the records, but then stopped again. A third warning letter was followed by much the same pattern: a single large payment but no payments immediately following, with a period of payments beginning some months later.

The fourth letter came in November 1970, over two years after the divorce. Herman's arrearage was then $253. He called his officer, arranged to pay an extra two dollars a week, and then began a period of uninterrupted payments at twenty dollars a week that continued for at least two and a half years, until the end of our recording in the summer of 1973. One more pay-or-appear letter was nonetheless sent to him in early 1972, apparently to induce him to pay off the remainder of his accumulated arrearage. When Herman called and reminded the officer of the agreement that he could pay at the rate of twenty dollars a week, the officer wrote a note in the file that the man had indeed been living up to his earlier arrangement.

We have 410 Hermans in our sample, 1,600 pay-or-appear letters, and 2,100 enforcement efforts in all. For each pay-or-appear letter we recorded two sorts of payment responses: lump-sum payments and periods of regular weekly payments. In order to include only those payments for which there was a plausible causal link between the warning letter and the payments, we recorded only lump sums that were paid and regular-payment periods that began within three weeks of the mailing of the letter. A lump-sum payment for our purposes was a payment equalling at least three weeks' worth of payments or $100, whichever was less. A period of regular payments was coded only when payments continued for at least three weeks. Thus, we counted as a lump-sum payment Herman's payment of $120 ten days after his second warning letter but did not attribute to the letter the period of payments that began some months later, even though we had no evidence of any other event that might have sparked the revival of payments.

We also faced frequently the problem posed by the last letter to Herman. In 15 percent of all the efforts, a warning was issued when the father was already paying steadily or had at least made payments within recent weeks. (Such efforts were made to induce men to make up for an old arrearage.) Because of burdens of time we did not code whether the weekly payments that followed such warnings were in an amount greater than the weekly order. Accordingly, we have simply excluded these letters altogether in reporting on payment responses to the warnings. Herman is thus treated as having been sent four, not five, letters.

Of course, even when a warning letter is preceded by a long period of nonpayment and followed within a few days by the onset of a period of steady payment, we cannot safely conclude that the warning letter "caused" the payments. In some of the instances that we report, the impression of a causal tie is no doubt mistaken: a man out of work, fully intending to pay again, returns to work and to payments a few days after a gratuitous warning letter. Although we have tried in general to use neutral verbs like "follow" rather than "produced by" to describe the relation between payments and efforts, the form of our reporting will inevitably invite inferences of causation.

We came in the end to believe that the warnings did in fact contribute to the renewal of payments in a large portion of cases. The incidence of periods of steady payments following warning letters after substantial gaps in payments is sufficiently high that it became implausible to believe that most of the payments would have occurred anyway. Large numbers of men promise—and then make—lump-sum payments. Larger numbers promise to resume paying—and do.*

Some payment periods following enforcement efforts, such as that following Herman's fourth letter, are quite long—two, three, even four years. One can reasonably argue that at some point we should have ceased to attribute payments to the letter, for after a year, if not a few months, it is unlikely that the man adverted to the warning letter when he wrote his weekly check. Fear, if it was ever present, was surely replaced at some point by habit. On the other hand, it is also not at all improbable that the payments in the third year after the letter was sent

---

*In reporting on all the pay-or-appear letters sent to our sample, we see many of the men several times. Some men, it is to be recalled, received none at all and thus do not figure in these data; a few received ten or fifteen letters, all of which are reported here. Of course, more efforts were expended on the subgroups who paid less well on the whole than others. Men who were unemployed at divorce or worked as unskilled laborers received, on the average, twice as many warnings as the managers and professionals. Thus, when considering the responses to the warnings, it is important to remember that the responses are to warnings mailed to men who, if we treat each effort as a separate case, may be thought somewhat less likely to respond than many other people.

would not have occurred but for the letter: if left alone, the man would have slipped into a well-entrenched habit of nonpayment. This latter possibility seems to us sufficient to justify reporting payments that continue for years after a warning even though we inevitably invite causal inferences between the letter and the long course of payments. Although the same rationale might justify attributing to the effort payments made years after the letter but after a gap in payments following the effort, we have not done so. We count and report only payment periods that continue in an unbroken string after a warning. If a gap occurred of more than three weeks or if another letter or other contact with the father intervened, we regarded the period as ended, even though the later resumption of payments might well not have occurred but for the earlier warning.

Now let us return to the question with which we began. What patterns of payments followed warning letters? Figure 7.5 reveals that, by our conservative criteria, 24 percent of the letters are followed by lump-sum payments and 34 percent are followed by periods of regular pay-

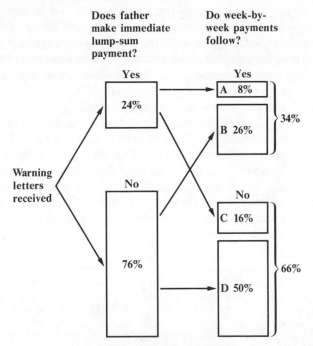

Fig. 7.5 Payments following "pay-or-appear" letters (Genesee Random Sample, N=1,358).

ments. Half the letters (box D in the figure) were followed by no payment responses at all.

One oddity is apparent from this figure: the payment by a man of a lump sum does not signal a high likelihood of the beginning of a period of regular payments. Of the 24 percent of men who make a lump-sum payment, a third (those in box A) begin a period of regular payments. Similarly, of the 76 percent who do *not* make a lump-sum payment, a third (those in box B) begin regular payments. Thus, those who pay a lump sum are no more likely to begin to pay with regularity than those who do not pay a lump sum. We had expected the lump-sum payment to signify a renewed commitment to pay. On the contrary, it seems as often as not to be nearly the opposite: a one-shot effort by the man to keep the agency at bay.[18]

When lump sums did follow warning letters, how large were they? When periods of steady payments suddenly began, how long did they last? The sums were big enough and the payment periods long enough to make all those letters worth mailing. Lump sums, when paid, averaged $215 or about eight weeks' worth of payments. The sum of $215 is not enormous, but most men who paid lump sums did not have an enormous arrearage: the average lump sum represented over 70 percent of the man's accumulated arrearage.

Periods of regular payments were quite varied, with about 30 percent lasting only three to ten weeks. On the other hand, in 20 percent of the cases they lasted over a year. Because of these longer responses, the mean length of the periods of steady payments was about thirty-eight weeks. The median was about twenty-two weeks. What were the overall effects of these letters, considering the combined effects of the lump-sum and weekly payments? We took the lump-sum payments expressed as weeks of payments and added to them the weeks of steady payments following letters. This gave us the total weeks' worth of payments that followed letters. When we divided this sum by the total number of pay-or-appear letters, including those that were followed by no payment response, we found that for every pay-or-appear letter dropped into the mail (and not returned "addressee unknown") the agency averaged about fifteen weeks of payments immediately following (see table 7.8).

Fifteen weeks' worth of payments is not a bad return for a postage stamp and a multilithed form. It remains a profitable rate of return even after one recognizes that people on salaries must make decisions about when to mail letters and keep the books that identify the nonpayers.

In gauging the returns from warning letters, we must remember that

letters were not mailed at random. Indeed, one might guess that the
substantial rate of return from warnings was due to a highly selective
process that led to their being mailed only to the most promising persons, for it is true that enforcement officers made a judgment about
which men to warn and when to mail the warning. We do not, however,
believe that letters were mailed to an elite. Nearly all persons with less
than a nearly perfect payment record received at least one pay-or-
appear letter, and among those who received any the average number
received was about five. In general, the decision not to mail a pay-or-
appear warning to a person who had begun to fall behind appeared to
turn not on a judgment that he was unlikely to respond but on a fore-
knowledge that he had an acceptable excuse for temporary nonpayment (when the man was known, for example, to be employed at a
company out on strike). In only one respect—and it is not a significant
respect—were the men to whom warnings were mailed elite: enforcement officers did not mail warnings to men for whom they had no

Table 7.8   **Payments Following Pay-or-Appear Letters, Genesee Random
                             Sample (N = 1,266)**

Lump sums	
Among lump-sum payments, average equivalent in weeks of payments	8.2 weeks
× Portion of all letters followed by lump-sum payments	× .24
Among all warning letters, average return in lump-sum payments measured in weeks	2.0 weeks
Week-by-week payments	
Among letters that are followed by payments, average length of payments in weeks	38.4 weeks
× Portion of all letters followed by week-by-week payment	× .34
Among all letters, average return in weeks of weekly payments	13.1 weeks
Sum of lump-sum and week-by-week	2.0+13.1=15.1 weeks average total return.

NOTE: Excluded are cases in which the man was
already making payments at the time the warning was
sent and cases in which the man made contact
with the agency, claimed to be out of work or laid
off, and worked out an arrangement, accepted by the
officer, to begin to pay after resuming work.

address. This limitation inheres, of course, in any system of enforcement by mail.

The rate of return may seem even more impressive when we remember the task for these warning letters: they have to trigger an *act*. They have to induce the father to bring to mind the necessity of doing something. For most behavior treated as criminal—robbery or shoplifting, for example—the task of the threat of punishment can be achieved by curbing the potential offender's impulse to commit the act after he develops the temptation to do it: he is tempted, and the temptation can trigger recollection of the threat. With child support there may be no conscious temptation not to pay. Thursday may simply pass without the recollection that a payment is due. The threat must be sufficient in itself to force weekly recollection of the obligation.

Within the large pool of faltering men who received warning letters, what factors seemed to predict the sorts of men most likely to respond with payments? One man's scratch may be another man's tickle. As a general matter, we find again, as we did with payment levels in general, that background characteristics about the men or their marriages tell us little or nothing: after controls, black men respond as well as white, men with short marriages as well as men with longer ones, men for whom we had indications of alcohol problems as well as those for whom we did not. Managers and professionals, perhaps because of easier access to cash, were more likely than blue-collar workers to make lump-sum payments, but they were no more likely to begin periods of week-by-week payments. Nor were men of higher earnings at the point of divorce more likely to pay than persons who were working but earning less. Response was not, however, utterly unrelated to employment: The 953 pay-or-appear letters sent to men working full-time at divorce produced average net payments of 19.6 weeks (counting lump sums and week-by-week payments from payers and nonpayers), whereas the 248 sent to the smaller group of men who were unemployed or irregularly employed at divorce averaged a return of only 7.5 weeks. Two other factors also accompanied lower returns: the higher the man's arrearage at the time of the effort and the more efforts previously tried on him, the lower the returns (see appendix table 7Q).

That a pay-or-appear letter that was the tenth or twelfth effort used in a case produced fewer payments than did the first or second is surely expectable. A man whom the agency has not been able to jostle into a pattern of regular payments after several efforts is likely to be either especially resistant or especially hard-pressed to make payments.

There may, however, be a subtler aspect of later efforts that needs to be explored—the strident words of a form letter may eventually lose their punch. Genesee's pay-or-appear letter ends with a snarl: "If you fail to appear [at the Friend of the Court office] as ordered, immediate court action will be taken. This is your final and only notice."

It is this notice that fathers who fall behind first receive and typically continue to receive whenever patches of nonpayment follow periods of payment. The threat made by this letter surely propelled many men into paying, but the men who didn't make a payment and either ignored the letter altogether or called and made a promise that they never fulfilled did not in fact always find themselves the subject of "immediate court action." Faced with an enormous caseload, the enforcement officers only sometimes followed the letter with a warrant and used varying degrees of effort to serve the warrant once issued. Thus men who "got away with" nonpayment after an earlier pay-or-appear letter may well have felt less fearful upon receiving later ones.

A second danger posed by the tough content of the initial warning was the likelihood that it conveyed to many of its recipients the implication that they were already viewed as deadbeats. The desire to avoid this label may of course have spurred many men toward payment. On the other hand, research into other forms of nonconforming behavior suggests that, for some men, the imputation to them of unreliability ironically comes to confirm the view they are beginning to have of themselves and will reinforce rather than end their nonconforming behavior.[19]

Would these potential drawbacks in the harsh pay-or-appear letter be alleviated by using, at least initially, a less threatening communication? We have little on which to base a judgment. Most other Friends of the Court in Michigan use form letters closely similar to Genesee's. One other form letter, the "contact" letter, occasionally used in Genesee does have a gentler tone—"please get in touch with us about your arrearage"—but it is difficult to draw conclusions about the impact it would have had if more widely used. The payment responses to it were approximately as frequent and as sizable as the responses to pay-or-appears, but in the overwhelming portion of cases in which a contact letter was used, a pay-or-appear or some other threatening letter had already been used at least once before. Thus, although gentler in tone, the contact letters may have borrowed much of their impact from the drum rolls of the past.

If failure to respond to a warning did in fact always lead to immediate judicial action, considerations of fairness, wholly apart from the agency's desire to scare the father into payment, would certainly suggest that the father deserved to be warned of what would come. The question raised but left unanswered by the contact letters is whether it is wise or necessary to leap from a warning letter directly to a warrant without other intermediate steps.

In a few counties in Michigan with collections as high as Genesee's, the Friend of the Court, prior to taking any judicial action, routinely sent a second warning letter to the fathers who failed to respond to the first. Moreover, in almost all counties other than Genesee, the failure to respond to a letter of warning leads not to a warrant but to the issuance of an "order to show cause," an order directing the man to appear at a hearing to explain his arrearage. The "order to show cause," which is mailed, operates in practice as a second warning letter, for the men who receive one generally come into the Friend of the Court before the hearing and make arrangements that eliminate the need for them to appear before the judge. Several of the counties that routinely used orders to show cause collected at higher rates than Genesee, even after taking Genesee's population into account.

Effects of Wage Assignments

A wage assignment is not a warning. It is an order to an employer, backed by the authority of a court, directing the employer to send part of the man's wages each week to the Friend of the Court.

Pay-or-appear letters, arrests, and jailings are jolts that threaten or inflict pain. Their success depends upon the father, who must decide whether he will pay. The efficacy of the wage assignment is in one sense within the control of the father, for he can evade its operation by quitting his job. For most men, however, the decision to quit a job is not taken lightly. Unless another good job is available, he is unlikely to cut off his primary source of income in order to ensure that nothing goes to his former wife. Thus, it is understandable that we find that wage assignments are much more likely than warning letters to be followed by periods of steady payment.

The high rate of return may seem even higher once the conditions under which wage assignments are imposed are understood. Under Michigan law, courts may order wage assignments only for parents who have fallen behind in their support payments and been held in contempt. Although in practice there is seldom a formal adjudication of contempt, since the man "voluntarily" signs the wage assignment on the urging of his enforcement officer, they are nonetheless employed as a remedial device only after a man has fallen into arrears and usually after he has not responded to a warning letter.

In Genesee County, for example, over 40 percent of the men in our sample were placed under a wage assignment at least once, but none of the men were asked to execute, or in fact executed, a wage assignment at the time of the entry of their first decree. For only seventeen men in our sample was the wage assignment the first recorded enforcement effort. More than half the wage assignments were entered when men had accumulated arrearages of at least five hundred dollars. Thus, as with the pay-or-appear letters, when a wage assignment in Genesee County was followed by a period of steady payments, we can rarely be confident that the payments would have come anyway. On the other hand, as with the warning letters, we can never say that the payments would not have come. In the analysis that follows, we have, however, as we did with the letters, excluded all wage assignments entered when the man was already making steady payments.

Three out of every four wage assignments imposed after a gap in payments were followed by periods of steady payments (173 out of 229). When periods of regular payments did follow, many lasted for a long time; nearly 40 percent lasted for over a year and the average length of payments was seventy-three weeks. Including both those wage assignments followed by regular payments and those not followed by such payments, we find the expectable return upon imposition of an assignment to be about 57 weeks of payments (table 7.9).

In reflecting on table 7.9 it is perhaps less striking that 77 percent of wage assignments are followed by payments than that 23 percent are not. If a person has a job when he signs the wage assignment, should there not be payments in every case? Several recurring circumstances explain why wage assignments fail: the man didn't have a job at the time of the assignment; the man quit the job; the employer fired the man soon after receiving the notice of the assignment; and the employer simply ignored the court order. The first explanation—the wage assignment for the job that doesn't exist—may seem unlikely but

Table 7.9   Responses to Wage Assignments, Genesee Random Sample
                             (N = 229)

a) Average number of weeks of regular payments when
   payments followed   73.4 weeks
b) Portion of wage assignments followed by regular payments   × .77
c) Net weeks of payments for all wage assignments including
   payers and nonpayers (line *a* × line *b*).   56.5 weeks

apparently did occur from time to time when the officer did not check with the alleged employer to ensure that the man was actually working for him.

Of the three remaining explanations, the first two—the man quitting or being fired—account for most of the cases of unsuccessful assignments, but it is impossible to measure precisely the extent of either. Employers frequently wrote the Friend of the Court shortly after being served with an assignment saying they no longer employed the man, but these letters are often equivocal as to the reason for the man's departure and when they assert that the man had resigned there is the possibility that they are self-serving and untrustworthy. Jerry Neal, for example, told me that he was fired from a job by an employer who, according to his file, had written the Friend of the Court that Jerry had quit. On another occasion, Jerry and his employer conspired to evade an assignment imposed by the judge through the employer arranging for Jerry to switch to work at another apartment complex managed by the same persons but incorporated under a different name.

When we try to explain what sorts of men do not pay even after a wage assignment, we find that among the factors available to us two are most important in predicting which men are particularly likely to quit, evade, or be fired: age and occupational category.

Wage assignments were most often followed by periods of payment when the men whose wages were assigned worked in the auto industry or were over thirty-five at the time of the assignment. The likelihood of regular payments was least when the men were either skilled or unskilled blue-collar workers outside the auto industry or were twenty-six or under at the time of the assignment (see appendix table 7R). Men who worked for the auto industry were regarded as having the cream of the unskilled work in Genesee County and were probably less likely than other unskilled men to quit their jobs simply to avoid the effects of a wage assignment. Perhaps more important, General Motors, long accustomed to processing wage assignments for credit unions and garnishments from creditors probably fired none of its factory workers simply because of a wage assignment. It is thus likely that nearly all of those men recorded as working for the auto industry at the point of divorce, and for whom the wage assignment failed, were either working for some other employer at the time of the wage assignment or were working for GM but quit their job. Older, nonauto workers, because they anticipated special difficulties in finding other work or had pensions or other benefits they cared about, were probably less likely to quit a job in response to a wage assignment. They were also probably less often fired because of their likely seniority in the places where they worked.

Social scientists seem to be most contented when they find differences among groups, but surely the most important theme to sound about the wage assignment is its high return across nearly all groups. One of the factors closely related to the success of pay-or-appear letters had no relation to the success of the wage assignment: on the average, wage assignments produced steady payments as often when it was a later enforcement effort as when it was one of the first. For persons concerned with regular payments, the wage assignment appears to be the method of choice for parents with steady jobs and a prior history of not responding to other efforts.

The reasons for the high success rate of the wage assignment may include one that is not obvious. It is not merely the case that one must quit one's job to avoid paying; it is also true that the wage assignment may remove some of the sting of paying. Even the man inclined toward payment is subject to the emotional turmoil of the divorce. Each week's payment, when it requires an affirmative act by the father, may be invested with symbolic content. Forgetfulness and tardiness may be conscious or unconscious means of communicating feelings to the other parent. So long as the wage assignment remains in effect it necessarily forces a change in the man's mode of communication. He may still feel some twinge when he sees the deduction listed on his pay stub, but by then the deed is done and he cannot act on his feeling by withholding payment for that week.

The Genesee enforcement staff knew the value of the wage assignment. It is thus easy to understand why we found that in Genesee 43 percent of men with any recorded enforcement efforts were placed under a wage assignment at least once. At any given time, however, only a small portion of the men in Genesee were under an assignment. We were somewhat surprised to find in our survey of twenty-eight counties that, in the nine counties in which it was possible to code from the pay records whether men were under wage assignments, in none were more than 18 percent of the men under an assignment at the time of coding.

Why, given its obvious value, is there not more use of the wage assignment? We are uncertain. For some persons with the spottiest payment records, men with frequent patches of unemployment and many short-term jobs, the wage assignment as it operates today is not particularly useful. A wage assignment works, of course, only when a man keeps his job. It is not automatically reimposed if the man changes employers. However, Friends of the Court often refrain from using wage assignments even with men with erratic payments who have long records of employment with the same employer. Some men strongly resent wage assignments and some employers regard them either as an annoyance or as a sign of weak moral fiber. In the last chapter, we will explore alternatives to the current system of enforcement which depends so much for its effectiveness on the threat and use of penal sanctions. A system of universal wage assignments, traveling with men wherever they are employed, is one of the systems that seems obvious for exploration. Such systems are employed in at least a few European countries. When we do explore it, however, we will need to consider with care the reasons that may lie behind the current limited use of assignments.

Effects of Warnings When Jail Is Not a Threat—A Comparison with Washtenaw County

In Genesee County, most of the men who pay at the highest rates are subjected to several enforcement efforts. Sixty percent of Genesee's men in our sample paid 80 percent or more of everything due over the lives of their orders up to the point that we sampled, but most did not pay at this rate without official intervention. They were the targets of an average of five enforcement efforts, or an average of one effort every nineteen months. Most received warning letters only. Many were also placed at least once on a wage assignment. One in eight, however, had some sort of hearing before a judge. The inference invited by our earlier discussion of the twenty-eight counties is that Genesee collects as well as it does in large part because of the intensity of its enforcement process. The earlier part of this chapter suggests further that the process works not because men hear about enforcement efforts used on others but because they themselves are the targets of efforts and they respond.

A major question left open by the examination of Genesee information alone is whether the warning letters used in Genesee depend for much of their force on the recipient's belief that jail lies in wait if he ignores the letter or whether the letters would have much the same effect, even if jail were rarely used.

The twenty-eight county study does suggest that the prospect of jail gives force to less aggressive efforts: we saw there that counties that were "self-starting," in the sense that they sent warning letters without awaiting complaints, collected far more if they were also high-jailing counties than if they were not. This finding suggests, but does not prove, that those actually receiving warning letters are more likely to respond if they have reason to believe that the warnings have real teeth in them.

Washtenaw County was a non-self-starting, low-jailing county. Our sample in Washtenaw should permit us to test what the twenty-eight county study suggests. It should, that is, permit us to see how men there responded to warning letters even though the prospect of jail did not meaningfully lie behind them.

Washtenaw County makes use of an arrearage notice that is closely similar in its content to Genesee's pay-or-appear letter, a fill-in-the-blanks form that pointedly reminds the recipient that his account is in arrears (see figure 7.6—compare with figure 7.4, above). In capital letters just above the signature line, the form carries an ominous threat: "Enforcement proceedings (including arrest) may be instituted without further notice." The threat is repeated elsewhere on the form. The overall tone is as stiff as that of the pay-or-appear letters in Genesee.[20] The Washtenaw letter also played about the same central role in Washtenaw's enforcement system that the pay-or-appear letter played in Genesee. The warning letter constituted 68 percent of all efforts in Washtenaw not involving a judge, just as the pay-or-appear constituted 75 percent of all such efforts in Genesee.

In comparing the responses to warnings in Washtenaw to the responses in Genesee, we are hampered to some degree by the fact that we were unable to gather data about enforcement efforts in Washtenaw in precisely the same way that we did in Genesee County. We cannot simply compare whether there are, on the average, periods of steady payments for roughly as long a time after individual warnings in Washtenaw as there were in Genesee, because we gathered payment information at a different time than we gathered enforcement information and, because of constraints of time, could not link particular enforcement efforts with the payments in the period that immediately followed. On the other hand, we can draw some telling overall comparisons on the basis of the data we have.

In each county, there were large numbers of men in our samples who were never arrested or jailed. These men were, at most, the recipients of warnings or subjects of wage assignments. Do such men in Washtenaw on whom the gentler methods alone were used pay at rates as high as those of the comparable gently treated men in Genesee? No indeed. We find that the never-arrested-or-jailed group in Genesee, about 71 percent of its sample, paid at a much higher rate than the comparable group in Washtenaw, about 80 percent of that sample for whom we had enforcement information. (We'll call these men the "never-arrested" groups.) The never-arrested men in Washtenaw have an average lifetime index of .59 whereas the comparable group in

RICHARD S. BENEDEK
FRIEND OF THE COURT
WASHTENAW COUNTY BUILDING
ANN ARBOR, MICHIGAN

DATED:

MR.

YOUR ACCOUNT HAS JUST BEEN
REVIEWED. THE FOLLOWING IN-
FORMATION, RESULTING FROM
THIS REVIEW, IS FURNISHED AS A
COURTESY TO YOU. ENFORCE-
MENT PROCEEDINGS (INCLUD-
ING ARREST) MAY BE INSTI-
TUTED BY THE FRIEND OF THE
COURT WITHOUT ANY FURTHER
NOTICE.

☐ IMMEDIATE REDUCTION IN
ARREARAGE IS EXPECTED.

☐ CONTEMPT PROCEEDINGS
HAVE BEEN AUTHORIZED.

☐ PETITION FOR WRIT OF AT-
TACHMENT (ARREST) HAS BEEN
AUTHORIZED.

PLEASE TAKE NOTICE that you are
in arrears $_____

as of

OTHER:

in the payment of support ordered by the Circuit
Court.

DEMAND FOR PAYMENT IS HEREBY MADE.
ENFORCEMENT PROCEEDINGS (INCLUDING
ARREST) MAY BE INSTITUTED WITHOUT
FURTHER NOTICE.

RICHARD S. BENEDEK, Attorney
FRIEND OF THE COURT

By
_____

Fig. 7.6 Form notice of arrearage used in Washtenaw County.

Genesee has an index of .79, about 35 percent higher. That's a large difference, but several explanations might exist for it.

An initial one would be that the unarrested men in Washtenaw are less able to pay than Genesee's unarrested group: Washtenaw may not arrest the poor or disabled, and these may be the ones in the low-paying group. This is in fact not the case. Just as is true with the samples as a whole, Washtenaw's unarrested group was richer, not poorer, than Genesee's: 36 percent of Washtenaw's unarrested group were white-collar (mostly executives and professionals) as opposed to only 20 percent of Genesee's; 30 percent of Washtenaw's unarrested men earned over $150 a week at divorce as opposed to 17 percent of Genesee's. Nor were Genesee's unarrested men older or more likely to have had longer marriages.

If socioeconomic characteristics cannot explain the enormous differences in collections between the payments of the unarrested men in the two counties, several aspects of the enforcement process might. One would be that most men in Washtenaw were left largely alone and were not reminded about arrearages with the surly form that we have seen. That is, Washtenaw may have used this stern reminder but perhaps just didn't use it much. This is an attractive hypothesis, attractive but again unsound. In fact, Washtenaw sent warnings more frequently, not less frequently, than Genesee. The accurate explanation seems to be that Washtenaw's men, though prodded more often, were simply less responsive.

As table 7.10 reveals, Washtenaw County's unarrested men pay less well but are the subject of more efforts, more closely spaced, than are the men in Genesee. Washtenaw used more warnings but brought in less money overall.[21]

The differences between Washtenaw and Genesee can be conveyed more dramatically by comparing the efforts and payments for men of

Table 7.10   Comparison of Payments by, and Enforcement Efforts
                    Used on, Men Never Arrested or Jailed in
                    Washtenaw and Genesee Counties

	N	Pay Index	Average No. of Efforts	Average No. of Months between Efforts
Washtenaw County's never-arrested men	312	.59	4.7	11.3
Genesee County's never-arrested men	292	.79	3.9	19.2

the same occupations in the two counties. Again we see, for comparable occupational groups, the same pattern we see for the never-arrested
group as a whole. In every occupational group from unskilled blue-
collar workers to professionals, the men in Genesee pay markedly
better over the lives of their decrees than the men in Washtenaw and
are, at the same time, the subject of fewer enforcement efforts. Consider the unskilled blue-collar workers, for example. Genesee's never-
arrested workers paid at an average rate of .78, with efforts averaging
once every 17 months; Washtenaw's paid at an average rate of .58 with
efforts averaging once every eight months (see appendix table 7S).

The conclusion seems almost inescapable that similar efforts are
producing more in Genesee than in Washtenaw. It still does not necessarily follow, however, that the difference between the two counties
results solely from the men's differing perceptions of the prospects of
jailing. It could be that Washtenaw's enforcement efforts are ill-timed
or in some other way, apart from the fate that befalls nonpayers, fail to
carry the moral authority that Genesee's do, or that they lack some
guilt-evoking quality that Genesee's have.

It is nonetheless our strong suspicion that, despite the closely similar
threats of the warning letters in each county, the men in Genesee come
to fear the letters they receive more than do the men in Washtenaw. In
each county, a disproportionate number of the efforts are crowded into
the first years of the order before the man has established a long history
of nonpayment. Thus initial timing does not seem to distinguish the
two. What is different is what happens after the letter is sent. In
Genesee, it is simply far more frequently the case (though by no means
always) that a warning letter that is ignored leads in fact to a warrant
and perhaps an arrest, just as each letter threatens.

In Genesee, around 80 percent of men made contact with the agency
after receiving their first warning. They would then have learned, if
they hadn't already, that there was a specific full-time officer assigned
to their case and they would likely have found that the officer talked
serious business. The officer sometimes told the man that he (the
officer) had the power to make arrests and did so. In Washtenaw, we
did not code data about the father's contact with the agency after each
letter, but by agency practice calls from fathers were referred to a
person other than the one in the bookkeeping office who had mailed the
warning. The person to whom the man spoke would generally be a
lawyer who spent only part of his time on enforcement matters and
who had probably never previously reviewed the man's file. When the
man called a second time, he might well speak to someone else.

If the Washtenaw man failed to respond to the warning, the next step was to mail him an order to show cause. Except in welfare cases, no order would be mailed unless the mother requested it in writing. Genesee generally moved directly from an unheeded warning to an arrest warrant served by the man's own enforcement officer without awaiting a complaint, oral or written, from the mother. In Washtenaw, when the wife did request an order to show cause and the man failed to respond, warrants were frequently issued, but it was a sheriff's deputy, not a Friend of the Court officer, who was charged with serving them. The sheriff's department often ignored warrants from the Friend of the Court except when its officers had already arrested or already wanted to arrest a man for another reason. The difference in the overall flavors of the two Friends of the Court is conveyed by the fact that we have many cases in Washtenaw, but very few in Genesee, in which three or four warnings, with no follow-up, are mailed in the first year of the order. It would hardly be surprising if the threat of arrest in the Washtenaw letter quickly lost its potency.

Not all men in Washtenaw become immune to its toothless warnings. The vast difference in collections between Washtenaw and Dane County, Wisconsin, with no system of official warnings at all, probably derives in substantial part from Washtenaw's reminders. Washtenaw's collections, it is to be recalled, generally fell over the years of the life of a case but quite gradually. Dane's fell precipitously. After six years 40 percent of Washtenaw's men, but only 17 percent of Dane's, are still paying nearly everything due.

We also find internal evidence within the Washtenaw data of the effectiveness of the warnings for some men. A significant number of men in our Washtenaw sample end with high overall payment records and indications in their files of large numbers of warning letters over the years—several with well over thirty. This record suggests either men with unusually edgy former wives constantly and unnecessarily requesting warning letters or, more likely, men who do fall behind and for whom a reminder, whether backed with a meaningful threat or not, serves to induce them to begin paying at least for a while.

Let us give an example of a group apparently responsive to Washtenaw's system. Among all of the identifiable subgroups in Washtenaw of any substantial size, there is only one which pays nearly as well over the life of its decrees as its counterpart in Genesee. The members of this group, you may recall, are the men who served as plaintiffs in their suits for divorce. We have examined this group earlier in this chapter (see page 120 above). These eighty-two men in Washtenaw paid at a mean rate of .70, over 30 percent higher than the mean rate of payments for the county (see appendix table 7I). If this group had been fully self-propelled toward payments, we would expect to find that they reach their comparatively high level of payments with fewer enforcement efforts than were used on others. This is partly the case, for substantially fewer of this group were ever the object of a warrant. On the other hand, the seventy-three who were never the object of an arrest or jailing received as many or more warnings and other less formal enforcement efforts as the rest of the unjailed population—an average of one each 10.4 months.

This pattern has suggested to us a significant group whose members are as responsive to Washtenaw's looser enforcement system as the general run of men in Genesee are to its more rigorous system. Since the significance of higher payments by the group of fathers who were plaintiffs persists after controls for other factors that might correlate with serving as plaintiff (such as father's occupation), we are invited to speculate about what it is about serving as plaintiff that indicates a receptiveness toward Washtenaw's enforcement system. We cannot be certain, of course, but it seems possible that the man who serves as plaintiff is a person with special regard for the formalities of the legal system. The letters that come from the agency—whether backed by believable force or not—are nonetheless "official" reminders, and it is that quality that induces the plaintiff group to respond. As a useful contrast, we have found in each county, as reported earlier, that the men who were not merely not plaintiffs but failed even to attend the predivorce interview that they were told in court papers to attend were consistently among the worst payers—a lifetime rate in Washtenaw of .34 and in Genesee of .52, despite the fact that in each county most such men were showered with warnings.

Summary

We had expected to find that Genesee County, with its militant enforcing agency and high rate of jailing, would extract regular payments from nearly all groups of men who were able to pay. Faced with giving up dollars or giving up freedom, most men would eventually give up dollars. And, to a large extent, that is what we did find. White-collar workers, skilled blue-collar workers, and men with indications of remaining with the same employer pay, for example, at very high rates indeed. But we also found that high rates of payments were produced from groups of men who seemed least likely to feel able to pay. Men earning the lowest wages among our sample, men with high orders in relation to earnings, and even men who were identified as having alcohol problems at divorce all paid at rates not far lower than the average for the sample as a whole. Their high rates of payment may simply suggest that, so long as a man is employed, he will choose to pay rather than go to jail, even if the financial pinch is severe.

To be sure, going to jail was not the only choice for men who preferred not to pay. Leaving the county and, safer yet, leaving the state provided sanctuary to many nonpayers. In our Genesee sample, about 30 percent of the men paid less than half of everything they owed; well over half of this low-paying group apparently left town. Rather few men stayed in town and failed to pay year after year.

Our findings are not, however, free of mysteries. In the first place, we are able to explain far from all the variation in payments in Genesee County. Among all the remaining reasons we can easily imagine, which ones in fact explain why some men fail to pay? Some men surely suffered financial problems not detected by us. On the other hand, there appear to have been many men able to pay among those who fail. Most of those who left town were working full-time at decent-paying jobs at the point of divorce. We have few clues about their state of mind. Most of the men who fell greatly in arrears seem to begin their nonpayment early in the life of the order. (The later remarriage of either party, for example, seems to have affected few men's payments.) What it was that made certain men especially resistant from the outset remains beyond us to explain. Something important seems to have been signified by a man's failure to attend the predivorce interview with the Friend of the Court and by his later failure to visit his children, but these are probably symptoms of the ailment, not its source.

Our comparisons with collections in softer-toned Washtenaw County simply deepen the mysteries. We found it no surprise that there was more variation in payments in Washtenaw—which had as many men who paid very little as it did those who paid regularly—and no surprise (though discouraging) that most men in Washtenaw respond less well to warnings since the warnings are not actually followed with forceful action. At the same time, the characteristics and life-events available to us to explain differences in payments served to identify few groups of men in Washtenaw who took special advantage of the opportunities not to pay. Most groups do pay less well than their counterparts in Genesee but typically by about a constant 20 percent difference. Although this finding that Genesee's pressures produce responses from nearly all groups is a valuable finding, it still leaves hidden the reason for especially low payments by some men in each county.

Part Four

Jail

Eight

"All Right, Mr. Connors, Bring up Mr. Neal"

The Story of the Jailing Process

Up to this point, we have examined the collections from random samples of men under support orders in twenty-eight Michigan counties, with a closer look at samples in two counties. We have been looking at everybody in those samples. For most of the rest of the book we will be looking at just some of the bodies—the men brought before the judges for nonpayment and the men that the judges actually sentenced to jail. There are thousands of such men jailed in Michigan every year. And these thousands appear from our earlier analysis to affect the payments of tens of thousands of other men who never go to jail. Given the current system, jailing seems useful.

The nonsupporting men who reside in such large numbers in Michigan's jails nonetheless occupy a quite anomalous position in the American system of penal justice. When we consider crimes for which people are jailed, we picture varied offenders—drunken drivers, embezzlers, rapists—but we tend to imagine a single enforcement and judicial process through which they will pass. For either the embezzler or rapist, the police will make the arrest and a court will set bail. A prosecutor will appear on behalf of the state, and another attorney, perhaps appointed, will appear for the defendant. A jury of local citizens will, if the defendant wishes, decide his guilt after a trial, and, if he is convicted, a judge who was not a personal victim of the offense will decide what punishment to impose.

The men who are jailed for nonpayment of support in Michigan pass through such a vastly different process that the model of the traditional criminal justice system provides at most a point of comparison for judging fairness but offers little basis for predicting the details of the process. In Genesee County, at the time of our study, a man who had not paid his child support was typically arrested not by police but by an agency enforcement officer (who was not trained as a police officer), held for several days at the jail without bond or preliminary hearing, prosecuted by the same enforcement staff member who had arrested him (who was also not trained as an attorney), not represented by counsel or heard by a jury, convicted without sworn testimony, and sentenced by the same judge whose order he had allegedly violated.

In one formal and largely nonsensical regard, a ready explanation exists for the vast difference in procedures. The nonsupporter is sentenced for contempt of court for failing to make payments under an order of support in a "civil" case. The hearing that leads to his jailing is treated as simply one stage in a long "civil" divorce case, not a new and separate "criminal" proceeding. The case remains "Neal v. Neal," rather than "People v. Neal" or "State v. Neal." In civil proceedings, custom and the Constitution have traditionally been viewed as permitting far looser protections for defendants. At a minimum, the label "civil" frees judges from thinking in terms of certain procedures and protections they would extend as a matter of course to a drunken driver or a murderer. The man behind in his child support, who is sitting in jail under a six-month sentence after a five-minute hearing, is likely to take cold comfort in being told his trial was denominated "civil" rather than "criminal." Let us postpone, however, judgments about fairness. There may be more than one model of fair procedure. Here then is a description of the process in Genesee County. It may seem like an anthropologist's tour through the legal system of another culture.

The Genesee Enforcement Staff

Here is an exchange of letters between Jerry Neal, when serving his third one-year sentence of contempt for nonsupport, and the enforcement officer at the Friend of the Court assigned to his case. The officer was a recent college graduate with a liberal arts degree, who had worked with the agency about a year.

September 14, 1974

Dear Sir:
I would like to see you about getting out of jail.
If you let me out now I could get my job back and then I will send you $25.00 every week, because there is only 2 to pay for now. I sure would like to get out now because my wife is going to have a baby and I would like to be with her. I don't have my money order stubs now but I am sure there should be more money paid to you last year. They got mixed up once on me with the other Jerry Neal you have on the books. Why don't you check up on it?
Like I said, if you want to get this cleared up, please let me out now and I can start sending you $25.00 or sometimes more a week. Thank you.

Jerry Neal
Genesee County Jail
917 Beach Street
Flint

September 17, 1974

Dear Mr. Neal:
I am sorry that jail is an inconvenience, but you are over $18,000 behind on your child support and have been sentenced to one year in the County Jail by Judge Cheever. Unless you make a payment of at least $1000 and sign a wage assignment for $50 per week, there is no possibility of a recommendation for your release at this time.
Due to your past record of neglect and indifference, there is nothing to warrant any seeming privileges or favors such as passes. No passes will be recommended to Judge Cheever, except in an emergency situation.
If you can arrange a realistic plan of payment that would include a large cash payment and a wage assignment, your release would undoubtedly be considered by Judge Cheever.

William Booth
Enforcement Officer

The man whom I call William Booth was one of twenty-two enforcement officers working at the Friend of the Court in Genesee County in 1974. Every new case was assigned to one of the enforcement staff as soon as the court entered an order of support. In these officers resided nearly total power over the nonpaying men they found.

Jerry Neal's judge would never have listened to a request from Jerry for early release unless it had come with the officer's blessing. Only by understanding the officers and the functions they perform can one grasp the jailing process.

In 1969 and 1970, the base-point years for data in Genesee County, the enforcement staff was entirely male and, except for one person, entirely white. Mr. Connors, the enforcement officer at the hearing that led to Jerry Neal's first jailing, was one of these men. By the summer of 1974, Mr. Connors had been replaced by Mr. Booth. The staff was still nearly all white and male, except that the one black male officer had been joined by a black female officer. Sixteen of the twenty-two enforcement officers were college graduates. The remainder had completed high school. For half the officers, nearly all of whom were under thirty-five, their position with the Friend of the Court was their first after finishing their formal education. Of the remainder, four had joined the Friend of the Court after working in sales or business, and two each after working in law enforcement, teaching, and the military services. Among urban Friends of the Court, Genesee's was unusual but not unique in having no attorneys on its staff. By contrast, the Friend of the Court staffs in Macomb and Washtenaw Counties, for example, were dominated by attorneys. In these two, the Friend of the Court was himself an attorney, as were his deputies, and, in Macomb, most of the other principal staff persons concerned with enforcement.

From conversations with a large number of officers in Genesee, I derived a sense of a group with widely differing personalities but with a broadly shared perception of mission. Some loved the chase and could sit for hours telling anecdotes of particularly elusive men brought to justice. Others, more sedentary, described their work as just a job. All, however, believed strongly in the duty of fathers to support their children. And all took this work seriously, justly viewing themselves as professionals charged with a serious task.

As a group, the officers were also confident of the efficacy of their efforts and confident especially of the value of Genesee's heavy reliance on jailing. This faith was made evident when we asked them in a survey what they thought would happen if their judges began to sentence defaulting fathers to sixty- or ninety-day terms rather than to the six-month and one-year terms the judges typically imposed. To me, such a change seemed unlikely to have much effect. Twenty of the twenty-two, however, believed that fewer sentenced men would be willing to pay large lump sums for their release. Seventeen also believed that if sentences were shorter the "general run of fathers under support orders would be less frightened about the prospect of jail and total collections would decline." Not one officer believed that with shorter sentences people under orders would behave the same as before.

Operating within only a few announced agency guidelines, these officers exercised nearly total control over the enforcement efforts employed on the men in their caseloads. This power extended to all the men under orders. Even in cases in which the mother had independent resources, she rarely retained an attorney of her own to enforce the court order. Rather, like everyone else, she relied on the agency. In a few counties, the Friends of the Court, in cases in which the mother was not receiving public assistance, waited for complaints from the mothers to prompt them to initiate enforcement efforts. In Genesee County, a "self-starting" county, however, the principal manner by which enforcement officers learned of delinquency was not from the mother but from computer printouts distributed every two weeks. The printout listed, for each case on an officer's caseload, the date of the last payment and the total arrearage in the case stated both in dollars and weeks' worth of payments due. The officers moved delinquent men swiftly from the printout of payments to the jail's register of inmates.

Efforts That Precede Apprehension

For the men who were jailed, jailing typically came early in the life of their orders. Among the men in our separately examined subsample of 191 men who were sentenced in Genesee during 1969 or 1970, two-thirds had been sentenced for the first time by the end of the second year after the final judgment of divorce. Indeed, a quarter were first sentenced for nonpayment under the temporary order before the divorce even became final.

Despite this swift movement toward jail for nonpayers, nearly all jailed men had received earlier warnings. Indeed, in more than half the cases of men brought before judges for nonpayment in the random sample, the man had been the target of at least three earlier efforts before his first court appearance. These earlier efforts were typically the same sorts of pay-or-appear letters and wage assignments used on everyone else. What characterized the jailed population—though it did not distinguish them from everyone else not jailed—was that they had generally failed to respond to these early efforts. Three-fourths of those who had at least two informal efforts before being sentenced—warnings or wage assignments—either made no payments immediately afterwards or made payments lasting in sum less than three months.

In Genesee County, the man who failed to respond to even his first pay-or-appear letter and did not begin paying after receiving it stood in some peril. So did the man who phoned in with an excuse that the officer considered unacceptable. Such a person might have received a second, more threatening, letter,[1] might conceivably have been forgotten, but he was quite likely to have become the subject of a warrant for his arrest.

Much of the power of the enforcement officer lay in his freedom of choice about the fitting response to an unheeded warning. At least as of the early 1970s, the agency had no firm rules that told the officer what steps to take next. He did not have to check his proposed actions with a supervisor or with the judge assigned to the case. In fact, the judges played no role at this stage: they did not receive copies of the computer printout; they did not meet with the enforcement officers to review the caseload; they did not issue directives to the officers specifying a pattern of enforcement efforts they expected for the men under orders. The judges' passivity was understandable because divorce cases consumed only a modest portion of their time in a weekly calendar crowded with felony cases and civil actions other than divorces. Thus, if the officer decided that an arrest was the next step called for, he prepared a writ of attachment, functionally the same as an arrest warrant, which was reviewed perfunctorily by the Friend of the Court, and forwarded for signature to the judge, who almost invariably signed it.

In many counties, perhaps most, there were few guidelines for the enforcers, but there was a division of functions. In most large counties, the enforcement officer who decided to seek an arrest gave the warrant (after it had been signed by the judge) to someone else on the agency staff deputized to perform arrests. In most small counties, warrants were served by sheriff's deputies, who were generally said to assign the warrants low priority among their tasks. In Genesee, however, during the period we examined, the same officer who watched over the computer printout and received complaints from former wives was responsible for serving the warrants he drafted. He became the policeman on the beat. The officers handling nonwelfare cases spent most of three days out of the five work-days each week in the field serving warrants.

Most Genesee officers carried loaded revolvers whenever they went into the field, though they received no formal training in the use of firearms. Occasionally, an officer who had some training would take a junior officer to a firing range. The officers arrested and handcuffed fathers at their place of work, at home, or at the bars they frequented. At least one of the officers claimed to have handled his arrests just as a police officer would handle the arrest of a felon—with drawn gun, he frisked the man, handcuffed him, and recited a warning that anything the man said could be used against him. The Friend of the Court claimed that no suspected nonsupporter (or officer) had ever been shot, though one suspect did disarm two officers and, after shackling them in his basement with their own handcuffs, drove off in their car.

The formality of some officers with hardened nonsupporters amused the sheriff's deputies I interviewed at the Genesee jail. They regarded nonsupporters such as Jerry Neal as friendly, hapless wastrels and called some of the Friend of the Court officers "TV Cops." "Often," one sheriff's deputy told me, "they bring in the nonsupport person in handcuffs behind his back. We don't do that to armed robbers unless they are violent." Why some agency officers behaved in this way is not fully clear to me. Some feared violence because of the anger many nonpayers feel toward their former wives. Others feared the men who believed themselves wanted for more serious offenses and who would not know the officer's purposes when he approached. How frequently these were the thoughts on the officer's mind and how frequently the guns and handcuffs were viewed simply as valuable instruments of humiliation I cannot say.

Frequently when the local police arrested men on charges other than nonsupport, particularly drunkenness or traffic offenses, they found that the men were wanted by the Friend of the Court. Friend of the Court officers frequently traveled to nearby counties to pick up men arrested on other charges. On the last of his three jailings, for example, Jerry Neal was arrested sixty miles from Flint for driving with a loud muffler; as is routine, the police in the other county checked him through a statewide police computer system that revealed that there was a writ for his arrest in Genesee County; and two officers from the Genesee Friend of the Court drove the sixty miles to retrieve him.

Even in these cases the Friend of the Court officers in Genesee exercised judgment about whether they wanted to take the time to pick up the arrested person. And indeed at each stage, because there were always too many nonpayers to track down, the officers, like police officers everywhere, had to make judgments about which of the offenders to spend their time on—whom to look for in the field, whom to send another sort of warning, whom to make calls about.

Officers occasionally became determined to track down particularly elusive men. One officer in Genesee, not by reputation the most aggressive, described to me his recent search for Steve Dancey, a man with alcohol problems jailed three times before for failing to pay support. The offiicer said he had searched steadily for a week checking out leads to find Dancey. He finally tracked him down visiting the parents of his new wife. Dancey put up no resistance and indeed began to laugh. "Today you're laughing, tomorrow I'll be," gloated the officer to Dancey, repeating the story to me with obvious relish. Later in the day I went over to the jail to interview Dancey, by then in the sixth week of his fourth sentence. He called the officer a "big-mouthed little bastard" and admitted to having spent most of the preceding year hiding out from the Friend of the Court. During this most recent jailing, the officer, according to Dancey, had refused to discuss possible terms for a release short of the payment of his full arrearage.

The absorption with fieldwork and arrests exemplified an individualized and particularized approach to the enforcement process—a me-against-him approach. The officers were not charged, any more than are individual police officers, with developing techniques for improving the overall efficiency of the system. They were, rather, charged with pursuing individuals who violated the law. Whether it is the cause or the result of this focus on particular individuals, the enforcement officer's relationship to the men he hunted down necessarily became charged with moral content. I reported earlier that we surveyed the staff officers about the probable consequences of various changes in the enforcement system, asking what they thought would be the consequences of reducing maximum sentences from a year down to sixty or ninety days, and found that a large portion thought that men would be less deterred from repeating. But that isn't all they thought. Many also stated that they thought ninety-day sentences would be less than nonpaying men "deserved" for their misconduct.

Enforcement Efforts Involving a
Judicial Appearance

Within our study, the portion of men in Genesee who passed from warnings to the judicial enforcement stage was substantial. Ninety-three of the 411 men, almost all of whom were arrested first, made at least one appearance before a judge because of their arrearage. An additional twenty men were arrested and booked but avoided a judicial appearance by paying their entire arrearage prior to being brought before the judge. Thus 113 men, or over a quarter of our sample, spent at least some time in jail. Since ours is a random sample of all men under orders of support, the startling implication of this finding is that in Flint, Michigan, one in four divorced fathers with children ordered to pay support is confined at least briefly in jail.

In Genesee, the judicial phase of the enforcement process almost always began with the man's arrest. In nearly all other counties, the judicial phase began with mailing a man the circuit court's traditional "order to show cause" why he should not be held in contempt. The order directed the man to appear at a hearing before a judge. In these counties, only if the man failed to appear at the hearing would an order for his arrest issue. Under Michigan court rules, the Friend of the Court is required to use such orders to show cause before arrest except in cases of emergency.[2] The Friend of the Court in Genesee simply treated all cases as emergencies.

Because of its omission of the "show cause" stage, we see a pattern repeated over and over in Genesee: a pay-or-appear letter is sent; the man either makes no response or phones with an excuse or a promise; no week-by-week payments follow; a warrant is issued; and the man is arrested and brought before the judge. Sometimes this pattern appears very early in the life of the case. We find in the random sample fourteen men who were arrested on warrants issued after the men failed to respond to the first warning letter in their cases, half of them while the cases were still under temporary orders before the divorces became final. In other counties, when the failure to respond to a warning letter is followed by a show-cause order, the man gets a second chance to respond and an opportunity to appear voluntarily before the judge, rather than being brought in in handcuffs. The Genesee men, typically having been arrested first, stood before the judge looking especially remiss and stubborn.[3]

In Genesee, after arrest by the enforcement officer, the man would be held in jail until his hearing before the judge, unless he paid his entire arrearage prior to the hearing. Those who did appear before the judge faced a period of waiting that averaged around three days for the men in our jailed sample. The period was sometimes longer. About a quarter of the men eventually sentenced spent five days or more waiting for their appearance before the judge. During this time no bail would be set. No preliminary hearing would be held to determine whether the officer had a reasonable basis for the arrest.

The enforcing officers could arrange for a particularly recalcitrant man to be arrested at a time, such as Friday afternoon, when he would be certain to be held several days before the judge next conducted hearings. As described by five different officers, the men they arrested in such a way as to ensure that they would have to spend a weekend in jail were those "who are continuous problems and need some time to think it over," "smart-asses," "the troublemakers," "the guy who needs an extra kick," and "the guy who needs to be sentenced but won't be." We found, for example, that men who had never had a period of steady payments prior to their first arrest were held, on the average, 46 percent longer before a hearing than the men who had had at least one prior period of steady payments, a difference that persists after controlling for other information available to us.

In most cases, by the time of a hearing, the officer had prepared a brief written report for the judge that set forth the man's arrearage, his past record of jailings for nonsupport, and the enforcement officer's recommended disposition. In the vast majority of cases, the recommendation was a jail sentence. That was always the recommendation that accompanied Jerry Neal to court.

The Hearings before the Judge

In most American courts, a verbatim record is made of all hearings but is usually left untranscribed except when a party appeals. In Genesee men never appealed (most of them certainly did not know that they could), but the court reporters always transcribed their notes of contempt hearings. A copy of each transcript was kept in the Friend of the Court file. For each case in our samples in Genesee in which there was a court hearing, we read the transcript and coded information. There were over three hundred transcripts in our cases conducted by the dozen circuit judges who sat between 1954 and 1973. These transcripts make disheartening reading to anyone steeped in the traditions of due process of law.

The participants were always the same: a man in arrears, a Friend of the Court officer, and a judge. For the first time, someone other than the officer played a critical role in the enforcement process. The officer shifted into the positon of prosecutor presenting the agency's case. A defense attorney was never appointed for any man, though on occasion a retained counsel did appear. Jury trials were never offered and would not have been held, even if requested. Sworn testimony was never taken. Witnesses were never called. Objections were never raised to evidence, though men were often committed to jail on the basis of hearsay evidence introduced by the enforcement officer. Men were never informed that they had a right not to speak, though judges often ended hearings by saying, "on the basis of your admissions I find you in contempt."

The ostensible issues at the hearing were three: Was the man in arrears? If he was, was he, in the peculiar language of the Michigan statute, "of sufficient ability to comply with the order, or by the exercise of diligence could be of sufficient ability and has neglected or refused to do so"?[4] If this second question about ability to pay was also answered in the affirmative, the man could then be held in contempt and the final question was what to do with him. By statute, he could be sentenced to any term in jail up to a year, subject to his immediate release as a matter of right upon payment of the full arrearage. He could also be released on any other terms found acceptable to the judge, or given a suspended sentence, or placed on probation, or placed under a wage assignment.

In reading the transcripts or watching the hearings, one is struck immediately by the brevity of most of them. The reader often gains as little sense of the defendant as a driver does of a country village driven through at a high speed. Here is the full transcript from one hearing. It recalls the Queen's retort to Alice at the trial of the Jack of Hearts, "Sentence first—verdict later."

The Court:	In the matter of File No. 76550 entitled Ruth Ellis against Bobby Ellis. (Whereupon the defendant came forward, was addressed by the Court as follows:)
Q.	This is pursuant to a case of Ruth Ellis. Now, on April 15, 1963, a judgment of divorce was entered by this Court wherein Bobby Ellis was ordered to pay support in the amount of $16 per week for two minor children. As of October 15, 1973, he is $9,708.86 in arrears. Do you have anything to say before the Court pronounces sentence on you?
A.	Yes. I have been paying this last summer as much as I possibly could and due to the weather and the work conditions I have been on unemployment now for five years.
Q.	Why didn't you give them some of that money?
A.	Well, the price of food and everything.
Q.	What food? They are supposed to starve?

A.   No, they ain't.

The Court: The sentence of the Court is that you be confined
                        to the County jail for one year. You may be re-
                        leased on the advancement of a satisfactory
                        method of making the payments on the support
                        order.

It all took less than a minute.

In one sense, part of the hearing may have taken place before the
man ever saw the judge. From the officer's written report, which the
judge may have read just before the case was called, the judge could
learn the man's arrearage and the enforcement officer's views about a
sentence. He may even have discussed the case with the officer briefly.
In a criminal setting, such written or spoken communications between
a prosecutor and judge in advance of a hearing on the merits would be
grounds for reversal, because they are too likely to cause the judge to
decide that the defendant is guilty before hearing the evidence.

The Ellis hearing was shorter than most. Others took longer, not
because of a dispute about the existence of an arrearage—that was
almost never seriously contested—but because in most hearings the
defendant took more ample occasion to explain his reasons for nonpayment. The judge often took the time to explain why the defendant's
position was unacceptable and to berate him for his inadequacies. Recall Jerry Neal's hearing in the opening chapter.

The part of the hearing that dealt with the defendant's capacity
seemed firmly patterned for most of the judges—patterned in a way
that helped the judge avoid listening with care to the often painful
stories men tried to relate. The judges developed their own patterns
because the statutory language regarding "sufficient ability" to pay
had little firm content and because the state's appellate courts, despite
the language having been in the act for half a century, had as of 1974
never been asked to interpret the language more explicitly (another
effect of the absence of lawyers).

One Genesee judge, until he was recently reversed,[5] regularly took
the view that "sufficient ability" meant only that a person must be
physically able to work; the judge rejected any responsibility to consider whether there were any jobs available or whether the man had
made the best efforts possible to find one. He thus jailed a man who
was receiving welfare benefits and was certified as enrolled in a job
placement program, although he had not yet been placed. The only
issue, the judge said, was whether the man was "in reasonably good

health, not...hospitalized, not...required by doctor's directive or order to be unemployed because of physical hazard.'' He had found a standard that made his task of judging easy.

Other judges at different times took even more extreme positions, however difficult that may be to imagine. One unemployed man was jailed not because the judge believed he was currently able to find work but because the judge believed that he should have found steady work ten years before (nine years before his separation) and that, if he had, he would not have been unemployable today. Another man pointed out that he had been in prison in another state during part of the time he had not been paying, to which the judge replied, "Should your children go without help because you get yourself arrested on some other charge, Mr. Morris? Is that your reasoning?" "No, sir," mumbled the dazed man.

For several other judges the issue was not whether the man could have been paying in full but whether he could have been paying at least in part, a view that was plausible and was especially inviting because most of the men brought before them had paid nothing at all for a substantial period and typically did not claim to have been unemployed during the entire period of nonpayment. Even Mr. Ellis of the one-minute hearing claimed only to have been unemployed for five years, although he had not paid in over ten years.

When the men did get to explain their problems at length, the stories were often pathetic ones—of bouts with alcoholism and delirium tremens; of short-term jobs in "bump and paint" work, maintenance work, or car-washes; of new debts and new families they were barely able to support.

A man who had gone through a Chapter XIII bankruptcy in the federal courts explained why he had left a job where he was subject to a large wage assignment:

> I was paying Chapter XIII 20 percent of my paycheck. I was paying the Friend of the Court 60 percent. Income tax, social security and the rest too—all the rest. I got checks out of the Chevrolet [plant] for 8 cents, $2, $3, so I quit.

Another man explained his problems in these terms:

Mr. Sawyer: I couldn't find work around here in that time, and I was having trouble with my back, so I tried to find work elsewhere, and I went to...first I went to Tucson, Arizona, and there was no work there, so I went to California and I found work at

Hopkins Electronics, and I worked there only approximately two and a half months, and I wasn't making out, and they told me that there was better jobs and more money in Houston, Texas. I went to Houston, Texas, and got a job with Sheppard's Electric, and I worked there for two weeks and one day, and I had ... they said I had a stroke in my right side, and I couldn't work anymore, and I stayed down there, and I thought that I could get better so that I could get the job back, but I didn't get too much better, so I came back here on December the 29th, and I tried to find work here. I found work at an Allied Tool and Engineering Company in Owosso, and I worked two weeks there and they then laid me off. Then ...

The Court: During these various times that you have worked, what, if anything, did you pay your wife for the support of your six kids, sir?

Mr. Sawyer: None, sir. I had to borrow money to go out there and find work, and I had to pay that back, and I had to borrow the money to come home on. I haven't been able to pay any room and board, and I have had no transportation.

The Court: Is there anything else that you would like to say?

Mr. Sawyer: I would like to pay. My employer said he would go along with a wage assignment. He likes my work, and we get along well. This is the first job I have had ... the first decent job that I can depend on, since last July when I lost my job at Ternstedt.

The Court: Well, the court is required to find that you, Mr. Sawyer, are of sufficient ability to pay and comply, at least in part, with the order of the court requiring you to pay for the support of your minor children, and that you have failed and refused to do so, and that you are, therefore, guilty of contempt of court, and committed to the county jail for one year.

You can purge yourself of contempt by paying $3,000 or by making another agreement satisfactory to the friend of the court and to myself.

No judge ever recognized, or tried to read into the statute, a defense that men need not pay at all, even if working, unless they earned enough to meet their individual basic needs for subsistence. Judges were also brusque with claims of expenses for new families. As Jerry Neal was told when he mentioned to the judge his responsibilities to his second wife, a diabetic, "Now, isn't that too bad. . . . If and when you have enough money for a second wife, then you get a second wife." In another hearing, the Friend of the Court officer, Mr. Diamond, seemed to be sympathetic to the father:

Mr. Diamond:	His financial circumstances in July and now are that he has remarried.
The Court:	That is his hard luck.
Mr. Diamond:	There is a child born of the second marriage . . . and she had other children.
The Court:	That is his hard luck. His first children come first. The fact that his second wife has children by another man, those are not his obligation. She is supposed to get support for them from her first husband.
Mr. Diamond:	She never has.
The Court:	If she never has, then, that's her hard luck and why should he deprive his children by his first marriage to give to her children whom he is not even obliged to support.

The judges rarely seemed interested in the men before them as individuals with problems. Occasionally, the judges used the defendants to make jokes for the amusement of others in the courtroom:

The Court:	How much is your rent?
Defendant:	$16 a week.
The Court:	I can cut your expenses by $16 a week. I bet you know how.
Defendant:	Yes sir, I know.
The Court:	Because I know a landlord who demands nothing in rent and will even provide meals for you.

Except for the sneers at the end, the judges' hardened attitude toward men's problems was understandable at least from the perspective of persons who are punctilious about the details of their lives. The men who stood before them may have had financial troubles, but hundreds of Flint men who also had financial problems paid regularly and, when they couldn't pay, called the Friend of the Court in response to warning letters and worked out arrangements to pay. Often the men were jailed less for the sin of failing to pay than for the sin of failing to call the officer. One judge commented at a hearing:

> If you would contact the Friend of the Court—this is true so often, that if fellows would contact the Friend of the Court and say, "Well, look I have got financial problems," quite often something can be worked out. So when you ignore it completely, then the only assumption we can make is that you don't care and you are in contempt.

Indeed, one Friend of the Court in another county said to me, "No one is ever jailed here for not paying. They are jailed for not cooperating."

In Genesee, we found that 70 percent of the pay-or-appear letters were followed by the father's contact with the agency. Many of the remaining 30 percent of the letters had surely been sent to men who simply had grave difficulty coping with the public aspects of their lives or with persons in authority. Even when they had valid excuses, they may have assumed that the officer would not believe them. (These men are matched by mothers who need child support payments but are embarrassed or afraid to keep calling the agency with complaints, even in counties in which complaints are the only trigger for sending warnings.)

When the man, having failed to "contact," stands before the judge under arrest, he faces a further problem in that his excuses now seem almost inevitably less believable than they might have seemed if he had called. After reading large numbers of transcripts, I too began to feel that I would not have been able to tell whether a man was lying about his problems in the labor market. The stories all began to sound much the same. Two-thirds of the men in our sample of jailed men had never paid steadily for more than a month or two prior to their first jailing, had never had, that is, a period in which they had demonstrated at least some concern for the support of their children. As one judge said during a hearing in response to a defendant's plea for a little more time,

> It's amazing.... It just occurs to me ... as if every time we arrest somebody we have been looking for, they are just now on the way to the job they have been waiting for for two years.

Had these cases been tried as criminal cases, the prosecutor would have borne the burden of proving beyond a reasonable doubt that the man had been working or, if not working, that he could have been. In the contempt proceedings as they were carried out in fact, the defendant, once shown to have failed to pay in full, had the burden of "showing cause" why he should not be found in contempt and thus of demonstrating his total incapacity to pay. He then had no resources available to him to make his defense—no lawyer to marshall witnesses, no witnesses to support his story. The history of civil contempt provides precedent for imposing the burden on the defendant, and so in some measure does common sense, since it is impossible for the enforcement officers (acting as prosecutors) to learn what the defendant has done month by month during the period of nonpayment. With men who have been unemployed, the prosecutor's problem is especially thorny. Even if there is no factual dispute about the man's unemployment, the prosecutor would have to prove—as usual, beyond a reasonable doubt—that the man could have been employed. In a county such as Genesee with unemployment above 8 percent during much of the period, and higher than that for young blue-collar workers, it would seem nearly impossible to prove beyond a reasonable doubt that any given man could have had a job.

Unfortunately, of course, if the prosecutor cannot prove the man's employability, it is no more possible for the fathers to prove the converse or even to tell their own story credibly and persuasively. They too are put into a position of accounting for their lives week by week over an extended period. The problem for the judges and defendants was compounded by the almost inevitable differences in their perceptions about life and about work—class differences that made it impossible for the judges to see the men's behavior in the way the men saw it. To the judges, *any* nonpayment that could have been avoided in any part provided a basis for holding the men in contempt. To the men, looking back over a year or two of nonpayment, the painfully memorable parts were probably not the moments, now found contemptuous, when they could have paid, but the stretches when they didn't feel they could.

At an early stage in the project, two law students interviewed about twenty men who were in jail for nonsupport in Detroit and asked each, among many other questions, "Do you think, overall, that the court was fair to you?" Most men thought not, and by far the most common complaint was that the judge didn't listen to their side of the story. As

Jerry Neal put it, in Flint, of a woman judge, "You couldn't tell her nothing." My guess is that most of the time men were permitted to say whatever they wished, but that the judges heard something different. None of them had ever worked at a car wash or had been pressed to avoid remarriage and a fresh start with a new family because of obligations to an earlier one. "What is the trouble between you and employment?" asked one puzzled Genesee judge. Asked another, "Don't you have any pride in being a father? There is something wrong with you but I don't know what it is."

The judges' puzzlement grew in part out of their inability to understand how any decent person could fail to insure that his children were provided for. Moral indignation sometimes boiled through to the surface. The judge who jailed Jerry Neal and fumed about Jerry's unconcern about whether his children "get food in their little stomachs" and "boots in the wintertime" was more colorful than her colleagues, but I believe that most of them, when sentencing, if they had said what they felt, would have joined her in saying "I'm going to teach you a lesson."

As another Genesee judge stated at another hearing:

> If a man is not going to pay support for his lovely offspring, I would prefer that he should not enjoy the sunshine, the flowers, the trees. I think I'd rather not have him pay while he's in jail. You're not paying either way so you might as well spend your time in jail.

When I interviewed yet a third judge, one who was regarded by many on the Friend of the Court staff as too lenient (though still a substantial sentencer by most other counties' standards), I asked him what were the most important purposes he was seeking to serve in sentencing. I expected to hear about deterrence. "Well," he replied to my slight surprise, "collection of monies is secondary in my view to my moral belief that a man should do right by the children he has brought into the world."

The judges themselves had families. A firm stand reaffirmed their own moral commitments. When a man who had just been sentenced to a year made the familiar complaint that he could not make a large lump-sum payment without starving his new family, this was the exchange:

Judge: Well, I'm sorry. If you'd asked us before you had
                     all the children, why perhaps we could be in a
                     better position to sympathize with you. I've got
                     six.

Defendant: Yes, sir.

Friend of the Court Officer:	I've got three.
Judge:	Thank you, Mr. Andrews. If he can work out something with you, I'll consider it, but it better be something pretty good.

The misbehavior of the nonpaying men not merely offended the judges as parents, it also offended them as taxpayers, for a significant portion of the men before them for failure to pay were men whose children currently received welfare benefits. One judge exploded at a defendant: "I'm getting sick and tired as a taxpayer of supporting your children and other fellows' because they are just too doggone lazy to support their own."

Another tied his anger even more explicitly to the punishment he decreed:

> Before this man is released, I want the files brought to me. I will not release him simply on the payment of arrearages. I understand that the ADC benefits this woman has received are substantial. This is an important factor that I take into consideration.

In an interview this judge kept returning to the theme of his special irritation with AFDC cases: there were far too many women on the dole; they should live on their other resources. It was, however, difficult to verify the impact of his views on his sentencing practices, since he gave nearly every man who appeared before him the maximum permissible sentence, whether or not the man's children received public assistance.

All the judges in Genesee were given ample opportunity to take into account the fact of receipt of welfare; it was generally indicated on the face of the report the judge had before him when the man was brought before him for a contempt hearing. I myself have always had difficulty understanding why a judge should be any more indignant when the nonpaying man before him was the father of a child receiving welfare than he was when the child was not. The father who knows that his child is not receiving welfare knows that his nonpayment is reducing his child's standard of living.

Men's nonpayment also offended some judges in their special role as judges. As a formal matter, men are found in contempt not because they have been contemptuous of their children but because they have been contemptuous of a judge's decree—typically the decree entered earlier by the same judge now sentencing the man. One of the judges stated in hearing after hearing his concern that orders be followed because they were orders: "When the court makes an order, the court should enforce its orders. We are not just signing a piece of paper to be thrown out the window."

Offended as parents, as taxpayers, as issuers of violated orders, judges nonetheless did not always, or even generally, openly express rage. Coping with dozens of nonpaying men, the judges' collective anger was apparent through the sentences they gave but often not through any comments they made directly to the men about their irresponsibility. Some judges let the men speak, and then, without directly responding to the excuses given, simply mouthed their finding, under the statute, that the defendant had the ability to pay and meted out a sentence. Comments on the men's conduct were common but not the rule. Some of the judges spoke at hearings as if the actions they took were beyond their power to control: "The only choice that a court has when someone ignores the order of the court is, very frankly, to put him in jail, and I have no choice in this matter but to do this."

Of course, the judges in Genesee knew that they had a choice and sometimes exercised it to impose a disposition other than jailing. In a few other counties, judges held large numbers of hearings but put very few men in jail, preferring suspended sentences, probation, or wage assignments. In Genesee County, however, by far the most common result of the hearings was a jail sentence with release conditional on the payment of a lump sum. Of the ninety-three men in the random sample who were ever brought before a judge for nonpayment, we know for eighty-four of them the results of their first judicial appearance. Fifty of the eighty-four (60 percent) were sentenced to jail. In only three cases did the judge find that the man was not in contempt. Of the thirty-four men not sentenced the first time they appeared, ten more were eventually sentenced at least once in later judicial proceedings. Thus a total of sixty men—more than one in seven of all the men in the random sample of divorced cases—were sentenced to jail at least once for failing to make payments. Consider this figure: of all divorced men in Genesee County under support orders, counting all those paying regularly week after week, one in seven served some time in jail under a sentence of contempt within an average of the first seven years of the decrees. The portion of the men who had been jailed was even higher in the cases that had been open for a substantial number of years. Nearly 20 percent of the men in our sample, whose cases had been alive six or more years (32 of 163), had been jailed at least once.

As we have seen earlier, the rate of jailing among Michigan counties varies widely. Although judges in most counties sentence a much smaller portion of the men in their cases than do the judges in Genesee, the rate was higher in six of our twenty-eight counties than it was in Genesee. Among men brought before the judges in Genesee, whom do the judges choose to jail and whom do they choose to release? In the next section we will see how the men jailed differ from the rest of the men under orders of support. Here we merely glimpse the judge's behavior in dealing with that much smaller group of men actually brought before them by the enforcement staff, for in many ways the pattern appears to confirm the overarching power of the enforcement staff.

When we examined the dispositions of men brought before the judges for the first time, we found that most men were sentenced and that there was only one highly significant factor that seemed to account for dispositions other than jail: whether the father did or did not have an attorney at the hearing. Only two of ten men with attorneys were jailed at their first judicial appearance, whereas jail befell forty-two of sixty-three men who did not have attorneys ($p < .01$). Disproportionate numbers of those with identified alcohol problems were jailed, and disproportionately more of those who were unemployed were jailed than those who were employed full-time; but in neither case were the disproportions at levels of statistical significance.

Several groups that we expected to be more frequently jailed when brought before the judges in fact showed no significantly greater likelihood of being jailed: for example, of those brought to a hearing, blue-collar workers were no more likely to be jailed than white-collar workers. Moreover, there was no difference whatever in the mean arrearages of those jailed and those given another opportunity to pay. Each group had a mean arrearage of around $1,350, though it appears that the jailed group had built up the arrearage over a slightly (but not statistically significantly) shorter period.

There also did not appear to be any foolproof excuses. We have too few cases and too many different excuses to speak with confidence of the impact of any particular type. Nonetheless we can report that two large, rough groupings of excuses—those relating to difficulties in obtaining or retaining employment and those relating to new debts or responsibilities of the fathers—seemed no more likely to avert a jailing than making no excuse at all.

Why did attorneys make an important difference in the outcome of hearings? From an examination of the transcripts, part of the answer seems reasonably clear. It was not because they effectively raised issues of law or procedure, though many might have been raised.

Lawyers in the cases we read never raised legal defenses. They never denied the fact of an arrearage or even that their clients could have been paying at least part of what was due. What they did do was to devise a plan and put it before the judge—worked out a wage assignment, helped the man find a job, sometimes brought in a relative to vouch for him, and always themselves vouched for the existence of the plan. This outside person, the lawyer, was probably known personally by the judge and was at least seen as a fellow member of the bar. The lawyer did not challenge the judge's power but acknowledged it and enticed the judge into treating his client as a person with special problems. The same judge I've quoted before, who said in many hearings that he had no choice but to sentence, said in another, when an attorney proposed a plan for an employed man deeply in arrears, that he was glad to give the man a chance "to straighten this all out." The same judge best conveyed his own view of the value of having an attorney in yet another case in which he gave an adjournment to a man two thousand dollars behind in payments:

Defendant: Your honor, could I say something?

The Court: No. I think you are better off if you let your attorney speak for you.

Perhaps because of the effectiveness of attorneys, no issue that I discussed with judges or enforcement officers generated a more heated response than the question whether counsel should be provided to indigent defendants in contempt proceedings. One enforcement officer, when interviewed, said that if attorneys were provided "we might as well close up shop." One of the judges told me he thought providing counsel would be "ludicrous." Another said that he thought attorneys might help in working out settlements with the Friend of the Court but still opposed providing them because it would cripple the judges' capacity to get their job done.

The view on the part of judges and enforcement staff was not unique to Genesee County. We surveyed by mail the Friends of the Court all over Michigan, asking them, among many things, several questions about changes in the law that might be considered. Thirty-eight of the forty-six who responded opposed providing free counsel to indigents in contempt proceedings and twenty-three opposed it "strongly," by far the most intensely negative reaction we received to any of the changes about which we inquired.

The Supreme Court of Michigan, after we completed the gathering of our own data, agreed with the Friends of the Court: in a case coming to the court from Genesee County, the justices held unanimously that an indigent person facing jail for contempt for failing to pay child support had no constitutional right to an appointed attorney.[6] Their decision was reached despite earlier decisions directly to the contrary by other state supreme courts[7] and despite the fact that the Supreme Court of the United States had held that indigents charged with misdemeanors were entitled to appointed counsel.[8] To one Michigan Supreme Court justice, a critical distinction between contempt for nonpayment and a misdemeanor was that the person charged with contempt had "the keys to the jailhouse in his pocket" since he could get out of jail at any time by showing his willingness to pay. That reasoning was simply disingenuous rubbish. Judges never inquired whether men had cash on hand equal to the portion of the arrearage demanded as the price of release. Nor was any man released simply on saying that he promised to begin paying. The real rationale for the Michigan decision was probably that the justices knew that to provide lawyers would cost money and that county officials were already complaining about the costs of providing lawyers in other settings.

Why such strong feelings about appointed counsel among the local judges and the Friends of the Court? On their part, such feelings seemed unlikely to be due simply to the dollars lawyers would cost, even though the cost might be substantial. My suspicion is that, at least in part, judges and staff knew that lawyers would force them to treat as individuals men whom they have been accustomed to treating as stereotypes and that locking people in jail is less easy when a person of respectability—the lawyer—starts proposing individual plans that sound reasonable. The staff members of the Friends of the Court enjoy the power they have.

Lawyers made a difference in determining who, among men appearing at a hearing, was sentenced to jail. Among men sentenced, however, they had no impact on the length of sentence in fact imposed. Judges in Genesee used long sentences in large part to place the maximum pressure on the men to disgorge a substantial lump-sum payment as the price for an early release. Thus, among the jailed men, 63 percent of the sentences were, on their face, for a full year, the maximum permitted by law, and only 8 percent were for ninety days or less. Yearlong sentences were the tradition. As one of the judges informed a defendant at sentencing:

It is customary for me to sentence a man to a year in the county jail for contempt of these court orders and you . . . [should] know that is the standard practice of most of the judges here to do the very same thing because we want these children taken care of.

Among Michigan counties, the pattern of sentence length of the judges in Macomb County, a heavily populated suburban county adjacent to Detroit, seems to have been more common and nearly the reverse of Genesee's. There, over two-thirds of sentences were for ninety days or less and only 8 percent were for a full year. Around 20 percent of the sentences were for six-month terms (see appendix table 8A). The judges in most other counties chose even shorter sentences than the Macomb judges. In our survey of twenty-eight counties, the judges in seventeen counties, during the year we coded, imposed sentences of six or more months on fewer than 10 percent of the men who appeared before them.

Yet another difference between Genesee County and most other Michigan counties was that in most places the judge would at the moment of passing sentence state an amount far short of the full arrearage that he would accept as a payment for release. In Genesee, it was the practice for the judge to leave up to the enforcement officer the task of determining an amount short of the full arrearage that he would accept or of framing some other arrangement such as release on a wage assignment.

The adjudication and sentencing moment marked the only point in the enforcement process when the judge—or anyone other than the enforcement officer—performed an official function of any more than a perfunctory sort. And even at this stage the judges in Genesee typically followed the officer's recommendations and sentenced the vast bulk of the men brought to them. They did not sort out any men for more lenient treatment by any systematic scheme we could detect. Thus, even here, the enforcement staff's power seems to be confirmed. To be sure, the officers' decisions about whom to bring to the judges were tempered by their knowledge of what the judges would be likely to do, but the officers alone made the decision about whom to bring to court and, except in the rarest cases, the judges never knew whom they had filtered out.

Moreover, the Friend of the Court staff has provided a continuity of attitude about support enforcement that seems almost certain to have affected the Genesee judges. The judges seemed markedly different from each other—one resigned during the period studied in part on the ground of the terrible conditions in the state prisons—but all, including this judge, sentenced to long terms most of the men brought to them for nonsupport. The judges' habit of following the recommendations of the staff may have been reinforced in part by their awareness of how much the staff had invested in its efforts. The staff members felt disappointed when a judge released a man at the hearing. As one officer described his frustration, "You bust your butt for six months trying to find someone. You hate like hell to see all your work go down the drain." The judges knew that the officers cared.

Life in Jail and Negotiations
for Early Release

Here are excerpts from an interview with Jerry Neal, then several months into his third term in the Genesee jail for contempt of court. He had been sentenced in late May. It was now nearly Thanksgiving. His new wife, Judy, a warm, resilient woman, was expecting a child within a few weeks. She visited Jerry twice a week, bringing Billy, the youngest of her four children from a previous marriage. Billy was four, and looked forward to seeing "Daddy Jerry" on their Wednesday and Sunday trips to the jail. Jerry is "good with kids," Judy later told me.

Jerry was then a "trusty" in the jail, the term for an inmate with a job inside the jail who has a few more privileges than other inmates. In his current job, he helped run the inmate store.

Chambers:	I'd like to talk a little bit about what life is, what happens while you're here in jail? How many of the times that you've been here have you been put on trusty?
Neal:	Every time.
Chambers:	Tell me what kinds of jobs they've put you on to.
Neal:	Well, the first time I was in here when I had to spend the whole year they had me in charge of all the other trusties. I was almost the head one.
Chambers:	What would that entail for you? What would your day be?
Neal:	Well, seeing that everybody had a job and that it got done.
Chambers:	I see. A foreman.
Neal:	Yeah. If somebody went home I got to get somebody to replace him and see that everything was going O.K. If they ever needed anything, like the

	lieutenant needed something done he'd holler to me first and then . . . then . . . .
Chambers:	You'd holler at the next guy down the chain?
Neal:	See what kind of job they wanted. I'd get some-body to do it.
Chambers:	What would they have had to do if they hadn't had you to do that kind of work?
Neal:	Well, they'd had to do it theirselves.
Chambers:	How many trusties are there now?
Neal:	There's about forty-seven or forty-eight.
Chambers:	Trusties?
Neal:	Yeah.
Chambers:	Of that group, could you take a guess as to how many are in here for nonsupport?
Neal:	I'd say out of the forty-seven, about forty of them are nonsupport. . . .
Chambers:	Now when will your time be up this time?
Neal:	March, I got half the time in now.
Chambers:	So what are your chances of getting out early this time?
Neal:	Well, for the looks of Booth,* he don't want to talk or nothing.
Chambers:	How much do you think he'd accept before . . .
Neal:	Well, on that last letter he said to me, he said a thousand dollars.
Chambers:	Oh was that right? I'd forgot.
Neal:	A thousand dollars and a wage assignment.
Chambers:	Coming up with a thousand is more than you can possibly do?
Neal:	Well I had it, I could have given it to them at the beginning, but now she spent it for medical bills and everything, she had to spend it.
Chambers:	Have you ever tried to borrow that money from anybody?

*Neal's enforcement officer. See letter above, p. 167.

Neal:	No, because I don't want to go in debt again otherwise I'd be, have to make it up again. That'd be the heck of it.
Chambers:	Do you have any family members who could come up with that kind of money, if you asked them?
Neal:	Yeah, probably could, but like I said, I hate to borrow because then you just catch yourself in debt again. . . .
Chambers:	What is life like for you while you're here?
Neal:	Well it ain't easy.
Chambers:	What are the hardest parts of it?
Neal:	Well knowing that she's sitting there and going to go in any day [to have her baby].
Chambers:	Oh that's right, isn't it. What about the way you're treated?
Neal:	Why, you mean here?
Chambers:	Yeah.
Neal:	Treated O.K. as far as that goes, I mean, can't complain on that. I was thinking about writing a letter to the judge and see if he'd be any easier to talk to than Booth, but I don't know if he'd go back to the Friend of the Court anyway and talk to Booth and that'd be the end of it there.

In Genesee, as the jailhouse door clanged shut after sentencing, it was again the enforcement officer, now functionally similar to the parole board, whom the sentenced man had to please. The only way a man could secure his early release as a matter of right was by purchasing it with a payment equal to his full arrearage. Of the 182 men in our Genesee County jailing sample for whom we know the reason for release, however, only eighteen paid their full arrearage (or an amount so close to it that the officer would almost certainly have felt bound to accept it). A few others worked out release plans that circumvented the officers, by escaping from custody (principally by walking away from an unguarded work assignment), by reconciling with their former spouse, or by securing her "acknowledgement" that she had received payments in full.

The early release of the remaining men, constituting over eighty percent of the men sentenced, lay almost entirely within the discretion of the officer, who proposed a dollar amount as the price for release or in some cases accepted a wage assignment. A third of these men never came up with the amount set by their officer or devised a plan satisfactory to the officer. They thus served their full term (see summary of reasons for release, appendix table 8B). That was Jerry's fate on two of his three sentences.

Some judges conveyed informal instructions to the officers about the portions of the arrearage or the dollar amounts that they would consider acceptable, but if the officer did not forward an inmate's proposal to the judge, the judge in all likelihood would never have known it had been made. If an inmate wrote the judge from jail, the judge generally simply forwarded the letter to the officer without direction. Most officers reported that, when they proposed plans for release, the judges almost always accepted them.

There was a rough pattern to the bargaining between the jailed father and the officer. The closer it came to the end of the man's term, the smaller an amount the officer would typically accept. Often the officer would persuade the man to couple a small lump-sum payment with a wage assignment. In Genesee and Macomb, many officers would begin late in the term of the sentence to recommend release on a wage assignment alone, sometimes to jobs where the officer was not at all certain the man would stay for more than a few days. We occasionally heard of the officers proposing release on a low sum or a wage assignment alone and the jailed man, angry or stubborn, held for months already, preferring to serve out his short remaining time, even though he still owed the full arrearage upon his release including what had accrued while he was in jail.

When we compare the lengths of time actually served in jail in Macomb and Genesee, we find again that the periods are much longer in Genesee. It need not have been so, of course, since deals could have been struck in either county within a day or two after sentencing, regardless of sentence length, but it turned out to have been so in fact. The median time served in Genesee County was eight times longer than the median time served in Macomb—fifty-two days as opposed to six (see details in appendix tables 8C and 8D). The long periods of time served by most men in Genesee astonished us. Whereas in most counties, the object of jailing as reported by the Friend of the Court was to give men a brief, painful jolt, for over half the men in Genesee the jolt was so substantial that it probably cost them whatever job they had at the time they were confined. Much of the disparity between Genesee and Macomb in time actually served must be attributed to the original sentence lengths themselves: while 40 percent of Genesee's jailed men *served* more than ninety days, only 30 percent of Macomb's men were given initial *sentences* that were that long.

Within Genesee County, where nearly everyone received a long sentence, the original sentence length in months provides only a small part of the explanation for the differences among men in time served. Rather, we again find that one important factor in determining the length of time served is the enforcement officer assigned to the individual judge. For example, although the sentences imposed by two of the judges averaged about the same length, the men sentenced by one of them spent on the average two and one-half times as long in jail as the men sentenced by the other—145 days as opposed to 56 days.[9] Since virtually all decisions over early release were left to the individual officers, we see here more evidence of the nearly unfettered powers of the officers.

The figures about the long terms actually served do not adequately convey the place of jail in the lives of the jailed men. We have already mentioned that most men jailed are first jailed early in the life of their orders. After a first jailing, often for a substantial period, many men are jailed again.

For a quarter of our sample of jailed men, the jailing in 1969–70, the base of our sample, was not their first jailing for nonsupport. For 9 percent of the men, it was at least their third. One man had been jailed six times by 1970. By the summer of 1973, when we completed our coding of this sample, 55 of the 191 men who had been jailed in 1969 or 1970 had been jailed again. The man who had been jailed six times had been jailed a seventh. Nearly half of the men jailed in 1969–70 had been sentenced to jail at least twice during their careers by 1973.

And jail not merely came early and frequently, it absorbed a large portion of many men's lives after their divorce. Only 40 of the 191 men jailed in 1969 or 1970 had spent less than a week in jail by the summer of 1972. By that time, when no case in which a man was jailed had been opened less than three years and most had been open more than eight, a sixth of the men in the jailed group had spent at least 20 percent of their days in jail for nonsupport in the period after their support order had been entered. Forty-three men (23 percent of the jailed sample) had served three hundred or more days for nonsupport. The mean days served by all men had risen to 173 and the median to 86. A pound of flesh? It seems to me a pound and a half.

The place these many days were served has little to commend it. Our county jails are among America's most soul-deadening institutions.

Genesee's is no exception. Like jails everywhere, it is blockish, drab, airless. There is far less here for inmates to do to kill time than is typically available in prisons. Men are crowded into double bunks in dormitory cells, where temperatures and tempers rise during warm-weather months. They are fed meal after meal of heavy, starchy food—macaroni, bread, potatoes. At the time we studied, they were permitted two visits a week with family members.

It is nonetheless conceivable that, for some men, the experience of being jailed for nonsupport is not as traumatic as those of us on the outside would consider it. At the time of their first jailing for nonsupport, 47 percent of the men jailed in 1969 and 1970 had been previously booked into the Genesee jail on other charges at least once.

It is also the case that the nonsupporters were in a somewhat special position in the Genesee jail. On any given day, the fifty to sixty non-supporters in jail typically represented over three-fourths of the persons there under sentence. Those making up the remaining and larger portion of the jail population were not under sentence but, unable to make bail, were awaiting trial for felonies or misdemeanors. Since persons awaiting trial were barred by sheriff's policy from holding trusty positions, most trusty slots were held by nonsupporters, and nearly all nonsupporters got the opportunity to serve as trusties.

As Jerry Neal reported in the conversation quoted above, when he was in jail in 1974 about forty of the forty-seven trusties were nonsup-porters. Jail staff corroborated these rough proportions as the typical distribution over the years. Despite the fact that the nonsupporters were, in the words of one of the deputies, the "slave labor" of the jail—cooking the food, cleaning cells, running the elevator—they themselves probably preferred the freedom of movement, physical activity, and unofficially sanctioned larger food portions of the trusty to the lot of those confined to cellblocks all day. Responding to the men's desires for trusty slots, the jail staff seemed to permit more men to work as trusties than were really needed, so that much of the time during the day, in the entry area to the cellblocks where two officers oversaw the traffic into locked parts of the jail, a few men jailed for nonsupport could almost always be found sitting around waiting for nothing to happen.

I nonetheless suspect that jail caused pain for most jailed men both while they were there and when they later reflected on the experience. Enough is known from research of others about the impact of being confined on people's feelings of self-esteem to justify such a suspicion.

We also know that about a third of the men jailed in 1969 and 1970, and over 40 percent of the men serving more than ninety days, left town or disappeared soon after release, a strong sign that they had found jail an experience they wished not to repeat. However painful that experience was, we must also remember the pain of life for the women caring for children the men were not supporting. The reader will have to decide whether the men's pain was their just deserts. We can also think, if we wish, of the enforcement officers as the agents of the mothers' revenge.

Whatever they deserved, the men typically left jail worse off than they were when they arrived. They were stamped with a jail record. They were lucky if they could return to the job they had held when sentenced. And they were deeper in arrears than they had been when sentenced, for they now owed for all the weeks that they had not been paying while in jail. During his several jailings, Jerry's arrearage grew by more than three thousand dollars.

The Power of the Officers

We are now at the end of the enforcement cycle. At every stage, from first warning to release from jail, the enforcement officer can act in several ways or fail to act at all, and no one is ever likely to know what he does or what he fails to do beyond the affected man. Are there other examples in our system of laws where a single official exerts such unscrutinized discretionary authority at every step of a process that can end in incarceration? Very few.

When I have at various points drawn analogies between the enforcing staff of the Friends of the Court and police officers, prosecutors, probation officers, and parole boards in the criminal justice system, I have identified steps in the traditional criminal process each of which is typically performed by a different person. In the traditional system, these diverse roles probably serve to introduce checks on abusive power and to promote a randomness of outcome that is its own modest protection against tyranny. Perhaps some hospital psychiatrists in the system of civil commitment of the mentally disabled and some probation staff in juvenile courts play as many or nearly as many of these multiple roles, but those systems operate from very different premises than those of the support enforcement system. Not even their most enthusiastic proponents would paint the support enforcement officers as therapists. The larger analogy the support enforcement officers invite is ironic. In some ways, they resemble parents, who, within a narrow sphere, are the ultimate repositories of near total authority in our society. They are parents, diligent and vigilant, in much the way that the men they seek to punish were not. Consider the exchange of letters that opens this chapter. Neal asks petulantly for release. The officer replies with sarcasm, "I am sorry you find jail inconvenient," and insists on a concrete demonstration of willingness to pay. One can almost hear the officer saying, "And you stay in your room until all your toys are picked up."

The nature of the conduct of nonsupport provides a further source of power for the enforcement officers. If a bank is robbed or a person is murdered, police nearly always want to arrest the offender. If a payment of child support is missed, the nonpayment may well be an offense, but there may be many extenuating circumstances or justifications that would make almost everyone agree that there should be no arrest. Discretion with regard to apprehension and with regard to arrangements for future payment seems indispensable, but the problem with according vast discretion over people's lives is that other people, not gods, have to exercise it. All of us have preconceptions about different groups of people in our society—about alcoholics or car washers or doctors or young people generally. We also have preconceptions about the labor market and how easy or difficult it is to find work. A problem for enforcement officers is that most of them, like the judges, do not share a common background or experiences with the unskilled blue-collar men with whom they most commonly come into contact.

While discretion and the class distance between the offender and the policing officer are perhaps unavoidable in this setting, there are curbs on discretion that could enhance the possibilities for fairness and regularity. In many counties, the person responsible for requesting a warrant is not the same person who serves it. Separating these functions may somewhat retard the progress of individual vendettas. Genesee's Friend of the Court has, for other reasons, moved to this bifurcated system in the last few years. Much the same function could be served further by separating the enforcing function from the prosecutorial function, so that at hearings in support proceedings, as is the case universally in criminal trials, the enforcing officer, like the police officer on the beat, would be a witness and the prosecutor would be a person who had not participated in the chase.

Administrative regulations within the Friend of the Court office can also circumscribe the range of agent discretion without eliminating it altogether. Rules regarding the minimum arrearage before warnings are sent or warrants issued, rules regarding the checking to be done on assertions of layoffs or changes in income, rules regarding the number of extra dollars per week to demand from a person who has developed an arrearage—all are possible and used in some places. If jailing is to continue, divisions of functions and other constraints on officers' powers seem necessary for purposes of fairness even if they reduce the efficiency of the enforcement system.

Nine

The Jailed Men

Who is jailed? How do those who are jailed differ from those who are not? How did the men jailed respond to the experience of being jailed? Did they begin paying again? Would they have responded as well, or nearly as well, to less drastic sanctions?

Jerry Neal was a white, unskilled worker, over twenty-five at divorce. He was, in these regards, like more than half the jailed men and more than half the random sample as a whole. In several other ways, however, he shared characteristics with the jailed men that distinguish them from the majority of the men under orders of support: most particularly, he changed jobs often and experienced many short periods of unemployment, he displayed indications of an alcohol problem, and he had a prior arrest record for offenses other than nonsupport. (Recall the days he spent in jail under arrest for assaulting Dolores with a hammer.)

Jerry was jailed three times for failing to pay support. On the first two occasions, he paid nothing for release and nothing afterwards. His only patches of regular payments in the entire life of his decree up to the point of his third jailing had been for about a year immediately after his divorce and for a short while during the second jailing when he was released during the day to work as a maintenance man at an apartment complex. After his third jailing, however, Jerry at first paid little but then, upon receiving a letter warning him that a warrant had been issued, began to pay with regularity. He paid fairly steadily thereafter for at least eighteen months.

In my interview with Jerry when he was halfway through his third sentence, I asked him why he had never made a lump-sum payment for release. He said that too much had always been demanded as the price (a thousand dollars on the current occasion, for example) and that, though he could have borrowed money, he didn't like piling up debts. It is not fully clear to me whether he could have borrowed a thousand dollars or even half of it, since he rarely had any salable or pawnable possessions and since he was largely estranged from his parents and brothers. In any event, his mother confirmed what Jerry himself claims—that Jerry never asked for a loan or a gift of money.

Regarding the payments after release, I tried to understand why he had paid nothing after the first two jailings—laying himself open each time to the jailings that followed—but then began paying after the third. Had he simply been like the celebrated mule who had to be hit on the head three times before his attention was captured? Or were different problems or attitudes involved at different points? At the time of each of the jailings and thereafter, Jerry's former wife was a welfare recipient. After each release, Jerry found work and worked steadily. These factors remained constant. Although he stressed the competition of other expenses as his reason for nonpayment after the first two jailings, his other expenses were in fact greater after his third, when his new wife had just given birth to a baby.

When I interviewed him again a year after his third release, at a point when he was paying regularly, Jerry did mention one difference about the third jailing—by that time, three of the five children covered by the order had reached eighteen and the agency had not sought to increase the order size for the other two. Thus, his order size—ten dollars per week per child—had declined to twenty dollars per week. Twenty dollars a week in 1975 was far easier to come up with than fifty dollars a week had been in 1964.

He offered no other explanation for the differences in response. I abandoned indirection and asked whether he might be paying in part because he was simply tired of going to jail—having been sentenced three times and served over two full years. He simply chuckled, but not in a way that conveyed agreement. Then in his customarily indirect way he said that the Friend of the Court had written him a few months before, warning him that a warrant was out for his arrest: "They wanted forty dollars a week [twenty of it applied to the arrearage] and I wrote and told them that they'd better be satisfied with thirty dollars or to hell with them."

The letter that Jerry sent was close in bravado to the summary he gave of it:

> I am sending $30.00 a week in to you. I know I signed a paper for $40.00 but I cannot send that much in and live to. So I hope $30.00 a week will do it O.K. and I want you to call off that warrant you have out for me, because if I am picked up again you wouldn't get nothing and I will lose my job.

It seems probable, as Jerry hinted, that another distinguishing feature of the third jailing was that, when he did not pay immediately after release, the Friend of the Court sent him first a pay-or-appear letter and then a believable personal warning that another jailing was at hand, rather than simply following the form pay-or-appear letter with the arrest itself. The warning about the warrant gave him a chance to pay before it was too late.

Jerry's erratic responses to jailing are by no means unique within our jailed samples. On the other hand, the jailed men and their responses to jailing are far too varied to capture through a single person. In fact, almost every identifiable subgroup in the random sample was represented in the jailed sample. Here are four brief descriptions of other men in our sample of jailed men. They may help the reader appreciate the diversity of the sample men's backgrounds and the range of responses to jailing we undertook to explain.

Tom Andrews could scarcely resemble Jerry less. He was the prosperous manager of a small business. Divorced after ten years of marriage, he paid steadily for several years, then stopped altogether for over a year, apparently displeased by the fact that his wife had moved with their children to another state. The agency sent a warning letter. He ignored it and was arrested. Brought before the judge, he was sentenced to a year in jail, but was released on the same day after paying a thousand dollars. He paid steadily thereafter to the end of our records.

Paul Mazzo was a factory worker, thirty-one at divorce. He was jailed early in the life of the decree when only a few weeks in arrears, probably because he had been labelled as uncooperative. A file note by the enforcement officer reads: "feels he can pay when he pleases." Paul was jailed for two days, then released on a wage assignment. He paid steadily for six months, then stopped for six. Threatened with arrest, he started paying again under a wage assignment, paid steadily for about three months, and then left the state and never made another payment.

Charles Devine was an unskilled blue-collar worker, employed erratically and divorced after a marriage of fifteen years. Repeated statements about alcohol problems dot his file, including notes about arrests and convictions for alcohol offenses. He was jailed twice for nonsupport, in 1967 and 1969. His only period of steady payments in the life of the decree was a few months while in jail for the second time when he was placed on work release with a job in the community as a laborer, returning to the jail each night.

Johnny Lizabehr was a bartender divorced in 1959 after a ten-year marriage. He paid steadily for the first few years, then only erratically. Between 1963 and 1970, he was sentenced to jail for nonsupport on six different occasions. Following three of these sentencings, he made substantial lump-sum payments to purchase an early release (on each occasion an amount between three hundred and four hundred dollars), but only once was the release followed by a period of steady payments. By 1970, he had spent about two full years in jail. His wife was unrelenting. The agency's records indicate that she complained at least thirty-five times about nonpayment, including some complaints after the sixth jailing.

How Men Who Were Jailed Differed from Men Who Were Not

Who Was Jailed at Least Once?

So few men were jailed in Washtenaw that its experience provides little guidance to the sorts of men jailed in Michigan. Our Genesee data, however, provide two views. Sixty men were sentenced to jail among the 410 men in our random sample, and the characteristics of those who were jailed can be compared with the characteristics of those who were not. We also drew a representative sample of 191 men in Genesee sentenced during 1969 and the first ten months of 1970. This group constituted about 80 percent of the total sentenced to jail during this period. Since our random sample of the caseload as a whole was drawn from among all cases alive at precisely the time from which we drew the jailed sample—during 1969 and the first ten months of 1970—the two samples are directly comparable: if there are many people with a certain characteristic among the jailed group and comparatively few with that characteristic in the random sample as a whole (or in its unjailed members), we have a strong indication of an overrepresentation in the jailed group.

Like the general sample of the whole caseload, a majority of the jailed group worked at blue-collar jobs, but the majority is even greater among the jailed men. In comparison to the men in the random sample, twice as large a percentage of the jailed men were unskilled blue-collar workers not working in the auto industry (42 percent as opposed to 21 percent). Few white-collar men go to jail, especially few of the managers and professionals. By the same token, the overwhelming majority of both the jailed and general sample were white, but a larger portion of black men ended in jail. So did a larger portion of the men whose wives received welfare benefits. (See appendix table 9A.)

Essentially the same patterns appear when we look just at the random sample and compare the 60 men within that sample who were ever jailed with the other 351 men in that sample. For example, of the men in the random sample, 14 percent of the whites were jailed in contrast with 21 percent of the blacks; 12 percent of the men whose wives never received welfare were jailed in contrast with 20 percent of the men whose wives did receive it. (A comparison of these and other characteristics is set forth in appendix table 9B.) Virtually every subgroup we see in the general population is also represented among the men within the population who are jailed. On the other hand, the jailed group contains a larger proportion of men with apparent alcohol problems, criminal records for other offenses, men with high orders in relation to their earnings, and men who failed to attend their predivorce interview.

We must, however, deal with these figures on the incidence of jailing with great care. The fact that a disproportionate number of black men or unskilled workers outside the auto industry are jailed alerts us to possibilities of bias in the enforcement process. It remains quite possible, however, that the Genesee enforcement staff sought to jail all men seriously in arrears but that the jailed men, who happened to be more frequently blue-collar or black or low earners than the population as a whole, were more commonly the ones who did not pay or flee. That is a possible explanation, but it is not quite accurate. Lots of men stay in Flint, miss large numbers of payments, and avoid jail. It is thus important to compare those who were jailed not with the sample as a whole but rather with the others in the sample who became in arrears and were not jailed. Only in this way can we learn what explains why some *delinquent* men are jailed and others are not.

Grave problems are posed, however, in deciding the appropriate group with whom to compare the jailed men. The problem is that virtually no one in the population was a perfect payer. At one time or another nearly every father slipped at least a few weeks behind and at that moment became at least in theory subject to jailing unless he could prove that the arrearage he had accumulated was not due to his "neglect" or "refusal" to pay. Even in hard times—during a layoff, for example—most men could probably have borrowed or scrimped and managed to pay, if they had given their support payments the highest priority in their budgets, above their own and any new family's minimal well-being.

Rather than try to make case-by-case decisions about which men ever reached an arrearage they could have avoided (decisions for which we simply did not have enough information), we decided to set a measure of falling behind in payments that would be large enough to be widely accepted as calling for action and see how the agency treated the group that accumulated such a debt. There were many measures that could have been used to define the group that developed a large arrearage—the dollar amount paid or not paid during any year, the portion paid of all that had been ordered, regularity of payments. We tried several, and elected to treat as the pool of nonpayers all men who had ever accumulated an arrearage of twenty-six weeks' worth of payments by the end of any calendar year.[1] Within the constraints of our data, this seemed to be as revealing a measure as any available to us, for twenty-six weeks of nonpayments is not only a sum that all would agree was substantial—a half-year's worth of payments—but it was also visible to the agency officers whose printouts listed the man's arrearage in both dollars and weeks' worth of payments owed. Moreover, four-fifths of the men in our sample of jailed men had an arrearage of at least twenty-six weeks at the time of their jailing.

How many in the caseload as a whole developed such a high arrearage at any point? Given the high overall collections we found, it may come as somewhat of a surprise that more than half of the men in Genesee developed an arrearage of at least twenty-six weeks' worth of payments at some point. To be precise, 233 of the 410 men in our random sample accumulated by the end of some calendar year an arrearage of at least twenty-six times the weekly order amount. These 233 cases represent 57 percent of the entire caseload. Moreover, of these 233, five out of six (83 percent) had an arrearage of at least that high at the end of two or more calendar years.

Of the 233 who built up this very substantial arrearage, only 55, or slightly under a quarter, were ever jailed.[2] When we compare the characteristics of the 55 men who were jailed with the men who were not but who built up this large arrearage, the results are rather different from the impression conveyed by comparing the jailed men with all the men in the sample including the perfect payers (see figure 9.1).

Occupational Groups

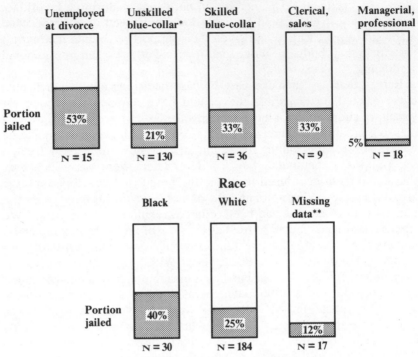

Unemployed at divorce — **53%** N = 15

Unskilled blue-collar* — **21%** N = 130

Skilled blue-collar — **33%** N = 36

Clerical, sales — **33%** N = 9

Managerial, professional — **5%** N = 18

Portion jailed

Race

Black — **40%** N = 30

White — **25%** N = 184

Missing data** — **12%** N = 17

Portion jailed

Wife Receives Welfare

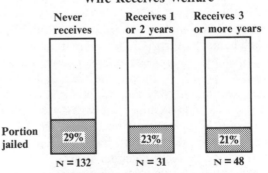

Never receives — **29%** N = 132

Receives 1 or 2 years — **23%** N = 31

Receives 3 or more years — **21%** N = 48

Portion jailed

Fig. 9.1 Rates of jailing among 231 men who accumulated arrearages of 26 or more weeks' worth of payments (Genesee Random Sample).

*Among blue-collar men who accumulated 26-week arrearages, there were no differences in the rates of jailing for auto and nonauto workers.

**Regarding missing data on race, see p. 110 in text.

Once we have limited our inquiry to those who became significantly in arrears, we find, within the random sample, that neither unskilled blue-collar workers nor fathers of children receiving welfare are over-jailed in relation to their frequency of falling into arrears. The earlier appearance was due to the fact that, as a group, unskilled blue-collar workers outside the auto industry and men whose wives receive welfare benefits are simply more likely not to pay significant portions of what they owe. Thus, despite the judges' strong feelings about the burden on taxpayers, fathers of children receiving welfare were not overrepresented among the jailed group, after payments are taken into account. Perhaps whatever tendency there might have been toward harshness in welfare cases was balanced by the fact that enforcement officers were also responsive to the needs of nonwelfare mothers who were not receiving their payments and to the information such mothers sometimes provided about the fathers' whereabouts.

While the limitation of our inquiry to those who fall deeply into arrears has explained the overrepresentation of unskilled blue-collar workers and fathers of welfare recipients, it does not affect a couple of other disproportionate representations: even among men who fall into arrears, black men remain overrepresented, and managers and professionals underrepresented, among the jailed groups. We similarly found, although this is not revealed in figure 9.1, that men with high orders in relation to their earnings are overrepresented and men with low orders in relation to their earnings are underrepresented even among those who end up in arrears. So also overrepresented are men with alcohol problems and men with other criminal records.

Why do these disparities occur? Are there explanations other than overt prejudice or favoritism? Overrepresentation of some groups might occur simply because some nonpayers are more easily found than others. It might also occur because some men who become deeply in arrears are more responsive than others to less drastic enforcement techniques. Our inquiry tried to focus on the extent to which these relatively benign explanations undercut the hypothesis that inappropriate forms of prejudice or favoritism were in operation.

Using multiple classification analysis to sort for explanations of the jailed and never-jailed groups among the men who ever are twenty-six weeks in arrears, we do find that part of the explanation lies in responsiveness to efforts and long prior records of high payments before the arrearage is developed. Among people who build the large arrearage, jailing was far more likely to befall those who were unresponsive to early nonjudicial enforcement efforts and those who built the twenty-six weeks of arrearages in the early years of their order. Nonetheless, even after these factors are taken into account, most of the disproportions that we have reported remain. Of all the overrepresentations, that of black men is surely the most disturbing, given this nation's history and the racial composition of the Friend of the Court's staff in Genesee. Forty percent of the black men but only 25 percent of the white men who fell into arrears were jailed. As an initial matter, there is a possibility within the random sample that the overrepresentation is due to chance. We doubt it, however, for, as we have seen, the difference is also present in our sample of 191 men jailed at the same time.

What the true explanation for the higher rate of jailing of black men is we do not know.[3] The staff, on the questionnaire we administered to them, indicated that they did not view black men as likely to be lower payers, although it is perhaps unrealistic in our society today to expect public employees to give candid answers to such questions. It is possible that the staff viewed black men as less likely to be responsive to milder efforts, and it is in fact the case that a somewhat smaller portion of black men began a period of steady payments after either of the first two nonjudicial enforcment efforts (57 percent for blacks vs. 66 percent for whites), not enough of a difference to be statistically significant for social science purposes but still statistically more probably true than not and thus perhaps fairly perceived as fact by the officers. A few officers made openly racist remarks to our research staff, and in the random sample we find that blacks were far less likely than whites ever to receive nonthreatening contact letters or nonthreatening personal letters.

Just as racial suspicions come easily, however, so charges of racism should not be made lightly. We are about to see that black men are *under*represented among men jailed more than once. We have also found that black men are held, on the average, for shorter periods of time after arrest than are white men before being brought before a judge. I do not believe on the slim data we have that we can conclude that the overrepresentation of black men flowed from perceptions or feelings about race rather than from other factors appropriately related to the payment system.

Let us look at a few other under- and overrepresented groups that suggest troubling aspects of the enforcement process. Why, even among persons in arrears, managers and professionals should be far less frequently jailed is also troubling. We are again dealing with small numbers in the random sample as a whole, but managers and professionals are underrepresented both in the sample of jailed persons and in the men jailed within the general sample. Perhaps the explanation is simply that nonpaying professionals were pursued as ardently as others but that, when the pursuit got hot, professionals and managers had easier access to a substantial sum of money. While as a general matter, managers and professionals were no more responsive to warnings than unskilled auto workers or skilled blue-collar workers, it remains possible that they were more responsive when the risk of jail was most palpable. Another explanation is that nonpaying managers and professionals were more frequently represented by attorneys at any court hearing and that attorneys, as we have reported earlier, were often successful in producing a "second chance" for their clients. Even this is not a full explanation because managers and professionals are also underrepresented among nonpaying men ever brought before the court for a hearing. The discrimination in their favor, if it occurs, occurs earlier. From all evidence available to us, it thus remains possible but not fully proven that, at the point of the most serious interventions, professionals and managers—those with the highest incomes—are treated with a special gingerliness that reflects a favorable predisposition toward people of their status.

If jail fell only rarely on the nonpaying professional, it fell particularly heavily on nonpaying men who were periodically unemployed. We have spoken earlier of the men who appear before the judges with employment-related excuses, and of how brusquely their excuses were often treated. These cases are not rare. In our sample of men jailed in 1969 and 1970, 33 percent appear to have been unemployed at the point of their jailing (at least the agency made no effort to refute their claims of unemployment) and another 11 percent appear to have been employed only part-time or sporadically. While these men may well have been quite unresponsive to warnings and gentler enforcement efforts, their high numbers among the men jailed point up even more the difficulties posed by the Michigan statutes permitting the jailing of men who are unemployed but believed by judges to be employable.

A final worrisome group within the jailed sample was made up of men with other signs of deviant behavior apart from nonpayment of support—either criminal records or signs of alcohol problems. For the jailed sample but not for the general sample as a whole we checked the records of the Genesee jail regarding other occasions when men had been arrested and held. Nearly half of the men in the jailed sample (47 percent) had at least one arrest in Genesee County for offenses other than nonsupport prior to their first jailing for nonsupport. Of this group with prior arrests, about a third had been charged with felonies. For most of these men it does not appear that the agency had sought to jail them for nonsupport simply as an alternative way of dealing with an otherwise undesirable person. Indeed it was often the case that a bona fide arrest on another charge led to the discovery that a warrant was outstanding for nonpayment of support and, after the other charge had been disposed of, the man was turned over to the Friend of the Court. Thus to some degree we expect that the high representation among the jailed population of men with records is due to the happenstance of the arresting process.

For nearly half the men with other criminal arrests before their first nonsupport jailing at least some of the other offenses involved alcohol. And, in the end, if there is any especially striking characteristic of the jailed population, it is the frequency with which there are reports of alcohol problems in their file or in the police records. The indications we had of problems with alcohol came from the woman's complaints at divorce, from police arrest records, from transcripts of the contempt hearings, and from notes while the man was in jail that he was participating in an alcohol rehabilitation program.

Using these indicators, we find, as table 9.1 indicates, that three-fifths of the men in the jailed sample have signs of alcohol problems. We did not search as thoroughly for signs of alcohol problems in the records of the cases in the random sample as we did in the cases in the special sample of jailed men. It is difficult, however, to believe that the incidence of alcohol problems among divorced men with children generally (our random sample) is as high as 60 percent. As we saw earlier, about 20 percent of mothers in the random sample complained of alcohol problems at divorce. Twenty percent is not a trivial incidence of alcohol problems but it is small in comparison to the 60 percent level within the jailed group. It is thus our belief that alcoholics are greatly

Table 9.1	Indications of Alcohol Problems among Men Jailed in Genesee County, 1969–70		
		N	%
	No indication of alcohol problem	75	39%
	One indication in file	51	27
	Two or more indications	65	34
	Total	191	100%

overrepresented among the men who are jailed. The simple explanation for the vast numbers of alcohol-problem men in the jailed group would be that such men just will not pay their support and will not respond to lesser techniques. As we have reported earlier, however, with some surprise, men in the random sample about whom their wives complained of an alcohol problem paid no less well than men about whom no such complaint was made (see Chapter 7). It is still possible that within the group of men with alcohol problems there is a core of men especially unwilling or unable to pay.

Two additional explanations for the high incidence of alcoholics within the jailed population also seem plausible. One is that jailing for nonsupport was sometimes a mask for punishing men for their alcoholism or a means of drying them out—in either case the alcoholism would have been taken into account in the jailing decision. One of the judges, who jailed a smaller proportion of his caseload than any of the others, was nonetheless described by several enforcement officers as being tough on alcoholics and only on alcoholics.[4] We found in the transcripts that this judge frequently justified his sentence in part on the ground that it would give the man a chance to dry out.

The other explanation for the overrepresentation of alcoholics is that, although alcoholics were treated like everyone else, they were simply easier to find among the nonpayers. For example, nonpaying alcoholics left town less frequently after their 1969 or 1970 jailing than did other nonpaying men. Conversely, alcoholics were more likely than other men to fall into the agency's hands when arrested on other charges (drinking offenses mostly) that would trigger the execution of an outstanding warrant for nonsupport.

From the men's side, we suspect that for many of the alcoholics the prospect of jail evoked little terror. Indeed for some it seemed to beckon as a place of refuge. I interviewed several sheriff's deputies working at the jail and nearly all told tales of alcoholics who had served three or four terms for nonsupport, men who apparently could not hold jobs on the outside but who performed valuable services on the inside. "The best damn booker we ever had," said the jail administrator of one celebrated four-timer whose jail job was to register freshly arrested persons into the jail. When I interviewed a few of the repeaters, none claimed to enjoy jail, but each was proud of his responsibility and status there. When I asked the "best damn booker" what he planned to do upon release, he replied without much feeling, "I get out on March 10 and I'll sit around the trailer and wait for them to pick me up again."

What can be said in the end about the selection process that leads to jailing? The factors available to us explain only a small part of the reasons why some nonpaying men were jailed and others were not. Our analysis takes into account some benign factors, such as how quickly an arrearage developed, that help explain differences, but much that we cannot measure in numbers is relevant to the question of whether officers tried to bring each unresponsive nonpayer to court, except when persuaded that the man was truly unable to pay. We can hardly fault officers with a caseload of a thousand, who try but fail to arrest all who are unresponsive to warnings and other efforts. The agency's own view of itself was that it was tough, but evenhanded, with the scale of the effort directed at each man determined solely by what was needed to get him to pay.

In the end we remain unpersuaded that the agency's self-portrait is fully accurate. We believe that undesirable though unmalicious factors, factors more subtle than race or social rank, were inevitably at play. The presence of so many men with alcohol and employment problems suggests to us dubious judgments about men's capacity to pay. As we will see, the postrelease payments of the men in these groups is so low that officers had little to support a belief that they were employable. Worse, though this is hard to measure, we believe the agency officers could not avoid being arbitrary in much that they did. As we have discussed in Chapter 8, no human could do otherwise. The easy cases for the officers were the men who made no contact with them in response to warnings, but 70 percent of the warning letters were followed by contact and, as we have already reported, most of the contacts were not followed by a resumption of regular payment. It is here that we worry most. For men in arrears the most critical decisions the officers made were whether to believe their excuses and how long to give them to turn their payments around. Here it seems inevitable that the officers responded differently to different personalities. Some men like the alcoholics may have consciously or unconsciously baited the officer, challenging him with flippant or evasive comments not recorded in the files. Conversely, some men were extraordinarily adept at keeping the agency at bay. There are many cases in which a warning was sent, the man made contact with the agency, apparently promising to start paying soon, but no payments came for many months and no further threats were recorded during the period. Nor was a warrant recorded as having been issued.

The agency is to be commended for having avoided the blatant discrimination that has characterized some law enforcement systems in this country. On the other hand, one can hardly feel comfortable that so many of its judgments—judgments on which the question of a person's freedom turns—have to be made on the basis of partial information and instinct.

Who Is Jailed More Than Once?

There were 191 men in our sample of men jailed in 1969 or 1970 in Genesee County. At the time of their jailing in either of those years, forty-eight had been jailed before for the same offense. By the end of our coding in midsummer 1973, an additional thirty-five men for whom the 1969 or 1970 jailing had been their first had been jailed at least twice. Thus, by the end of our coding, eighty-three men, or over 40 percent of our sample, had been sentenced to jail at least twice for nonsupport. Twenty-four men, about a seventh of the entire group, had, like Jerry Neal, been jailed three or more times. Which men are singled out for rejailing? This question invites an initial inquiry into the functions actually served and purported to be served by the first jailing.

If the Friend of the Court were primarily concerned with maximizing returns from the men jailed, we would expect to find that rejailing was used primarily on men for whom the previous jailing had been a short-run success—particularly, perhaps, on those men who paid a substantial lump-sum payment for release but little in week-by-week payments later. If, on the other hand, the function was simply to punish the misbehavior of nonpayment or to deliver a message to the population under orders generally, we would expect to find no particular pattern in the rejailed men in their response to a previous jailing (except of course, that they had not become perfect payers). And in fact, the latter pattern is what we do find.

Of the thirty-one men for whom the 1969 or 1970 jailing was their second, seven had served their full first term, and the seventeen men who had paid a lump-sum payment for their release had paid a median of $300, substantially smaller, as we will see, than the median lump payment of $490 extracted from initial jailings among all those in the jailed sample. The prior performance in lump-sum payments or post-release payments of those for whom the 1969 or 1970 jailing was their third had been even less promising.

We thus received the impression that, in deciding whom to rejail, the enforcement staff was not guided primarily by a desire to reach men for whom prior jailings had produced substantial initial returns. We derived further support for this impression from interviews. Enforcement officers in Genesee and elsewhere did not seem particularly reflective

OFFICER'S REPORT

NAME   Jerry Neal   DATE   May 2, 1974

EMPLOYMENT   Riverside Garden Apartments   CHANCERY NO. 70768

DATE OF ORDER   June 22, 1963   AMOUNT OF ORDER $10.00 per child/per wk.

AGES OF CHILDREN NOW INVOLVED   16, 14, 13

ARREARS $17,998.22 AS OF 5-1-74 LAST PAYMENT $80.00 ON 6-26-73

AVERAGE WEEKLY EARNINGS (GROSS)   AS PER LAST EIGHT PAYS.

1. $ DATE   2. $ DATE

PREVIOUS COURT HEARINGS
1.   3-29-69   Before Judge Martin - Sentenced to one year.

2.   1-11-71   Before Judge Martin - Sentenced to one year.

3.

PAYEE NOW RECEIVES WELFARE OR A.D.C.   Yes   SUBJECT ARRESTED AT

$ Oakland County

SUMMARY

On June 22, 1963 a Judgment of Divorce was entered by this Court wherein the Defendant was ordered to pay support in the amount of $10.00 per week per child.

As of May 1, 1974 he is $17,998.22 in arrears; the last payment was made June 26, 1973.

He was stopped on April 8, 1974 by the State Police in Oakland County and a hold was placed on him.*

He is currently employed by Riverside Garden Apartments in Pontiac at $3.50 per hour.

RECOMMENDATION: Confinement in the County Jail with release on a substantial payment and signing of a wage assignment.

Respectfully submitted,

William Booth
Program Officer
Enforcement Division

*[Note that Jerry had been held over three weeks before he was brought before the judge in Genesee County. The Genesee enforcement staff apparently did not come to get him right away.]

Fig. 9.2 Report of enforcement officer to judge, Genesee County.

about their policies toward rejailing: when we asked officers why they continued to jail certain men for whom prior jailings had failed, they usually had little to say. It had not occurred to them not to rejail the men. If pressed, they stressed that to give up was to announce to the world that men could get away without paying. When Jerry Neal was serving his third term, after two prior terms in which he had paid nothing for release and virtually nothing afterwards, I asked his enforcement officer why he had bothered. "I'm just doing my job," he said, and then, not finding any reaction from me, he added, "and it's not fair to other men who are paying not to enforce the order."

The officer could quite properly claim to be just doing his job. He had no individual responsibility to maximize collections in the caseload as a whole. He simply knew that Neal was still not paying. A warning letter produced nothing. He secured a warrant. Neal was picked up on a traffic charge by police in a nearby county, who learned of the warrant in Genesee. Neal was returned and sentenced. No one, including Neal, found anything peculiar in the process.

Here are the surviving court records of Neal's third jailing. Figure 9.2 presents the report that the enforcement officer prepared for the judge to read before the hearing. The entire transcript for the hearing follows. Justice is blind but fleet of foot.

Transcript of Jerry Neal's
Third Court Hearing

The Court:	In the matter of Case Number 77— Strike that. —70768, Dolores Neal Fisher against Jerry Neal. Mr. Neal. (Whereupon the defendant approached the bench.)
The Court [reading from report]:	On June the 22nd of 1963, a judgment of divorce was entered in this court and you were ordered to pay $10 per week for child support. As of May the 1st of 1974, you are $17,998.22 in arrearage. The last payment was made on June the 26th of 1973 in the amount of $80.
	And, you see, you were stopped by the state police for driving, a hold was placed on you. It states that you are currently employed at the Riverside Apartments in Pontiac at $3.50 an hour.
	Is that correct?

The Defendant:	Yes, sir.
The Court:	All right. Let me advise you that you have a right to a hearing in this matter either by—Strike that.
	You have a right to a hearing in this matter by the Court, and you also have the further right to be represented by an attorney if you choose [to hire one]. You understand that?
The Defendant:	Yes, sir.
The Court:	Now, do you wish a hearing in this matter?
The Defendant:	No.
The Court:	You do not wish a hearing. Then, all right.
	Then you acknowledge or admit that you're $17,998.22 in arrearage in this matter, that you have failed to support your children?
The Defendant:	Yes.
The Court:	All right. The sentence of the Court is that you be confined to the county jail for a period of one year.
	You may be released once you come up with a satisfactory plan to support your family. You are making $3.50 an hour, so surely you could come up with something whereby you can support these children. They are your children.
	You may have a seat.
Mr. Booth:	Thank you, your Honor.

Whether all this seems mindless or commendably efficient, rejailings are nonetheless not without pattern. In a multiple classification analysis that we used to isolate the factors that best explained what sorts of persons were subjected to repeated jailings within the jailed population, five factors stood out. Most likely to be rejailed were men with repeated signs of alcohol problems, men with low overall payment records, men whose cases had been open more years than other jailed men's, men who were white, and men about whom their wives had made frequent complaints (see appendix table 9C). Men with several indications of alcohol problems were three times as likely—and men with even one such indication were over twice as likely—to be rejailed as men with no signs in the file of alcohol problems.

Three of these factors—the father's cumulative payment record, the years the case had been alive, and the frequency of the mother's complaints—have self-evident relationships to rejailing. We have already discussed men with alcohol problems and see further evidence of their repeated presence. Whatever the reasons for the high representation of alcoholics, their incidence of rejailing could hardly have been justified in terms of expectable returns: they served the longest first terms among identifiable subgroups, were least likely to pay a large lump sum for release, and were among the lowest paying subgroups in week-by-week performance after release.

That fewer black men than white men are jailed more than once is more puzzling, especially since, as we have seen, they are overrepresented among men ever jailed once. After their jailings in 1969 and 1970, black men paid no better or worse than white men, either in lump-sum payments or week-by-week payments and were less likely than whites to leave town.

Effects of Jailing on Payments

Given the indecency of the conditions in American jails, it is unfortunate that the design of this study appears to accept the payment effects of jailing as the principal appropriate measure of jail's effect. Conducting a file-based, retrospective inquiry, we limited ourselves to the information in the public records of the agency. We could thus develop subtle measures of payments from several vantage points, but we can only speculate about the other impacts of jailing on peoples' lives. We have no capacity to measure the extent of harm of lengthy jailing on the emotional well-being of the men jailed or on the well-being of the new families of which many of the men had become a part. We cannot say whether many former wives felt avenged. Nor can we speak of the responses of the children of the original marriage to the jailing of their fathers, although it is for their benefit that the fathers are being jailed. It is possible that many children come to blame themselves for their father's jailing: "If it were not for me, Dad wouldn't have gone to jail." In much the same sad and inverted way, children often blame themselves for their parents' divorce. The Friend of the Court in Washtenaw County feared this possible effect of jailing and cited it as one of the reasons his office avoided penal remedies. All these possible costs of jail we cannot measure.

What we have done is to examine the agency records of jailed persons in two counties. One of the counties, Genesee, we have discussed throughout. There we drew upon our sample of 191 men jailed in 1969 and the first nine months of 1970. The other county is not our usual comparison, Washtenaw: almost no one was jailed there. The other county is Macomb, which we have drawn upon earlier in comparing sentencing behaviors among Michigan counties. The Macomb sample of all 309 men jailed in 1970 offers us the opportunity to examine the effects of much shorter sentences and terms in jail than were common in Genesee.

In Genesee, we looked for four sorts of indications of jail's possible effects on the behavior of the jailed men: (1) periods of steady payments from earnings from jobs in the community to which a few men were released during the day; (2) lump-sum payments made to purchase freedom from jail; (3) periods of regular payments that began after release from jail; and (4) evidence that the man left the county shortly after release, an event that we found nearly always corresponded with nonpayment. In Macomb County we were able to measure only payments for release and payments afterwards. For both counties, we are a bit like cold-blooded analysts of America's balance of payments. Our measures, like theirs, are of dollars in and dollars departed, not of quality of life.

Our findings in a nutshell are these. Most jailed men had paid poorly in the period prior to the jailing. While in jail, a few men in Genesee County were released during the day to work at jobs, and some of these men made regular payments during the period. Far more common in both Genesee and Macomb was the payment of a substantial lump sum as the price of an early release. After release, many men pay nothing and a third of the men in Genesee apparently leave the county. On the other hand, a substantial number with prior erratic payments begin to pay. Half the jailed men in Macomb and nearly a third of the jailed men in Genesee pay over half of everything due in the period from their release from jail to the end of the calendar year that follows, though in Genesee many of these became nonpayers again by the end of our records.

The remainder of this chapter fleshes out these findings and explains the characteristics of the men who do and do not respond. The records available to us provided a uniquely rich base for examining the efficacy of penal sanctions in altering the very behavior at which they were addressed. Among human behaviors punished with penal sanctions, few have ever proven as susceptible as nonsupport to close observation. Some readers, more interested in the problems of divorced families generally and less in penology, may find here a bit more than they want to know about just one subgroup—the jailed men. For them, I suggest jogging across the pages that immediately follow, pausing only here and there, and resuming at a walk at the beginning of Chapter 10.

Forms of Payment Response to Jailing

The Comparison Point: Payments in the Period before Jailing

We do not know how the jailed men in Macomb performed in the period prior to jailing. We do have the performance rates of the jailed men in Genesee County. Nearly all the jailed men had failed to pay anything for several months before their appearance before the judge in 1969 and 1970. There were a few exceptions. One man was jailed who had paid regularly but had stubbornly insisted on paying a few dollars less each week than the judge had ordered. Several others had responded to a warning letter in the recent past with a small lump-sum payment or a couple of weekly payments. But most had paid nothing at all.

Indeed, of the 145 men in the jailed sample for whom the early pay records are adequate and whose cases had been open more than a few months, two-thirds had never had a period of steady payments of more than a month or two prior to their first jailing. When there were prior periods of payments, they tended to be quite brief, the vast majority being under a year, more likely than not in response to a prior warning letter or wage assignment. Only thirteen men, 9 percent of the jailed sample, had paid steadily for two years or more at any point prior to jailing.

Payments to Secure Release from Jail

As we have seen earlier, a long stretch of nonpayment and the failure to make contact after a warning letter, frequently led enforcing officers in Genesee to secure a warrant for arrest. If apprehended and taken to jail, the nonpayer suddenly found himself with a greatly altered psychological setting for payment. Payment became ransom: to secure his release he either had to pay his entire arrearage or make a substantial enough payment to please the enforcing officer.

Some arrested men—about a tenth of those arrested at least once in the random sample in Genesee—did avoid ever being brought before the judge by paying off their entire arrears. The remainder appeared before the judge. In Macomb and most other Michigan counties, the judges at hearings fixed an amount at sentencing that they would accept as a payment against the arrearage and gave a sentence that otherwise sounded like the common fate of the public drunk: "That will be sixty days or five hundred dollars." Five hundred dollars was in fact the typical amount demanded in Macomb of men whose arrearage was as high or higher. In Genesee County, the judges typically imposed a sentence in days only and refused to set an amount for release or to discuss with the man an acceptable amount. As one judge told a man who had offered a hundred dollars, "This isn't any rug dealers' convention." Rather, as we glimpsed in Chapter 8, the judges relegated the man to a bargaining process with the enforcing officer. (A Michigan Appeals Court has since found this refusal to specify an amount to be a violation of the contempt statute under which fathers are sentenced.)

Most of the men jailed in Genesee and Macomb did purchase their release—52 percent of the men in Genesee and 68 percent in Macomb. The patterns of payment were somewhat different in the two counties (see appendix table 9D). In Genesee, slightly more than half the men made lump-sum payments for release, with a median of five hundred dollars for the men who did. Thirteen percent of the men paid over a thousand dollars. Exactly half the men released on a lump-sum payment also executed a wage assignment at the point of their release. In Macomb, a larger portion of the jailed men paid a lump sum for release but the lump sums are generally smaller—a median of $360—and fewer men apparently executed wage assignments concurrently with the lump-sum payment. Because Macomb obtained money from more men, even though obtaining less on the average in each payment, the net yield to the counties from lump-sum payments was about the same.

Some of the difference in the sizes of the lump sums paid in the two counties is almost certainly due to the simple fact that less money was demanded of the men in Macomb at the point of sentencing than was demanded by the enforcement officers in Genesee. The mean amount initially *demanded* by Macomb's judges as the price for release from the men who paid lump sums for their release is in fact slightly lower than the mean amount actually *paid* in Flint by the men paying lump sums.

In both counties, the amount initially fixed by the judge or enforcement staff as the acceptable price of redemption was flexible. As a man's sentence wore on, the officers would accept less. In Macomb, for example, among the men who paid a lump sum for release, there was a strong negative correlation ($-.50$) between the length of time the man spent in jail and the percentage he paid on release of the amount originally demanded. Partly for this reason, the size of the lump sums ranged widely. In Genesee, the smallest was $50, a token accompaniment to a wage assignment. The largest was $3,000, representing three hundred weeks of payments in an odd case indeed: the man had been jailed three times before, departing for California after each jailing. On his fourth jailing in 1970, he paid $3,000 after being held for less than a day.

In Genesee, the total amount paid by the eighty-five men for whom we know the precise dollar amount of their lump-sum payments was $53,900. In Macomb the total was around $84,000 in 190 cases. As a portion of total collections in either county during the relevant time period, the amount collected was slight—well under 1 percent of collections for a year in either county. It was nonetheless a substantial amount in absolute terms and represented a core of payments that might well have been unobtainable, in most cases, in the absence of jailing or the credible threat of its imminent imposition; for in most cases, at least in Genesee where we have the information, it had been a long time since the last preceding payment. (That these men were in general not inclined toward making lump-sum payments out of the blue is indicated by the the fact that in Genesee, in the years prior to the first jailing, only about 10 percent of the men in the jailed sample had ever made a lump-sum payment of two hundred dollars or more and the majority of these lump-sum payments were themselves made after recorded jail-threatening enforcement efforts.)

Several warnings however, need to be given to anyone tempted to conclude from the record of Macomb and Genesee that jailing men to extract lump-sum payments is a sensible policy. The first is that we have little hard information—none of it computerized—on the sources of these lump-sum payments. Few men crack their own piggy banks. The lore among staff at the jail—supported by occasional file notations at the Friend of the Court—was that the man's parents or siblings were the most common source of the lump-sum and the man's new wife or woman companion the next most common. If many of these men never repay these "loans," the final effect of the lump-sum-payment transaction was to relieve the financial privation of one group (the former wife and children) by transferring the burden to other persons, perhaps no less in need but willing to pay a ransom for a son or brother. In welfare cases in which the beneficiary of the lump-sum payment is the government, the transfer seems to me to operate as a tax on the wrong persons.

By the same token, if the source of the lump-sum payment is someone other than the jailed man himself, it is unsafe to read such a payment, even a large one, as indicating that the father has the capacity to maintain week-by-week payments. Over and over again, in Michigan and elsewhere, I have heard support enforcers claim that they jail only persons capable of paying and allude to the lump-sum payments as part of their proof of the men's capacity to pay regularly. What evidence is available indicates that is not a reasonable conclusion.

A second warning about a strategy of jailing to extract lump-sum payments is the short duration of their benefit. Six hundred dollars, the mean size of the lump-sum payments received in Genesee, was, to be sure, a substantial sum—around twenty weeks of payments in the average case. When that money passed through to the former wife and children, it might well have been eagerly received but it would have been quickly gone. Most jailed men were divorced when at least one of their children was quite young and were first sentenced in the early years of an order. For them, there were likely to be over seven hundred weeks left in the life of the case after their release. Unless the man can confidently be judged to be otherwise beyond persuasion, the wisest enforcement strategy would appear to be one that focuses less on extracting a quick twenty weeks of payments than on the seven hundred payments yet to come.

A final warning derives from the converse of our finding that half the men in Genesee made a lump-sum payment: half did not. As we have seen earlier, those who did not languished in jail for long periods of time (see appendix table 8D). In Genesee, of the 191 jailed men, 29 who did not come up with a lump-sum payment were eventually released on a wage assignment but only after serving a mean of 114 days in jail. Forty others were held for their full term and averaged 231 days in jail. The lengths served by the comparable men not paying lump sums in Macomb were not as long but still averaged eighty-seven days. Unless these long-serving men begin paying regularly after release, jailing for them has been an expensive failure. If they do begin paying, it has been an expensive success.

Steady Payments from Jobs Held While in Jail

Of the 191 men jailed during 1969 and 1970 in Genesee County whose files we examined, thirty were approved by the judge for a "work-release" program permitting them to leave the jail each day and return each night. We cannot determine from the files for how many men a job was actually found, but eight of the men had a period of steady payments of at least a month during their jailing. On the other hand, five of the thirty, three of whom had been among the eight with a period of steady payments, walked away from their work-release jobs and failed to return to the jail. (Some of these were later reapprehended and served the balance of their sentences.)

Very few of those on work-release secured their release through making a lump-sum payment, but a third of the group was released early on wage assignments, typically to work-release jobs, and in the postrelease period the work-release group as a whole performed as well as the median of all persons jailed in Genesee. On his second jailing, Jerry Neal was one of this group. He was placed as a maintenance man at an apartment complex and after release continued his job for a short while. Those who escape, however, thereafter perform at a lower rate than any other group (as measured by the reason for leaving jail), which is hardly surprising given the fact that payments, even if the fathers felt inclined to make them, might tend to reveal their whereabouts.

At least in part because of the escape rate, the Friend of the Court in Genesee County has not been particularly enthusiastic about work-release programs. Such programs are apparently not widely in use elsewhere in Michigan but appear to be used to some degree in other parts of the country. I have heard enforcing officials in other parts of the country speak of them with great enthusiasm.

Week-by-Week Payments after Release from Jail

What happened after the men were released from jail?

We developed a common measure for both Macomb and Genesee Counties of the payments that followed release from jail. Closely comparable to the payment index we have used for measuring year-by-year payments for the random population in Genesee, the index is formed simply by dividing the total dollars paid by the man from the point of release from jail to the end of the next following calendar year by the total dollars he was under an order to pay during that time.

Using this index, we examined payments for each case for thirteen to twenty-four months after release, the precise length depending upon the month of the year when the man was released. For three-quarters of the cases, we have an index based on at least sixteen months of postrelease payment history. Comparisons among cases would have been more precise, of course, if we had been able to report our findings in terms of a common time-length of payments after release. Our method of coding, which was based on the arrearage at the point of each enforcement effort and at the end of each calendar year, did not permit us to do so. On the other hand, the form of the measure does not appear, upon examination, to have injured substantially the reliability of our findings.[5]

For the jailed samples in Genesee and Macomb, our findings revealed some close similarities and some puzzling differences (see details in table 9.2). In both counties a substantial number of men begin to pay with some regularity—over half the men in Macomb and nearly a third of the men in Genesee pay over half of everything due from the point of their release to the end of the following calendar year. Since, at the point of jailing, the jailed men in each county were typically far behind in payments—around two-thirds of the men in each county

Table 9.2   **Payment Performance among Jailed Men in Macomb and Genesee Counties in the Period Following Release**

Performance Week-by-Week after Release	Macomb (N = 224)		Genesee (N = 172)	
Overall measures				
Mean length measured	17.9 mos.		17.9 mos.	
Mean portion paid of everything ordered*	.53		.33	
Median portion paid*	.54		.13	
By ranges (portion paid of		% of all		% of all
fore end of following year**)	N	cases	N	cases
Cases paying .00–.10	54	24%	82	48%
Cases paying .11–.50	54	24	39	23
Cases paying .51–.90	62	27	21	12
Cases paying .91 or more	54	24	30	17
(Missing data or case closed before end of following year**)	(85)	—	(19)	—
Total	309	99%	191	100%

* Portion paid of everything ordered from release to end of next calendar year (not including lump-sums).

** Twenty-nine cases in Macomb closed before the end of the next calendar year. Other information we have for the remaining fifty-six men for whom payment data for the period were missing suggests that, as a group, they paid at least as high a rate as the group for which payment data existed. The nineteen cases in Genesee with missing data are all cases that closed before the end of the next calendar year.

were in arrears by at least a half year's worth of payments—the sudden renaissance in payments for so many men is striking.

The second obvious observation to be made about postrelease payments is that many men did *not* begin to pay again after release—half the jailed men in Genesee and a quarter of the jailed men in Macomb paid 10 percent or less of everything due in the period after their release to the end of the next calendar year. While we are probably on safe ground in attributing to the experience of jail (and the fear of its repetition) much of the motivation for payment of the vast majority of the men who did begin to pay after release, we cannot confidently determine the relation between jailing and the nonpaying men's continued failure to pay. Jail may have renewed some of the nonpaying men's will to pay (if only to avoid pain) but left them no more employable than before. It may indeed have caused many to lose the job they held at the point of sentencing and, for some, hindered their capacity to get another. For still others, it may have hardened their resistance to pay.

After these two observations comes the puzzlement. Many more of Macomb's jailed men than Genesee's began to pay. Twice as large a portion of Genesee's men (48 percent vs. 24 percent) paid nothing in the period after release. We do not have socioeconomic data on the men in Macomb, but by the few measures that permit comparison of the men in the two counties they seem much the same: within the jailed samples in each county about the same portion of men were being jailed for the second (to sixth) time and the men in each county had closely comparable and high arrearages. In the last section of this chapter we discuss the only factor that appears to offer a clue to the differences between the two places: Genesee's jailed men are held in jail much longer, and the longer a person is confined the less well he pays after release.

Persons Who Pay Better Than
Others after Jailing

During the period immediately following their release from jail (the period from release to the end of the next calendar year), the members of the jailed group in Genesee paid, on average, about a third of all that was due from them. That is a much lower rate than was the case for the men in the Genesee caseload as a whole. During any given year, the men in our random sample paid, on average, between 65 and 75 percent of all that was due. Within the jailed group, only one small identifiable group paid after release at above 70 percent—the ten jailed men employed as managers or professionals. For them, whether jail was necessary or not, it certainly appeared to have remarkable restorative powers. (Perhaps Mao was right: periods of forced labor and moral reeducation should regularly be imposed on the professional classes.) We can't identify within the jailed sample many other groups that paid even 60 percent of the amounts due.

On the other hand, we have little trouble identifying groups within the jailed population who paid especially poorly after release. Consider the forty men who served their full sentences (an average postrelease payment rate of .22); the largely overlapping group of sixty-six men who served more than ninety days in jail (an index of .13); the thirty-eight men who had been sentenced for nonsupport before (a payment rate of .23); the forty-six men with signs of physical ailments (a payment rate of .20); and the seventy-six men with criminal records for offenses other than nonsupport (an index of .25). All these factors continue to explain variations in the response to jailing after taking other factors into account. For all these groups, as groups, jail should probably be regarded as a particular failure. Indeed, as with the alcoholics, who are greatly overrepresented in the jailed population but whose low payments seem largely due to their employment problems, the large numbers in these groups of low payers raise questions about the goals the judges and Friends of the Court were seeking to serve through jailing, for we have coded the information about these men's maladies largely out of the agency's own records.

Table 9.3 sets forth in summary form the factors most strongly related to week-by-week payments after release. (In appendix tables 9E and 9F we set forth in greater detail some of the findings regarding lump-sum payments and week-by-week payments.) With regard to regular payments, we found that of all information that is available at the point of release from jail, information about the length of time the man is held tells more about his later probable payments than any other information. After controlling for other factors available to us, we continued to find that the longer a man is held the less well he pays. In a section at the end of this chapter we pull together the several findings we have that suggest the pointlessness of long sentences in this setting.

Other factors strongly tied to performance include the man's record of other offenses and his employment status and occupation. In various ways these factors relate to men's capacity to pay and their attitudes toward payment. A closer look at a few of them sheds further light on the utility of jailing.

Table 9.3   **Principal Factors Relating to Higher Postrelease Week-by-Week Payments in Year after Release from Jail, Genesee Jailed Sample (N = 163)**

	Rank and Beta with Factors Knowable at Jailing		Rank and Beta with Factors Knowable at Release		Rank and Beta with Factors Knowable at End of Our Record	
Factors ascertainable at time of jailing	*Rank*	*Beta*	*Rank*	*Beta*	*Rank*	*Beta*
Man employed full-time at jailing	①	.30	③	.22	④	.20
Man employed as manager or professional	②	.23	⑤	.20	⑤	.19
Man has no prior record of other criminal offenses	③	.20	②	.23	(see last factor)	
Man's wife remarried before jailing	④	.19	6	.15	7	.14
Man is jailed for the first time	5	.15	10	.09	10	.10
Man's wife not receiving AFDC	6	.15	9	.11	11	.10
Man shows no sign of illness at jailing or before	7	.13	8	.12	9	.11
Man does not show signs of alcoholism	8	.09	7	.13	8	.11
Adding factors first knowable at release from jail						
Man serves 3 or fewer days, does not serve over 90	—	—	①	.24	③	.21
Man released on payment of lump sum and execution of wage assignment; man does not serve full term	—	—	④	.21	⑥	.19
Adding factors knowable only in retrospect						
Man does not leave town within 12 months after release	—	—	—	—	①	.28
Man never has other criminal record before or after jailing for nonsupport	—	—	—	—	②	.21
Total explained variance (adjusted)	32.1%		38.4%		47.1%	

NOTE: Excluded are nine cases of men who escaped from jail. Remaining excluded cases are those that closed before end of calendar year after release from jail. The table represents a summary of three Multiple Classification Analyses.

Men with Employment or Alcohol Problems

Men for whom there are indications of employment difficulties before jail pay substantially less well after release than men for whom there is no such indication. The seventy-eight men employed full-time at the time of their jailing have a payment rate after release of .50, while the fifty-eight men who were unemployed or employed off and on have a payment rate of .17. Of all information available at the time of sentencing, the man's employment status at the point of jailing was the strongest predictor of later payments.[6]

Closely interacting with problems of employment—partly absorbed but not swallowed by it in our multiple classification analysis—were problems of alcoholism and signs of physical illness. After taking all other factors into account that are ascertainable either in advance of jailing or at the point of release, these two remain the seventh and eighth most significant factors in determining variation in response to jailing. Table 9.4 displays the payment performance of these groups.

To the extent that the Friend of the Court sought to use jail to convince men who had not been working steadily that they must find work and begin to pay, the agency largely failed. The most straightforward explanation for the failure is, of course, that those who have

Table 9.4   Postrelease Payment Performance Rates of Jailed Men in Relation to Employment, Alcohol, or Physical Illness Problems, Genesee Jailed Sample

	N	Payment Index
Total Population	172	.34
Employment status at time of jailing		
Employed full-time	78	.50
Employed part-time	5	.27
Not employed (or employed erratically)	58	.17
Employment status unclear	31	.27
Indications of alcohol problems		
No indication in file	67	.42
One indication in file	45	.38
Two or more indications in file	60	.21
Signs of physical illness		
No indication in file	124	.40
At least one sign of physical illness	48	.20

unemployment problems before jailing continue to have them afterwards. It is the most straightforward explanation because it plausibly
explains a reasonably high performance by the fully employed men and
the much lower performance of the unemployed. It is nonetheless possible that men with unemployment problems are more likely to have
other psychological resistances to payment, and it is these other resistances that explain the later low payment (and perhaps some of the
employment problems as well). One equivocal piece of evidence in this
regard is that the men in the jailed group with employment problems
were far more likely than the employed men to have failed to show for
the initial Friend of the Court interview.[7]

The more carefully the figures are examined the more disastrous the
jailing of men with employment difficulties appears. Of the sixty men
who were unemployed, or irregularly or only part-time employed at
jailing, twenty-seven, or 45 percent, seem to have left the county
within a year after release and paid at a mean rate of .06 of everything
due in the period after release. Of the thirty-three men who remained in
the county we have adequate postrelease payment information on
thirty-one, and of these only one man paid more than 80 percent of the
amount due over the period that followed. More than half paid 10
percent or less of everything due. These sparse results suggest, when
taken together with other findings, that many of these men were, as
they claimed at their jailing, not merely unemployed but unemployed
for reasons beyond their current capacities to remedy. If so, many
should never have been jailed at all under the statutory standard that
permits jailing only for willful refusal to pay. Statutes aside, wise policy
for the agency would suggest some other approach than jailing for this
group. What other approach should be taken is unclear. Agency participation in or referrals to job placement comes easily to mind but is a
tool of uncertain worth. Of the men with employment problems,
slightly more than half show two or more signs of alcohol problems and
40 percent display signs of physical problems apart from or in addition
to alcoholism.

What prompts the Friends of the Court and judges—or at least
Genesee County's Friend of the Court and judges—to continue to jail
so many men with such problems? One reason may be that the payment responses of these men, though slight, are better than nothing,
and nothing, after all, was their payment rate before jailing. A third of
the unemployed men did unearth from somewhere or someone a lump-
sum payment for release and one in six did pay more than half of
everything due in the period after release.

Judges in Genesee would probably offer at least two reasons for continuing to jail the men with employment problems whether or not the return from jailing them exceeds the cost. In the first place, the men with such problems are often, in the judges' view, morally responsible for having become unemployed or unemployable and deserve to be punished for their irresponsibility. In the transcript that begins this book Jerry Neal is upbraided for having left GM to bounce "from one insignificant job to another."

A second reason for jailing such men despite low returns is that to fail to do so would set a bad example to the rest of the population. More than one enforcement officer conjured for me a picture of men sitting around a bar while one deadbeat tells the other customers that the Friend of the Court knows where to find him but leaves him alone. The listeners are all Friend of the Court clients. Some are in arrears. They feel discriminated against if they have been pressed by the agency to pay. Worse, some of the men are regular payers. They now feel inspired to try getting by without paying.

Whether the unemployed man talks to anyone in a bar or elsewhere, we have reported in Chapter 6 that in counties well organized to collect payments overall collections appear related to the overall incidence of jailing. The jailing of these unemployed men somehow lets the world know that Genesee County means business.

We have looked at the jailing of unemployed men. Now the other side of the coin. How wise and successful is the jailing of employed men? On the surface, it certainly appears appreciably more productive. While only one of the thirty-one men unemployed at jailing paid more than 80 percent of the amount due in the period after release, twenty-three of the fifty-two fully employed men who stayed in town paid at that rate or a higher one. The problem is that there were twenty-two fully employed men who did not stay in town but left shortly after release, and at least six of the men who did stay appeared, from evidence we have in the files, to have lost their jobs by reason of the jailing. The question for the employed group then becomes whether they could as a group have been goaded into equally high or even higher payments, with lower rates of leaving town, by techniques short of jailing. A later section considers this question in greater detail. It can at least be said that some important lesser techniques had rarely been tried on those who paid well after release from jail in Flint. Of the men who were employed at the time of their jailing, two-thirds had never been placed on a wage assignment before being jailed and four-fifths had never been brought before a judge and given some lesser sanction than jailing, such as a suspended sentence or probation.

The Effects of Jailing on Psychological
Disincentives to Payment

We have seen that men with employment problems before jailing generally continue failing to pay after release. What of the men who had been failing to pay before jail not because they had been unable to do so but because, for one reason or another, they had been unwilling? In one sense we have just looked at this group. The men who were employed full-time at jailing could presumably have been making at least partial payments in the period before jailing, but almost none of them were. Thus for them, the barriers to payment must have been largely psychological. (We say "largely" rather than "entirely," because some of them, though employed at jailing, claimed to have been unemployed during much of the period of nonpayment.)

After release, as we have seen, the employed men pay much better as a group than the unemployed men, but the spectrum of their payments is wide. About 30 percent paid nothing or nearly nothing while 30 percent paid over 80 percent of all that was due. Their mean rate of payments was .50. If we can learn what explains the differences in rates of payments among the employed men, we may be able to learn which psychological barriers to payment jailing overcomes and which barriers it leaves unaffected. The theory we would apply in looking for the impact of jailing on psychological barriers or disincentives is as follows. We identify factors about the cases of the jailed men that may have posed psychological barriers to payment before the jailing—the former wife's remarriage, her receipt of AFDC, and so on. If we find that men whose cases exhibit that factor pay after release at a significantly higher level than other men (and that the difference persists after controls), that finding will suggest two conclusions at once: (1) the factor was indeed a psychological hindrance to many of the men and (2) jailing overcame it. Conversely, if we find that the men with the factor pay after release significantly less well than other jailed men, this suggests that the factor was a psychological barrier for many of these men and that the barrier remains intact after release.[8]

We're in a bit of trouble when men whose cases display the factor pay no differently than men whose cases do not (men who had "shotgun" marriages provide one example), for then it is possible either that the factor really was not a psychological barrier at all for the men who were jailed or that it was a barrier but that jail overcame the barrier for some men but left it unimpaired for a comparable number.[9]

The beginning of our inquiry was to examine the postrelease payment index of the employed men who displayed various sorts of possible psychological barriers to payment (appendix table 9G sets forth these initial findings).

No factors that especially suggested frictions within the marriage while the marriage was intact marked notable differences in performance after release from jail. For example, neither men whose wives were pregnant at marriage nor men who failed to attend the predivorce interview paid at lower rates than the rest of the jailed group. On the other hand, three factors suggesting psychological barriers to payments because of factors existing after divorce do bear a significant relationship to payments. All three suggest a reluctance to pay because the women and children have an alternative source of income. Men whose former wives remarried before they were sentenced to jail and men whose former wives had an occupation at the time of divorce paid substantially better than the average after release from jail. Conversely, men whose former wives received welfare benefits at the point of jailing paid decidedly worse than the average.

When we perform multiple classification analysis with other factors that might bear on payment performance, we find that the impression that men whose former wives receive welfare are especially resistant to payment is largely false, for its significance greatly diminishes. On the other hand, the men whose wives work and the men whose wives remarried do remain significantly more likely to pay better (betas of .31 and .19). Indeed it is in large part they who make the former husbands of welfare recipients appear worse; women who are currently remarried and women who are employed are far less likely to be receiving public assistance.

The suggestion thus conveyed is that within our jailed sample there was a group of men who were, on the whole, able to pay but felt absolved from payment by their former wife's remarriage or by her earnings from work. The jar of jailing brought more of them, on average, into regular payments than it did other jailed men, perhaps because this group of men's reluctance to pay, related in no way, even indirectly, to their financial capacity to make payments.

There is a dissonance between our findings here regarding the higher payments after release from jail of men whose former wives had remarried or were employed and our earlier reported findings in Chapter 7. There we said that within the random sample of all men under orders of support we found no suggestion that men paid less well because of their former wives' remarriage or employment. Our findings suggest that there may well be many men who are inclined toward lower payments by reason of these alternative income sources of their former wives. For most men, Genesee's routine system of warnings is sufficient to keep them paying. For a small core, however, the warnings are not enough and only jailing overcomes their unwillingness to pay.

Total Returns from Jailing: Would
Other Techniques Have Worked as Well?

Most jailed men in Genesee and Macomb Counties made a lump-sum payment to secure their release. A significant number in both counties began making payments after release. A large portion in both counties did both. When we created a combined payment index that included both the lump-sum and the week-by-week payments, we found that the mean rate of payments during the period after jailing for all jailed men was .50 in Genesee and .64 in Macomb (see appendix table 9H). Put another way, when lump sums and weekly payments were combined, we found that 40 percent of the jailed men in Genesee and 60 percent of the jailed men in Macomb paid half or more of everything due from the point of their release to the end of the next calendar year.

That is a substantial payment rate from a group of men who had seemed quite unpromising as payers. The response may seem even more remarkable when we look more closely at the forms of payment. The pattern of lump sums and weekly payments is strikingly different from that which we have discussed earlier when examining the payments following pay-or-appear letters.

There we found that, while many men made a lump-sum payment and many began periods of regular payments, fewer than 10 percent of the men did both (see box A in figure 7.5). With jailing we find that most men who did either did both. The difference is surprising. The man who makes a lump-sum payment to purchase his release from jail—even a very large payment—would hardly appear to be indicating a change of heart that foretells the beginning of regular payments later, but we find nonetheless that five of every six men who made a lump-sum payment made further regular payments in the period after release. Part of the difference in pattern from that observed for pay-or-appear letters is due to a difference in the way we recorded postrelease payments after jailing,[10] but in larger part the difference seems attributable to the strong desire of some of the jailed men not to be jailed again.

We also found notable the large number of men who made no lump-sum payment for release but then began to make some payments. In Genesee, there were twenty-six men who came up with nothing for release and thus typically served long terms—a mean of 139 days—but then upon release made at least some payments. For some of the men, the postrelease payments were slight, but twelve of the twenty-six men in Genesee paid more than half of everything due. This group did include a few who were released from jail very quickly on wage assignments alone, but most were men who apparently could not find anyone to bail them out. They nonetheless began to pay after release. Jerry Neal was such a person on his third jailing.

All this sounds like quite a remarkable return. At least within Genesee County, however, there is room to ask whether the agency, in its use of jail, has killed a lot of geese for a few golden eggs.

Half the jailed men in Genesee made virtually no postrelease payments. For this group, file records contain evidence that over half left town within a year of their release,[11] a much higher rate of movement than we found for men in the general sample as a whole.[12] After release, the group that left paid at an average rate of only .09, the lowest-paying group we can identify anywhere in our study. The very low payments of the men who left town strongly suggest that their motive in leaving was to avoid paying without rejailing.

The costs of a jailing policy that induces so many men to flee are high. Once gone, the man is highly likely to sever permanently his social ties to his children. Even a nonpaying father may love and want to see his children. The likelihood of strong ties sadly broken may be especially high in the cases in which the man had not been paying because of employment problems that the Friend of the Court staff had refused to believe. When I pointed out these possible losses to a senior staff member at the Friend of the Court, he said that if men weren't going to pay they might as well leave, and dismissed my concerns for the loss to the family as merely "sociological." Had I been a sociologist I'd have been offended. (I remembered a cartoon of two preteenage girls standing at a storefront labeled "Adult." "Adult," one informs the other, "means dirty.")

"Sociology" aside, the men who depart may also cause a dollar loss to the family and the Friend of the Court. The man who leaves the county is largely lost to the agency, and the opportunity to try gentler methods of persuasion is largely ended. In Genesee County, the man who failed to respond to a warning letter and became a subject of a warrant often found himself in jail before a wage assignment was ever tried and before a judge tried stern admonishment or some form of probation. It is possible, of course, that the man who left after jailing would have left after milder efforts as well, but we have many fewer indications of departures in the wake of nonjudicial enforcement efforts in the random sample than we do after sentences to jail. Moreover, a large portion of the men who left were men who might well have been able to pay. The strongest factor associated with whether a jailed man left town was signs of alcohol problems: those who had such problems tended to *stay*. Those without them were the group most likely to leave. Though it is true that men who had been employed at the point of jailing were somewhat less likely to leave town than men who were unemployed, it is nonetheless the case that nearly half of the men who left town and whose employment status we knew were in fact employed full-time at the time of jailing (twenty-two of forty-eight).[13]

What about those who did stay and paid after release? Even though many of these men paid for a while, for most their period of payments after release was of short duration. Over half of those who began to pay after release (forty-one of the sixty-nine) had stopped again by the end of the calendar year after their release even when other warnings or wage assignments had been used after release to spur them on again. A substantial number of those who had some period of steady payments were in fact rejailed within the next two years. The record is bleaker if one moves farther down the road. Of the men jailed in 1969 and 1970, the cases of 166 were still alive by spring of 1974, at least three years after the release of all the men and over four years for most of the men. During the first quarter of 1974, only 35 percent of the jailed men whose cases were alive made any payments. Only 60 percent of the jailed men had made any payments whatever during 1972, 1973, or the first quarter of 1974. Thus, 40 percent of the jailed men had disappeared totally from the system for over three years. The high rate at which men leave the county and the high rate of attrition from the system even from those who pay week by week for a while poignantly raise the question whether less severe techniques than jail would have worked as well.

What would have happened if, at the time when they were arrested and sentenced to jail, the sentenced men had instead been mailed another warning, perhaps more sternly worded, or placed on a wage assignment by the enforcement officer, or brought before the judge and the judge had then imposed some other sanction than jailing? Such questions are the stuff of experimental studies in which similar persons are randomly channeled into differing treatments. These questions cannot, however, be confidently answered by us. We can report only

on how men whose situations were somewhat similar to those of the
jailed men performed when techniques other than jailing were tried, but
we are without the capacity to control for the factors that caused the
Genesee enforcement officers and judges to make the nonrandom
choices they did among the techniques used.

In order to make rough comparisons, we sought to identify efforts
within the cases in the random sample that were applied at the point in
a faltering payment record when jail had often been used on other men.
Specifically, we looked at the response to warning letters (either form
or personal letters) that were sent within six months of an earlier effort,
when the earlier effort had been followed by either no payments or
payments that had soon ceased. We excluded efforts used more than
four years after the judgment, because most jailed men (80 percent) had
been jailed by the end of four years after judgment. We also excluded
any efforts that had been preceded by appearances before the judge for
nonsupport, because of the possible long-term effects of those appearances. We thus had a group of efforts occurring early in the life of the
decrees, preceded by earlier efforts that had produced no or few results.

Table 9.5 reveals that, when such comparisons are drawn, wage
assignments seem highly promising, but that further warnings and
techniques short of jailing used by the judges do not appear to work as
well as jailing, at least in the short run. Warnings typically produced
periods of regular payments with less frequency and of shorter duration than did sentences to jail, but only slightly less in each case. The
great difference between the responses was in terms of the lump-sum
payments—hardly surprising given the special burden pressing the man
while in jail. Once lump-sum payments are considered, the return from
jailings is over three times as great as the responses to the warnings
(putting aside for the moment the dollar costs of jailing).

A different pattern, but one with comparable net effect, is found in
those cases in which there was a hearing before the judge but the judge
chose to impose some sanction other than a sentence of time in jail.
Sometimes the judge imposed a wage assignment; at other times he
found the man in contempt and placed him on probation or gave him a
suspended sentence. These occasions produced lump-sum payments
far less frequently then jailing did and produced shorter periods of
regular payments. In net effect, jailings were followed by payments
two and one-half times as great.

It seems possible that these slender returns in Genesee, after repeated warnings, would have been even more slender in a jurisdiction

making less use of jail. Our findings in Washtenaw County suggest that the same warnings would be likely to produce even fewer returns in a county that does not back the warnings with the realistic threat of more severe consequences to follow (see Chapter 7 above).

What conclusion can we draw from these returns? That jail might as well be used because nothing else will do any better? That the golden

Table 9.5   **Comparison of Payment Responses to Jailing with Payment Responses to Other Efforts, Genesee Random Sample**

Responses	Nonjailed Comparison Group Sent Another Warning* (N = 283)	Nonjailed Comparison Group Placed on Wage Assignment* (N = 70)	Group Brought before Judge, Not Jailed (N = 45)	Jailed Group (N = 79)
Lump-sum payments				
Portion making lump-sum payments	20%	6%	22%	55%
Size when paid (mean)	$199	$438	$737	$691
Net weeks from lump-sum payments**	1 wk.	1 wk.	5 wks.	19 wks.
Regular payments				
Portion making payments beginning soon after effort	25%	79%	39%	30%
Length when paid (mean)	30 wks.	73 wks.	18 wks.	38 wks.
Net weeks from regular payments***	8 wks.	57 wks.	7 wks.	12 wks.
Total response from lump-sum and regular payment	9 wks.	58 wks.	12 wks.	31 wks.

* Defined to include efforts (a) employed within forty-eight months of the final order, (b) preceded within six months by another enforcement effort, and (c) employed when there had been no payments in the immediate period preceding the effort.

** Dollars obtained in lump-sums expressed in weeks' worth of payments divided by total efforts including those not followed by lump-sums.

*** Regular payments in weeks in all cases with payments divided by total efforts including those not followed by any payments.

goose was never golden and might as well be slain? Perhaps, but just perhaps.

We must flirt with any such conclusion with great caution. In the first place, the high returns from wage assignments suggest again that they should be preferred to jail whenever the man is employed, except perhaps in cases in which the man has previously resigned from a job expressly to avoid an earlier assignment. Moreover, before leaping to conclude that jailing is much more effective than probation, we must remember again that these sanctions were not employed at random. By examining the files of the men upon whom judges used other techniques, we find that judges sometimes chose a sanction other than jail not because the man was less blameworthy than the men he typically jailed but because the judge, although finding that the man was in contempt, believed that the man was currently unemployed and with time and encouragement might find work. If we look only at the twenty-nine occasions in which a judge used a sanction other than jail in circumstances in which he appeared to be trying to secure the immediate revival of regular payments, periods of regular payments do begin after nineteen of those occasions (66 percent), a record substantially better than in the jailing cases.

Finally, even as to the use of further warnings, it is true that they seem to produce far lower returns, but it is also true that they are far less expensive. A few dollars probably represents the fully distributed costs of sending out another form. Jail by contrast entails not merely the costs of incarceration but the high costs of the arresting process.

Several years have passed now since we drew our jailed sample. According to the Friend of the Court in Genesee and some of his deputies, the judges in Genesee shifted after 1975 to the much more frequent use of alternative sanctions, away from their prior habit of imposing a jail sentence in well more than half the hearings brought before them. In so doing, they are falling into line with the pattern of judges in most, though not all, other Michigan counties, including those in which jail is used with frequency. From our study of twenty-eight counties we cannot report on the impact of the use of alternative sanctions on the men on whom they were employed, but we do know that several such counties were among those with the highest overall levels of collections.

The Impacts of Long Terms in Jail

We have reported several aspects of the practice of jailing in Michigan that may make jailing seem attractive as an instrument of enforcement.

Since Genesee's judges routinely sentenced men to long terms in jail—80 percent were sentenced to six months or more—readers may assume that long sentences are part of the reason for Michigan's high levels of collections. The members of Genesee's enforcement staff believed that the long sentences were responsible for their success. Economists might make similar predictions. For example, Professor George Stigler of the University of Chicago, an economist and theoretician about sanctions, has written, "the offender is deterred by the expected punishment, which is (as a first approximation) the probability of punishment times the punishment. . . . Hence, increasing the punishment would always seem to increase the deterrence."[14] Except in one small regard, we find no evidence to support either the enforcement officers or Professor Stigler.

Let us look briefly at our findings about sentence length, time served, and the returns from jailing.

For jailed men, one might guess that the longer the sentence imposed the more that men would be willing to disgorge as the price for an early release. A man might, that is, wait out a one-month sentence but pay a thousand dollars to avoid a one-year sentence. We could not test this hypothesis in Genesee County, since nearly everyone jailed there received a long sentence. In Macomb, however, sentence length varied widely among judges: a quarter of those jailed received sentences of thirty days or less, another quarter received sentences of six months or more, and the rest received sentences of lengths in between (typically sixty or ninety days). Within Macomb we find that men are willing to come up with lump sums of significant size regardless of the length of the sentence imposed. So long as the amount demanded was no more than twenty weeks' worth of payments, as large a portion of those receiving short sentences came up with a lump sum as did those receiving the longest sentences.

In the small percentage of cases, however, when the lump sum demanded was more, men given long sentences were significantly more likely to purchase their release than those given sentences of thirty days or less. This finding does suggest that, when the dollar demand is high, some men (or perhaps their relations contemplating lending them money) will make a cold calculation of days in relation to dollars. Even here our findings are murky, however, for many of those with long sentences who did make a lump-sum payment for their release did not actually pay as much as was demanded and made the lump-sum payment only after they had been held over thirty days, by which time the men sentenced for shorter periods had been released without payment.

What small gain long sentences offer in producing large lump-sum payments from a few men is more than offset by the apparent negative effect long terms in jail exert on week-by-week payments after release. In each county we found that the length of sentence as originally imposed by the judge bore no substantial relation to payments after release. Men initially given thirty-day sentences paid at about the same rate after release as men given much longer sentences, after taking time served into account. On the other hand, the number of days actually served (often, if you recall, much shorter than the conditional sentence imposed) bore a strong negative relation to postrelease payments. In Genesee County, men held three or fewer days paid at five times as high an average rate as men held more than ninety days (a rate of .64 vs. a rate of .13). There was a less strong but still negative relationship in Macomb County as well (see table 9.6).

On its face, there are many reasons why the number of days served might be related to lower payments. Two hypotheses seem most plausible: first, that the men who served long terms were simply those who were less employable or more resistant before sentencing and that the failure to come up with a lump-sum payment and the later low weekly payments have a common earlier origin; and, second, that the longer men serve, the more bitter and less employable they become, and hence in some sense long terms "cause" lower payments. The first hypothesis, that a long term served suggests a preexisting incapacity, is subject in part to testing within our data. In our multiple correlation analyses of factors relating to postrelease payments in Genesee, we included as controls not merely time served but also whether the man

Table 9.6   Performance of Jailed Men in Genesee and Macomb Counties in Relation to Time Served

| | Genesee* | | Macomb** | |
Days Served in Jail	N	Mean Index	N	Mean
3 or less	29	.64	80	.68
4–10	26	.40	45	.52
11–30	19	.39	43	.42
31–90	26	.37	31	.37
91 or more	66	.13	25	.45
Total	169	.33	224	.53
		p < .001		p < .001

* Men jailed in Genesee County in 1969 and first ten months of 1970.

** Men jailed in Macomb County in 1970.

was employed at arrest and whether he made a lump-sum payment for release.[15] If days served had been simply a surrogate for the man's financial capacity, then, once employment and lump-sum payments had been taken into account, we would expect to find that days served would largely cease to explain performance. But it didn't. It increased in strength and remained the strongest factor determinable at release among all we included in the analysis (see col. 4, table 9.3). It is thus tempting to conclude that the second hypothesis has some substantial merit—that long terms in jail do themselves decrease men's will or capacity to pay. We cannot test this hypothesis directly, but in a finding consistent with this conclusion we did learn that leaving the county after release was significantly more common for men held for longer terms than for men held for short terms, especially among men not identified as having alcohol problems.

Whatever the reason for lower payments by those who served long terms, the lower payments are indisputably there. There is not the slightest shred of evidence to suggest that any group of men is frightened into *better* payments after release, the longer they are held. Nor is there any evidence that if a man is given a long sentence—say six months or a year—but serves only three or four days, he is more likely to be frightened in the future into paying better than if he serves only three or four days of a thirty-day sentence. And, of course, short terms in jail cost the counties far less. At twenty dollars per inmate per day, a common figure today for urban jails, the difference in the costs of holding a man for six days (the median in Macomb) as opposed to fifty-two days (the median in Genesee) is close to a thousand dollars.

If all this is true, only a finding that the longer sentences somehow induce the general run of men under orders who never go to jail at all into higher payments would offer a justification, apart from revenge, for holding men for long periods. There is, however, no support for such a finding within our data.

Within the twenty-eight-county study, we examined this question with care. The reader will recall from Chapter 6 that the rate of jailing, its frequency in relation to county population, was an important explainer of performance. In each county, we multiplied the rate of jailing by the average length of sentences imposed to produce an index that weighted the rate of jailing by sentence length. We created a second, similar index by multiplying the jail rate by the percentage of sentences that were for six months or more.

Counties such as Genesee that jailed large numbers of men for long terms had the highest score on these indexes. When used in our regression analysis, however, the indexes were of no utility whatever in sorting the higher- from the lower-collecting counties. In every regression run with the rate of jailing in unaltered form, the sentence-length indexes offered virtually no additional explanatory power. Looking more closely at the data, we can see why sentence length tells nothing: the judges in most of the highest-collecting counties used jail frequently but rarely used long sentences. In several of the counties with the highest rates of collections, the judges rarely used sentences of more than thirty or, at the most, sixty days.

Why are the general run of men under orders of support affected by the incidence of jailing of their local judges but not by the length of sentences imposed? Is sentence length unimportant because most men under orders learn something of the incidence of jailing but not of sentence length or time served? Or is it that, even though some men do learn of sentencing or release practices, their knowledge of sentencing adds nothing to the alarm already instilled by the knowledge that jailing of any length is widely used? We cannot answer the question, but little turns on it for our purposes. What is critical is that our study suggests that, given the realistic prospects of broadcasting information about sentencing or actual time served, counties have nothing to gain from locking men up for long periods.

Ten

Justifying the Continued Use of Jail

Jerry Neal's mother is seventy-eight. I called and asked her if I could see her sometime and, weeks later, called again and paid a visit. Jerry's father wasn't home. Mrs. Neal was reluctant to talk. She repeated several times that she knew she was going to get into trouble for speaking to me.

We sat at her kitchen table. She pulled at the folds of her dress and talked about her family. Jerry was her baby, the last of her four sons. The other three, like their father, had spent their adult lives to this point working in the local General Motors plants. They had jobs to be proud of. They went to church and stayed married to the same women.

To her, Jerry had many of the good qualities of his brothers. He was "a good hard worker." He came out and fixed the cars from time to time. He helped his Dad in other ways. "He'd give the shirt off his back for you."

"Then what made Jerry different?" I asked. After a long pause, she replied, "I don't know. That's the way it goes, I guess." I could hear the same words out of Jerry's mouth.

She said that, when she heard that Jerry had been jailed for nonsupport, she cried and cried. "He hadn't killed anybody or hurt anybody, had he?"

Yet, Mrs. Neal's own life is the visible proof of Jerry's sin. Her man—she always referred to her husband as "my man"—had always

241

taken care of her and brought home his paycheck for his family. They lived on five acres in a small, well-tended farmhouse that he had bought over forty years before. Cared for financially, Mrs. Neal had looked after this house and raised her sons. She had never been on welfare. She had never felt compelled by need to take a job outside the home. Mr. Neal had shared with her the task of raising the sons, had disciplined them when they needed it, had provided an image of reliability for them to emulate.

Throughout her life, Mrs. Neal had been cared for and protected—as Jerry himself as a child had been cared for and protected—in ways that Jerry had failed to provide for Dolores or for his children. Maybe Jerry had not killed anyone, but by Mrs. Neal's moral code it could hardly be said that he had not hurt anyone.

If we share Mrs. Neal's code or even that part of the code that makes parents responsible for their children, Jerry's moral failure alone might appear to justify locking him up in jail. Jail can serve admirably as an instrument of retribution. Many women wish their former husbands some unspeakable torture, and in this country the county jail is about the best we have to offer. Remember Dolores Neal's smile as she recollected that two of her husbands served time in jail together for failing to pay. Especially if the nonpayer's children are receiving welfare benefits, judges and many members of the public might join Dolores in her chuckle.

Chapters 6 and 9 were devoted in substantial part to more measurable benefits of sentences to jail: their use and their threat produce dollars from men who are jailed and men who are not. Not just a few dollars but many. So long as states rely on a child support system that depends on divorced parents making payments after earnings are in their pockets, there is probably no sanction other than jail that will work as well: threatening fines seem pointless given the sort of behavior the government is trying to induce; cutting off fingers or branding foreheads would be rejected as barbaric; other forms of public mortification—such a publishing the names of defaulters—might be tried but such lists have never been a favored form of sanction in this country and might have little effect on the large numbers of persons who pay little attention to newspapers.

If jail induces high payments and the extra dollars collected outstrip the dollar costs of the jailing policy, can there be any serious objections to its continued use? The measure of jail's justifiability cannot lie alone in its effectiveness in deterring undesired conduct. America keeps a larger portion of its citizens in prisons than any other Western nation.

The reason is not merely that we suffer from a high incidence of violent crime; it is also that our judges and legislators prescribe jail easily. If a person is "bad," he belongs in jail. Thus, today, even many liberals who deplore the conditions in our jails advocate the greater use of penal sanctions on men who beat their wives or assault them sexually.

I think jail should be selected as a sanction with greater caution. Except for the death penalty, our society inflicts no more serious sanction than sentences of jail or imprisonment. Sentencing a man to jail involves two steps of greater significance than most of us consider on first reflection: first, there is a determination that the man has engaged in some sort of conduct serious enough that we are willing to place a stamp of social condemnation on him—willing to saddle him with a "criminal record." Though nonsupport proceedings are formally denominated "civil," the public surely makes no such distinction when hearing of a man sentenced to jail for six months or a year. Second, there is a decision to sever the man's ties for some period from the activities in the community that he depends upon—access to friends, the satisfactions of work, heterosexual contacts, religious ceremonies of his own choosing, strolling, chatting, and chewing the fat with friends on his front stoop. We accomplish the severance by locking him in an institution in which he will be subjected to complete loss of privacy, to the substantial likelihood of physical and sexual assault, and to the degradation of placement in a servile relation to guards with power to punish, ignore, or humiliate. We have commented earlier on the conditions of the jail in Genesee County. Most jails in this country are older and in worse condition than Genesee's. Indeed, the county jails that house misdemeanants, nonsupporters, and persons awaiting trial are America's vilest institutions of incarceration[1]—typically far worse than our prisons, for unlike prisons, jails, generally in the middle of cities, offer little opportunity for physical exercise. Most people in jails just sit or sleep.

Over the last few decades, a great deal that is unsettling has been learned about the effects of labeling a person "bad."[2] The label sticks in the man's own head and often reshapes his vision of himself: he is as likely to accept the label as a confirmation of his own sense of worthlessness as he is to resist the label and resolve to live up to the expectations of society. Moreover, in a seemingly perverse manner, many men become dependent upon the loss of autonomy jail affords. They become "institutionalized," to use the term adopted by students of institutions of confinement.

That we find men staying around Flint who make no payments and are jailed four or five times for long terms surprises no social scientist who has examined the behavior of other men with contact with the criminal justice system. The rate of reimprisonment of previously convicted men remains so high that many social scientists and penologists despair of the utility of either jail or prison to deter, by fear of recommittal, most of those put there or to rehabilitate by programs that instill new attitudes. Given these attributes of jailing and the conditions of jails, does nonsupport still seem an appropriate offense for jail's use, even if it has useful general deterrent effects?

One part of the answer should lie in answering another question: how heinous an act is willful nonsupport? At first blush it seems particularly vicious—the conscious disregard of one of a person's most sacred duties. Nonetheless, two aspects of jailing for nonsupport should give us pause: first, it is a form of jailing for debt; and, second, it arises as an offense between family members.

By any commonsense understanding, jailing for an arrearage in court-ordered support is indeed a form of jailing for debt. Jailing for debt. The very phrase transports us back to Fielding, Defoe, and Dickens, to eighteenth- and nineteenth-century England when thousands of debtors were jailed each year in the vilest conditions. In the 1750s, three-quarters of the prisoners in London's jails were debtors, committed on the bare assertion of an unpaid bill for owing as little as a sixpence or a shilling.[3] In this country most state constitutions, including Michigan's, bar jailing for debt.

Why do most Americans, even today, recoil from the idea of jailing for debt? If there are good reasons to recoil, can jailing for nonpayment of child support be distinguished from jailing for debt? To many people, failing to pay a commercial debt simply does not seem sinful enough to justify a criminal record and penal incarceration. We do not think in terms of the criminal law as a part of business transactions between consenting persons. Rather we think in terms of commercial remedies—suits in contract, refusal to continue to deal, refusals to extend credit—and consider them adequate. In a commercial context, jailing becomes simply another collection technique of creditors, a powerful supplement to garnishment and default judgments. The debtors who would be subjected to jailing today would probably be persons of low income involved with loan companies and with furniture, automobile, and appliance dealers. In these transactions, many would feel that adding to the seller's arsenal the power to secure the buyer's commitment to jail would simply add weight to the stronger side of the transaction. Moreover, tending to consider crimes in terms of victims, many would find it hard to picture a relation between a single person's nonpayment and any significant harm to the creditor. It is indeed typically the case that the loss suffered by the corporate creditor is significant only when there has been default by large numbers of debtors. Ma Bell is really no one's mother.

In most respects the failure to pay child support seems vastly different from the failure to pay commercial debts. With child-support nonpayment outside the welfare setting, there is for each nonpayer a victim—a child, visible and often hurting. Moreover, the victim has not been in an overweaning bargaining position with regard to the transactions that led to the debt. Nor can the child victim adequately protect himself for the future by tightening his credit practices or relying on repossession. Perhaps, most compellingly, the welfare of children is simply more important than the welfare of automobile dealers. These differences may explain why Congress has long provided that commercial debts can be discharged in bankruptcy but arrearages in child support obligations cannot.[4] It also explains the underlying reason why state courts have almost uniformly read their constitutional prohibitions against jailing for debt as not including debt arising from court-ordered obligations of support. If analogies to old practices of jailing for debts were the only reason to feel queasy about jailing for nonsupport, we might well decide that nonsupport is justly considered different.

What, however, do we make of the fact that we are dealing with a "family" offense? While the family nature of the child support debt makes nonpayment seem more egregious than nonpayment of commercial debts, there are other aspects of the "family nature" of the child support offense that may make nonpayment seem less appropriate for criminal sanctions. A recent British government committee that studied all aspects of the problems of one-parent families criticized the continued wide use in Britain of jailing for nonpayment of support. Citing the "emotional stress" of the postdivorce period and child support's connection with an "intimate personal relationship," the committee recommended that Parliament eliminate penal sanctions for nonpayment of support.[5]

The stress of the postdivorce period is important to remember. In many cases the nonpaying male who appears to have a callous disregard for the welfare of his family is in fact caught in a much more nearly forgiveable struggle, often the continuation after divorce of patterns of behavior that were a part of the marital relationship: withholding as a form of communication. Divorced men thus often "forget" to pay from quite prosaic human feelings of jealousy or anger, just as divorced women similarly forget that Tuesday is the day the father planned to visit the children. At one hearing, a Genesee man confessed to the judge with some embarrassment that he had withheld support, in an effort he admitted was childish, to make the woman realize her dependency on him and come back. Jailings commonly occur during this period of particular stress. The reader may recall that nearly half of the men in our sample of jailed men had been first jailed for failing to pay within a year of their final judgment of divorce.

To be sure, men who murder their wives may similarly claim that they acted during a moment of "emotional stress," growing out of an "intimate family relationship." If there is a difference between killing and nonpayment, it lies in the seriousness of the act of killing. When an addled man or woman kills his or her spouse, the law recognizes and juries commonly concur that the act deserves punishment, although often not for first-degree murder. Second-degree murder or manslaughter are more common verdicts. With nonsupport within the family, the emotional turmoil may suggest to us that the act simply no longer seems to justify criminal sanctions at all. "Second-degree" nonsupport may not seem an appropriate occasion for jail.

Another aspect of the "family" nature of the offense is also troublesome, although it may apply in only a small portion of cases. Courts commonly refuse to intrude on controversies between spouses during an ongoing marriage.[6] Their abstention can be justified in part as a recognition that spouses need to work through the terms of their own relationships. Sometimes those terms are rather bizarre, but bizarre behavior behind the closed doors of the home deserves protection in a heterogeneous society. Consider the following case within our sample in which the tacit terms of a couple's relationship included the man as a person not contributing to his family's support. The husband in the case had rarely ever been employed or even sought employment. He drank heavily throughout adulthood. At marriage, he and his wife moved into his parents' home where they remained until separation. They lived largely off his wife's earnings. After divorce, he stayed at home and behaved just as he always had—and was shipped away on a one-year sentence by a judge outraged at his indolence. This seems to me a case in which the judge imposed new and very different rules on a game entered into by two people with very different expectations. Much of the jurisprudential hostility to "victimless crimes" can be similarly viewed: controls on fornication or marijuana use have often operated as simply an imposition by force of majoritarian values on people who do not share them. With regard to support, it is highly probable that most nonpaying men accept a notion of an obligation to support, but it is also probable from the evidence we have that a large portion of the jailed men had long histories of alcohol problems and sporadic work records that had formed part of the complex relationships they had maintained for many years with their spouses.

Our exploration of the propriety of jailing for failing to pay support has thus far focused on the nature of the offense. To many persons, what we have examined so far points in opposed directions: the intrafamily nature of the offense makes nonpayment at once more serious and more pardonable, in differing degrees in different cases. Whatever one's judgment to this point, however, the nature of the offense is not the sole basis for doubt about the appropriateness of penal sanctions in this context. The offense itself cannot be separated from the process through which the offender must pass before jailing, and it remains important to ask whether the offense is sufficiently susceptible to evenhanded and fair administration to meet some minimum notions of justice. Our review of the actual administration of the collection of support in Genesee County, a system with many disturbing attributes, is relevant to our inquiry here but not dispositive. Our inquiry is whether, given the limits of human competence, discriminatory or unfair administration inheres in the nature of the offense and whether any system widely relying on jail can meet tolerable standards of fairness. We have suggested in our discussion of Genesee that it is unlikely that such standards can be met, but some points need emphasis and generalization.

The task of assessment is difficult at best. It involves paring away the day-to-day facts of administration that we viewed in Michigan to get down to some core of characteristics nearly certain to be shared by all systems of enforcement—the task of separating the dancer from the dance. And then, once we have divined the core, we must make judgments about fairness in a context in which there is, in this country, no widely agreed upon set of minimal standards for appraising systems of criminal justice. The United States Constitution suggests some important shared values about evenhandedness and just methods of arrest and adjudication, but the divergent views of the current justices of the Supreme Court mirror the diverse feelings of Americans generally about how much fairness "guilty" people deserve. For all these difficulties, we can identify a few characteristics, almost certain to be present in any system of child support enforcement, that many people, perhaps most, can agree are troubling. The first is that vastly more parents will fail to pay at one time or another than will ever be arrested or jailed, creating countless opportunities for abuses in selecting who shall be punished and who shall be spared. The second is that, even with conscientious efforts at evenhandedness, the task of sorting out those who "deserve" to be arrested from those who do not will involve troubling questions about acceptable excuses and acceptable plans for deferred payments about which there will be much disagreement. The third is that those who will in fact end up in jail—and particularly those who will stay there for any significant period of time—will almost certainly include a large portion of the persons whose "guilt" will seem more dubious.

We have seen that even in Genesee County, over 60 percent of the men ended up in arrears by at least twenty-six weeks' worth of payments at some point, but fewer than a third of this group were ever jailed. Wayne County, a large urban county reasonably well-organized for enforcing, provides even starker figures. During 1974, of over a hundred thousand men under orders of support in divorce or paternity cases, over half paid less than 10 percent of everything due. Of the more than 50,000 defaulters only 914 were sentenced to jail. This low rate occurred despite the fact that the identities of all offenders were known to the agency.

Given the experience across Michigan, it seems likely that other states will continue to have large numbers of nonpayers, even if they develop enforcement systems that mirror Michigan's system. The defaulters will include men who fail to pay for all sorts of reasons—anger over visitation, unemployment, layoffs, jealousy, competing expenses, distaste for the child, and so on. And, everywhere, as in Michigan, human beings—enforcement officers or police and judges—will have to decide who shall be branded with a penal record.

Statutes provide little guidance for sorting out who should and should not be punished. Today, courts can hold someone in contempt only when the violation is willful, but only a few nonpayers are persons utterly unable to make any payments. The vast bulk of nonpayers, including those who are unemployed, are persons who could pay more—a few dollars at the very least—if they placed payment of support above all other uses of their money. Even for the limited number of unemployed men who literally can pay nothing more than they do, statutes invite courts to ask the impossible suppositional question, "Could this man have been employed if he had really tried?" Especially in the context of mass administration of justice, that question seems beyond the capacity of judges to answer except by reference to their own skewed experiences in the labor market and their own ill-informed guesses about employment opportunities.

Can legislatures write statutes that would provide better guidance? Even if courts or legislatures recognized a defense for the unemployed as well as for persons with incomes below the single-individual Lower Standard Budget level—both of these are changes I would recommend—there would still be vast numbers of offenders for both enforcing officers and judges to pick among. The problem is not in defining the undesirable conduct but in developing a system of responses that is both equitable and flexible—a nearly impossible task. Nonsupport is hardly unique in this regard. The closely comparable offense of willful failure to pay taxes calls similarly for judgments by enforcers.

What is troublesome, however, about selective enforcement in the area of child support is that there are many inviting subgroups of nonpayers likely to be singled out inappropriately for especially disfavored treatment. Within Michigan, for example, there are counties in which it appears that most of the jailing befalls those whose children receive welfare benefits, despite the fact that no just claim can be made that this group is either more villainous for failing to pay or that it constitutes an especially visible group to scare other potential defaulters. In Dane County, Wisconsin, fathers in welfare cases were similarly singled out, as was another worrisome group: those with criminal records for other offenses. Like other offenses thought easy to prove as a matter of law, nonpayment of support lends itself to use by police or prosecutors as a way of holding men suspected of offenses more difficult to prove. Enforcement is also certain to fall unevenly on those who have difficulty communicating with middle-class persons in authority. To many men, nonpayment involves a series of excuses to fend off prying enforcement persons. As stated by one Friend of the Court we have earlier quoted, "No one gets jailed for failing to pay. They get jailed for failing to cooperate."

Those who do not communicate with the agency after warnings and those who do, but are inept, are the ones whom enforcing officers are most likely to carry through the discretionary screens to arrest. Nearly all the filters before jail lead to an overrepresentation in the jailed population of blue-collar males and an underrepresentation of white-collar males, just as we found in Genesee County. It is similarly inevitable that those who spend any substantial length of time in jail, unable to come up with lump-sum payments, will be the most down-and-out among these men, those with the fewest resources of their own and those with the fewest relatives warmly disposed to bail them out. It seems quite probable that the high representation of alcoholics in Genesee County among men who serve the longest terms would be repeated under any system. It is ironic that this group should bear so much of the brunt of the enforcement system since there must be more doubts regarding its capacity to pay than there are about almost any other group of nonpaying men.

My impression from staffs of Friends of the Court is that they expect little from the long-servers, viewing them as generally worthless men who deserve what they get and whose jailing is justified, if for no other reason, by the general deterrent value of scaring the other fathers. Sacrificing these blue-collar men for the common good finds its analogues in our society in the use of jailing for street corner gambling as well as in medical experimentation on prison inmates. It is also reminiscent of old patterns of jailing for debt, a phenomenon we suggested was distinguishable from jailing for nonsupport but seems less so now in light of probable and actual patterns of jailing for nonsupport.

For the last few pages we have been examining the possible inequities and dangers of jailing, largely from the perspective of the men who go to jail. Whether one worries about the treatment these nonpaying men receive will turn on whether one's anger at nonpayment is more intense than one's devotion to evenhandedness.

No matter how we regard the defaulting parents, we should also examine the jailing system from the perspective of the children it is intended to benefit. When we do so, we encounter a bit of a puzzlement.

For some children, the effect of a jailing policy will be an unalloyed gain, for others both a gain and a loss, and for still others solely a loss. We have frequently noted the dollar gains for some children. For some other children, however, there will predictably be a dollar loss. We learned in Genesee County that significant numbers of the jailed men leave town and do not pay again. While it is probably the case that most of these men were determined not to pay, for some others it is probably the case that they could have been cajoled into better payments through less severe measures. Their jailing may have contributed in some small measure to overall collections at the expense of their own children. The same is probably the case for some families of men never jailed: the man, resistant to paying and aware of jail's possibility, leaves town before lesser forms of cajolery can be applied.

The effects on children cannot be measured in dollars alone. A jailing policy will have psychological effects on children that may be similarly unevenly distributed. For those children who receive more money than they would in the absence of jailing, there is not only the fact of more dollars available for food and clothing, there may also be a psychic value in payments: they may make the child feel that she is loved and lovable. Many fathers will never consciously recognize the place of jail in their decision to pay, and the continuity of payments will help sustain a relationship with their children. We have no measures whatever in our study of the extent to which steady payments increase the warmth of relationships between father and child. Even assuming that they do, and it seems plausible that they do, if only by reducing friction between the parents, there is little evidence on the importance in the development of a child of sustaining a close tie to the parent who ceases to live with her or participate regularly in the decisions affecting her life. What speculative literature there is about the relation of a noncustodial parent to a child points in two directions—some of it suggests that the relationship between the child and the custodial parent almost inevitably dominates and that the other relationship becomes relatively insignificant,[7] some of it suggests that the relationship with the noncustodial parent remains critical to the child's image of herself and to her growth.[8]

But let us accept for the moment what is probably the case: for some children, a jailing policy induces, in subtle ways, higher payments from their fathers, their long-term ties with their fathers are thereby improved, and they (and perhaps their fathers) are happier. The dilemma is that it is no less plausible, and equally beyond this study's capacity to prove, that other children will be harmed by a jailing policy. The children whose fathers flee not only lose the money, they lose a tie with the father and quite possibly with other members of the father's family. For some men who flee, their nonpayment before leaving town will not have been because they did not care. They may have been truly unable to pay but fearful of being jailed anyway. They may also have been fathers of children on welfare who knew that their payments did not affect the income available to the child. While government may wish to combat this latter father's nonpayment, it is still the case that the father's leaving can produce an unfortunate loss for the child.

Even more elusive to measure is a loss that may occur for some children whose fathers do not leave and continue in fact to maintain contact with them. Especially for those children whose fathers are most conscious of jail's possibility, the hovering image in the father's mind of a clanging cell door may alter the tone of the relationship between him and his child. At some level, the relationship may shift from one based solely on affection to one based in significant part on fear. To be sure, simply the entry of a formal court order to support may produce a partial shift in the father's view of his relationship to the child, but it is surely possible that the potential of jail may distort the relationship further. If the child becomes at some level a spectre of jail, one would expect the father to avoid the spectre or to feel uncomfortable in its presence. Moreover, in some cases of men actually jailed, it is possible that some fathers will view the child as the "cause" of their jailing and that the child, in a no less great inversion, will accept the view and feel guilt.

The serious problem posed by these possible psychic harms is not merely their impossibility of measurement but also that the harms accrue to some of the very group whom the entire enforcement process is intended to help. If there is a serious possibility of harm to any substantial number of children, a good case can be made that jailing should be avoided, even if many more children will be aided than will be hurt.

Consider a case in a very different setting. Meteorologists, I recollect, are working on techniques for seeding hurricanes with chemicals that absorb and dissipate the force of a storm. Let me pretend I know more about their progress than I do. The problem the scientists face is that, according to their calculations, of every ten seedings they try, four will succeed at least in part, five will have no effect whatever, and one will, for reasons not fully clear to them, cause the storm to accelerate and cause more extensive damage than it otherwise would. They are confident that they will save more lives and property in the successful seedings than will be lost by the occasional misfiring.

In this setting, should a seeding program be launched? One might suppose that if all possibly affected persons were polled in advance of the hurricane season, they would vote overwhelmingly in favor of seeding. And perhaps they would. But I suspect that large numbers would vote "no" on the following reasoning: "If we do nothing, we can blame fate, the gods, or whatever. If we seed, the blood is on our hands for those who die who would otherwise have lived." Not coldly rational thinking perhaps—we can as well say that the blood is on our hands for those whose lives we could have saved—but most of us have a strong sense that there is a meaningful difference between letting nature take her course and botching a rescue.

When a state jails men for nonsupport, it hurts some children in the process of aiding many others. Is jailing for child support meaningfully different from cloud seeding? The fact that the effect of some jailings is harm to the emotional well-being of children rather than something more tangible, like lives lost in a storm, would seem to make no difference if we conclude that children are actually injured. The only difference would appear to be that the nonpaying man, unlike the hurricane, is morally "bad" and needs to be punished. The weight we assign to revenge needs to be included in our calculation of the values and costs of jailing for nonsupport. I'd say it wasn't worth much.

Summary

Stack up all the dubious aspects of jailing for nonsupport: the offense is an intrafamily one with complex emotional roots; jails are debilitating institutions—they exceed rather than fit this crime; jailing in this setting is difficult, nearly impossible, to administer in an evenhanded manner; when widely used, the prospect of jailing may well affect adversely the relationship between children and the parent under an order of support, even when the parent pays with unflagging regularity. On these grounds taken together, I, were I a legislator, would vote to remove the sanction of jailing for contempt from the permissible range of techniques for enforcing support. Many others, however, would hear my complaints about jailing and admit them to be troubling, but at the same time they would also hear another small voice whispering compellingly in the background, "But jail works." It works not merely in the sense of satisfying a public need for retribution. It works by altering the very behavior toward which it is addressed, an impact so rarely demonstrated for penal sanctions that we may wish to hold on to it for its very rarity—a whooping crane in the criminal justice system.

To my view the effectiveness of jailing is largely irrelevant, if my reasons for deploring jailing are sound. Nonetheless, persons troubled by jailing but strongly moved by its success in extracting dollars should lose much of their enthusiasm for jailing if equitable alternatives exist that permit even more reliable support for children without the unfortunate aspects of jails. And I too would say that if effective alternatives exist—"less restrictive alternatives" than jailing, to borrow a term from constitutional law—it would be immoral for government to continue to rely on jailing. It would be immoral in much the same sense that it would be immoral to use a sledgehammer to swat a mosquito on a friend's back. The last chapter considers some of the possible alternatives.

Part Five

"Food in Their Little Stomachs, Boots in the Wintertime"

Eleven

Alternatives and Limits

Every Friday afternoon, Jerry Neal collects his paycheck at the manager's office in the apartment complex where he works. He cashes the check and joins others from the maintenance crew for two or three beers at Marble Lucy's. As the weekend passes, he may or may not remember the thirty dollars he promised to send the Genesee Friend of the Court. Even if he does remember, he may or may not actually buy and mail a money order. On those Saturdays when he does send it, there is little doubt that his action will have been prompted in part by the desire to avoid another jailing. Our findings suggest strongly that, if Michigan were to abandon jailing as a collection tool while retaining the current system that depends on payments by fathers after they have cashed their paychecks, the state would collect less not only from Jerry but also from many other men under orders. Smaller collections would leave thousands of Michigan children who live with one parent worse off financially than they already are.

In this chapter, we first consider various schemes for obtaining money from parents before each week's paycheck reaches their pockets. Under some schemes, money would be collected even before the couple separates. Each scheme has some advantages and drawbacks in relation to the present system. Among the plans discussed, a system of universal wage deductions seems most promising. The others, various sorts of insurance schemes with payments before separation, are enticing but unworkable.

We end the chapter—and the book—by exploring some root issues with which we might appropriately have begun the book. Why are parents the ones who are held financially responsible for the costs of raising children? We examine the source and the scope of the duties that parents have toward their children and ask whether the duties might wisely be characterized somewhat differently when a parent is living with a child than it is after several years of separation. Our inquiry leads us to speculate whether, over the decades to come, we can expect changes in the laws that hold absent parents liable for the support of their children throughout the period of their minority.

Two New Approaches

Mandatory Wage Deductions

The biggest money-collecting enterprise of governments is, of course, the collection of taxes. How do they do it? In this country, prior to World War II, the federal government simply required all persons owing taxes to pay whatever they owed at the end of each tax year, relying on a sense of duty and the fear of civil suit or criminal prosecution as the principal motivations to pay.

During World War II, the government shifted to a new system for most individual taxpayers, requiring employers to withhold an estimate of the taxes that would be due. The employed taxpayer no longer made a choice about paying. The pay-as-you-earn system has continued to the present and all states with income taxes have followed suit.

Today, the collection of child support largely resembles prewar tax collections. The payments men are to make are due weekly, not annually, but the expected motivations of duty and fear are essentially the same. Although many states authorize the use of wage assignments to collect support, and such assignments operate like a tax withholding system, assignments are rarely used in more than a small portion of cases. Moreover, in most states, including Michigan, courts may not impose a wage assignment except on a person already in default, and in all states a wage assignment ends when a person ceases to work for the employer against whom it was ordered.

Could child support collections be increased and fewer men end up singled out for penal treatment if governments instituted a system of mandatory deductions from wages that followed an employee wherever he went?

If a federal system were established under which withholding occurred from the first moment of an order and traveled with a person wherever he took work within the country, the need for much of the current enforcement system would largely disappear. To make such a system work, the federal government would need to create a national computerized system probably tied to the man's Social Security number. Employers would be required to make a check on a new employee through a Social Security office to learn whether support payments were to be withheld from his wages. Under such a system, payments would be nearly perfect except by the unemployed, the self-employed, and those able to evade the floating wage assignment by falsifying their Social Security numbers or by colluding with the employer. Jerry Neal, for all his problems, has nearly always held a job. He started on the line at General Motors. Over the years since, he has painted houses, installed mufflers at an auto-repair shop, and, in recent years, performed maintenance work at apartment houses. At least in theory, under a wage assignment scheme, Jerry would have been nearly current in his payments in 1974 instead of $18,000 in arrears. He would also have avoided the pain, and Genesee County the expense, of three long terms in jail.

An additional advantage of the assignment system is that it could be set up to allow judges to fix orders in terms of a percentage of the individual's earnings. Employers in turn would deduct the fixed percentage of the worker's earnings, the dollar amount varying over time, just as they do with Social Security. Today, in nearly all places, courts set a fixed *dollar* amount as the order size. Although courts currently have the power to modify an order to reflect changes in earnings, the procedure is cumbersome and in many places infrequently used. The consequence is that, as men's earnings and their children's living costs rise, the order remains the same.

A national compulsory deduction system would, however, have many troublesome aspects. It would be cumbersome to administer, a fountain of details inviting errors. Unlike income-tax withholding, deductions for child support would be required only for certain employees. Also, unlike income taxes, support payments would generally have to be funneled to a recipient other than the federal government, a process likely to take several weeks, even months. At varying intervals, as children reached majority, the amount to be withheld would change.

Some of these problems are not insuperable. The federal government could speed the process of passing payments through to the custodial parent (and to state welfare departments) simply by starting payments to recipients upon receiving notice that withholding had begun but without waiting until payments were actually received. Withholding ·from the noncustodial parent could continue beyond the children's majority, if that were necessary to recoup the money advanced.

Some other troubling aspects of a compulsory wage-assignment system would not be so fully remediable. Many people feel strongly about their right to decide for themselves what to do with their earnings. They would resent involuntary wage assignments for child support as much as they would resent involuntary deductions for their Master Charge bill, even though they could agree that it was reprehensible not to pay. Whether seeing it as a right or an obligation, many noncustodial parents attach importance to their weekly act of writing a support check, viewing it as an occasion to demonstrate their love for their children.

A wage-assignment system would also involve another sort of federal intrusion on matters many consider private and personal. We can appropriately worry about a federal computer system carrying detailed information about the failed marriages of millions of citizens. Indeed, the employer would invariably learn through the system if his employee was divorced or was the parent of an illegitimate child. Today, some Friends of the Court hesitate to impose wage assignments in cases in which they fear that the father is likely to be fired by an employer who either does not want the bother of making an additional deduction or thinks ill of persons who are divorced or the parents of a "bastard." In Genesee County, General Motors cooperated in full with the Friend of the Court with regard to wage assignments for its blue-collar workers but regarded a wage assignment as a blot on the record for its white-collar workers. (The Friends of the Court were not badly hobbled by this odd bit of class bias. They simply informed the defaulting white-collar worker at General Motors that if he didn't begin regular payments they had a wage assignment ready to mail in.) The problem of employer resistance could well continue under the system proposed here.

For all these reasons, it is easily understandable why only a bare majority of the Friends of the Court indicated in a mailed survey that they would favor a change in Michigan law to permit the imposition of a wage assignment at the moment the support order first takes effect and before any arrearage develops. There was no uniform enthusiasm despite the fact that nearly all the Friends of the Court are strongly committed to improving collections of support. All, I believe, favored wage assignments for men substantially in arrears, for these men had lost their just claim to control the disposition of their earnings.

In the end, however, the issue when contemplating a mandatory deduction system is not the drawbacks of such a system in the abstract. Rather, it is whether a system of automatic wage assignments would be worse than the sin-based system that we have now—the system in which we dangle before men the opportunity not to pay and, then, when men respond to the opportunity, clap them into jail.

If state and federal governments remain committed to compelling long-absent parents to support their children and remain determined to enforce the obligation aggressively, I for one would choose the compulsory-deduction system over the system now found in Michigan. It would be my preference not so much because it would almost certainly lead to even higher collections than Michigan obtains today but because of the doubts I have expressed about the justness of a jail-based system and about the atmosphere that system creates. The choice may seem easier because the new system does not yet exist. It is, however, hard to believe that a new system, however intrusive, could be as distasteful as one that depends heavily on imprisonment and the fear of imprisonment. Readers who have doubts in this regard should turn themselves in for a weekend at the nearest county jail.

Insurance Schemes

Choosing between child support squeezed out under pain of imprisonment and child support removed from wages through an all-knowing federal system may seem like a choice between death by fire and death by ice. Neither has much appeal. Are there other workable alternatives? The opposite pole of our current individualized system of support would be a purely public system of welfare benefits. Noncustodial parents would not be compelled to support their children at all (except through their payment of income taxes, as for any other taxpayers). The custodial parent, if in need, would turn to the public assistance system for support. No reimbursement would be sought from the other parent.

Such an alternative would have little appeal in this country. It would be acceptable only if Americans came to view all children as everyone's children, with parents no more responsible than anyone else for the support of their own children. It is hardly likely that Americans will ever see the children of a divorced bank president as everybody's children.

The private system and the welfare system do not, however, represent the full range of possibilities. In between there are some well-developed alternatives that may be loosely grouped under the heading "insurance," for dealing with events such as death or automobile accidents that, like divorce, are both predictable in their incidence and catastrophic in their financial consequences. Under such schemes, a pool of funds is created in advance of an event so that it is available when the event occurs. Let us consider briefly three forms of "divorce" or "marriage" insurance, each with familiar analogues, to see whether they offer promise as substitutes for, or supplements to, the current system.

Private Voluntary Insurance

People buy life insurance to provide for their families upon their deaths. Couples might similarly buy marriage insurance to provide for their children in the event of their separation. Insurance companies would offer policies to couples who wanted them, set premiums, and then if a couple separated, pay a benefit, perhaps in periodic form, to the custodial spouse. How much would be paid and for how long could all be matters of choice for individuals (or the insurers) and would affect the size of the premium. Just as is the case with term life insurance, if a sufficient number of couples bought the policy and the insured event befell only a small portion of the participating couples, premiums could be kept small in relation to the benefits paid to those families with claims.

As a scheme for dealing with the problem of inadequate income for single parents, a system of private voluntary insurance may sound appealing but it is wholly unworkable. As long as it is voluntary, how many American couples, most of whom consider themselves living at the margin, would choose to participate? Very few, and those who would participate would be likely to be those who felt their marriages in greatest risk. If the latter problem, known as "adverse selection" in the insurance business, occurred, it would mean that within the pool participating the ratio of divorcing couples to other couples would be higher than in the population as a whole and thus that premiums would have to be higher than if the pool contained a random representation of couples. The premium cost is a serious problem, but even if the premium were quite quite small—which it could not be—the problem with voluntary insurance would be that it is almost certain that those parents in greatest need would not be participants.

Private insurance carriers are unlikely to be interested in carrying divorce insurance even for well-heeled couples. They have indeed already shown little interest in suggestions by women's groups that they carry it. Apart from the fact that some carriers may regard divorce as a nasty business, they are likely to be greatly bothered by the problem of adverse selection. The problem is aggravated by the fact that the insured event is within the control of the insured couple. In some ways, such insurance would be like a property insurance policy that explicitly permitted the owner to collect even when he intentionally burned down his own plant. The very existence of marriage insurance might cause some couples to separate who would otherwise stay together. The financial security promised by such insurance would be an attractive feature for women who feel trapped in unhappy marriages, but it would be a most unattractive feature to insurers.

For all these reasons, the only place voluntary insurance would seem to have would be as self-insurance for a few farsighted, well-off people. This would hardly be insurance at all; it would be like a savings account in which a couple would simply salt away money. If they separated, the fund, grown over time, would be available to them. If they did not separate, the money would still be there for their middle years or for their retirement. Many couples have something slightly comparable to such a plan today without thinking of it in those terms, for in most states savings during a marriage will, of course, be divided between the spouses at divorce.

Compulsory Insurance Plans

Today, in nearly all states, the continued validity of a person's license to drive an automobile is conditioned on his carrying liability insurance to protect those who may be injured in an accident. Could a somewhat comparable form of child support insurance be devised as a condition to marriage? Each couple as a condition of marriage would be required to produce proof of insurance, just as they are required to provide proof of a blood test. They would then be required to continue the insurance throughout their marriage or for some fixed period of years. The premiums would be set forth in such a way as to provide adequate income after divorce for those who become single parents.

If such a system could work, consider the virtues it would have: it would reach all married couples with children, not just the few who would choose to participate in a voluntary plan; it would provide income to a custodial parent after divorce in a form (unlike welfare) that would clearly be seen as a contractual or legal right. Payments would come without the unpredictability and unreliability of periodic postseparation payments by the father. Even if some periodic payments by fathers were required after divorce, the insurance scheme would provide a valuable supplement—if it worked. But it won't.

In the first place, it would not reach the illegitimate child at all. Unless every young person had to purchase intercourse insurance or a high-priced intercourse license, there would be no period of premium payment before the insured event (a child living with a single parent) would have occurred.

Even assuming that every married couple participated, with benefits paid only to custodial parents after divorce, the premiums would have to be very high. There are simply a lot of minor children of divorced persons, in an era in which one out of every four or five couples with minor children divorce before the children reach their majority. To be able to pay three thousand dollars a year to each divorced parent with custody of one child, forty-eight hundred dollars to each parent with two children, and six thousand dollars to each parent with three or more, all married couples in the country would have to pay premiums of at least $450 a year throughout their marriage, even after they reached their fifties. To most American families, $450 will seem a lot of money. And forty-eight hundred dollars for a woman with two children would still leave her living in poverty.

Considerations of fairness might well force the premiums even higher. Legislatures might consider it inequitable to require insurance to be carried by couples who had no children, couples in which the woman was beyond childbearing age, and couples whose children had all reached their majority. Requiring older couples to pay for insurance would be like requiring a person to continue to pay automobile insurance after he had given up driving. If the pool of required contributors were limited to younger married couples who had a minor child, premiums for those included in the plan would have to be raised substantially higher—doubled or tripled perhaps.

The problem with compulsory insurance lies not only in the size of premiums but also in their collection. What do we do to the couple who cannot or will not pay the premium? Denying the right to marry to those who cannot afford to pay would surely violate the Constitution.[1] Jailing after marriage those later refusing to pay would pose many of the same problems of jailing for nonpayment after divorce. Indeed jailing during marriage may seem even more dubious, if the couple is happily united, living with children, confident in their capacity to hold the marriage together. Collections could, of course, be made through payroll deductions in the manner of the mandatory wage assignment

system discussed above. If they were, the system would closely resemble an expansion of the Social Security system, an idea to which we
now turn.

Expanding the Social Security System

Yet another form of insurance that is familiar to all of us is the public
insurance known as Social Security. Today, for the overwhelming
majority of workers in this country and their dependents, the Social
Security system provides benefits to those who reach a certain age or
become disabled, as well as to the survivors of those who die. The
benefit scheme, evolving since its creation forty years ago, is extremely
complex. The benefits paid depend upon the length of time a worker
has made payments prior to the occurrence of the insured event and
upon his earnings during the period he was making payments. Funds
for the benefits are obtained by wage deductions from employees
matched by an equal contribution from employers. Today, in 1978, the
rate is 6.05 percent of the employee's wages, with an additional 6.05
percent paid by the employer.

It would be possible to add the event of becoming a single parent to
the list of covered incidents. Since "single-parentness" is not an event
likely to befall workers over a certain age, contributions might not be
required from workers over, say, the age of fifty.

If the contribution rate for both employers and employees were to be
substantially raised, a sufficient amount of money could be obtained to
pay benefits approximately equal to those obtained through the compulsory insurance scheme discussed above, although pegged in some
way to the parents' actual level of contributions.

Such a scheme would have several attractive attributes. For those
covered, the problem of collecting premiums is largely cured: if a person works, he or she makes payments. The current scheme of individual collections after divorce could be largely scrapped, depending
on the level of support one wished to assure. Moreover, the current
welfare system could be dramatically cut back. Workers whose children today receive payments through the AFDC system would support
their children instead through Social Security benefits. In turn, payments through the Social Security system would be largely free of the
stigma attached to the receipt of welfare. They would be free for what
most Americans would consider the right reason: that is, the children
would be supported in a manner that bore a relation to actual contributions from the parents.

Such a scheme, however, would not reach all children living with single parents. At the psychological heart of the current Social Security system is the notion that it provides benefits only to those who have made contributions over a certain period. Most illegitimate children whose parents do not live together and a significant portion of children of divorce have young parents neither of whom has long participated in the labor force and neither of whom would today be eligible for full benefits on becoming disabled. Indeed many illegitimate children have parents who have never participated in the labor force at all. While a very short period of contributions might be justified on the ground that, with this form of covered event (unlike death, disability, or old age), the probability is high that one or both parents will have many more years as contributors to the fund, it would do violence to the central concept of Social Security that many people have by providing benefits in some cases in which neither parent has made any contribution.

Much more fundamental objections can be raised to the scheme than that it does not reach everyone. Many feel the Social Security system is already overburdened. Congress has recently increased both the rate of the tax and the income levels up to which the taxes are paid. Workers feel the cost of the system when it reduces their take-home pay. They would be likely to acknowledge that the additional deduction was worth it to them only if they perceived themselves as one of those significantly at risk of needing the benefits. Many workers would readily admit the risk of death, disability, and old age but would not consider themselves at all likely to become a parent of a child living with a single parent. They would object to such an alteration of the Social Security system just as they would object to the mandatory "divorce insurance" scheme we discussed earlier. The objectors would include not merely older couples but also the millions of young single people who either abstain altogether from sexual intercourse or, if they engage in it, invariably use reliable contraceptive devices.

In addition, death, old age, and disability are seen by most Americans as largely free of fault. Though there are exceptions, people do not generally die or cripple themselves either on purpose or in ways that make us think ill of them. Divorce is different. To many, it has the flavor of sin or at least of insufficient resolve to live up to a solemn commitment. Even more frequently viewed as sinful is the conception of a child out of wedlock by a woman not living with the father of the child. The compulsory system I suggest would require some people to support others they view as irresponsible. Indeed they would see the system as encouraging people to act irresponsibly.

If the Social Security system were expanded to insure against the event of single parenthood, the entire system might thus become tainted, whereas one of its signal features in this country has been that its recipients have always been permitted to feel that they were receiving payments that they deserved for reasons that they need not feel badly about. This feature is one about which we may justly feel ambivalence—it is related to the tendency to distinguish between the "worthy" and the "unworthy" poor—but it is nonetheless a feature of American civilization that policy-makers and citizens accept. And for these reasons, and the costs, it is probable that Congress would refuse to expand the Social Security system to include single parents.

Conclusion

We have looked at many different schemes to assure adequate support for children living with a single parent. Some are appealing but all have problems. If we try to collect from the noncustodial parent after separation, we find that we either must use distasteful means, such as the threat of jail, or cumbersome ones, such as universal and mandatory wage assignments. Insurance schemes to collect from parents before the insured event have no fewer administrative problems and suffer from the additional difficulty of forcing us to define the persons who are going to be compelled to make payments into a fund whether or not they receive any return. I personally am drawn to the mandatory wage-assignment idea because it spares us the politically touchy task of defining who, besides already separated parents, shall contribute while at the same time offering an opportunity largely to eliminate the need to rely on jail as an instrument of enforcement. Moreover, unlike the various pay-in-advance insurance schemes, the wage-assignment system retains whatever psychological benefit may accrue to the parents and to the child from knowing that the absent parent is making current and substantial financial contributions for the child.

There is another alternative to the heavy use of jail or to mandatory wage assignments. Weaker than either, but politically feasible, it is simply for states to create efficient full-time collection and enforcement offices, comparable to Friends of the Court, with courts empowered to use sentences to jail but rarely actually doing so. Remember that in many of our twenty-eight counties the judges jailed few people, but the full-time agencies in each still collected vastly more than Dane County, Wisconsin. To those to whom jail is repugnant or at least distasteful, this is a possible middle ground that would almost certainly lead to much higher collections in the many places where mothers not receiving welfare are now left to the same inadequate private remedies available in Dane.[2]

Even if one of the more audacious schemes were adopted, however, one fundamental limit needs to be kept in mind. Like the current system, neither mandatory wage assignments nor any of the insurance schemes alone will provide an income that will permit custodial parents and children to survive at anywhere near the standard of living they maintained when the family was intact. Recall that child support for a parent taking care of two children is typically set at 33 percent of the noncustodial parent's net earnings, but that the custodial parent needs around 80 percent of the family's former total income to maintain the prior standard of living. We have also seen that it is not feasible to demand dramatically higher percentages of earnings to be paid by the noncustodial parent. While insurance schemes could be tailored to provide higher benefits simply by raising the premiums, premiums high enough to assure a parent of young children a standard of living equal to what he or she had before would be considered prohibitively expensive. Even under the Social Security system today, the goal for the disabled or the aged is to meet 60 percent, not 100 percent, of their prior level of earnings.

Thus, regardless of the system devised, custodians of small children must either adjust to a significant decline in income or, as we have discussed much earlier, find either high-paying work or a new spouse. None of these choices may seem palatable, but they will continue to be the ones that have to be made. Public officials worried about the financial plight of parents, especially the plight of mothers with young children, will need to devote as much attention to improving employment opportunities for women—and for the population generally—as they do to finding new ways to collect child support. And even if they succeed, they will not cure the dilemma for many single parents of choosing between full-time work and full-time parenting. Remember that nearly 60 percent of the mothers in our Genesee sample had at least one child under three at the point of separation.

The Future of Parental Obligations of Support

Implicit in every plan for the support of children that we have discussed is the assumption that it is appropriate to charge absent parents with all or part of the costs of providing for their children. Even in the insurance schemes, our goal was to tailor the plan to require contributions only from persons who might become the absent parent of a minor child. We were in short looking for systems different from public welfare systems that are paid for by all taxpayers out of general tax revenues.

Most readers have probably been comfortable with our assumptions, but some of the findings of our study may suggest that something is amiss. We have found that most absent parents, if pushed, will pay support after divorce but, if left alone, will eventually stop. Neither affection nor concern for their children's well-being will propel them to pay to the level of their capacities.

What do these findings tell us?

When millions of Americans violated the prohibition laws it suggested (or confirmed) not merely that the laws were unworkable but also that most people did not view the use of alcohol as immoral. The use of marijuana seems similarly to be losing its odor of sinfulness.

Does the widespread disobedience of orders of support suggest that the majority of American noncustodial parents reject the notion that they are morally responsible for contributing to their children's support? I greatly doubt it. Stated so abstractly, my guess is that nearly all Americans would affirm a belief in the obligation of parents to support their children until majority. Many liberals criticized the recent federal legislation pressing the states toward more vigorous enforcement of support in welfare cases, but none, so far as I can find, questioned the justness of requiring parents who can afford it to contribute to their children's support.

But if belief in the obligation is so nearly universal, how should we view equally widespread failure to pay? Two possible ways suggest themselves, each with different implications for public policy. One is that the beliefs of nearly everyone about obligations to support are out of kilter with the psychological demands of the postdivorce period and that, if we examined our beliefs more closely, we would find that we have principled grounds on which to be queasy about imposing long-term obligations of support on noncustodial parents. If this suggestion is sound, it invites a reconsideration of the current laws obliging parents to pay support—or at least invites some reconsideration of their scope.

The other view of nonpayment is simply that, although the imposition of the obligation is still fully justified, nonpayment flows from human frailties that must be combatted in order to be overcome. Lots of people engage in shoplifting from time to time, but few would conclude that we should remove the sanctions for doing so. If the problem is one of human weakness, it reduces the question of relying on court-ordered child support to practical questions of the comparative effectiveness of other approaches that might be taken to insure adequate income for children. It similarly leaves the question of how to enforce court-ordered support, if that route is chosen, to decisions about what is practical and to the morality of particular techniques. Which of these views seems more persuasive depends in substantial part on one's view of the nature of the obligation to support.

Where does the idea that parents can appropriately be held liable for their children come from? Why is it appropriate to bill an absent parent for the costs of raising a child? To begin with, someone must care for babies. Left alone, they will starve or freeze. No one rationally considers children morally lax for failing to feed or clothe themselves. The observation that someone must provide support for children, however, does not necessarily lead to a conclusion that it is their parents who must do so. We could expect tasks to be shared by a large group of relations. After parents separate, we could send part of the bill for support to next-door neighbors or the children's aunts and uncles. Why are parents in a special position? In some regards, the question may seem too obvious even to ask. Parents have always been the ones who took care of their children. The notion is so deeply imbedded in our sensibilities that we may respond to the question with the tautology that they must support the children because the children are "theirs," even though, in a different society, with a different set of norms, we might accept a view that the children belong to the tribe and everyone shares equal responsibility for them.

Enforcing support against absent parents is not a uniquely American phenomenon. So far as I can find, every European nation requires that absent parents make financial contributions for the support of their children. At least as of a few years ago, for example, the Soviet Union not only imposed an obligation of support but fixed the obligation at essentially the same percentage of the absent parent's income and for essentially the same duration as we have reported for Genesee County, Michigan.[3]

When we strive to justify the liability of parents in principled terms, and not by merely adverting to custom, we can start by reasoning that the parents should be responsible because they "caused" the child to come into existence. Moreover they did so by a volitional act (intercourse) known to each to entail a child as a possible consequence, and each had the capacity to avoid the act if he or she had wished. Such reasoning provides a basis for liability derived from reasoning familiar to us from the law of torts, under which we hold people financially responsible for the consequences of automobile or other accidents caused by their carelessness or for the consequences of harms intentionally inflicted on others.

For married couples, an alternative basis for liability may be offered from the law of contracts. As traditionally portrayed, husbands agree, upon getting married, to earn money and wives agree to bear and raise children and take care of the home. This ancient view, however repugnant to many women today, still adequately captures the unspoken beliefs of many married "partners" about their obligations.

These arguments in the language of tort and contract are inviting. They are the two primary modes of reasoning in Anglo-American law when courts advance principled grounds for compelling one person to make payments to another. They capture well the responses I receive when I ask people about their personal view of the source of parents' obligations of support. They are, nevertheless, only starting points for defining liabilities. The contract arguments are especially brittle—largely a fiction to the extent that we would try to apply them to a couple after they have separated. Young people do not in fact hammer out bargains between themselves as they enter into marriage. They often harbor loosely formed expectations about the later conduct of the other that each is entitled to rely upon, but they surely almost never discuss, let alone agree upon, what will happen if they divorce after having children. What they do at most is to step into a contract whose terms have been prescribed by the state; and it is precisely the justifiability of the state's imposing those terms that we are here throwing open to question.

The alternative ground for liability—simply the causal link between the parent and child—rests on no such fictive assumptions about the expectations of the parties. Indeed, it is a particularly appealing way of thinking about support responsibilities today, both because the contract arguments cannot reach the many children born outside of marriage (or marriage-like relationships), and because the availability of contraception and abortion makes more reasonable the emphasis in tort argument on the volitional act that produced the child.

At the same time, we need to recognize that the arguments in terms of causation do not compel a just government to impose liability. Rather they provide a justification resting on principle for a result— parental liability—if we choose to impose it—a way of distinguishing parents from taxpayers generally and from everyone else in the world around the child.

The tort arguments do not compel governments to impose liability on parents any more than the recognition that drivers cause automobile accidents requires that drivers be held personally liable. Governments can justly create no-fault schemes for accidents if they decide such schemes are wiser or more equitable than personal liability systems. Moreover, if we look to the laws regarding compelled financial support within families that have existed over time in this country, we will discover that there is no set of immutable principles—tort or otherwise—that have guided the selection of persons held liable. Rather, support laws derive from judgments of the majority about relationships that are felt as significant at a particular moment in history and that are based in large part on actual living arrangements and proximity. The laws regarding support that have existed in this country over the last century and the changes in such laws over time may indeed cause us to think afresh about the appropriateness of holding liable for support a parent who, though doubtless the "cause" of a child, has not lived with the child for many years.

Parents of minor children are not the only relatives upon whom American governments have placed formal obligations of support. At various times, in various states, grandparents and siblings both of persons receiving welfare benefits and of persons held in public institutions (particularly for the mentally ill and retarded) have also been compelled to reimburse the state for part of the state's costs.[4] So likewise, in some states, children who have reached their majority have been required to contribute to the welfare and institutional costs of their parents and even their grandparents. Holding a person liable for the public support of his brothers and sisters can be justified neither by reasoning in terms of causation nor by reasoning in terms of contract. We could, of course, on these grounds dismiss the sibling support laws as unjust. But at the time these laws were originally passed, many of them in the nineteenth century, patterns of living in which grandparents and siblings lived in the same town and shared a more general sense of responsibility for others in their family were more common than today—or at least a nostalgic recollection of such patterns was fresher in the public mind.

Today, when patterns of residence have changed and the nuclear family of parent or parents and minor children is generally considered the one critical unit, the old laws imposing grandparent and sibling liability seem oddly anachronistic, like Sunday-closing laws or laws prohibiting horseless carriages on city streets. And in fact, many states with such laws have repealed them in recent years during a period when legislators have been no less concerned about the public costs of the welfare system than they were when the laws were originally adopted.[5]

The existence of laws imposing liability on one sibling for another or on a grandchild for his grandparent illustrates the fact that liability has not always turned on notions of contract or causal tie. On the other hand, they do not demonstrate the opposite: that liability has not at least been unvarying when the parental link did exist. There have, however, been eras when even parents have not in fact been held liable for the support of their minor children. For example, until well into the nineteenth century in this country, many states did not hold the father of an illegitimate child liable for the support of his child, despite the fact that there were ample British antecedents for doing so. Indeed, until the United States Supreme Court held their laws unconstitutional a few years ago,[6] Texas and two other American states still denied illegitimate children support from their fathers. Laws in most states had changed not, to be sure, because the causal link had changed, but because there had been changes in public attitudes. Most Americans had come to believe that it was inappropriate to visit the "sins of the father" on innocent children and thus inappropriate to continue to treat illegitimate children less favorably than legitimate children. When attitudes change, the causal link provides a justification for changing the law but the link alone has not always been seen as requiring liability.

Drawing lessons from laws as discredited as those that denied support to illegitimate children is a hazardous enterprise, but I will attempt it anyway. The point is that, principles aside, laws concerning the family evolve over time to ratify those relationships perceived as significant or as "normal." When support laws have changed to remove liability—for example, the liability of grandparent or sibling—the change comes because we no longer perceive the relatives as so significantly involved with each other as to justify the imposition of liability.

How does all this bear on the issue of the liability of parents for their minor children today? Whether one relies on causation or custom, no relationship in our society seems more intrinsically significant than this one. The human species has survived not because laws have required parents to be the ones to care for children but because of much deeper drives. The mother of the newborn has the physical capacity to provide sustenance for the infant and throughout human history in almost all cultures has provided psychic supports as well. Fathers, though physically indispensable only for the purposes of conception, have throughout recorded history formed dwelling units with the woman and child—attracted by sexual and economic links to the woman, and perhaps to the child as well. The economic link has varied among cultures, often resting on a strict division of labor, sometimes on jointly shared tasks, but generally serving the function of leaving the partners better off than if they were alone, as well as ensuring the continuation of the species. Although in many societies the core unit has included other relatives in addition to the mother and father, it has nearly always included, as a starting point, the mother, the father, and their children. Indeed, the very trend in this country that has led to the exclusion of other relatives from the common conception of the core unit—and has led in most states to the repeal of the financial liability of grandparents—reinforces the image of the parent-child relationship as the one truly significant relationship for the child.

In the mythic view, the nuclear family of mother, father, and child lives together contentedly under one roof. Each parent plays an important role in the raising of the child. Nothing could be more elemental in our society than the expectation that the parents will assume responsibility for the child's financial support—or more reasonable than the income-tax laws that provide an exemption for dependents, a provision applied with the fewest limitations and proof requirements when the person claiming an exemption is the parent of a minor child living with the child. But what of the relation of a child to a parent after divorce and long after the parent has ceased to live with the child? What then of laws imposing liability on the absent parent? It is perhaps improbable that we will ever conclude that the fact of separation makes a difference, but let us look at the changes that occur over time, after separation, in the relationship of parent to child and see whether they suggest a change in the law.

For some period after separation, varying widely from family to family, the emotional life of all family members is likely to remain closely bound up in each other, while each passes through a period of severe emotional strain. Each adult is likely to pass through a stage remarkably similar to bereavement upon death.

The period after separation is also one of great difficulty for children, a time of confusion, loneliness, and depression. It is common for children to feel that they caused their father to leave them and to suffer feelings of guilt and inadequacy. Visits by the noncustodial parent may help persuade the child that he or she is loved and valued. During this period, payments of support may provide critical relief from the exigencies with which the woman and the children are suddenly faced. For children old enough to be aware, payments may also have important symbolic value—the payments confirm that they are worthy in the eyes of a person of central importance to them.

As time passes—and typically not that much time—the partners reorient themselves to life without each other. Some noncustodial fathers continue to see their children almost daily and continue a major role in decisions about their lives. More commonly, visits taper off in frequency. They do so for varying reasons, and they often have an uneasy quality for both parent and child—staged events at the parent's new apartment or the park or the zoo. Even parents determined to be "reasonable" discover that the arrangements for visits cause tensions; the children themselves find that visits disrupt their play with neighborhood friends, and fathers sense the children's uneasiness. As time passes, more and more of the fathers no longer live in the same town as the mother. Either the father or the children will have moved away.[7]

If they had not done so before the divorce, each partner is soon likely to develop new sexual and romantic alliances. Within a year after divorce, most divorced women, even if they have not remarried, have developed regular dating relations with men. The vast bulk of parents of both sexes will remarry.

The remarriage of either parent typically has important psychological content for all the parties. For many couples, it probably marks more effectively than the divorce itself the end of the relationship between them. When the woman has custody of the children and she remarries, she is likely, according to Goode, to wish that her first husband would reduce the number of his visits with the children. While her reasons may be selfish (and not flow from an altered belief about the impact of visits on the children), her attitude may nonetheless be communicated to the children. Her new husband, as a stepparent, stands in a most ambiguous position in our society, but, as a general proposition, the children are likely to turn more and more to him for decisions that affect their lives. The mother will rely on the stepfather for aid in discipline and the stepfather will bring his paycheck home to all of them. He will become the one to enjoy the pedestrian pleasures of life at home—teaching his new "daughter" to ride her two-wheeler, playing catch before supper with his new "son," hearing at the supper table about a loose tooth or a new friend in the neighborhood. And their "real" father will know or sense what he is missing.

The father's remarriage may have no less significant consequences for him and for his children from his first marriage. He now has a new family. If his new wife has children from a previous alliance or if she and he have a new child, he will likely feel the baby's needs more pressingly than the needs of the children from his first marriage. If he now has a relationship that is satisfying, he may find himself thinking less and less about his earlier marriage and the children of that marriage.

The actual payments of child support under the current system of long-term obligations suggest that there are indeed changes of feelings over time. The Wisconsin study by Kenneth Eckhardt found that in a county in which enforcement was haphazard most men paid some or all of what was due in the first year after divorce, but over 70 percent were paying nothing whatever by the seventh year. In our own study, we found that Washtenaw County, with a modest level of enforcement, could sustain over time at least a majority of men making some or all payments, but that within a few years the number of men making no payment rose from about a sixth of the men to more than a third. In Genesee County we found that the men, as a whole, pay better over time. Since it is somewhat unlikely that the affection of Genesee men increases with time or that they are simply more affectionate toward their children, it is probable that the Genesee experience simply indicates that for most men insistent prodding can overcome the resistances that accumulate with the passage of time.

To my reading, the suggestion from this review of the period after divorce is that, at some indeterminate point in that period, many non-custodial parents probably lose a psychological sense that they have a moral obligation to contribute to the support of their children, apart from an obligation to obey a court order whatever it provides. This loss of feeling does not come from a crass or all-too-convenient disregard of obvious duties but is rather the inevitable product of the altered position of their lives and the lives of their children and their former wives. At some unconscious level they come to feel that child support is a form of taxation without representation. They would still say that they "love" their children, but the quality of the feeling would not be the same as it had been before separation.

There has been much discussion in recent years of the proposition that, from the perspective of a child, a blood tie is far less important than a tie to an adult or adults fulfilling the role of the "psychological parent." In a widely read book, Joseph Goldstein, Anna Freud, and Albert Solnit have spoken of the psychological parent as a person who "on a continuous, day-to-day basis, through interaction, companionship, interplay, and mutuality, fulfills the child's psychological needs for a parent, as well as the child's physical needs."[8] Payments by the absent parent can help meet a child's physical needs, but after divorce the absent parent typically cannot sustain the more intimate aspects of the psychological relationship; according to Goldstein and the others, the child's sense of attachment to that parent will necessarily alter over time.

It is possible that the absent parent, although he or she as an adult is in a far different position than that of a child, must also necessarily undergo a comparable loss of attachment; in some sense, the child ceases to be the parent's "psychological child." The timing and the degree of detachment are likely to vary widely among parents. We have a hint of the process in our own study, where we know that the men married for the shortest periods before separation—those separated within a year of marriage—pay significantly less well over the lives of their orders than do other men, even after controlling for men's ages and earnings at divorce.

The forces that pull a divorced father into a different orbit from that of his first family are comparable in a way to those that have come to exclude grandparents from an inner core of most families. The father and the grandparents are special people, but they are in the end just visitors.

The increasing incidence of divorce also seems likely to add to the attenuation of ties between noncustodial parents and their children. The rate of divorce has been climbing annually—up 80 percent between 1960 and 1972—and, though it must level off, it is almost certain to remain high. The higher it becomes, the more "normal" the single-parent unit becomes, a force in itself toward encouraging divorce and toward permitting noncustodial parents to view the units they have left behind as complete in themselves.

What do we make of this somewhat bleak portrait of the expectable relation between the long-absent parent and his or her child? For purposes of decisions about legal obligations, states could ignore it and fall back on the causal tie that will always persist as a reason for retaining current laws. Or, as they have done in the case of grandparents, states could yield to the trend by altering in some ways the laws of support, for example, by reducing the number of years an absent parent could be held liable.

Of course, the impetus is powerful to ignore any decline in absent parents' feelings of ties. The obvious effect of any reduction in one parent's liability is to increase the financial burden on the other. Even if most mothers remarry, some will not, and those who do not are generally unable, on their own income, to maintain even close to the family's preseparation standard of living.

For those divorced mothers who receive public assistance, a reduction in liability would mean that the government would forego an opportunity to recoup some of its costs. It is likely to be many decades before taxpayers will view absent parents, however detached the parents may come to feel about their children, as no more responsible for their children's welfare than the public is generally. Moreover, some may view it as important for other than financial reasons to resist policies that recognize a deterioration of relations between absent parents and their children. They would attach importance to fostering a continued active involvement between parent and child and would view compulsory support payments as a way of encouraging such involvement on the part of the absent parent. It would in fact be valuable to learn whether, in states (or counties) that are especially successful in collecting support, absent parents and their children maintain more regular and healthy contact.

All these factors make a change in the law unlikely. On the other hand, it remains the case—as illustrated by the repeal of the liability laws for relatives—that laws regarding support do change over time and that, on occasion, relatives are recognized as no longer having the same central position we once thought them to have. It is at least conceivable that at some distant point in the future we will come to a rather different view of the family than we have today. The family will be seen as whatever group lives together at a common moment in time and views itself as family. During a child's upbringing, he may stay continually with his father, while two or three mother figures pass through the household. That is not to say that children will be better off than they are today. That is just the way it will be. In this setting, child support payments that continue to be made fourteen years after a marriage has broken up and ten years after each parent has remarried and moved to a different town, may seem an anachronism.

How might the law of child support evolve to reflect a different vision of the relationship between the absent parent and the child?

A first step would apply only in those places in which an agency enforces support obligations without awaiting complaints from the custodial parent. The success in collections of the Michigan counties with such "self-starting" systems may well encourage other states to set up comparable systems. The considerations advanced in this chapter suggest, however, that any new laws might be wisely framed to permit enforcement to operate on a self-starting basis for only a few years after separation. After a few years, agencies would enforce orders only upon complaint from the custodial parent. If the noncustodial parent would prefer not to pay and the custodial parent has become indifferent, restraint by the enforcing agency will permit the divorced couple peaceably to end their relationship together. To be sure, the custodial parent's decision not to seek enforcement may reduce the total income available to the child, and it is for the child's benefit that these payments are made. But in almost every other regard we permit the custodial parent to decide what resources will be made available to the child, and that reasoning should lead us to a similar result here.

For welfare cases there are special problems. Shifting after a few years to enforcement in these cases only upon the mother's complaint will not be a satisfactory way to mark the changes that have occurred in the relationships within the family, because the government, not the custodial parent, keeps whatever money the other parent pays. The question for Congress and the state legislatures is whether they too should recognize the likely effective end of relationships and resist enforcement after a few years.

It is unlikely that legislatures will be so self-denying, at least so long as support collections are made available to the nonwelfare parents who want them. Thus, let me suggest a final step in the metamorphosis that would apply to everyone. The year is 2025 and the law provides: (1) that courts are permitted to enter orders of support in divorce or paternity actions but that these orders are legally enforceable for only three years after separation or for a period equal to half the length of time the man and woman resided together, whichever is longer;* (2)

---

*An initially inviting alternative to a fixed number of years of liability after divorce would be a system providing for an automatic reduction or termination of the support order upon the remarriage of either party, whenever it occurs. The alternative is inviting because it would link a change in liability directly to a likely significant alteration in either the custodial parent's needs (in the case of her remarriage) or in the man's likely costs of living (in the case of his remarriage), as well as to the likely changes in the father's perceptions of his primary duties. Rules of liability in terms of marital status are, however, likely to alter both parties' decisions about remarriage and to produce subterfuge and misery—causing men to remarry precipitously and vindictively to escape or reduce liability and causing women to live out of wedlock to avoid the decline in income. At least until recently, large numbers of older widows and widowers apparently lived together in slightly uncomfortable sin without remarrying because marriage would have reduced their total income from Social Security benefits when one of them was receiving benefits as the widow or widower of another person. Because of impact on remarriage, Congress that this change would be balanced by a comparable change in the law to make visitation by the noncustodial parent enforceable through the courts only for the same period; and finally (3) that after three years, or half the length of the relation, payments by the noncustodial parent would be voluntary and visits by the noncustodial parent would be entirely within the discretion of the custodial parent. After the initial period, that is, the noncustodial parent would be free to contribute to the child's support and free to visit, if invited, but would have no enforceable rights in or duties to the child. The state, as it does with most family matters, would return to the position of neutrality, and the parents themselves would arrange the terms of any continuing relation they wished to have.

If such a change in the law were to occur, it would parallel a development taking place in some states today with regard to alimony paid after divorce for the support of a spouse. In a declining number of states, "innocent" divorced wives remain entitled to permanent partial support so long as they remain single. In many states today, however, court-decreed alimony has largely disappeared. In some, an intermediate step, "rehabilitative" alimony, is apparently becoming somewhat common: payments are agreed upon or ordered to be made for a few years to permit a woman to return to school or at least to help meet her expenses in a period of transition to life on her own. Child support might similarly come to be viewed as transitional, with the overt recognition that after some period the noncustodial parent might well cease to have much contact with his children.

How does this vision of the year 2025 strike you? Men and women bounce in and out of each other's lives like bumper cars at a carnival, children riding always with at least one of their parents but rarely with both. The children indeed scarcely know one parent and live in near poverty with the other. Is that the picture I've painted?

That is not my own vision. Mine is of many coexisting forms of family life. Just as today, most children will spend their childhood in a family dwelling that includes both parents. In some cases, when parents divorce, children will live part of each week or each year with each parent and no child support will change hands. Other children will live with one parent only but maintain close contact with the other, who

---

changed the law, as of January 1979, to permit remarriage without a reduction in benefits. Occasionally rules turning on voluntary changes of status are unavoidable, but they nearly always produce unwanted side effects: a bonus or preference for any marital state, advantages for marrying or not marrying, necessarily create penalties for other states.

will in a significant portion of cases make financial contributions to the former spouse. Finally, many others will live with one parent only and after a while receive little or no money from the other parent. It is these last children, of course, about whom we are concerned.

These children would generally be worse off financially under the change in law forecast here than they would be under a system in which absent parents continued to pay if ordered to do so. But other aspects of the world will be different in my version of 2025. Placement of children with one parent on the basis of the parent's sex will have disappeared both as a matter of law and as a matter of social expectation. Moreover, young people of each sex will be equally free to participate in the labor market, and jobs at decent levels of pay will be available to persons returning to the labor force. There would no longer be "women's jobs" into which women were funneled at lower wages.

If all these changes were to occur, the worst financial exigencies of the postdivorce period would be relieved for custodial parents. And with these changes, we could revel in the principal value of the termination of liability: it would remove government from coercive involvement in people's lives. Americans are quick to use the power of government to suppress undesired behavior. We have seen in this book that suppression can work. But we have also seen its other faces: the vast discretion inevitably vested in enforcers, the alcoholics jailed over and over again, the arrogance of judges. And even if we shifted to a more bloodless, automated system of wage deductions, we are still fixing for men and women the terms of their relationship well after their lives have settled into other patterns. I'd prefer a world in which, even after separation, adults worked out the terms of their own relations just as we permit them to do in nearly all matters during the period they live together.

Jerry Neal has reached his middle forties. His children from his marriage to Dolores are grown. His support order now covers only the youngest of the five children, and she will soon reach eighteen. Two of his other children are married and have begun families of their own. One of them, Pearl, married a few years ago at sixteen, a year younger than Dolores was when she married Jerry. Pearl now has a son of her own. Jerry saw his children rarely as they grew up. He has never met his grandson.

Free after sixteen years of a court obligation, Jerry may well soon become subject to a new order, for his marriage to his third wife, Judy, has not worked well. Their child, Jerry, Jr., is now over two. Jerry was in jail when little Jerry was born. If Jerry and Judy divorce, Jerry will begin at the beginning again, for Jerry, Jr., will need "food in his little stomach" and "boots in the wintertime." Welfare payments will meet Judy's needs only slightly more adequately in 1979 than they met Dolores's in 1965.

Will Jerry's payment record be any different this time than it was before? Will the fact that there is only one child and hence a smaller order, or the fact that Jerry will be more than fifteen years older than he was when Dolores divorced him, make a difference? What will be the effect of him of his three jailings? Judy thought the jailings had an effect. When I chatted with her one afternoon, she noted that Jerry, who was working in another town forty miles away, was sending very little of his paycheck to her, even though he was making regular payments to the Friend of the Court. She commented with a shrug, "He knows that if he don't pay them, he'll go to jail."

And for Judy, will her life be any different from Dolores's? Her house was small and in bad repair. As I sat talking to her, she was worried that she was going to have to move to someplace even worse because of a rise in rent. Will she feel as angry as Dolores and feed information to the Friend of the Court to keep Jerry in jail, off and on, for another couple of decades?

What will the rest of us have to show for thirty-five years of overseeing Jerry's life?

Mulling these questions as I sat with Judy Neal at her kitchen table, I watched Jerry, Jr., then eighteen months, toddle about, chewing, pointing, bumping around. He picked up a fishing pole that had been leaning against the wall and brushed against his mother. "Boys," she said, patiently removing it from his hands. "Boys. Heaven help us."

Yes, indeed. Boys and girls. Men and women. Fathers and mothers. Heaven help us.

Methodological
Appendix

Terry K. Adams

Introduction

In the period from 1972 to 1975 during which data were collected for this study, various techniques and data sources were used to accumulate eleven primary and six derivative datasets. Our work places heavy reliance on five of these primary datasets and five of the derivative ones. In this appendix we describe, for each dataset: the sampling universe, the sampling technique, our evaluation of the representativeness of the sample, and the contents of the final dataset. For those datasets not discussed extensively in the text, we also include a brief description of the results of our analyses.

The samples on which we placed heaviest reliance were selected from lists of fathers sentenced to jail in a particular time period and from lists of support orders alive in a particular time period. For example, in Genesee County, we selected from a list of persons sentenced to jail in 1969 and 1970, and from a list of orders alive in 1969 and 1970. We could have employed an alternative method used by Kenneth Eckhardt.[1] Eckhardt selected from among all orders entered in a particular period and followed them for several years. (We did use this method in some of our secondary samples.) Because our focus was on the use of jail as an enforcement technique, we needed a rather large list of jailed fathers, which as a practical matter was not available for all orders entered in a particular year. More important, we wanted to have a period of time after the jailing in which to measure payment and other responses. Our desire to minimize the impact of historical changes in judicial and Friend of the Court behavior dictated that we look at jailings occurring within a limited time period.

As initially conceived, the random samples of orders were intended primarily as comparison groups for the jailed men. Thus, once it was decided to sample from among fathers jailed in a particular time period, the obvious comparison group was all fathers subject to an active order during that same time period—these were all the men who *could* have ended up in jail during that period for nonpayment of support, the men whose payments the enforcement officers were then scrutinizing. Cases where the order was not "active" (that is, had no *new* obligation accruing each week or month) were excluding from both the jailing and random samples. These sampling frames gave us a sample of cases with orders and enforcement histories dating from as early as 1950. This variety in dates poses some difficulty in comparing incomes and order sizes among our cases but has the advantage of allowing us to see historical, "generational" changes in enforcement and payment patterns.

All of our random samples were drawn on a systematic basis. Starting with a list of names of fathers under orders, arranged alphabetically or chronologically (by order date), we calculated the sampling fraction by dividing the number of cases in the list by the final sample size desired (plus a margin for unlocatable and inappropriate cases). We worked through the list at a constant interval (the inverse of the sampling fraction) from a randomly selected point (less than the interval). If we underestimated the number of unusable cases, we supplemented with an entirely new sample. This procedure is the equivalent of a purely random sample unless there is some periodicity in the ordering of the names on the list which corresponds with the sampling interval. There is no reason whatever to believe that our alphabetical or chronological lists of cases have *any* periodicity, much less a fifteen- or twenty-case period. We are confident that every valid case on our lists had an equal chance of being in its relevant sample, and that the samples are therefore, by definition, random.

Two computer software packages developed at the University of Michigan were used to create and analyze the computer-readable datasets—MIDAS[2] and OSIRIS.[3] Both packages are designed for easy use by social scientists in that they readily accommodate the creation and use of "categorical" variables (those in which the numbers designating a response have no real quantitative meaning, e.g., the variable "race" where "1" represents blacks and "2" represents whites) and reduce the amount of "programming" that must be done by a user to filling in a few numbers and choosing among a few options on a dozen or so standardized control cards associated with each data management or analysis package.

Our analysis of the data relied upon five principal techniques—univariate frequency distributions, bivariate frequency distributions, one-way analysis of variance, multiple regression, and an OSIRIS technique known as Multiple Classification Analysis (MCA), which obtains regression-like results for sets of categorical variables through treating each response category as a binary variable and applying a combination of analysis of variance and multiple regression statistical techniques.[4]

Lists of variables in the various datasets can be obtained from the author.

The Datasets

Dataset A: Genesee Random

The Genesee Random Dataset is a sort of motherlode for the data we used to analyze payment performance and enforcement efforts other than jail in Chaper 7, and for the descriptions of divorced families in Chapters 3 and 4. Because of its case-by-case longitidinal structure and consequent enormous size (1,021,098 bits of information), we never intended to use, and did not use, the full Genesee Random Dataset for any but very preliminary analysis. Rather, it formed the basis for a series of more usable restructurings and subsets listed below as A-1 through A-4.

Collected during the summer of 1973 from files at the Genesee County Friend of the Court, the Genesee Random Dataset consists of 507 (411 divorce and 96 paternity) cases, each of which has 2,014 variables. In fact, these 2,014 variables represent only 328 unique variables: 71 that apply to all cases; 82 that apply only to divorce cases; 60 that apply only to paternity cases; 33 variables for each of the nineteen possible years in which support payments could have been ordered and paid; 31 variables for each of the twenty-eight possible nonjudicial enforcement efforts (the maximum actually observed); and 51 variables for each of the six possible judicial enforcement efforts (the maximum actually observed).

The universe for the Genesee Random sample consisted of all those divorce and paternity cases filed in the Genesee County Circuit

Court that had an active support order for at least eighteen months, at least one day of which was in 1969 or 1970. These years were chosen as the base years for the Genesee Random sample primarily because they were the base years for the Genesee Divorce Jailings sample (drawn earlier and described below as Dataset B); in turn, those years were chosen for the Divorce Jailing sample in order to allow at least two and a half years to have passed after the central event—a jail sentence— until our data collection was made, so that we could evaluate long-term effects. This purpose was also well served in relation to all the types of enforcement efforts on which we collected data in the Genesee Random sample. The Genesee County Friend of the Court had, since 1966, kept a computer-based record of orders and payments, and the principal tool for our sample was a computer printout of the 15,132 cases regarded as "open" cases by the Friend of the Court on November 1, 1970. These were alphabetically arranged by the father's name. In addition, we used the FOC handwritten lists of cases closed during January 1969 through October 1970 and of cases opened during November and December 1970.

The sampling technique was simple—we selected every fifteenth divorce or paternity case on the list after choosing a starting point from a table of random numbers. Since the printout included as the first coded item for each case the "case-type" (divorce, paternity, in-state and out-state Uniform Reciprocal Enforcement of Support Act, Family Support Act, and Probate Court cases were the six categories used by the Friend of the Court), we were able to exclude from the interval count, and the sample, all but divorce and paternity cases.

Of our 683 selections of divorce and paternity cases from the printout, we located FOC enforcement case files on 664 (97.2 percent). Of those enforcement files we found, 527 (79.4 percent) appeared appropriate for coding; the 136 inappropriate cases fell almost wholly into two categories: (a) those in which the order was not truly legally active in 1969–70 but was erroneously still on the printout; and (b) those in which the support order lasted less than eighteen months. A case was closed in less than eighteen months primarily due to reconciliation prior to final judgment and to adoption of the children by the wife's new husband.

Our luck in finding the case files closed before or opened after the date of the printout was less good. Of the 182 divorce and paternity cases selected from the complete handwritten lists, we located enforcement files on only 90 (49.5 percent). Of those 90, only 13 (14.4 percent) appeared appropriate, the exclusions being almost wholly due to orders lasting less than eighteen months. It is our strong feeling that the reason we did not locate so many enforcement files in this "previous closure" group is that no enforcement files ever existed; the clerks in the office often waited until a support order was entered to open an enforcement file (rather than open it immediately upon the filing of a divorce or paternity complaint as they did with the "social services" files used by the staff making custody recommendations), and in many cases the complaint was dismissed (due to reconciliation or lack of progress) before any support order was entered.

During the coding process, we eliminated 33 of the 540 cases on which we had collected data, most of them because on closer examination we found they did not have live orders for the requisite eighteen months (usually due to a reconciliation not reported to the FOC until several months later) and the rest because the cases were not supposed to have been active in 1969–70 but were because of a failure to remove the case from the computer file. Thus we ended with 507 valid cases.

The representativeness of our sample may have been affected by three factors. First is the possibility that the 12.8 percent of the cases we selected, but for which we were unable to locate enforcement files, were in fact appropriate for our sample and in some way different from the cases for whom we found files. As indicated above, our strong conviction is that these were cases in which there never was a support order and which therefore were inappropriate.

Second, there were about 3.6 percent more orders listed in the printout than there were fathers. One reason for this does not affect the representativeness of the sample—some fathers are subject to more than one divorce and/or paternity support order. Over 12 percent of our divorced fathers had been divorced before, as were 17 percent of our divorced mothers; 29 percent of the previously divorced mothers had children from the previous marriage for whom a support order existed. Similarly, among our paternity cases, 9 percent of the fathers had other illegitimate children and another 20 percent had legitimate children. It does not seem at all unlikely that our 3.6 percent "excess" of orders over fathers is almost entirely due to multiple orders. However, it is clear that a few types of cases are overrepresented by our interval sampling technique. In those cases where a temporary order for both alimony and child support was in effect on November 1, 1970, the order was divided for FOC accounting purposes into separate alimony and child support lines in the printout. Although alimony was virtually never granted in final divorce orders—the temporary alimony amount was typically added to the temporary support amount to obtain a final support amount—the presence of that extra line in the printout means a very slight overrepresentation for cases with temporary alimony orders in November 1970; we attempted to treat such dual orders as a single case but may have failed to do so in a few cases. Similarly, there were a few cases where the printout contained erroneous lines, as where a temporary order is not deleted on the computer file after a final order is entered. In neither of these situations of "extra lines" in the printout, however, do we have any reason to believe that the overrepresented cases have any systematic differences from the rest of the sample.

Our worst fear about the representativeness of the sample was based on what we heard about the practices of some other county Friends of the Court—that when no payments are received under an order for a period of time, e.g., one year, the case is put in "closed" or "inactive" status, no further attempts at enforcement are made, and the cases are not included in the calculation of statistics of compliance with orders. Obviously, such cases must be included in any sample that purports to be representative. Our repeated questioning of the administrators and enforcement officers convinced us that the Genesee County Friend of the Court never considered a case "closed" or "inactive" until the term of the order had run—usually when the youngest child reached eighteen or was adopted by the wife's new husband—*and* every cent had been paid (though the enforcement tactics appeared considerably less harsh after the order had run its term). We were able to verify this by looking at what had happened by November 1970 to all of the 995 final divorce and paternity support orders entered in 1967. We found a clear reason *unrelated* to nonpayment in 97.5 percent of the cases which had been closed; in the remaining 2.5 percent of the cases we were unable to find the files in order to determine the reason.

What we did not count on, and did not discover until our data collection was virtually over, was a practice of the office's bookkeepers, seven and more years before we began our study, which could have had a similar effect. Prior to computerization of the payment records in 1966, the bookkeeping clerks, for reasons of space, periodically removed from the "pay-card" file cabinets those payment records on which there had been no payment made for over six months and stored them in cardboard boxes nearby. This practice had no impact on the enforcement officers—they were not even informed of it—and if payments were received, or the enforcement officer asked for a current arrearage figure, the record was moved back to the main file. The problem arose in 1966 when the changeover to computerization took place. The task of transferring the over 12,000 records was so huge, and the computer programs so full of "bugs," that the chief book-keeper decided to transfer only the records in the main file at once, and to transfer those in the "inactive" file only if a payment was later received or the enforcement officer requested it.

To determine the extent to which cases that should have been included in our sample were not included because they were not transferred to the computer files in 1966, we drew the special "remedial" samples described below as Dataset H: Genesee Remedial. In brief, we think that if the nontransfer problem had not occurred in 1966, our sample would have included a few more divorce and paternity cases with very low payment rates. This means that, instead of a mean payment level of .74, the Genesee divorce cases really had one of .72. We report and use this lower payment rate in Chapters 6 and 7. We cannot, however, describe the personal characteristics of this small group of men whose cases would have been in our sample but for the computer transition problem.

Although we believe the Genesee Random sample is quite representative of the sampling universe, we should make absolutely clear the fact that it is *not* representative, nor was it intended to be representative, of all fathers subject to support orders in Genesee County in 1969 and 1970.

There were several types of orders being enforced by the Genesee County Friend of the Court in 1969 and 1970 that were excluded from our sample. Had our sampling frame included all orders being enforced by the Friend of the Court, our sample would have included approximately 21 Uniform Reciprocal Enforcement of Support Act (URESA) orders entered originally in other states, 43 Circuit Court Family Support Act cases (mainly welfare department actions in cases in which there had been separation but no divorce, to reimburse the department for AFDC payments to the mother and children), and 6 Probate Court orders (the predecessor act to the Family Support Act). When the father was in the military or receiving Social Security benefits, the order typically was for the standard child's allotment to be paid directly to the mother; our sample originally had 12 cases of this type, but we excluded them because the Friend of the Court took no collection or enforcement responsibilities for them. These 82 additional cases would have increased the sample by 16 percent.

It would be an even worse mistake to assume that our sample is representative of all divorces involving children. First, as noted above, we excluded cases with orders lasting less than eighteen months. These were mainly cases of reconciliations but also included some rapid remarriages of the mother accompanied by adoptions by the stepfather. There were also a few cases in which the only child covered by an order married or reached eighteen soon after his parents' divorce. We estimated that about 5 to 10 percent of orders active at any moment would turn out to last less than eighteen months.

Moreover, in some divorce cases with minor children no support order is entered. Three sorts of cases merit mention. First, among the wealthy, the property settlement sometimes included substantial income-producing property in trust for the children's benefit as a substitute for periodic payments. Second, courts sometimes chose to enter no support order because they thought it pointless (the man was in prison under a long sentence) or otherwise inappropriate (particularly cases in which the father was awarded custody and the mother was unemployed). Finally, when a father had left town or otherwise avoided being served with a summons notifying him that a suit for divorce had begun, the courts in Michigan (and in other states) had no legal authority to enter a support order, although if the notice was published in a newspaper several times the divorce itself could be granted. We have no precise knowledge of the extent to which divorces involving children were granted without a support order, but our best guess was that the figure did not exceed 5 percent.

For the 507 cases that were included in our sample, there were three essential sources of information: the payment records, the enforcement log, and the general file. The payment records contain a record of every charge and every payment made during the history of the case, updated at least weekly since virtually all support orders are to be paid on a weekly basis. Not only is a running total of arrearage available, but also calendar-year totals of charges and payments and a year-end arrearage. Since computerization, one or two cards contain each person's calendar year's data. The biweekly summary printouts distributed to enforcement officers contain payment information for the preceding two months, so the payment records remained in a central storage area until and unless an enforcement officer asked for them in order to get a longer view of a particular case's payment history.

The enforcement log was an 8½-by-14-inch hard-stock card used primarily to record enforcement efforts in chronological order and their results (father's contacts, excuses, and lump-sum payments), although it also contained some information regarding the father's race, address, and employment that was useful for locating and identifying the father, and occasional notes on pending adoptions and other events of importance to the case. The log was kept at the enforcement officer's desk while the case was "alive," and filed with the enforcement file in the "dead files" after the case was closed. Using this log in combination with the payment records, we were able to study the results of judicial and nonjudicial enforcement efforts. Our general rule was that, if a father had not been paying for three weeks prior to an enforcement effort and began regular payments (three weeks in a row) or made a lump-sum payment (a hundred dollars or the equivalent of three weeks' payments, whichever was greater) within three weeks after the effort and prior to the next effort, the payments were treated as the "result" of the enforcement effort.

Each man's general file contained a variety of information: the original divorce complaint, temporary and final orders, and all other pleadings filed in the case; a questionnaire administered to both the mother and father in a divorce case to obtain information on their ages, addresses, legal representation, date and length of marriage, employment status, occupation, income, religion, previous marriage and children, attitudes to reconciliation, and names and ages of children; a much briefer questionnaire for the mother in paternity cases; copies of letters and warrants used as enforcement efforts; and transcripts of hearings before judges.

Dataset A-1: Genesee Random Analysis

The Genesee Random Analysis Dataset was used as the primary source for analyzing the overall payment performances of fathers in Chapter 7 and the characteristics of divorced families in Chapters 3 and 4. The set was created by transferring the general, divorce, paternity, and the summary payment and a few enforcement-effort variables from the Genesee Random Dataset. Most annual payment information and individual enforcement effort information was omitted from this set. To the variables transferred, we added several new variables regarding the fact and timing of fathers' movements in and out of Genesee County and the standards of living of the parties before and after the divorce. In all, it contains 327 variables for 507 cases.

The standard-of-living variables, the basis for most of Chapter 4, are available only for those cases in which we had valid (nonmissing) data on the earnings of *both* the mother and father at the time of the pre-divorce interviews; unemployed mothers and fathers were included and treated as having zero earnings.

Because our data on incomes and order sizes were collected in twenty different calendar years, we used several techniques to attempt to compare living standards of families (and subfamilies) in our sample. First, we adjusted the weekly earnings by the ratio of the average weekly earnings of nonsupervisory manufacturing workers in Michigan in December 1969 and the year of the order, to "standardize" earnings at a December 1969 level, the midpoint of our sample. (The ratios are derived from *Employment and Earnings, States and Areas, 1939–1975* [U.S. Department of Labor, Bureau of Labor Statistics Bulletin 1370–12], p. 354.)

Second, we assumed that the net after-tax earnings reported by fathers at divorce were based on their claim of the mother and children as income-tax dependent deductions (or of just the children if the mother was employed), and adjusted their income downward to reflect a postdivorce loss of a right to claim those deductions; a long series of computations of the impact of a deduction on net earnings after 1969 federal and state income and F.I.C.A. taxes demonstrated that each dependent was worth almost exactly 2.25 percent of gross income at all income levels, so that became the basis of the computation.

Third, we computed an estimated December 1969 weekly order by multiplying the ratio of the actual order to the father's reported earnings by the December 1969 net earnings estimated in the second step above. Fourth, we computed a variety of pre- and postseparation family and subfamily incomes, using various combinations of father paying or not, mother employed or not, mother receiving AFDC or not, and mother and father remarried to new spouses or not.

Finally, each of our series of family and subfamily incomes was categorized by where it fell among the thresholds for the Poverty, Lower Standard, Intermediate Standard, and Higher Standard Budgets as these categories are defined by the Bureau of Labor Statistics. The substance of these various measures of standards of living is explained in Chapter 4. The important point to note here is that, due to a quirk in the "equivalency ratios" used to convert the BLS budgets from the standard two-parent, two-child amounts to those for other family sizes and compositions, the poverty lines for one- and two-person families are *higher* than the BLS Lower Standard Budgets for those family sizes. Thus, for fathers living alone and mothers with one child, we did not categorize any case as having an income between the Poverty and Lower Standard Budget levels.

Dataset A-2: Genesee Random Payments

The Payments dataset is a transformation of the Random set so that each payment year is treated as a "case." From two to nineteen pseudocases could be created from each original case, since each case had at least two calendar years in which payments had been due (the minimum case length was eighteen months) and at most nineteen calendar years in which payments had been due (the maximum case length was eighteen years). Each set of payment-year data has appended to it the general, divorce, and paternity variables associated with the original full case from which the payment-year variables are derived. For example, an original case with three payment years becomes three pseudocases with different payment-year information but the same general, divorce, and paternity information. The effect of this is to "weight" the demographic and other case characteristics by the number of calendar years in which payments are due. After eliminating the pseudocases on which all of the relevant payment variables had "missing data" responses, we are left with 4,539 cases (3,639 divorce, 900 paternity) and 246 variables. The Payments dataset was used in Chapter 7 to analyze the patterns of payment over time, in relation to the order date, remarriage, and welfare receipt.

Dataset A-3: Genesee Random Nonjudicial Efforts

The Nonjudicial Efforts Dataset, used in Chapter 7 to analyze the impact of efforts not involving court appearances, contains a pseudocase for each nonjudicial effort, attaching to the nonjudicial-effort variables the general, divorce, and paternity variables associated with the original full case from which the nonjudicial-effort data were taken. In effect, the demographic and other data are "weighted" by the number of nonjudicial enforcement efforts, which ranged from 0 to 28; the cases with no nonjudicial-enforcement efforts (11.0 percent of the divorce cases, 11.5 percent of the paternity cases) are not represented in the nonjudicial-effort dataset at all. After eliminating the cases with all "missing data" on the nonjudicial-effort variables, the resulting dataset has 2,597 cases (2,159 divorce, 438 paternity) and 244 variables.

Dataset A-4: Genesee Random Judicial Efforts

The Judicial Efforts Dataset, which we used to analyze the impact of judicial efforts other than jail, is derived from a transformation of the Genesee Random Dataset, creating a pseudocase from each of the six possible judicial-enforcement efforts by attaching to the judicial-effort variables the general, divorce, and paternity associated variables from the original full case from which the judicial-effort data were taken. The dataset consists of 3,042 pseudocases (507 × 6) and 264 variables. Although we did not create a shortened dataset by eliminating the pseudocases with only "missing data" on the judicial-enforcement effort variables, if we had done so it would have reduced the dataset to 198 pseudocases (161 divorce and 37 paternity).

Dataset B: Genesee Divorce Jailing

The first data we collected, in the summer of 1972, were on the divorced men in Genesee County sentenced to jail in 1969 and in the first ten and a half months of 1970. The analysis of this data forms the basis for Chapters 8 and 9 on the jailing process and its impact on payments and other behavior of the men jailed.

The sampling universe was all those divorce cases in which the father received a jail sentence for nonpayment of a support order during 1969 and the first ten and a half months of 1970. We were assisted in our case selection by a list of persons arrested for nonsupport kept by the Friend of the Court on a stenographic pad for the benefit of the local newspaper, the *Flint Journal,* which published a "rogues' gallery" of persons arrested each week in the Sunday edition. Using this list and the courthouse logs of each judge's activities during the same period, we found that 234 divorced men were sentenced to jail during this period for failing to pay support. Of the 234, we coded data for 191, or 81.2 percent of the total group. In most of the remaining 43 cases, the reason for noninclusion was that we could not find the general file for the case. It is possible that these 43 cases differ in their characteristics from the remaining 191. We have no way of knowing with certainty. It is nonetheless the case that the characteristics of the men we do have in our sample mirror closely the characteristics of the 60 men in the Genesee Random Sample who were ever sentenced to jail. The primary reason a file would have been missing was that it was on the desk of an enforcement officer who was currently looking for the man. It is thus probable that the missing 43 cases were, as a group, even lower payers than the remaining 191 men we describe in Chapter 9.

The Genesee Divorce Jailing Dataset includes 191 cases and 610 variables, the great majority of the variables being associated with the demographic characteristics of the family and the circumstances and results of the 1969–70 jail sentence. Overall and year-by-year payment performance and other enforcement efforts were recorded and analyzed but in more summary form than in the Genesee Random Dataset.

Dataset C: Washtenaw Random Divorce

The Washtenaw Random Divorce Dataset was used primarily in Chapter 7 for the purpose of contrasting payments in Genesee County with payments in a county that devoted much less staff time to enforcement and rarely used jail sentences as a sanction for nonpayment. Washtenaw was chosen for this purpose because (1) it was one of only two large counties in Michigan that jailed fewer than a dozen men for nonsupport each year during the period we studied, (2) the Friend of the Court, Richard Benedek, was willing to cooperate by giving access to pay records and providing work space, and (3) Washtenaw was our home county, so we were within walking distance of the agency offices.

The sampling universe was all those divorce orders alive for at least eighteen months, one of which was January 1972. Washtenaw did not have computerized (or any other comprehensive) list of cases alive at any point in time; nor was there any unified record of charges, payments, and arrearages. Rather, individual payment records were updated when payments were received (and occasionally by auditors for a small sample). Our sampling technique, then, was to pull every twentieth payment record (from the alphabetically arranged "active" and "inactive" files in which they were stored) beginning with a starting point from a table of random numbers. If a record thus selected did not meet the eighteen-month or January 1972 criteria, we simply skipped it and went to the next (twentieth) payment period. As it turned out, the interval was too large, and we had to go through the alphabet twice to gather a sample as large as we wished.

The initial draws resulted in 700 cases being selected, of which 459 appeared usable and had questionnaires completed. The 241 exclusions included 154 that had been open less than eighteen months, 36 URESA, 30 paternity, 6 with incomprehensible pay records, 7 in which the judge had ordered the records suppressed from public view, and 8 in which we could not locate the enforcement files. At the coding stage another 39 cases were eliminated, nearly all for not meeting the eighteen-month requirement. In final form, the dataset thus includes 420 usable cases.

We are confident that our dataset is representative of the Washtenaw divorce cases alive for eighteen months, one of which was January 1972. The bookkeepers in Washtenaw never threw away a pay record; even after a case was closed (children eighteen or adopted) the records were retained in a cardboard box. Further, we were able to get the enforcement files in 684 of the 700 cases (98 percent), an extraordinarily high proportion. In one respect only have we a basis for fearing the results from the sampling. Since Washtenaw County's Friend of the Court sent warning notices and took enforcement steps only upon receiving a complaint of nonpayment in nonwelfare cases, parents could arrange between themselves for direct payments, and the Friend of the Court payment records would never reflect the fact of payments. We may thus record some cases as nonpaying when in fact full payments were being made directly to the custodial parent. To test for the possible scope of this problem, we identified all cases in the sample in which (1) the woman was *not* on welfare for at least a third of the life of the case, (2) in which there were at least twenty-six weeks of nonpayments without a recorded complaint or a mailed warning or other enforcement effort, and (3) in which there was no revival of payments (except when accompanied by an adjustment for direct payments). These seemed to be cases in which significant direct payments could have occurred, though we surely included large numbers of cases in which the reason for the absence of recorded complaints was due not to direct payments but to the wife's belief that complaint would be futile (or to the failure of an agency staff person to record receipt of the complaint). By this process, we identified 72 possible cases of direct payments, though it is our best guess, given the similarity of many of these men with the worst payers in Genesee (a large portion were no-shows at the predivorce interview) that far fewer of these men's apparent nonpayments are actually attributable to direct payments.

There were four major sources of data for the Washtenaw County divorce cases: the payment records, an address card file, the court file, and the enforcement file. The payment records gave us calender-year data on number and dollar amount of payments; year-end weekly charge and total arrearage; temporary and final order amounts; judge and judgment dates; and number, sex, and age of children. The address card file told us when and if the mother remarried and/or received welfare. The court file, which as our label implies was kept by the court clerk (and not the Friend of the Court) for the use of the judge, contained the complaint and other pleadings and the FOC report derived from the predivorce interview. This predivorce interview disclosed the parties' age; education; religion; previous marriages, children, and support orders; health problems; occupation, earnings, and length of employment; marriage and separation dates; stated reasons for wanting a divorce; chance of reconciliation; and contempt show-cause orders and warrants issued. Finally, the "enforcement file" kept by the FOC gave us a running log of contacts with the parties, including support-enforcement efforts (though custody and visitation disputes were given far more attention in the files).

We used the Washtenaw data to produce a dataset essentially similar to the Genesee Random Dataset. The major exception is that in Washtenaw we did not gather detailed information on the circumstances and results of individual enforcement efforts; rather, we simply counted the number of each type of effort in each calendar year. The 420 cases contain 772 variables.

Dataset D: Macomb Jailing

The Macomb Jailing Dataset is used in Chapter 8 to provide a description of a second county with substantial reliance on jailing and in Chapter 9 to permit a comparison of the effects of relatively short jail sentences with the effects of long sentences that we found in the Genesee Divorce Jailing Dataset. The sampling universe was all those persons sentenced to jail for contempt of a child support order in 1970.

The Macomb County Friend of the Court, for its own internal use, compiled a monthly list, organized by judge, of all persons sentenced to or in jail for nonpayment of a child support order. The twelve lists for 1970 provided us with the names of all those sentenced in 1970, which constituted our sample. The lists indicated judge, sentence date, sentence length in days or months, dollar amount set as a condition for release, date of release, amount paid for release, and whether the mother and children were receiving welfare at the time of jailing. If the father stayed in jail more than one month, his name would appear on the list for each month in which he was jailed, and the release information appeared only on the list for the month in which he was actually released. The lists produced 309 men involved in 341 jailings, all of which had usable information on the jailing.

Some additional information was obtained from the enforcement file (particularly the "computation record" which related payments to enforcement efforts) and the payment records: order size and arrearage at time of jailing, arrearage at end of first full calender year after release, whether and why the case was closed after the jailing, the number of prior and subsequent jailings. We located this information on 285 of the 341 cases (84 percent); all 341 are included in the dataset. There are 29 variables in the dataset.

Dataset E: Multicounty

The Multicounty Dataset is the basis for the attempt in Chapter 6 to explain variations in payment rates among counties. The sampling universe was to be all thirty Michigan Friend of the Court agencies with one thousand or more active support orders in calender year 1973, but two agencies had to be dropped because we were unable to arrange mutually convenient times for data collection. In this dataset, each case represents a county. The dataset contains a large variety of information for the county or counties in the jurisdiction of each Friend of the Court. First, for each of the eighty-three counties in the state, there is 1970 census data on population levels, density, and growth; migration, ethnic composition and country of origin; educational levels; labor force participation and employment by industry; and income levels. For 1970 through 1973, data on marriage, divorce, and illegitimacy rates were obtained from the state bureau of vital statistics.

Second, we had results from questionnaires completed in 1972 and 1974 by the chief executive of the agency or his or her deputy, regarding caseload sizes, definitions of active cases, frequency and arrearage threshold levels of various enforcement techniques, opinions about the current system and proposed changes in it, and staff size and credentials. We obtained completed questionnaires from forty-five and forty-eight of the sixty-five agencies in 1972 and in 1974, respectively. (There are fewer agencies than counties because some rural FOCs serve more than one county.)

Third, we had 1973 and 1974 reports by each of the sixty-five agencies to the Friend of the Court Association regarding the number of welfare-connected cases, collections, payment rates, and staff.

Finally, we have the results of the data collected in the twenty-eight counties during the summer of 1975. In each county, we planned and executed an interval sample calculated to produce around 450 orders alive during all of calender year 1974 (or fiscal year 1974 in a few counties that used a fiscal year other than the calendar year). If a county used an inactive file for cases in which no payments had been made for a long period, we also selected an appropriate number from the inactive file. We were able to locate full information on an average of 430 cases in each county, giving us over 12,000 cases in all. This dataset was used to produce a series of summary descriptions for each county which became variables in the multicounty set—several payment-performance indices, order-to-show-cause and jailing rates, mean jail sentence, and proportion of caseload in which the custodial parent was receiving welfare. We also gathered information about the agency's operations as of the summer of 1975—for example, whether the agency put its payment records on computer files, whether it had its own arresting officers, and whether a complaint from the mother was a prerequisite to initiating enforcement procedures in nonwelfare cases.

The twenty-eight counties on which we have complete data had populations of at least 37,000 in 1970; most are in the range of 100,000 to 500,000 that is usually termed "middle-sized." Although we have the impression that the Friends of the Court in very small counties operate in very much the same manner and with the same level of efficiency as the smaller ones in our sample—in part because several groups of small counties share consolidated Friends of the Court, thus producing caseloads similar to those in our sample—we cannot be sure that small counties do not have a distinct dynamic. It is at least possible that if we had performance data on the other thirty-seven agencies in the state, the relationships we found among variables in the twenty-eight would no longer hold.

The final dataset had 240 variables for each of the 28 counties.

Dataset F: Genesee Remedial

As mentioned above in the discussion of the Genesee Random Dataset, we discovered after completing our sampling in the files of Genesee's Friend of the Court that prior to 1966 the agency removed from the active files some cases in which the father was making no payments and that these cases were not placed on the computer records when the agency began computerizing recordkeeping in 1966. We thus felt it necessary to estimate the.extent of that loss and the impact that inclusion of a proportionate number of the missing cases would have had on our overall estimates of payment performance.

For this "remedial" purpose, we selected, on the basis of examination of photocopies of every order entered by the Genesee Circuit Court judges in 1960 and 1963, every divorce case in which a final child-support order was entered in those two years, and every paternity child-support order entered in 1960. This gave us a sample of 453 divorce orders from 1960, 535 divorce orders from 1963, and 117 paternity orders from 1960. We then examined the November 1966 master case-list of the Friend of the Court, one of the first full lists of all cases that had been placed in the computer records, to determine which cases were still listed and thus clearly *not* eliminated for nonpayment (once a case was listed it was never removed for nonpayment alone). We found 218 divorce cases from 1960, 92 divorce cases from 1963, and 42 paternity cases from 1960 which had not made it onto the early computer records and therefore *could* have been results of the "inactive" bin exclusion.

We then searched the payment records and enforcement files for these 352 cases, and located some records for 342 (97.2 percent). We found reasons for case closure clearly *other* than nonpayment in 269

(78.7 percent). In these cases, the most common reason for closure was that all the children covered by the order had reached the age of majority. In the remaining 73 cases (40 divorces from 1960, 22 divorces from 1963, and 11 paternities from 1960), we could not find any reason for closure, and nonpayment was a *possibility* we could not exclude. (The bookkeepers had told us that they did not consider a case "inactive" until six months had gone by since the last payment, but to be conservative we counted as "possibles" 9 cases in which one to six months had passed since the last payment prior to evidence of closure or "inactive" status.)

These "possible exclusion for nonpayment" cases were then used to formulate a rate-of-exclusion by calculating a regression line based on year in relation to judgment and cumulative percentage closed by a particular year in relation to judgment. Figures from 1960 were used, again to be conservative, since the total percentage possibly closed for nonpayment was higher in 1960 than 1963 for each year in relation to judgment. The regression equations that resulted are as follows:

		(Constant)		(Slope)	[Correlation]
Divorce	$Y =$	3.91	$+$	$1.007X$	[.820]
Paternity	$Y =$	0.25	$+$	$1.336X$	[.917]

where Y is the cumulative percentage closed in a given year after judgment; the constant is the Y-intercept (value of Y when $X = 0$); and X is the year after judgment (same year is 0, first year is 1, etc.).

Using the above equations, we calculated cumulative percentages possibly closed for nonpayment for each year from zero through eighteen, substituting actual 1960 values for regression estimates where possible; the values ranged from 1.3 percent in year zero to 22.0 percent in year eighteen for divorce cases, and from 0.0 percent to 24.3 percent in paternity cases. (We also calculated closure rates for *all* closings, nonpayment and otherwise, to ensure that we did not have estimates predicting over 100 percent closures prior to the eighteenth year. Gratifyingly, our regressions, based on years zero through ten data, predicted 100 percent closure at 17.6 years in the divorce cases and 18.1 years in the paternity cases).

By applying the complement of the possible nonpayment exclusion rate to the actual numbers of cases in our sample, and assuming *no* closures for nonpayment after computerization (1967–72), we are able to estimate the number of cases we would have had if no cases had been made inactive for nonpayment. For example, given a cumulative nonpayment "closure" rate for 1960 divorce cases of 8.6 percent by 1966, we can calculate that without such "closures" we would have had 10.9 cases in our sample instead of 10: $10/(1 - .086) = 10.9$. Carrying the calculations back through all our cases, we would have had another 20 cases, raising our total to 432 instead of 412. The comparable figure for paternity cases is 5 more than our actual 95, or 100.

If we make the extremely conservative assumption that the cases excluded for nonpayment had never had *any* payments prior to being placed in "inactive" status, then our divorce payment index would have dropped from .74 to .72, and the paternity payment index from .53 to .51.

As indicated, we have in the above calculations used "worst-case" assumptions, which are clearly false. Some of the cases for which we could not locate closure reasons other than nonpayment had such reasons. Closure rates in 1960 were markedly higher than those in 1963, yet only 16 percent of our cases began in a year nearer to 1960 than to 1963. And, although we did not record amounts, nearly all the cases possibly excluded for nonpayment had *some* payments prior to closure. It is our impression then, that the true magnitude of the problem caused by the nontransfer to computer records of cases "inactive" due to nonpayment is negligible for divorce cases—perhaps 10 missed cases and about .010 difference in the payments index. The effect on paternity cases is about the same as on divorce—perhaps 3 cases and about .010 in the payments index.

Dataset G: Genesee URESA and Family Support Act

We used the November 1970 master case-list to draw small samples of two case types that were enforced by the Genesee County Friend of the Court but were not otherwise represented in our study.

The Uniform Reciprocal Enforcement of Support Act is a model statute which has been adopted by all fifty states and the District of Columbia. It obligates an enacting state to enforce support orders, originally entered in other states, against the enacting state's residents. The process is initiated when a person under order in one state moves to another. The prosecutor in the state of the order formally notifies the prosecutor in the obligee's new state of the existence of the order; the second prosecutor begins a proceeding in a court of general jurisdiction, alleging the existence of the prior order and the request from the first state; the father is served with summons and has an opportunity to contest the entry or amount of an order; usually, an order of the same size as in the first state is entered in the second, and the father is subject to the same range of enforcement efforts and penalties as would be a person whose order was originally entered in the second state. The money collected is sent back to the originating state.

In November 1970, Genesee County was enforcing 510 orders originally entered in other states, and had responding orders in effect in other states in 549 cases. About 20 percent of these cases were paternity cases. We took a sample of the cases with Genesee orders originally, but later enforced out of state, selecting every other case. The result was a sample of 220 cases on which we had valid information on order date, November 1970 order size and arrearage, and a rough computation of a cumulative arrearage index like that computed in the Genesee Random dataset. The arrearage index for these Genesee orders, enforced for some period of time in Genesee but by November 1970 being enforced in another state, is .60 mean, .71 median. This compares to our overall mean arrearage index of .80 mean for the random divorce cases and .56 for the random paternity cases—for both divorce and paternity, a weighted mean of .757.

We also drew a 1 in 6 sample of the 1,091 cases on the November 1970 master case-list in which support orders had been entered under the Family Support Act or its predecessors; this act allows the Circuit Court to order child support among parties to a marriage without the necessity of bringing a divorce or separate maintenance action. The true plaintiff in nearly all these cases is the welfare department trying to reimburse itself for the AFDC benefits being provided to the mother and children. We selected 164 cases with usable data (the same variables as for the URESA cases) and calculated a rough arrearage index (as of November 1970) of .33 mean, .15 median, by far the worst performance of any case type, much lower than the welfare cases in our random sample.

Dataset H: Genesee Paternity Jailing

Since the initial jailing dataset we collected (in summer 1972) included only divorce cases, part of our efforts in summer 1973 involved attempting to sample the paternity cases jailed during 1969 and 1970. We used the judges' daily order logs as the sampling frame, so we are sure that the 58 cases in the sampling frame constitute the entire universe. We located full records on 56 of these (96.6 percent). Of the 56 cases we located, 16 were inappropriate since they did not last the eighteen months we set as a minimum standard. Thus our final dataset includes 40 cases.

The information coded was the same as that for the Genesee Random, and thus in most instances was more complete than that for the divorce jailing, due to the very limited analysis we were able to perform on the paternity cases. The full set of variables used in the Genesee Random Dataset is not available for the Paternity Jailing Dataset—nearly all the demographic and enforcement-effort information is there, but none of the computer-generated measures of overall or yearly payment performance or responses to enforcement efforts were calculated.

Dataset I: Genesee Brief Paternity

Because our Genesee Random Dataset ended with so few—95—paternity cases, we made an additional sample from the November 1970 master case-list; a 1 in 3 sample produced 657 cases. Our data came solely from the master case-lists for November 1970 and (if the case was active at those times) November 1966 and May 1973. The variables include judge, enforcement officer, order size, fees paid and owed (as an indication of the last date a payment was made), arrearage, weeks since order was entered, and a rough arrearage index. The mean arrearage indices were .75, .58, and .67 as of November 1966, November 1970, and April 1973, respectively. The medians were .89, .70, and .77.

Dataset J: Washtenaw Paternity

Our sample of paternity cases in Washtenaw was drawn independently from, but in the same manner as, the Washtenaw divorce sample described above—a 1 in 20 sample of all the active, inactive, and closed cases alive for at least eighteen months, one of which was January 1972. It took three passes through the alphabet to accumulate the 212 valid cases in the dataset. We collected the same sort of information as for the Washtenaw divorce, except that payment-year information was recorded only for 1966, 1970, and 1973. Thus far, none of the summary-performance and enforcement-effort variables have been computed for this dataset.

Appendix of Tables

Principal Samples Drawn during Project

	N	Group Selected
Random samples of divorce cases in 28 counties	12,000 (average of 430 per county)	Cases alive in 1974 or early 1975
Random sample of divorce cases in Genesee County	411	Cases alive at any time during 1969 or 1970
Random sample of divorce cases in Washtenaw County	420	Cases alive in January 1972
Sample of jailed men in Genesee County	191	Men jailed in 1969 and first 9 mos. of 1970
Sample of jailed men in Macomb County	309	Men jailed in 1970

Aspects of Sample Studied

Description of Divorced Men and Families	General Payment Performance	Incidence of Jailing	Impact of Jailing on Jailed Men	Impact of Jailing on General Population
	*	*		*
*	*	*	x	x
*	*	*		x
			*	
			*	

* Principal reliance
x Secondary reliance

Table 2B   **Comparison of Counties in Survey with United States as a Whole (1970 Census)**

	U.S. as a Whole	28 Counties*	Genesee County	Washtenaw County	Macomb County
Population (in 1,000s)	—	117 (median)	444	234	625
Education (median, in years)	12.1	12.1	12.1	12.6	12.1
% of workers in manufacturing	25.9	38.3	46.3	23.1	42.3
% of workers, white collar	48.3	41.4	37.8	64.6	47.2
% of families with female head	10.8	8.2	9.8	8.4	6.6
Median family income	$9,586	$10,716	$11,254	$12,294	$13,108
% of families earning under $5,000 (1970)	20.3	14.6	12.4	11.2	7.7
% of families earning $15,000 or more	20.6	23.7	27.0	34.8	36.1
% unemployed in civilian labor force	4.4	5.5	5.3	5.0	4.8
% white	89	95	86	91	98
% of population in urban setting	73.5	51.4	77.3	78.3	92.2

* Unless otherwise indicated, the figures in this column
are averages of the census figures for the 28 counties.
A county with a population of 40,000 was weighed
equally with a county with a population of 1
million.

Table 3A   **Weekly Earnings of Men, Genesee Random Sample**

	N	Mean Net Weekly Earnings*	Adjusted to October 1977 Cost of Living**
Unemployed	15	$ 0	$ 0
Blue-collar			
Unskilled auto workers	127	105	207
Other unskilled	88	92	179
Skilled workers	65	125	235
White-collar			
Clerical	25	111	202
Manager, professional	40	196	349
Other	8	89	158
(Missing data)	(42)	—	—
Total	368	$111 (mean)	$210 (mean)

* "Net" means earnings after deductions for income and social security taxes and, where applicable, union dues.

** The first step of the computation involved taking each man's earnings as reported at divorce and standardizing them in relation to 1969 earnings as described above in the Methodological Appendix, p. 291. To adjust from 1969 to 1977, we used a multiplier derived from BLS cost-of-living figures.

Table 3B   **"What Church Do You Attend?" at Time of Divorce,
                            Genesee Random Sample**

		Mothers			Fathers	
	N	% of All Mothers Answering	%, Excluding "None"	N	% of All Fathers Answering	%, Excluding "None"
None	142	36%	—	190	53%	—
Protestant	198	49	77%	111	31	67%
"Liberal"*	(125)	(31)	(48)	(65)	(18)	(39)
"Conservative"*	(73)	(18)	(28)	(46)	(13)	(28)
Catholic	57	14	22	47	13	29
Jewish	1	—	—	1	—	—
Other	2	1	1	6	2	4
(Missing data)	(10)	—	—	(55)	—	—
Total	400	100%	100%	355	99%	100%

> * We treated as "conservative" those who reported
> themselves as Baptists or members of other
> fundamentalist groups. We treated as "liberal" all
> other Protestants. Nearly all the "liberal" Protestants
> were Episcopalians, Lutherans, Methodists, or
> Presbyterians.

Table 3C   **Age at First Marriage**

		Genesee Random Sample	Ever-married Persons in Michigan, 1970*
Women	Median age at first marriage	18.0	20.6
	Portion 18 or under at first marriage	61%	29%
Men	Median age at first marriage	20.2	23.3
	Portion 20 or under at first marriage	49%	24%

> * U.S., Bureau of the Census, *1970 Census of
> Population,* vol. 1, pt. 24, table 159.

Table 3D   **Mother's Age at Marriage in Relation to Pregnancy
                                at Marriage, Genesee Random Sample**

Mother's Age at Marriage	N	All Mothers of This Age (%)	Mothers of This Age Who Were Pregnant at Marriage (%)
16 or under	73	18%	43%
17–18	125	32	39
19–20	87	22	28
21–24	55	14	21
25 or over	57	14	28
Total	397	100%	33%
			$p < .01$

Table 3E   **Number of Children in Family at Time of Divorce,
                                Genesee Random Sample**

No. of Children	N	% of Total
1	139	34%
2	134	33
3	67	17
4	40	10
5	15	4
6 or more	12	3
Total	407	101%

Mean: 2.26
Median: 2

Table 3F   **Length of Time from Marriage to Separation, Genesee Random Sample**

Time of Separation:	N	% of Total
12 or fewer months after marriage	42	10%
13–36 months after marriage	55	14
37–72 months after marriage	107	26
73–120 months after marriage	84	21
121–80 months after marriage	60	15
15 years or more after marriage	58	14
Total	406	100%

Mean: 92 months (7.7 years)
Median: 72 months (6.0 years)

Table 3G   **Relation of Length of Marriage to Number and Age of Children and Parents, Genesee Random Sample**

Amount of Time before Couple's Separation	N	% in Which Mother Pregnant at Marriage	Number of Children (Mean)	% with 3 or More Children	Age of Youngest Child at Separation (Mean)	Age of Mother at Divorce (Mean)
12 or fewer months after marriage	42	57%	1.1	0%	3 mos.	21.7
1.1–3.0 years after marriage	55	47	1.4	8	1.1 yrs.	23.5
3.1–6.0 years after marriage	107	40	2.0	18	2.0 yrs.	25.6
6.1–10.0 years after marriage	84	23	2.4	41	3.4 yrs.	28.9
Over 10.0 years after marriage	118	18	3.2	65	6.7 yrs.	35.8
Total	406	33%	2.3	34%	3.4 yrs.	28.5
		$p < .01$	$p < .01$	$p < .01$	$p < .01$	$p < .01$

Table 3H   Attitude toward Reconciliation, Genesee Random Sample

| | Mothers* | | Fathers* | |
	N	%	N	%
Willing to reconcile	28	7%	79	24%
Unsure, willing to consider reconciliation	14	4	29	9
Unwilling to reconcile	354	89	227	67
Total	396	100%	335	100%

* Excluding those who failed to attend predivorce interview.

Table 3I   Men's Age at Divorce in Relation to Other Factors, Genesee Random Sample (N = 398)

	Men 17–25* N = 91	Men 26–35* N = 195	Men 36–50* N = 112	Overall Mean N = 398
Age of father at divorce	22.6 yrs.	29.6 yrs.	41.2 yrs.	31.3 yrs.
Age of mother at divorce	20.9 yrs.	27.4 yrs.	36.6 yrs.	28.5 yrs.
Age of mother at marriage	17.4 yrs.	19.6 yrs.	21.7 yrs.	19.7 yrs.
Age of father at marriage	19.0 yrs.	21.7 yrs.	26.1 yrs.	22.3 yrs.
Mother's age at birth of first child	18.3 yrs.	20.4 yrs.	23.7 yrs.	20.8 yrs.
Length of marriage before separation	2.3 yrs.	6.7 yrs.	14.0 yrs.	7.7 yrs.
Age of youngest child at separation	10 mos.	3.0 yrs.	6.1 yrs.	3.3 yrs.
% with youngest child under 1 at separation	61	19	10	25

NOTE: In our sample of 411, there were 13 men for whom there were missing data regarding their age at divorce.
* Unless otherwise indicated, all figures are means.

Table 3I—Continued

	Men 17–25	Men 26–35	Men 36–50	Overall Mean
Oldest child's age at final divorce decree	3.0 yrs.	7.1 yrs.	13.0 yrs.	6.6 yrs.
Total children	1.5	2.3	2.9	2.3
% with 1 child only	63	29	22	34
% with 2 children	27	41	24	33
% with 3 or more children	10	30	54	33
Father's attitude toward reconciliation—yes or maybe (%)	21	32	39	32
Mother's attitude toward reconciliation—yes or maybe (%)	9	12	9	11
Father failed to attend interview (%)	19	14	19	17
Plaintiff or cross-plaintiff is father (%)	16	15	10	14
% unemployed or irregularly employed at divorce	16	10	15	13
% in white-collar jobs	9	21	22	18
Earnings per week	$84	$111	$131	$110
Order as a portion of earnings for full-time workers	.28	.31	.32	.31
% whose wives remarried	72	56	40	55
% whose wives ever received AFDC	46	29	24	31
% whose wives were working full-time at divorce	35	56	57	51
% of mothers who claimed:				
Infidelity	18	23	22	21
Alcohol	17	19	25	20
Physical abuse	20	24	23	23
Nonsupport	26	19	14	19

Table 4A   Mothers Working Full Time at Time of Predivorce
                             Interview in Relation to Age of Youngest Child
                             at Separation, Genesee Random Sample

Age of Youngest Child at Separation	N	% of Total	Portion of Mothers Working Full-Time at Divorce
Twelve months or younger	115	29%	.36
13–36 mos.	116	30	.47
37–72 mos.	83	21	.59
Over 72 mos.	79	20	.66
(Missing data)	(17)	—	—
Total	393	100%	.51
			$p < .01$

Table 4B   Welfare Payments Available to Mothers and Children
                             in Genesee County

| | Maximum Grant Levels in 1969 and 1976 | | | |
| | (Weekly) | | (Annually) | |
	1969	1976	1969	1976
1 Adult, 1 child	$50	$ 71	$2,580	$3,648
1 Adult, 2 children	58	85	2,993	4,404
1 Adult, 3 children	67	101	3,457	5,196
1 Adult, 4 children	75	116	3,870	5,964
1 Adult, 5 children	83	131	4,283	6,756

| | % of Poverty Line | | % of Lower Standard Budget | |
	1969	1976	1969	1976
1 Adult, 1 child	104%	109%	77%	64%
1 Adult, 2 children	102	99	67	58
1 Adult, 3 children	93	93	61	54
1 Adult, 4 children	89	87	56	48
1 Adult, 5 children	81	84	53	49

Table 4C   Factors Associated with Whether Mother
                            Received Welfare Benefits after Separation, Multiple
                            Classification Analysis, Genesee Random Sample

	N	Portion Ever Receiving Benefits	Portion after Control for Other Factors
Total Sample*	365	.348	.348
Mother's Occupation			
Not employed, no stated occupation	138	.57	.62
Unskilled auto worker	48	.17	.16
All other unskilled	81	.35	.29
White collar clerical, secretarial, sales	80	.15	.12
Professional, managerial	18	.00	.03
			(Beta .47)
Year of the Final Order			
1952–63	77	.30	.33
1964–68	161	.25	.26
1969–73	127	.50	.48
			(Beta .21)
Father's Cumulative Payments Index			
.00–.10 of everything due	29	.69	.65
.11–.50 of everything due	50	.52	.35
.51–.75 of everything due	47	.45	.41
.76–.94 of everything due	91	.29	.32
.95 or more of everything due	148	.23	.28
			(Beta .21)
Mother's Employment Status at Divorce			
Employed full time	191	.19	.37
Part time or irregularly employed	32	.41	.55
Unemployed	142	.55	.27
			(Beta .16)

* Excluded are 28 cases in which children and mother
moved permanently from Genesee County. They
are excluded because we could not tell how many
left the state. If they had left the state, the Friend
of the Court records might not have revealed whether
they later received welfare benefits.

Table 4C—Continued

Father's Occupation

Unemployed or missing	31	.39	.24
Blue-collar, auto	120	.37	.39
Other blue-collar, public service,			
military	141	.42	.39
White-collar clerical	22	.23	.37
Professional, managerial	51	.14	.19
			(Beta .16)

Youngest Child's Age at Separation

Under 1 yr.	99	.52	.45
1–3 yrs.	108	.36	.35
4–10 yrs.	124	.22	.27
Over 10 yrs.	27	.26	.34
(Missing data)	(7)	(.33)	(.33)
			(Beta .15)

Father's Job Stability

Same job throughout	70	.23	.36
Many jobs, always employed	12	.50	.56
Many layoffs or often			
unemployed	36	.56	.49
Always unemployed	20	.50	.34
(Missing data)	(227)	(.33)	(.31)
			(Beta .14)

Portion of variance explained by seven factors: 34.5% (unadjusted)
29.5% (adjusted)

Table 4D   **Factors Strongly Related to Remarriage of Divorced Women, Genesee Random Sample (N = 325)**

	B	Beta	Marginal R^2	Probability
Age of woman at divorce	−.023	−.32	10.3%	<.001
Whether woman black (yes = 1)	−.299	−.21	4.3%	<.01
Years between final order and year				
of our coding (1973)	+.017	−.15	2.1%	<.01

Total fraction of explained variance: 17.6% unadjusted
16.8% adjusted

NOTE: Table excludes cases in which the final order was entered in 1970 or later.

Table 6A   **Value on Critical Variables for Each of Twenty-eight Counties**

County Rank	Average Portion Pd. of Amount Due in Sample	Rate of Jailing per 10,000 Population	Self-starting for Several Years?*	Unemployment Rate (1970 Census)**	Population (1970 Census)***
1	.87	7	Yes	5%	S
2	.85	16	Yes	5	S
3	.80	4	Yes	6	S
4	.80	12	Yes	4	S
5	.78	4	Yes	6	S
6	.72	1	Yes	5	S
7	.71	3	Yes	4	S
8	.71	14	Yes	6	L
9	.69	3	No	5	M
10	.69	4	No	6	L
11	.68	3	No	7	S
12	.68	5	Yes	5	L
13	.67	7	Yes	5	L
14	.66	1	No	5	L
15	.64	1	Yes	4	S
16	.63	2	Yes	7	S
17	.63	2	Yes	5	S
18	.63	2	No	6	S
19	.62	3	Yes	5	M
20	.62	1	No	5	L
21	.62	6	No	7	M
22	.58	0	No	5	L
23	.57	8	No	7	M
24	.55	1	No	5	M
25	.52	1	No	7	M
26	.51	1	No	5	L
27	.46	5	No	6	M
28	.45	3	No	6	L

* A "self-starting" county was one that had a policy of initiating enforcement efforts in nonwelfare cases without waiting for complaints from the parent not receiving payments.

** The unemployment rate has been rounded to the nearest percent to preserve the anonymity of the counties. In our actual analysis, we used the unemployment rate rounded to the nearest tenth of a percent as reported in the Census.

*** We have categorized the county populations as follows:

S = Small (below 80,000)
M = Medium (80,001–200,000)
L = Large (more than 200,000)

In all regression runs, the $\log_{10}$ of actual county population was used. Persons interested in replicating the regression can obtain the actual values from the author.

Table 6B   **Relation of Jailing to Collections in Twenty-eight Michigan Counties**

Number of Jailings per 10,000 Persons in County	Number of Counties	Mean Rate of Collections
0–1 per 10,000	8	.60
2–3 per 10,000	8	.63
4–6 per 10,000	6	.67
7 or more per 10,000	6	.75
Total	28	.655 (mean)

Table 6C   **Variations in Income and Unemployment among the Twenty-eight Counties**

	Mean of 5 Counties with Lowest Representation of Characteristic	Mean	Mean of 5 Counties with Highest Representation of Characteristic	Standard Deviation
Median family income (1970)	$9,189	$10,716	$12,477	$1,171
% of families below low income budget line (1970)	4.8	7.2	9.7	1.8
% families earning $15,000 or more (1970)	16.5	23.6	34.4	5.8
% of males in labor force 16 or over working 50–52 weeks (1970)	59	67	72	5.0
% unemployment in civilian labor force (1970)	4.4	5.5	6.9	0.9
% unemployment during months studied in each county (1973–75)	5.5	10.2	15.2	3.5

Table 6D   **Indirect Indicators of Social Cohesion or Attitude
                            toward Legal Obligations in Twenty-eight
                            Michigan Counties**

	Mean of 5 Counties with Lowest Representation of Characteristics	Mean	Mean of 5 Counties with Highest Representation of Characteristics	Standard Deviation
Population (1970)	41,000	268,000*	1,011,000	511,000
% of population living in towns with 2,500 or more residents	17%	51%	90%	26.5
% population change 1960–70	+4.5	+19.0	+42.9	13.5
% population born in in different state	11	22	36	8.9
% population of foreign stock (1st or 2nd generation)	7	13	24	5.4
Reported crime rate/1000 residents	71	106	147	26.6
% of persons 18 & over voting in 1972 election	57	63	70	4.7
% of voters voting for Goldwater in 1964	30	42	49	6.8
% of county population who are church members**	27	41	60	11.6

* A more meaningful figure for population would be the
median, which was 117,000.

** In church censuses, all persons christened as Roman
Catholics are forever counted as church members,
even though many later do not consider
themselves church members. If we count Protestants
only, the smallest five counties have 15%, the
largest five 35% and the mean 23%.

Table 6E   **General Characteristics of Friends of the Court in**
1974 in Twenty-eight Counties

Does agency use computer for bookkeeping?
    Yes—17 counties (61%)
    No —11 counties (39%)
Does agency put some nonpaying cases in "inactive" bin?
    Yes—14 counties (50%)
    No —14 counties (50%)
Does agency have system in nonwelfare cases of initiating enforcement without
awaiting complaints (that is, is county self-starting)?*
    Yes, system in existence for many years—14 counties (50%)
    Yes, but only recently begun   — 3 counties (11%)
    No   —11 counties (39%)
Does agency have its own deputized arresting officers?
    Yes—14 counties (50%)
    No —14 counties (50%)
What was the budget of the agency in 1974 in relation to county
population? (Dollars per 1,000 population.)
    Average of:
                Lowest five: $498
                All counties: $837
                Highest five: $1487
What is the size of the staff in 1974 in relation to the population? (Staff per
100,000 population.)
    Average of:
                Lowest five: 6
                All counties: 9
                Highest five: 12

* See also Appendix table 6A.

Table 6F   **Aspects of the Use of Court Hearing and Jail Terms in Twenty-eight Counties (1974)**

	Mean of 5 Counties with Lowest Representation of Characteristic	Mean	Mean of 5 Counties with Highest Representation of Characteristic	Standard Deviation
Rate of orders to show cause per 10,000 persons in county (1974)	17	60	123	41.9
Rate of sentences to jail per 10,000 persons in county	0.6	4.3	11.4	4.1
Ratio of sentences to jail to orders to show cause	.02	.10	.33	.14
Mean sentence length imposed in jailings	1.1 mos.	2.4 mos.	4.8 mos.	1.5
% of jail sentences that were 6 months or more	0	14.5	51	20.1

Table 6G   **Incidence of AFDC Cases in Samples in Twenty-eight Counties**

	Mean of 5 Counties with Lowest Portion of AFDC cases	Mean	Mean of 5 Counties with Highest Portion of AFDC cases	Standard Deviation
% of sample in which mother received AFDC at time sampled	19	29	42	8.1

Table 6H   **Regression Analysis of Factors Accounting for Differences
in Rates of Collections among Twenty-eight Counties**

The measure of county performance used in the study was the mean for each county of the individual payment rates for each person in the sample for the period sampled. That measure is referred to here as the "Mean Payment Rate." For the manner in which the individual rate was computed, see Chapter 5, p. 75. This measure was used as the dependent variable here either in its natural form, its log to base 10, or its "Logit" form, as indicated.

A list of around forty control variables tested in the analysis can be obtained directly from the author. Below are the controls used in the analyses reported here:

1. *Self-Starting Factor.* A binary variable that records whether (coded 1) or not (coded 0) the county had used for several years an enforcement system in which the agency initiated enforcement in nonwelfare cases without awaiting complaints from the mother.

2. *Jailing Rate.* The number of sentences to jail in 1974 for contempt of court for nonpayment of support for each 10,000 persons in the county population. As explained in Chapter 6, n. 4, this rate closely parallels the rate of jailing for each 250 men in the county caseload.

3. *Population.* The $\log_{10}$ of the county's population from the 1970 decennial census.

4. *Unemployment Rate.* The unemployment rate in the civilian labor force according to the 1970 census.

5. *High-Jail/Self-Start Factor.* A combination of factors 1 and 2 above into a binary variable that treated as "1" counties that were both high jailing and "self-starting," and as "0" all others. Those counties that had both a jail rate of 4 or more per 10,000 and a self-starting system were contrasted with all other counties. The selected rate of 4 per 10,000 divided our counties at the median and had no other conceptual foundation.

6. *Jail x Self-Start Factor.* Factor 1 above multiplied by Factor 2. The multiplication produced a 0 for all counties without a self-starting policy (regardless of their jailing rate), and their jailing rate (from 1 to 17) for all counties that did have a self-starting policy.

Table 6H—Continued

A. Regression on the "Mean Payment Rate"

   1. *With three variables that explain most variance:*

	B	Beta	T-Ratio	Significance Level
Self-starting factor	8.62	+0.41	2.89	<.01
Jailing rate	0.92	+0.35	2.64	<.02
Log_{10} population	−7.91	−0.34	2.53	<.02

     Fraction of explained variance: 62.6 per cent (unadjusted)
                                        57.9 per cent (adjusted)

   2. *With four variables that explain most variance:*

	B	Beta	T-Ratio	Significance Level
Self-starting factor	7.00	+0.33	2.25	<.05
Jailing rate	0.96	+0.37	2.82	<.01
Log_{10} population	−8.64	−0.38	2.80	<.01
Unemployment rate	−2.35	−0.19	1.48	<.20

     Fraction of explained variance: 65.8 per cent (unadjusted)
                                        59.9 per cent (adjusted)

   3. *With the "High-Jail/Self-Start Factor":*

	B	Beta	T-Ratio	Significance Level
High-jail/self-start factor	14.8	+.64	6.36	<.01
Log_{10} population	−10.8	−.47	4.72	<.01
Unemployment rate	− 2.65	−.22	2.20	<.05

     Fraction of explained variance: 76.5 per cent (unadjusted)
                                        73.6 per cent (adjusted)

   4. *With the "Jail x Self-Start Factor":*

	B	Beta	T-Ratio	Significance Level
Jail × self-start factor	+1.33	+.55	4.30	<.01
Log_{10} population	−9.96	−.43	3.50	<.01
Unemployment rate	−1.94	−.16	1.25	—

     Fraction of explained variance: 64.4 per cent (unadjusted)
                                        60.1 per cent (adjusted)

Table 6H—Continued

B. Regression on Log_{10} "Mean Payment Rate"

With principal variables in log form:

	B	Beta	T-Ratio	Significance Level
Self-starting factor	0.047	+0.33	2.06	<.05
Log_{10} jail rate	0.052	+0.31	2.20	<.05
Log_{10} population	−0.059	−0.38	2.69	<.01
Log_{10} unemployment	−0.240	−0.23	1.62	<.20

Fraction of explained variance: 62.1 per cent (unadjusted)
55.5 per cent (adjusted)

C. Regression on "Mean Payment Rate" in modified "Logit" form:

$$Log_{10} \frac{\text{Mean Payment Rate}}{1 - \text{Mean Payment Rate}}$$

With principal measures in log form:

	B	Beta	T-Ratio	Significance Level
Self-starting factor	+0.13	+0.30	1.91	<.10
Log_{10} jail rate	0.19	0.38	2.75	<.01
Log_{10} population	−0.18	−0.37	2.67	<.01
Log_{10} unemployment	−0.79	−0.24	1.88	<.10

Fraction of explained variance: 63.9 per cent (unadjusted)
57.7 per cent (adjusted)

			% of Group Paying 80% or More of
	N	Mean Payment Rate	All Amounts Due

	N	Mean Payment Rate	% of Group Paying 80% or More of All Amounts Due
Total	409	.74	60%
Father's age at divorce			
25 or under	91	.66	46%
26–30	126	.75	61
31–35	69	.81	74
36–40	60	.80	70
41 or more	50	.77	58
(Missing data)	(13)	(.58)	(45)
		$p < .05$*	$p < .01$
Father's occupation at divorce			
Unskilled blue collar	223	.73	58%
(auto workers)	(135)	(.77)	(64)
(other)	(78)	(.66)	(49)
Skilled blue collar	69	.80	70
Clerical, sales	25	.86	72
Manager, professional	42	.85	74
Public service	14	.75	64
(Missing data and unemployed)	(37)	(.51)	(38)
		$p < .01$	$p < .01$
Father's net weekly earnings at divorce			
None, unemployed	20	.62	40%
$1–$60	26	.63	39
$61–$90	89	.77	65
$91–$120	126	.79	64
$121–$150	60	.75	63
$151 or more	53	.83	76
(Missing data)	(35)	(.54)	(34)
		$p < .05$	$p < .01$
Father's race			
Black	46	.68	52%
White	318	.74	60
(Missing data)	(45)	(.81)	(71)
Father's religion (What church do you attend?)			
None	190	.77	62%
Protestant, Liberal	65	.78	63
Protestant, Conservative, Fundamental	45	.78	64
Roman Catholic	47	.81	70
Other	7	.72	(71)
(Missing data)	(55)	(.54)	(40)

*In determining probabilities, missing-data cases have been excluded. If no probability is indicated, the differences were not statistically significant at the .05 level.

Table 7B   **Payment Performance in Relation to Characteristics**
                            of the Marriage, Genesee Random Sample

	N	Mean Payment Rate	% of Group Paying 80% or More of All Amounts Due
Total	409	.74	60%
Wife pregnant at time of marriage?			
Yes	134	.66	50%
No	268	.79	66
(Missing data)	(7)	(.68)	(43)
		p < .001	p < .01
Age of the mother at birth of the first child			
18 or under	140	.66	51%
19–22	163	.78	63
23–30	68	.81	72
31–40	22	.85	74
(Missing data)	(16)	(.70)	(47)
		p < .001	p < .05
Length of the marriage to separation			
12 mos. or less	42	.66	48%
13–36 mos.	55	.74	56
37–60 mos.	79	.68	51
61–120 mos.	112	.76	64
121 mos. or more	118	.82	71
(Missing data)	(3)	(.10)	(0)
		p < .01	p < .05

Table 7C   **Payment Performance in Relation to Facts about
the Children, Analysis of Variance, Genesee
Random Sample**

	N	Mean Payment Rate	% of Group Paying 80% or More of All Amounts Due
Total	409	.74	60%
Number of children			
1	138	.76	62%
2	134	.73	57
3	67	.80	70
4 or more	67	.66	54
(Missing data)	(3)	(.86)	(67)
Sex of children			
All boys	109	.77	64%
All girls	126	.76	61
At least One of each	170	.72	52
(Missing data)	(4)	(.83)	(50)
Age of youngest child at separation			
Youngest not yet born	29	.61	36%
Born, up to 12 mos.	90	.69	52
13–36 mos.	119	.73	60
37–72 mos.	85	.82	71
73 mos. or more	78	.81	72
(Missing data)	(8)	(.58)	(38)
		$p < .01$	$p < .001$

		Mean Payment Rate	Mean Rate after Adjustment for Other Factors
	N		

Table 7D   **Five Characteristics of Men or Marriages Most Closely Associated with Payments, Multiple Classification Analysis, Genesee Random Sample**

	N	Mean Payment Rate	Mean Rate after Adjustment for Other Factors
Total	409	.74	.74
Length of Marriage to Separation			
12 mos. or less	42	.66	.64
13–36 mos. (1+–3 yrs.)	55	.74	.74
37–60 mos. (3+–5 yrs.)	79	.68	.67
61–120 mos. (5+–10 yrs.)	112	.76	.73
121 mos. or more (10 yrs. or more)	118	.82	.86
(Missing data)	(3)	(.10)	(.13)
			(Beta .25)
Father's Occupation			
Unskilled autoworker	135	.77	.77
Unskilled, nonauto	87	.66	.68
Skilled blue-collar	69	.80	.81
Clerical, sales	25	.86	.82
Managerial, professional	42	.85	.82
Public service (police, fire)	14	.75	.84
Unemployed, never reported	37	.54	.57
			(Beta .24)
Number of Children			
1	138	.76	.80
2	134	.73	.74
3	67	.80	.77
4 or more	67	.66	.62
(Missing data)	(3)	(.86)	(.79)
			(Beta .20)
Father's Age at Divorce			
25 or under	91	.66	.73
26–30	126	.75	.79
31–35	69	.81	.78
36–40	60	.80	.77
41 or more	50	.77	.63
(Missing data)	(13)	(.58)	(.64)
			(Beta .18)
Mother's Age at Birth of First Child			
18 or under	140	.66	.68
19–22	163	.78	.78
23–30	68	.81	.79
31 or over	22	.85	.84
(Missing data)	(16)	(.69)	(.71)
			(Beta .16)

Portion of variance explained by five factors: 18.6% (unadjusted)
13.7% (adjusted)

Table 7E   **Relation of Payments to Attitudinal Information from Interview with Friend of the Court, Genesee Random Sample**

	N	Mean Payment Rate	% of Group Paying 80% or More of All Amounts Due
Mother's reasons for wanting divorce			
Father's infidelity			
Mother states as reason	85	.75	63%
Mother does not state as reason	319	.74	59
Father's alcohol problems			
Mother states as reason	81	.71	52
Mother does not state as reason	323	.75	62
Father's physical abuse			
Mother states as reason	90	.74	63
Mother does not state as reason	314	.74	60
Father's failure to support			
Mother states as reason	75	.69	48
Mother does not state as reason	329	.76	63
			p < .05
Father's attendance at predivorce interviews			
Failed to attend	68	.51	32
Attended	341	.79	65
		p < .01	p < .01
Father's attitude toward reconciliation			
Willing to reconcile or to consider reconciling	103	.78	62
Unwilling to reconcile	233	.80	66
Failed to attend interview	68	.51	32
		p < .01	p < .01
Father's attitudes regarding care of children			
Seeks custody of children (either in complaint or amendment)	49	.77	63
Complains at some point about care given children	18	.85	83
Neither of these	337	.73	59
Plaintiff			
Father	54	.79	63
Mother	348	.73	59

Table 7F   For Fathers Working Full-Time, Relation of Payments
                               to the Size of the Final Order as a Portion
                               of the Fathers' Earnings at Divorce, Genesee
                               Random Sample

Portion of Father's Net Earnings Represented by Order	N	Mean Payment Rate	% of Group Paying 80% or More of All Amounts Due
.20 or less	81	.78	63%
.21–.27	75	.83	72
.28–.35	64	.78	66
.36–.50	74	.80	69
.51 or more	27	.68	44
Unemployed or employed part time at divorce	(51)	(.60)	—
(Missing data)	(34)	(.58)	—
Total	321	.79	66%

Table 7G   Payments in Relation to the Year of the Divorce,
                               Genesee Random Sample

	N	Mean Payment Rate	% Paying 80% or More of Amounts Due
Year divorce became final			
1952–61	64	.81	67%
1962–66	139	.78	68
1967–68	75	.76	63
1969–72	130	.66	48
(No final order)	(1)	(.96)	(—)
Total	409	.74	60
		p < .001	

Table 7H   **Comparison of Men in Genesee and Washtenaw Counties Whose Wives Complained of Inadequate Support at Time of Divorce, Genesee and Washtenaw Random Samples**

| | Genesee | | Washtenaw | |
	N	Payment Rate	N	Payment Rate
Mean payment rates of:				
Men whose wives complained of inadequate support	75	.69	39	.36
Men whose wives did not complain of inadequate support	329	.76	331	.59
(Missing data)	(6)	—	(50)	—
Total	404	.74	370	.56

Table 7I   **Comparison of Payments in Genesee and Washtenaw Counties in Relation to Men's Roles in the Divorce, Genesee and Washtenaw Random Samples**

| | Genesee | | Washtenaw | |
	N	Mean Payment Rate	N	Mean Payment Rate
Mean overall payment rates of:				
Men who were plaintiffs in divorce	54	.79	82	.70
Men who were not plaintiffs but attended predivorce interview	280	.76	246	.59
Men who were not plaintiffs and failed to attend interview	68	.51	92	.37
Total	402	.74	420	.56
		$p < .001$		$p < .001$

Table 7J   **Relation of Payments to Men's Employment History
over Life of Decree (Based on Fragmentary Information),
Genesee Random Sample**

	N	Mean Payment Index
Same job, always employed	77	.92
Same job, often laid off	12	.83
Many jobs, always employed	15	.76
Many jobs, often unemployed	26	.58
Always unemployed when recorded	20	.52
Other combination	31	.58
(Inadequate information about employment history)	(229)	(.76)
Total	181	.73
		p < .01

Table 7K   **Relation of Evidence of Leaving Genesee County to Ranges
of Overall Payment Performance, Genesee Random
Sample**

	Number of Men Paying in This Range	Number of Men Who Left the County	% of Group Who Left the County
Men who paid at an average annual rate of:			
.00–.10 of amounts due	30	25	83%
.11–.50 of amounts due	56	24	43
.51–.80 of amounts due	76	14	18
.81 or more of amounts due	237	7	3
Total	399	70	18%
			p < .001

Table 7L   **Relation of Payments to Indications in File of Fathers'**
                                Contacts with Children after Divorce (Based on
                                Fragmentary Data), Genesee Random Sample

	N	Mean Payment Rate
Visited regularly	63	.85
Visited occasionally	51	.74
No contact with children	29	.33
(Missing data)	(266)	(.76)
Total	143	.71
		p < .01

Table 7M   **Payments by Men Who Remarried and by Men for**
                                Whom There Is No Evidence of Remarriage (Based
                                on Incomplete Data), Genesee Random Sample

	N	Mean Payment Rate
Men who remarried	151	.75
Men whose files contain no indication of remarriage	258	.73
Total	409	.74

Table 7N　　　　　　　**Payments by Men Whose Wives Did and Did Not Remarry, Genesee Random Sample**

	N	Mean Payment Rate
Men whose wives remarried:		
By the end of the calendar year after the year of divorce order	93	.75
More than one year after divorce	72	.72
An an uncertain time after divorce	55	.72
	220	.73
Men whose wives did not remarry	184	.76
Total	404	.74

Table 7O　　　　　　　**Payments over Time of Men Whose Former Wives Received Welfare Benefits, Genesee County**

	Men for Whom There Is Payment Data at Least 1 Year after First Welfare Receipt		Men for Whom There Is Payment Data at Least 2 Years after First Welfare Receipt	
	N	Payment Index	N	Payment Index
Year before mother's first welfare receipt	68	.67	51	.67
Year of mother's first welfare receipt	68	.68	51	.65
Year after mother's first welfare receipt	68	.70	51	.65
Second year after mother's first welfare receipt	—	—	51	.62

Table 7P **Excuses Given by Men Who Made Contact with the Agency in Response to Nonjudicial Enforcement Efforts, Genesee Random Sample**

Reason	N	% of All Who Made Contact	% of All Excuses
Loss of income	243	19%	54%
Direct payments	89	7	20
Other expenses	34	3	8
Mother's conduct	14	1	3
Other excuse	66	5	15
No recorded excuse	835	65	—
Total	1,281	100%	100%
100%	100%		

Table 7Q **Selected Factors Significantly Related to Responses to Pay-or-Appear Letters, Genesee Random Sample**

	N	Average Net Length in Weeks*
Total	1,269	14.8
Father's employment status at interview before divorce		
Full-time	953	16.9
Irregular	128	7.1
Unemployed	120	7.8
(Missing data)	(68)	12.3
Arrearage in dollars at time of effort		
0–$199	244	27.5
$200–$599	293	14.3
$600 or more	278	11.7
(Missing data)**	(454)	(10.2)
Overall enforcement effort number		
1st	253	22.8
2d	169	20.7
3d–4th	252	11.7
5th–8th	328	12.4
9th or more	267	9.4

* Sum of lump-sum and week-by-week payments in weeks divided by all efforts whether or not followed by any payment

We did not at the beginning of our recording note the exact arrearage at each effort. We began in midstream. Since we were moving through the alphabet, this late starting should not have prevented us from having a representative sample of men. The lower payments in response to warnings of the missing data cases thus remain quite puzzling.

Table 7R   **Principal Factors Predicting Whether Wage Assignment
                                  Is Followed by Period of Regular Payments, Genesee
                                  Random Sample**

	No. of efforts	Portion of Efforts Followed by Period of Regular Payments	After Adjust-ments for Other Factors*
Total	220	.79	.79
Father's occupation at interview before divorce			
None	23	.65	.53
Unskilled auto worker	107	.84	.86
Other unskilled	48	.67	.65
Skilled blue-collar	28	.68	.77
Other	14	.82	.76
			Beta .28
Father's age at time of wage assignment			
18–26 years	52	.67	.64
27–34 years	101	.77	.79
35 or more	67	.85	.84
			Beta .24

* The other factors were the length of the marriage (the
shorter the marriage the *better* the response to the
wage assignment), beta .16; the year of the final order
(the earlier the year the better the response),
beta .16; father's previous marriage (worse response if
previously married), beta .16; and arrearage at the
time of the effort (higher arrearage, lesser response), beta
.16. With these six variables, about 37 percent of the
variance is explained (unadjusted) and about 30
percent (adjusted).

Table 7S   Relation of Payments to Frequency of Enforcement
                            Efforts for Men Never Arrested or Brought before a
                            Judge, by Men's Occupation at Divorce, Genesee and
                            Washtenaw Random Samples

		Genesee			Washtenaw	
Occupation	N	Average No. of Months between Efforts	Overall Payment Index	N	Average No. of Months between Efforts	Overall Payment Index
Unskilled blue-collar	154	16.7	.78	65	8.9	.58
Skilled blue-collar	49	19.2	.81	41	12.0	.68
Clerical	18	38.5	.89	25	10.1	.61
Professional, Managerial	40	27.0	.86	67	16.9	.73
Other (including students, unemployed)	24	18.0	.65	56	9.4	.60
(Missing data)	(7)	(88.6)	(.78)	(58)	(15.6)	(.38)
Total	292	19.2	.79	312	11.3	.59

Table 8A   Sentence Lengths, Comparison of the Jailed Groups
                            in Macomb and Genesee Counties

Sentence Lengths As Imposed	Genesee*		Macomb**	
	N	%	N	%
30 days or less	5	3%	117	38%
45, 60, and 90 days	10	5	99	32
120–150 days	7	4	5	2
6 months	45	24	60	20
7–11 months	3	2	0	0
12 months	117	63	25	8
(Missing data)	(4)	—	(3)	—
Total	187	101%	306	100%

* Representative sample of men jailed in 1969–70.
** All men jailed in county in 1970.

Table 8B   **Reasons for Release from Jail in Relation to Officer's Role in Decision to Release, Genesee Jailed Sample (Jailings in 1969 and 1970)**

	N	% of entire sample
Men whose timing of release was determined by officers		
Man forced to serve full term	42	25
Man released on payment of less than 90% of arrearage	64	38
Man released with no lump-sum payment; executed wage assignment only	31	18
	137	81%
Men whose timing of release was not determined by officer		
Man paid lump-sum equaling 90% or more of arrearage	18	11
Man escaped	9	5
Man's former wife's action caused release (she acknowledged direct payment, reconciliation)	5	3
	32	19%
Other		
(Including lump sum paid but amount of arrearage unknown; other miscellaneous reasons for release; missing data)	22	—
Total	191	100%

Table 8C   **Days Spent in Jail, Sample of Jailed Men in Macomb and Genesee Counties**

Total Days Actually Spent in Jail	Genesee		Macomb	
	N	%	N	%
0–3	31	17 ⎫ 27	103	36 ⎫ 54
4–7	18	10 ⎭	52	18 ⎭
8–30	32	17	63	22
31–91	32	17	42	14
91–239	43	23 ⎫ 39	28	10 ⎫ 11
240 or more	30	16 ⎭	2	1 ⎭
(Missing data)	(5)	—	(19)	—
Total	191	100%	309	101%
Mean days spent in jail	99		34	
Median days spent in jail	52		6	

Table 8D   **Comparison of Days Served in Jail in Genesee and Macomb Counties by Reason for Release**

	Genesee		Macomb	
Reason for Release	N	Mean Days Served	N	Mean Days Served
Paid a lump sum (sometimes coupled with wage assignment)	74	29	188	10
Executed a wage assignment only	29	114	7	96
Served full term	40	231	71	87
Other	15	124	24	50
(Missing data)	(33)	—	(19)	—
Total	158	99	290	34

Table 9A   **Characteristics of Men in Sample of Men Jailed in Genesee County and in Genesee Random Sample**

	Jailed Sample		Random Sample	
	N	%	N	%
Total	191	100%	410	100%
Father's Occupation				
Auto Worker, unskilled	52	32%	135	37%
Other unskilled	61	42	78	21
Skilled	23	13	69	19
Clerical, sales	11	6	25	7
Professional, managerial	6	4	43	12
Public service	5	3	14	4
(Missing data, always unemployed, other)	(33)	—	(46)	—
Father's Race				
Black	29	18%	46	13%
White	131	81	319	87
Other	2	1	1	—
(Missing data)	(29)	—	(44)	—
Mother's and Children's Receipt of Welfare				
Received welfare during order	111	58%	121	31%
Never received welfare	80	42	264	69
(Missing data)	—	—	(25)	—

NOTE: Both samples were drawn from exactly the same time frame: orders alive in 1969 and in the first ten months of 1970.

	A Number in Sample	B Number Jailed for Nonsupport	C % of Group Ever Jailed (B/A)
Table 9B			

Table 9B   **Portions of Sample Ever Jailed for Nonsupport, by Various Characteristics, Genesee Random Sample**

	A Number in Sample	B Number Jailed for Nonsupport	C % of Group Ever Jailed (B/A)
Total sample	411	60	15%
Occupation			
Not employed at divorce interview	15	8	53
Auto—unskilled	135	15	11
Other unskilled	78	12	15
Skilled	69	12	17
Clerical, sales	25	2	12
Managerial	43	1	2
Public service, armed forces	14	0	0
Missing data	22	8	36
Race			
White	359	49	14
Black	50	11	21
Other	1	0	—
Indications of criminal record for offenses other than nonsupport			
No apparent record	360	39	11
Has arrest or conviction record	40	18	45
Father's attendance at predivorce interview			
Apparently attended	335	35	10
Apparently did not attend	75	25	33
Father's attitude toward reconciliation			
Unwilling to reconcile	278	39	14
Willing to reconcile	87	17	20
Uncertain	35	3	9
Birth of first child in relation to marriage			
Child born before marriage or seven months or less after marriage	134	29	22
Child born more than seven months after marriage	269	30	11
Mother's stated reasons for wanting divorce			
Father's infidelity	85	14	16
Father's physical abuse	90	14	16
Father's failure to support	75	21	28
Mother's receipt of welfare (AFDC)			
Ever receives	137	28	20
Never receives	274	32	12

Table 9C   **Which Men Jailed in 1969 or 1970 Had Been Jailed More than Once by 1973 in Cases Still Alive in 1973, Genesee Jailed Sample, 1969–70**

	N	Portion of Group Rejailed
Total	176	.44
Father's indications of alcohol problems		
0	69	.22
1	46	.48
2 or more	61	.67
		(Beta .29)
Father's cumulative payment performance over life of decree		
0–30% of everything owed	76	.59
31–50% of everything owed	53	.43
51% or more of everything owed	47	.21
		(Beta .26)
Years order alive in our records by mid-1973		
3–6	93	.35
More than 6	61	.59
		(Beta .17)
Father's race		
Black	26	.27
White	127	.51
(Missing data)	(23)	(.26)
		(Beta .15)
Mother's complaints over life of decree		
None or few	131	.40
Several	45	.56
		(Beta .14)

Table 9D **Payments of Lump Sums for Release from Jail in Genesee and Macomb Counties, by Men Sentenced to Jail**

	Macomb 1970		Genesee 1969–70	
	N	% of All Men	N	% of All Men
Lump-sum payments for release				
Jailed father made no lump-sum payment	88	32	82	48
Jailed father made a lump-sum payment	190	68	90	52
Missing data (or father released for reasons such as reconciliation with mother or adoption of children by step-father)	(31)	—	(19)	—
Total	278	100%	172	100%
Amount paid for release				
Including all persons jailed (other than missing data or other above)				
Mean	278	$302	172	$329
Median	278	$200	172	$100
Including only fathers who made a lump-sum payment				
Mean	190	$442	90	$628
Median	190	$360	90	$500
		% of Each Size		% of Each Size
Size of lump-sums when paid				
Under $200	29	15	11	13
$200–$500	120	63	41	48
$501–$1000	35	18	22	26
Over $1000	6	3	11	13
(Missing data)	(0)	—	(5)	—
Total	190	99%	85	100%

Table 9E **Principal Factors Associated with Lump-Sum Payment of $250 for Release (or Equaling Eight Weeks or More Worth of Payments), Genesee County Jailed Sample**

Men without alcohol problems	(beta .22)
Men whose former wives remarried	(beta .22)
Men being jailed for nonsupport for first time	(beta .17)
Men employed full-time at jailing	(beta .15)
Men whose wives were not receiving AFDC at time of jailing	(beta .14)
Men with arrearages under 26 weeks at jailing	(beta .12)

Total explained variance (adjusted)—17.2%

| Table 9F | | Factors Ascertainable at Release from Jail Relating to Postrelease Payments, Genesee Jailed Sample (N = 163) | |

Rank	N	Mean Index	Mean after Adjustment for Other Factors
1. Days served in jail			
3 or less	30	.65	.50
4–90	69	.43	.40
91–360	62	.14	.25
			Beta .24
2. Criminal record for offenses other than nonsupport			
Had a record at time of jailing	76	.26	.29
Had no record at time of jailing	81	.47	.44
			Beta .23
3. Father's employment status at jailing			
Full-time	73	.53	.45
Part-time	5	.27	.29
Irregularly or unemployed	56	.18	.25
Status missing	29	.28	.34
			Beta .22
4. Reason for release from jail			
Served full term	40	.14	.31
Released on lump-sum payment	41	.41	.30
Released on wage assignment only	30	.29	.40
Released on lump-sum payment and wage assignment	41	.62	.47
Other	11	.17	.17
			Beta .21

Other factors with some but less importance:
5. Father's occupation (managers high, clericals low)   Beta .20
6. Remarriage of former wife (men whose wives had remarried, high)   Beta .15
7. Indications of alcohol (the more indications, the worse the payment)   Beta .13
8. Signs of illness (if yes, lower)   Beta .12
9. Mother receiving AFDC at time of jailing (if yes, lower)   Beta .11

Explained variance: unadjusted—47.2%
adjusted—38.4%

Factors that might have been expected to be significantly related to high or low postrelease payments but were not:
Father's age at marriage, divorce, or jailing
Length of marriage
Mother complained of nonsupport at time of divorce
Payment performance in year prior to jailing
Arrearage at time of jailing
Man complains at jail hearing of high order or other obligations
Length of stated sentence imposed on father at jailing
Dollar amount paid for release from jail (among men making payment for release)

Table 9G   Postrelease Payment Performance of Men Who Had Been
                                Employed at the Point of Jailing in Relation to Various
                                Indications of Psychological Barriers, Genesee Jailed
                                Sample

	N	Performance Index
All employed men	78	.50
Mother had remarried by the time of jailing	15	.77
Father's excuse at jailing: he has new family*	13	.59
Marriage 7 months or less after conception of first child ("shotgun")	33	.48
Two or more signs of alcohol problems*	22	.40
Father failed to attend interview before divorce	29	.50
Mother had occupation at divorce	43	.61
Mother currently receiving AFDC	32	.34
Father's excuse at jailing: order too high or other debts*	33	.55

* These factors are equivocal. Alcoholism may prevent
employment in particular cases and mask true incapacity to
pay. The others indicate not incapacity but a placing
of a higher priority on other expenses.

Table 9H   Types of Payment Response of Jailed Men in
                            Genesee and Macomb Counties

| | Genesee | | | Macomb | | |
	N	% of Total	Mean Payment Index**	N	% of Total	Mean Payment Index**
Men who paid nothing for release or thereafter*	65	38%	.02	36	16%	.02
Men who paid a lump sum but nothing thereafter	13	8	.40	15	7	.15
Men who paid no lump sum but made some weekly payments	26	15	.55	45	20	.71
Men who paid a lump sum and made at least some weekly payments	68	40	.91	125	57	.86
Total	172	101%	.50	221	100%	.64

* Total payments in lump-sum payments or week-by-week
  payments did not equal 10 percent of what was
  due in the period from release to the end of the
  following calendar year.

** The formula for this index was $(1 + p)/(o \times w)$, where
  l = lump sum in dollars; p = week-by-week payments
  in dollars from release to end of following calendar
  year; o = order size in dollars per week and
  w = number of weeks from release to end of following
  calendar year.

Notes

Chapter Two

1. State of Michigan, Judicial Council, *Annual Report* (1935), pp. 63–64.
2. For a discussion of other groups not under orders of support, see the Methodological Appendix, pp. 289–90.

Chapter Three

1. See N. Glenn and C. Weaver, "The Marital Happiness of Remarried Divorced Persons," *Journal of Marriage and the Family* 39 (1977): 331.
2. See P. Glick, "Dissolution of Marriage by Divorce and Its Demographic Consequences," in *International Population Conference, Liège, 1973* (Liège, Belgium: Imprimerie Derouaux, 1973), 2:65–79.
3. $P < .05$.
4. P. Glick and A. Norton, "Frequency, Duration, and Probability of Marriage and Divorce," *Journal of Marriage and the Family* 33 (1971): 307; R. Schoen, "California Divorce Rates by Age at First Marriage and Duration of First Marriage," *Journal of Marriage and the Family* 37 (1975): 548.
5. Divorcing women were not asked whether they were pregnant at marriage. They were asked early in the interview the date of the marriage. Later in the interview they were asked the birth dates of each of their children. We counted a person as having been married after conception if the first child of the marriage was born before the marriage or within seven months after the marriage.
6. In 1968, HEW developed estimates that 16 percent of white women and 41 percent of black women who married between 1955 and 1959 conceived their first child before

marriage (U.S. Department of Health, Education and Welfare, *Trends in Illegitimacy: United States, 1940–63,* p. 3). Applying these national percentage estimates in proportion to the racial distribution of Genesee County in 1960, one would have estimated that 18.4 percent of couples in Genesee had been married after conceiving their first child. The actual rate of 33.3 percent among our couples is 80 percent higher than one would have expected were such couples represented in our sample in the same proportion as they were represented in the Genesee population.

7. That is, 73 percent of the 380 couples whose oldest child was not from a previous marriage of one of the two partners had had their first child. In eleven families, the oldest child of the couple (and perhaps others of their children) was adopted by the husband from a wife's previous marriage.

8. The product moment correlation between number of children and the length of the marriage to time of separation was +0.49.

9. William Goode, *Women in Divorce* (New York: The Free Press, 1965), pp. 133–36.

10. Only 6 percent of the 101 men with some sign of an alcohol problem filed for divorce as opposed to 20 percent of the 290 men without such a sign (p < .05).

11. Ours are the cases in which the designed purpose failed, but all Friends of the Court whom we asked reported a substantial number of cases every year that never proceeded to judgment, and they attributed a significant portion of these cases to reconciliation.

12. Thirty-nine percent of the men over thirty-five at divorce, but only 18 percent of the men under twenty-one, were willing to reconcile or to consider reconciling. Men twenty-two to twenty-five and twenty-six to thirty-five were in the middle (28 percent and 32 percent respectively) (p < .05).

13. Only 11 percent of the men accused of infidelity who attended the predivorce interview indicated a willingness to reconcile, as opposed to 25 percent of those not accused of infidelity (p < .05).

14. On adultery, see Alfred Kinsey, Wardell Pomeroy, and Clyde Martin, *Sexual Behavior in the Human Male* (Philadelphia: W. B. Saunders Co., 1948). On physical abuse, see Jean Renvoize, *Web of Violence* (Boston: Routledge and Kegan Paul, 1978); Terry Davidson, *Conjugal Crime* (New York: Hawthorn Books, 1978); Richard Gelles, *The Violent Home* (Beverly Hills, Calif.: Sage Publications, 1972).

15. See n. 14, above.

Chapter Four

1. On divorce among "nonwestern" peoples, see William Goode, *World Revolution and Family Patterns* (New York: The Free Press, 1970), pp. 195–99; E. Burch, Jr., "Marriage and Divorce Among the North Alaskan Eskimos," in *Divorce and After,* ed. Paul Bohannan (Garden City, New York: Doubleday, Anchor Books, 1971), pp. 171–204; Rennard Strickland, *Fire and the Spirits: Cherokee Law from Clan to Court* (Norman, Oklahoma: University of Oklahoma Press, 1975), pp. 8, 31.

2. Michigan Compiled Laws, §552.16.

3. See "New Child Support Schedule," *Seattle-King County Bar Association Bar Bulletin,* December 1974. For another effort to relate support-order sizes to actual costs of living, see Isabel Sawhill, "Developing Normative Standards for Child Support and Alimony Payments," working paper (Washington, D.C.: Urban Institute, 1977).

4. Angus Campbell, Philip Converse, and Willard Rogers, *The Quality of American*

Life: Perceptions, Evaluations, and Satisfactions (New York: Russell Sage Foundation, 1976), pp. 398, 420.

5. M. Orshansky, "Children of the Poor," *Social Security Bulletin* 26 (July 1963): 3.

6. The proper multiple, from the consumer expenditure data, should have been four, not three. Indeed, given that the consumer expenditures did not include taxes, but that the poverty level purports to do so, a multiple of *five* would be justified. The baseline, the Economy Food Plan, was devised for temporary, emergency use, and does not provide adequate nutrition over a longer period of time. The USDA "low-cost" food plan would have been far more appropriate. The basis for "cost-of-living" adjustments also has been changed twice with the effect of keeping the poverty line lower than it would otherwise be.

Had the Economy Food Plan (and its successor "Thrifty Food Plan") been used, with a multiplier of even four, the "Poverty Line" for a nonfarm family of four in the fall of 1976 would have been roughly $7,970, instead of the "official" $5,850, or 36 percent higher.

7. A full explanation of the construction of the standard budgets, and the detailed specification of the contents of each, can be found in U.S., Department of Labor, Bureau of Labor Statistics, *Three Standards of Living for an Urban Family of Four Persons, Spring 1967*, Bulletin No. 1570-5 (1968). See also J. Bracket, "New BLS Budgets Provide Yardsticks for Measuring Family Living Costs," *Monthly Labor Review* 92 (April 1969): 4. Summaries of the annual updates appear each year in the *Monthly Labor Review.*

The methodology used to convert the figures for the prototypical family (husband aged thirty-five to fifty-four, wife, two children, older child aged six to fifteen), to other family sizes and compositions, is explained in U.S., Department of Labor, Bureau of Labor Statistics, *Revised Equivalence Scale for Estimating Equivalent Incomes or Budget Costs by Family Type*, Bulletin No. 1570-2 (November 1968). Essentially, it is based on the squared ratios of food expenditures to after-tax income shown by the 1960–61 survey of consumer expenditures for various family sizes, compositions, and ages of the "head."

8. See Robert Weiss, *Marital Separation* (New York: Basic Books, 1975), pp. 139–42.

9. The 80 percent figure comes from a study of American families in which the spouses were divorced after 1967. During marriage, around 30 percent of the women in these families were employed. By 1973, after these women had been divorced or separated, nearly 80 percent were employed. See S. Hoffman and J. Holmes, "Husbands, Wives, and Divorce," in *Five Thousand American Families: Patterns of Economic Progress*, vol. 4, Greg Duncan and James Morgan, eds. (Ann Arbor: Institute for Social Research, 1976), p. 45.

10. P < .01.

11. See above, p. 65.

12. The women in this group were older and had been married longer than the rest of the women, as a group, but the seventy-one women in the sample who were employed at divorce but had never received welfare and never remarried had, as a group, been married even longer and were even older. The employed women were half as likely as those not employed (and not receiving welfare or remarrying) to indicate a willingness to reconcile or to consider doing so. The employed women may have felt more financially secure.

13. U.S., Bureau of the Census, *1970 Census of Population*, vol. 1, pt. 24, table 121. A comparable finding is reported in Hoffman and Holmes, "Husbands, Wives, and Di-

vorce," p. 45. Of a group of women married in 1967 but divorced or separated by 1973, only 30 percent were employed in 1967 but nearly 80 percent were employed in 1973.

14. In 1976, the median income for full-time working women in the United States was $6,326, which was 54.3 percent of the median income for full-time working men ($11,644). U.S., Department of Commerce, Bureau of the Census, *Money Income and Poverty Status of Families and Persons in the United States,* series P-60, n. 107 (1976).

15. Goode, *Women in Divorce,* chap. 16.

16. See Margaret Steinfels, *Who's Minding the Children? The History and Politics of Day Care in America* (New York: Simon and Schuster, 1973).

17. See, for example, Selma Fraiberg, *Every Child's Birthright: In Defense of Mothering* (New York: Basic Books, 1977).

18. A technical description of some of the techniques we used is included in the Methodological Appendix at the end of the book. Since we will be using multiple regression and multiple classification analysis throughout the book, a brief explanation of their functions in lay terms may be useful. Regression analysis helps estimate the relationship between factors through the use of numerical data. Complex in formula, readily accessible through computer programs, it permits one to test the relationship between some phenomenon one wishes to understand (here, the receipt of welfare benefits after divorce) and other measured factors that might have a bearing on that phenomenon (number of children, occupational types, and so forth). In the context of welfare receipt, it permits learning the direction and strength of the relationship of various factors to welfare receipt and helps strip away factors that initially appear to bear a relation to receipt of welfare but actually do not. Here and often in the book we will rely on a form of regression analysis called multiple classification analysis, especially devised for use with factors such as occupation types or religion in which, for computer analysis, groups (such as white-collar workers or Roman Catholics) are assigned numbers that have no quantitative significance.

19. For further discussion, see above, pp. 132–37.

20. Heather Ross and Isabel Sawhill, *Time of Transition: The Growth of Families Headed by Women* (Washington, D.C.: The Urban Institute, 1975), pp. 103–6; Barbara Boland, "Participation in the Aid to Families with Dependent Children Program (AFDC)," Working Paper 97–102 (Washington, D.C.: The Urban Institute, August 1973).

21. We actually had 130 women who were recorded as having received benefits in at least one year. For ten women, however, there was a gap in the records that prevented us from determining in how many years they received assistance.

22. For their predivorce standard, compare the first column of figure 4.1.

23. See Weiss, *Marital Separation,* pp. 303–4.

24. An earlier study that reached a similar finding for white women is Paul Glick, *American Families* (New York: John Wiley and Sons, 1957), pp. 137–38.

Chapter Five

1. Kenneth Eckhardt, "Social Change, Legal Controls, and Child Support: A Study in the Sociology of Law" (Ph.D. diss., University of Wisconsin, 1965).

2. See, e.g., Elliot Leibow, *Tally's Corner: A Study of Negro Streetcorner Men* (Waltham, Mass.: Little, Brown, 1967); Jonathan Cobb and Richard Sennett, *The Hidden Injuries of Class* (New York: Knopf, 1972).

3. Campbell, Converse, and Rogers, *The Quality of American Life,* p. 398.

4. Our payments index is a conservative measure of performance. It excludes from consideration any adjustments to the account in the man's favor—adjustments, for example, for unusually lengthy vacations spent by the children with the father or even for direct payments to the wife acknowledged by her to the agency. We counted only those payments actually made through the agency. We did develop a second payment index that took such adjustments into account, but it correlated so strongly with our payments index and we had such doubts about the reliability of the reasons recorded for some of the adjustments, that we will rarely allude to it.

We also developed a third, rarely used measure of the regularity of payments that was even more simply computed than the payments index. It was computed simply by dividing the number of payments made by the father during a year (regardless of payment size) by the number of weeks in the payment year (typically fifty-two). It was a measure that was intended to reflect the flow of payments as experienced by the recipient, on the reasoning that large lump sums arriving at unpredictable intervals would be less useful to the mother than a steady stream producing the same amount. As with the index that includes adjustments, there are problems with this one, for under this index a man who paid faithfully two weeks' worth of payments every fourteen days would have the same "regularity" index as the man who paid every week for the first half of the year and then stopped paying altogether. This measure also correlated quite highly with our payments index.

Chapter Six

1. The figures would be identical if all orders were of the same size. Within our samples in Genesee and Washtenaw, there were, of course, variations in the size of orders. There was in fact a very slight positive correlation between order size and payment rate, so that it is probable that the figure we use, the mean of individual payment rates, is quite close to (but slightly lower than) the portion the agency collected of everything due under all its orders.

2. This 68 percent is slightly lower than the collection rate of 74 percent that we report for the cases in our sample drawn from cases alive in 1970. Among many factors (other than chance) that may explain the lower average rate is that 1974 was a year of extraordinarily high unemployment in Genesee: 11.4 percent average monthly unemployment as opposed to 5.3 percent in 1970.

3. The product-moment correlation between the overall mean and the portion of the caseload paying less than 10 percent of everything due was $-.935$. The product-moment correlation between the mean and the portion of the caseload paying more than 80 percent was $+.899$.

4. The size of the caseloads of the Friends of the Court and the populations of the counties correlate very highly, largely because the divorce rate varies remarkably little among the Michigan counties in our sample. In fact, the correlation is so high that we were unable to test whether awareness of the possibility of jail, and thus the deterrent effect, depends on the size of the caseload or on the population. Within the counties in our study, the ratio of the county's population (in 1970) to number of men (or families) making up the caseload (in 1974) ranged from about 35:1 to 40:1. Thus our figure of the "number of jailings per 10,000 population" is roughly equivalent to the "number of

jailings per 250 men in the caseload." We have consistently used the population figure as the denominator because in a few counties we were never confident that we had a precise count of the caseload of orders still in effect.

5. Despite the diversity among our counties, from the perspective of the nation as a whole nearly all our counties look prosperous. Median family income in 1970 in the nation as a whole was $9,586. In only four of our counties was median income lower than the national median.

6. At approximately the same time, the comparable agency in New York City had over one thousand workers handling welfare cases alone. Interview with Florence Gittens, Director, Division of Location and Support, Department of Social Services, New York City, September 25, 1975.

7. See Franklin Zimring and Gordon Hawkins, *Deterrence: The Legal Threat in Crime Control* (Chicago: University of Chicago Press, 1973), pp. 264–66, 269; D. Baldus and J. Cole, "A Comparison of the Work of Thorsten Sellin and Isaac Ehrlich on the Deterrent Effect of Capital Punishment," *Yale Law Journal* 85 (1975): 170, 177–83.

8. In our analysis, we did not use actual population figures in unaltered form. Rather, we used the $\log_{10}$ of population as a more plausible indicator of the relation of population to performance. We used logarithms because we hypothesized that if population had effects, there would be more differences between two counties one of which had a population of 40,000 and the other 240,000 than there would be between two counties one of which had a population of 2,000,000 and the other a population of 2,200,000, even though in each pair of counties there were 200,000 more persons in one county than the other. Logarithms capture this "nonlinear" relationship.

9. Put slightly more technically, when we calculated what our counties should be expected to collect, using the regression coefficients for population, the jail rate, and the "self-starting" factor, the actual collections varied from the predicted collections by more than six percentage points for only nine of the twenty-eight counties. For eleven counties, the prediction was off by less than three percentage points. Only one county, our highest collecting county, collected over ten percentage points more than would be predicted. That county impressed us even before surveying its records as the most thoroughly organized of all. Conversely, only one county, one of our two lowest collecting, collected more than ten percentage points less than was predicted. This county seemed about the least well organized for collections. It was the only county in our sample with a population of over one hundred thousand whose agency head had only a part-time appointment.

10. In a regression on the performance index using as controls (1) the variable that combined "self-starting" and the jail rate into a single binary factor, (2) $\log_{10}$ population, and (3) the unemployment rate, the combined self-start/jailing factor had a coefficient of 14.77. Since the performance index is coded in percentage collected, the coefficient of 14.77 indicates that a county that had both a self-starting system and a high rate should collect after controls 14.77 percentage points more than those that did not have both. The mean collection rate among our counties was 65 percent. An added 14.8 percentage points collected would represent about a 25 percent increase in collections for counties pushed from a mean collection rate of several percentage points below 65 percent to a mean rate of several points above. See section A3 in appendix table 6H.

11. For example, in the six counties in our sample with the smallest populations, the median income (in 1970) and the unemployment rates during the months we surveyed averaged $9,600 and 12.5 percent respectively. By contrast, during the same periods

median income and unemployment for the six largest counties averaged $11,900 and 10.8 percent respectively. Similarly, in the six smallest counties the average portion of families living on incomes below the poverty line was 8.6 percent, whereas the average portion in the six largest was 5.9 percent.

12. We had for each case in our sample one indirect indication of the actual earnings of the men in the sample: the order size (based in part on earnings). The mean order size for our counties correlated positively with census information about median county incomes.

13. See above, p. 124.

14. The Bureau of the Census has no count of persons moving into or out of a county or of in-state migrations. Rather it computes how much the county could be expected to have grown over the decade through new births and deaths if no migration had occurred and then computes a rough "net migration" figure by comparing this derived figure with the actual population at the end of the decade. See U.S., Bureau of the Census, *County and City Data Book: 1972,* p. xxxii.

15. New York City provides another instructive example of the effects of lack of centralized organization. There, at least as of 1975, four different agencies had responsibilities for support enforcement—court administrators, probation officers, prosecutors, and the Department of Social Services. Though over three times as large as Detroit, New York's agencies collected far fewer total dollars than the Friend of the Court in Detroit. From interviews, it appeared that the agencies cooperated very little and barely knew what each other were doing. Because of its sheer size, New York will always have problems, but integration of responsibility could surely help.

16. By "high" rates, we mean men paying over 80 percent of everything due. A "low rate" is a rate of payment less than 10 percent of everything due. Genesee's pattern over the first six years is displayed in figure 5.1.

17. Numerous factors complicate the calculations of the costs of a jailing policy. For example, each Genesee judge spent a few hours a week on child-support cases, but removal of these cases from the dockets would not have led to a reduction in the number of judges. The long average jail terms in Genesee must have inflated enforcement costs, but a portion of these costs were probably avoidable without any loss in collections since, within the counties in our study, neither the length of the sentence nor the amount of time served affected county collections. Our calculation that Genesee incurred marginal costs of $400,000 in order to sustain an aggressive, high-jailing system is based on a generous estimate of the expenses. That is, we assumed that a shift to a passive enforcement system would have allowed a reduction by one-half in the size of the enforcement staff and a savings of $100,000 in court time. We further assumed that the average jail term served would be sixty days (far longer than that in most high-collecting counties) and that the costs of jailing were ten dollars per inmate per day, the figure used by the Genesee sheriff in preparing his 1974 budget. Even with these highly inflated figures, costs would barely total $400,000.

18. Given our finding that a high-jailing, self-starting enforcement system boosts collections by roughly 25 percent, Genesee's collections in 1974 would have been about $13.8 million, rather than the $17.3 million actually collected.

19. On the vastly different problems of measuring deterrence in other settings, including the difficult problem of measuring the actual incidence of various undesired behaviors, see D. Nagin, "General Deterrence: A Review of the the Empirical Evidence," in *Deterrence and Incapacitation: Estimating the Effects of Criminal Sanctions*

on Crime Rates, Alfred Blumstein, Jacqueline Cohen, and Daniel Nagin, eds. (Washington, D.C.: National Academy of Sciences, 1978), p. 95; Zimring and Hawkins, *Deterrence.*

20. Draft evasion is another crime nearly always committed after reflection. There is evidence that there, as here, there is a negative and significant association between draft evasion rates and conviction risks. See A. Blumstein and D. Nagin, "The Deterrent Effect of Legal Sanctions on Draft Evasion," *Stanford Law Review* 28 (1977): 241.

21. On the methodological problems of testing this hypothesis in other settings, see Nagin, "General Deterrence," pp. 111–17.

Chapter Seven

1. The thirty-five men for whom we had no information about earnings paid at an average rate of .54. The fifty-five men for whom we had no information about religion also paid at an average rate of .54.

2. The forty-five missing-data cases paid at an average rate of .81.

3. In multiple classification analysis, a researcher can either filter out all cases with missing data in any control variable (which has the unfortunate effect of eliminating cases that have valid data on all but one of the controls) or leave in the missing data as one category in the controls. We have typically performed preliminary analyses both ways. In any case in which "missing data" has been retained as a category, we do not include any control variable in our final reported analysis in which the missing-data category accounted for a substantial portion of the variance explained by the variable.

4. See explanation in Chapter 4, n. 18.

5. The total explained variance was 18.6 percent (unadjusted) and 13.7 percent (adjusted).

6. We later test and reject the expected explanation for lower payments by persons with four or more children—that these men had higher orders in relation to their earnings. See above, p. 114 and appendix table 7F.

7. Eckhardt, "Social Change, Legal Controls, and Child Support," p. 233.

8. See above, pp. 123–24 and appendix table 7J.

9. There is a danger that we have slightly understated the average performance-rate Washtenaw's Friend of the Court achieved. The Friend of the Court in Washtenaw was more tolerant of direct payments from noncustodial parent to custodial parent that bypassed the Friend of the Court. Our efforts to determine the extent of this phenomenon and to control for it are explained in the Methodological Appendix. pp. 295–95.

10. Of course, it is also possible that the kinds of persons who are complained about in Washtenaw are different than those complained about in Genesee. A smaller portion of the men were complained about in Washtenaw than in Genesee. On the other hand, the groups had roughly similar earnings in each county.

11. Our most common source of information was the card kept in the enforcement officer's desk. If the most recent card listed as the man's employer the same employer for whom the man had been working at divorce and no other employer is ever indicated, we treated the man as having been working for the same employer throughout.

12. Another group especially likely to leave town were men whose former wives received welfare benefits at some time during the life of the order. (After controlling for men's occupations and ages, we find that 27 percent of fathers in welfare cases but only 13 percent of other fathers left town.) Why should this be so? It may possibly be related

to a strong desire of some such men not to pay because the welfare department, not their children, got to keep any payments they might have made. On the other hand, the high rate of leaving town we record among these men may reveal an unevenness in the records we used. It is possible, though we sensed little evidence of it as we recorded our data, that the Friend of the Court staff took more efforts to locate men whose former wives received welfare and that evidence of having left the county was more thoroughly searched for in such cases.

13. See Goode, *Women in Divorce,* chaps. 16 and 20.

14. See Eckhardt, ''Social Change,'' pp. 249–55. A similar finding with regard to the effect of the woman's remarriage was reached by Goode, *Women in Divorce,* p. 226.

15. See discussion in Chapter 9, pp. 230–31, of one group of jailed men who were apparently affected by their wives' remarriage.

16. Before the MCA was run, welfare receipt—a binary yes/no variable—had an eta of .27, similar to a product-moment correlation. Its strength was exceeded only by father's occupation. In the MCA, welfare receipt had a beta of .13. No one of the other six robbed welfare receipt of its importance. It apparently required the combined effect of several or all of the six.

17. The agency had a fixed policy for handling men who claimed direct payments. If the mother was not receiving welfare benefits, the man was told that direct payments were greatly frowned upon but that the agency would credit his account if the woman acknowledged the direct payment in writing. (Reflecting perhaps on the truth of the claim that direct payment had been made, in only eleven of the eighty-nine instances in which men claimed to be making direct payments did the men eventually obtain written confirmation from the woman.) If the mother was receiving welfare benefits, the man claiming direct payments was out of luck. The money he paid her should have gone to the Department of Social Services and he still owed the money. Her acceptance of his money, if she failed to report it to the Department of Social Services and knew that she was supposed to, constituted criminal fraud.

18. Paying a lump sum alone did not in fact succeed well in keeping the agency from the door: among men who fell substantially in arrears, those who made a lump-sum payment in response to an early enforcement effort were not significantly less likely to end up in jail than men who made no response at all.

19. See chap. 10, n. 2.

20. About the only possibly significant difference is that, in Genesee, the letter instructs the recipient to come in to see the enforcement officer, whereas in Washtenaw the man is simply instructed to pay.

21. Efforts are more frequent in the early years of orders than in the later years, and Washtenaw's men were on the whole more recently divorced when we coded them than were the men in Genesee. Even when we control for length of time in the records, however, Washtenaw's men are the subject of more efforts, more closely spaced, than Genesee's.

Chapter Eight

1. In about 5 percent of the cases with enforcement efforts, men received personalized letters threatening arrest or jailing.

2. Michigan General Court Rules §§ 727.4(2), 727.4(5).

3. Of the fourteen who were arrested after failing to respond to their first warning

letter, ten were given jail sentences, five of them before their divorce became final. The Friend of the Court in several counties reported to us a much higher incidence of sentencing for men who were arrested having failed to appear at a show-cause hearing than for men, equally in arrears, who voluntarily appeared.

4. Michigan Compiled Laws § 552.201.

5. *Sword v. Sword,* 59 Mich. App. 730 (1975), *aff'd* 399 Mich. 367 (1976).

6. *Sword v. Sword,* 399 Mich. 367 (1976).

7. See *Otton v. Zaborac,* 525 P. 2d 537 (Alaska 1974); *Tetro v. Tetro,* 544 P. 2d 17 (Washington 1975).

8. *Argersinger v. Hamlin,* 407 U.S. 25 (1972).

9. This difference held as statistically significant after controlling for other differences—such as size of arrearage, employment status, original sentence length—that might have accounted for different lengths of time served among men.

Chapter Nine

1. The twenty-six weeks of arrearage need not all have been accumulated within a single year. A person was included if, for example, he accumulated ten weeks' worth of nonpayments in 1970 and, without paying off past arrearages, another sixteen weeks of nonpayments in 1971.

2. A total of sixty men in the random sample were actually jailed. Five of these had a smaller than twenty-six-week arrearage at jailing and never developed a larger one.

3. One ready explanation for an overrepresentation of black men might rest on the behavior of the Genesee police, not on that of the Friend of the Court's staff. Given arrest patterns for other offenses in our society, black men might have been thought more likely to have been arrested on other charges and thus simply to be more accessible to the Friend of the Court for jailing for nonsupport. Interestingly, we do not find that black men actually jailed have a higher incidence of earlier criminal records than white men who were jailed. (Indeed, within the jailed sample, black men were significantly less likely than white to have had recorded criminal records in Genesee County prior to their first jailing for nonsupport—21 percent of black men vs. 39 percent of white.)

4. Only slightly more of the judge's jailees showed signs of alcoholism (20 of 27, 74 percent) than did the jailees of the remainder of the judges (95 of 162, 59 percent).

5. We had feared that the cases that were measured over a longer period might have systematically lower performances, since two men who each paid for six months immediately after release would have widely different performance indexes if one was measured over a thirteen-month period and the other was measured over a twenty-three-month period. In fact, there turned out to be only a very slight negative relationship between the performance index and the length of time over which the payments were measured—a product-moment correlation of $-.09$ in Genesee County—and we have, of course, controlled for this effect, even though it is a modest one, in our analysis of the other factors affecting postrelease payment performance.

6. A substantial part of the predictive value of the employment status information is removed when time served is taken into account—the fully employed spend less time in jail largely because they more frequently make a lump-sum payment for release—but employment status nonetheless continues to have important explanatory power. Moreover, the relation between early release and employment status is certain to be tangled (see appendix table 8D).

7. Indeed, though failure to show for an interview appeared initially to be a predictor of lower postjail payments, most of its predictive power is removed when the men's employment status is entered into the analysis. The product-moment correlation of show/failure-to-show run against the performance index is .153. In an MCA analysis with employment status, and show/no show only, however, the beta of show/no show declines to .081. No other substantial predictor of postrelease performance, including indications of alcoholism, reduces the explanatory power of the show/no show variable to anywhere near the same degree.

8. The analysis is further complicated by the possibility that after release men who had been fully employed before jailing will suddenly be unemployed and will be unable to find employment. If new employment problems are not spread equally across groups of men with different psychological barriers to payment, then we may be deceived that what appears to be an impact (or the lack of it) of jailing on a psychological barrier to payment actually masks a problem in the labor market.

9. We might derive hints from a strong polarization in payments after release among men with the factor—more at the bottom and the top than in the rest of the population—that we do have a psychological factor producing different results.

10. On the measure used for jailings here we report any payments over the next eighteen months. For pay-or-appear letters we report payments beginning within three weeks of mailing.

11. A few whom we recorded as having left may in fact have remained but hid so well that they deceived a staff person at the Friend of the Court into an erroneous entry into the records that they had left. For most of the men we recorded as leaving, however, there is strong evidence in the file that they had indeed departed: most commonly, the evidence was either the record of an inquiry through the Social Security Administration revealing that the man was employed in another county or state or an indication of the arrest of the man in a distant county for another offense; less frequently, the evidence took the form of letters from the man to the Friend of the Court sent from elsewhere or notes by the enforcement officer that the former wife or another person had informed him that the man had left town.

12. See above, Chapter 7, pp. 124–26.

13. For eleven men who left town, we had no clear indication at the time of jailing whether they were employed or not. It is probable that nearly all were in fact employed because we would otherwise have expected them to have relied on their unemployment at the hearing. If they were in fact employed, employed men then constituted at least 60 percent of the group that left town.

14. Quoted in Zimring and Hawkins, *Deterrence*, p. 195.

15. We have recorded earlier that we were uncertain whether the making of a lump-sum payment was a reliable indication of greater capacity to perform (see above, pp. 219–20).

Chapter Ten

1. See, e.g., Ronald Goldfarb, *Jails: The Ultimate Ghetto* (Garden City: Anchor Press, 1975); President's Commission on Law Enforcement and Administration of Justice, *The Challenge of Crime in a Free Society* (Washington, D.C.: Government Printing Office, 1967), pp. 159, 178.

2. See Howard Becker, *Outsiders: Studies in the Sociology of Deviance* (London: Free Press, 1963), p. 31: "One of the most crucial steps in the process of developing a

stable pattern of deviant behavior is likely to be the experience of being caught and publicly labeled a deviant." See also, Robert Scott and Jack Douglas, *Theoretical Perspectives on Deviance* (New York: Basic Books, 1972); Walter Gove, ed., *The Labelling of Deviance: Evaluating a Perspective* (New York: Sage Publications, 1975).

3. See Paul Rock, *Making People Pay* (London: Routledge and Kegan Paul, 1973), pp. 120–21, 307–16.

4. See 11 U.S.C. § 523(a) (5) for the current codification.

5. Department of Health and Social Security, Committee on One-Parent Families, *Report* (London: Her Majesty's Stationery Office, 1974), pp. 128–32.

6. See the materials on "The Family Autonomy Tradition" in the widely used casebook on family law, Caleb Foote, Robert Levy, and Frank Sander, *Cases and Materials on Family Law* (Boston! Little, Brown, 1976), pp. 1–29.

7. See, e.g., Joseph Goldstein, Anna Freud, and Albert Solnit, *Beyond the Best Interests of the Child* (New York: The Free Press, 1973).

8. See R. Benedek and E. Benedek, "Postdivorce Visitation: A Child's Right," *Journal of the American Academy of Child Psychiatry* 16 (1977): 256.

Chapter Eleven

1. In 1978 in *Zablocki v. Redhail,* 434 U.S. 374, the United States Supreme Court held invalid under the equal protection clause of the Fourteenth Amendment a Wisconsin statute that denied marriage licenses to persons in arrears on a child support order from a previous marriage and to persons under orders of support for children receiving or "likely" to receive welfare benefits. In reaching its holding, the Court quoted an earlier decision characterizing the "freedom to marry" as "one of the vital personal rights essential to the orderly pursuit of happiness by free men."

2. In Chapter 6, we estimate that Dane County could have doubled its collections by creating a full-time enforcement staff, even if the enforcement staff did not initiate efforts without complaints and even if the rate of jailing had been low. See above, p. 98.

3. See E. L. Johnson, "Matrimonial Maintenance in Soviet Law," in *Parental Custody and Matrimonial Maintenance: A Symposium,* Josef Unger, ed. (London, British Institute of International and Comparative Law, 1966).

4. For a summary of such laws as of 1971, see Council of State Governments, *Reciprocal State Legislation to Enforce the Support of Dependents* (Lexington, Ky., 1971), p. 22, table VII.

5. Among states that have recently repealed all or part of their laws that impose liability on persons other than parents are: Colorado (1973), Illinois (1969 and 1971), Indiana (1971), Kentucky (1974), Minnesota (1973), Nebraska (1969), Ohio (1974), and Utah (1975).

6. *Gomez v. Perez,* 409 U.S. 535 (1973).

7. On all these points see Goode, *Women in Divorce;* Weiss, *Marital Separation.*

8. Goldstein, Freud, and Solnit, *Beyond the Best Interests of the Child,* p. 98.

Methodological Appendix

1. See "Social Change, Legal Controls, and Child Support."

2. Michigan Interactive Data Analysis System developed by the University of Michi-

gan Statistical Research Laboratory and described in Kenneth Guire and Thomas Fox, *Documentation for MIDAS* (Ann Arbor, Statistical Research Laboratory, 1976).

3. We used primarily version III, but made some use of versions II and IV. See Computer Support Group of the Survey Research Center, Institute for Social Research, *OSIRIS III*, volume 1, *System and Program Description* (Ann Arbor: Survey Research Center, 1973).

4. See Frank M. Andrews et al., *Multiple Classification Analysis: A Report on a Computer Program for Multiple Regression Using Categorical Predictors* (Ann Arbor: Institute for Social Research, 1973).

Selected Bibliography

Child Support—General

Baldwin, William H. *Family Desertion and Non-Support Laws: A Study of the Laws of the Various States*. Washington, D.C.: n.p. 1904.

Brandt, Lilian. *Five Hundred and Seventy-Four Deserters and Their Families: A Descriptive Study of Their Characteristics and Circumstances*. New York: Associated Charities, 1905.

British Institute of International and Comparative Law. *Parental Custody and Matrimonial Maintenance: A Symposium*. Special Publication No. 11, edited by J. Unger. London: British Institute of International and Comparative Law, 1966.

Brockelbank, William. *Interstate Enforcement of Family Support: The Runaway Pappy Act*. 2d ed. Edited by F. Infausto. Indianapolis: Bobbs-Merrill Co., 1971.

Cassetty, Judith, *Child Support and Public Policy: Securing Support from Absent Parents*. Lexington, Mass.: D. C. Heath, 1978.

Eckhardt, Kenneth. "Social Change, Legal Controls, and Child Support: A Study in the Sociology of Law." Ph.D. dissertation, University of Wisconsin, 1965.

Great Britain, Department of Health and Social Security, Committee on One-Parent Families. *Report*. London: Her Majesty's Stationery Office, 1974.

Jones, Carol; Gorden, Nancy; and Sawhill, Isabel. "Child Support Payments in the United States." Working Paper. Washington, D.C.: Urban Institute, 1976.

Massachusetts, Governor's Advisory Council on Home and Family. *Family Support Laws: An Inquiry Into Enforcement of Non-Support*. Boston: Advisory Council on Home and Family, 1972.

Sawhill, Isabel. "Developing Normative Standards for Child Support and Alimony Payments." Working Paper. Washington, D.C.: Urban Institute, 1977.

Child Support—Welfare System

Kaplan, Saul. *Support from Absent Fathers of Children Receiving ADC, 1955*. Public Assistance Report No. 41, United States Department of Health, Education, and Welfare, Social Security Division. Washington, D.C.: Government Printing Office, 1960.

United States, Congress, Senate, Committee on Finance. *Child Support and Paternity Determinations: Explanation of Committee Decisions*. 92nd Congress, 2d session, 1972.

United States, Congress, Senate, Committee on Finance, Staff. *Child Support: Data and Materials*. 94th Congress, 1st session, 1975.

United States, Department of Health, Education, and Welfare, Office of Child Support Enforcement. *Annual Reports to the Congress on the Child Support Enforcement Program*. 1976–1978. Washington, D.C.: Government Printing Office, 1976–1978.

United States, General Accounting Office, Comptroller General. *Collection of Child Support under the Program of Aid to Families with Dependent Children*. Washington, D.C.: General Accounting Office, 1972.

United States, General Accounting Office, Comptroller General. *New Child Support Legislation: Its Potential Impact and How to Improve It*. Washington, D.C.: General Accounting Office, 1976.

Young, Arthur, and Company. *Absent Parent Child Support: Cost-Benefit Analysis*. Washington, D.C.: Department of Health, Education, and Welfare, Social and Rehabilitation Service, 1975.

General Material on Divorce and on Single-Parent Families

Bernard, Sydney. *Fatherless Families: Their Economic and Social Adjustment*. Waltham, Mass.: Brandeis University Research Center, 1964.

Bohannan, Paul, ed. *Divorce and After*. Garden City, N.Y.: Doubleday, 1970.

Campbell, Angus; Converse, Philip; and Rogers, Willard. *The Quality of American Life: Perceptions, Evaluations, and Satisfactions*. New York: Russell Sage Foundation, 1976.

Duncan, Greg; Morgan, James; et al., *Five Thousand American Families–Patterns of Economic Progress*, 6 vols. Ann Arbor: Institute for Social Research, 1974–78.

Epstein, Joseph. *Divorced In America*. New York: Penguin Books, 1975.

Goode, William. *Women in Divorce* (originally published as *After Divorce*, 1956). New York: The Free Press, 1965.

Keniston, Kenneth and Carnegie Council on Children. *All Our Children: The American Family Under Pressure*. New York: Harcourt Brace Jovanovich, 1977.

Leibow, Elliot. *Tally's Corner: A Study of Negro Streetcorner Men*. Waltham, Mass.: Little, Brown, 1967.

Ross, Heather, and Sawhill, Isabel. *Time of Transition: The Growth of Families Headed by Women*. Washington, D.C.: Urban Institute, 1975.

United States, Congress, Joint Economic Committee, Subcommittee on Fiscal Policy. *The Family, Poverty, and Welfare Programs: Household Patterns and Government Policies*. Studies in Public Welfare, No. 12. Washington, D.C.: Government Printing Office, 1973.

Weiss, Robert. *Marital Separation*. New York: Basic Books, 1975.

Methodology

Andenaes, Johannes. "General Deterrence Revisited: Research and Policy Implications." *Journal of Criminal Law and Criminology* 66 (1975): 338–65.

Andrews, Frank. *Multiple Classification Analysis: A Report on a Computer Program for Multiple Regression Using Categorical Variables*. Ann Arbor: Institute for Survey Research, 1973.

Blumstein, Alfred; Cohen, Jacqueline; and Nagin, Daniel, eds. *Deterrence and Incapacitation: Estimating the Effects of Criminal Sanctions on Crime Rates*. Washington, D.C.: National Academy of Sciences, 1978.

Zimring, Franklin, and Hawkins, Gordon. *Deterrence: The Legal Threat in Crime Control*. Chicago: University of Chicago Press, 1973.

Index